DATE DUE

HANA-KIMI

For You in Full Blossom
VOLUME 9

STORY & ART BY HISAYA NAKAJO

Translation/David Ury
English Adaptation/Gerard Jones
Touch-Up Art & Lettering/Gabe Crate
Design/Izumi Evers
Editor/Jason Thompson

Managing Editor/Annette Roman
Director of Production/Noboru Watanabe
Vice President of Publishing/Alvin Lu
Sr. Director of Acquisitions/Rika Inouye
Vice President of Sales & Marketing/Liza Coppola
Publisher/Hyoe Narita

Printed in Canada

Published by VIZ Media, LLC, P.O. Box 77010, San Francisco, CA 94107

Shôjo Edition
10 9 8 7 6 5 4 3 2 1

First printing, November 2005

www.viz.com
store.viz.com

PARENTAL ADVISORY
HANA-KIMI is rated T+ for Older Teen and is recommended for ages 16 and up. Contains strong language, sexual themes and alcohol and tobacco usage.

CONTENTS

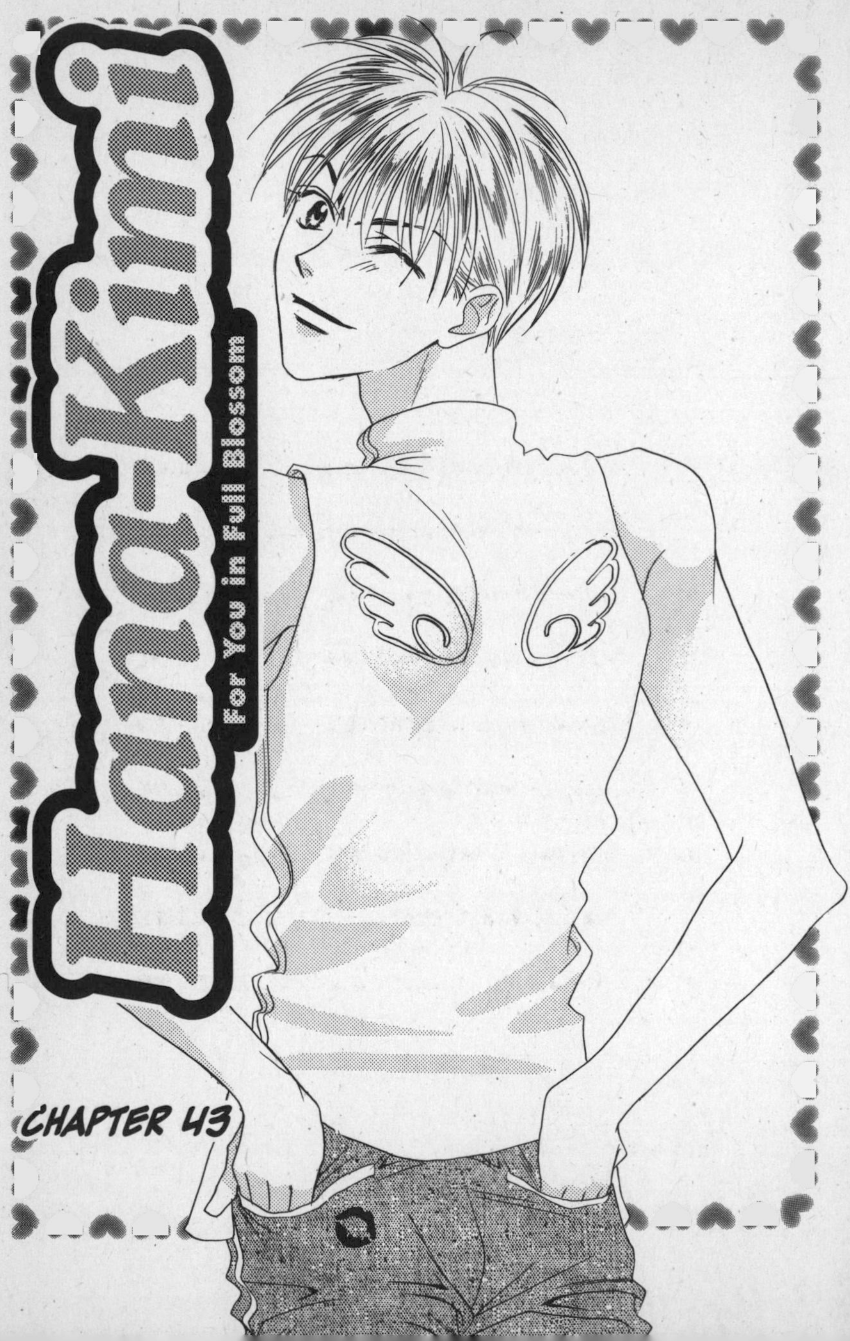

Hana-Kimi
For You in Full Blossom
CHAPTER 43

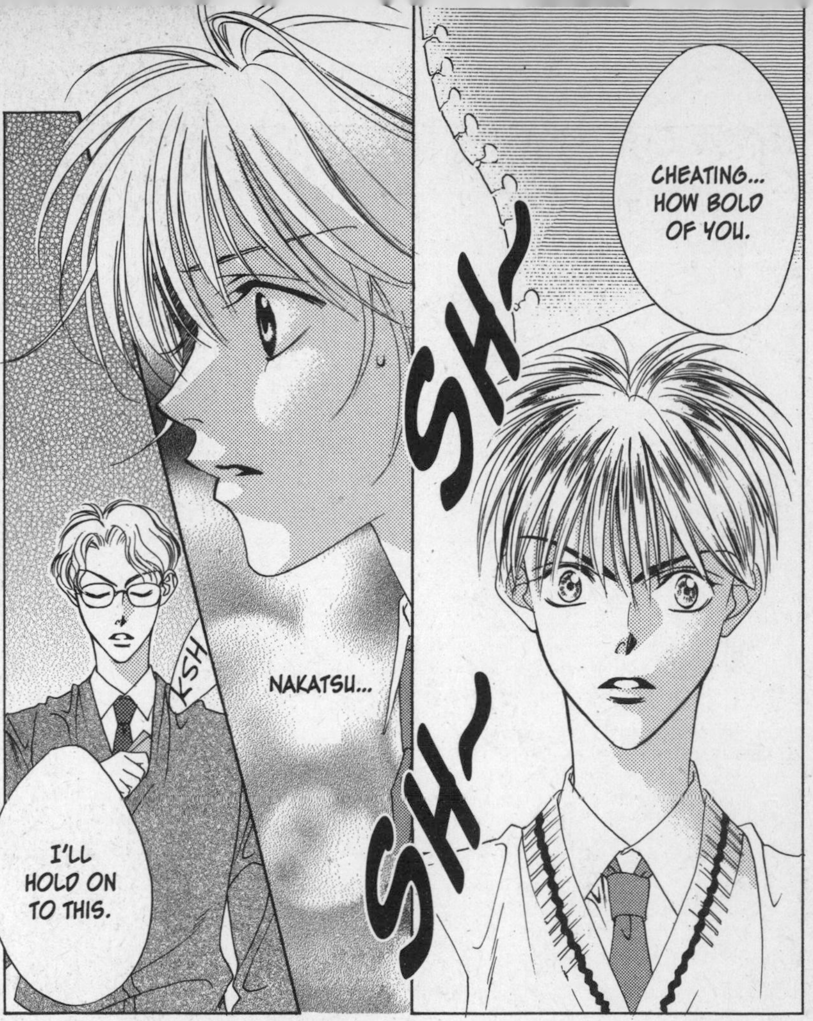
CHEATING... HOW BOLD OF YOU.
SH~ SH~
NAKATSU...
KSH
I'LL HOLD ON TO THIS.

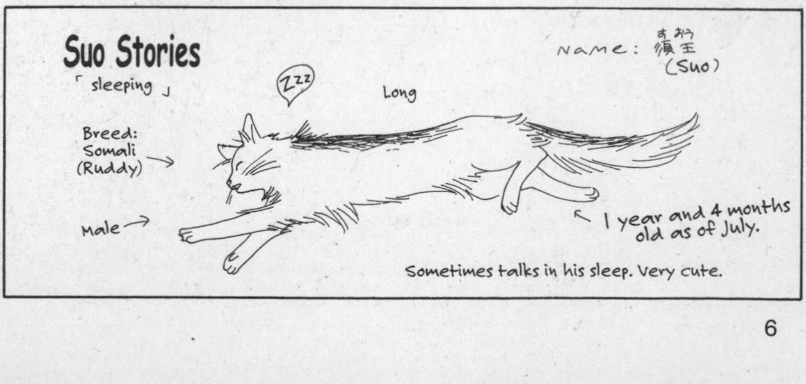
Suo Stories
「sleeping」
Name: 須王 (Suo)
Zzz
Long
Breed: Somali (Ruddy)
Male
1 year and 4 months old as of July.
Sometimes talks in his sleep. Very cute.

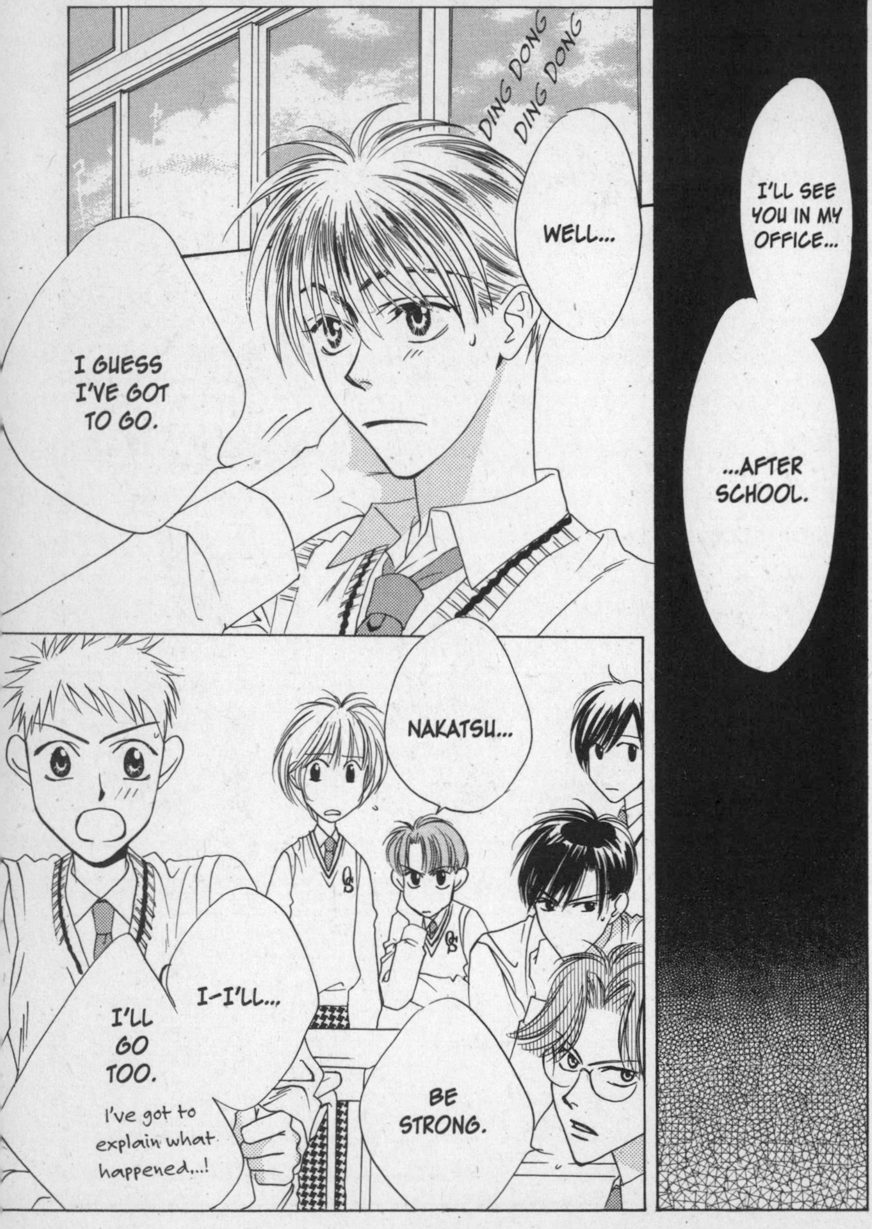
I'LL SEE YOU IN MY OFFICE...
...AFTER SCHOOL.
DING DONG DING DONG
WELL...
I GUESS I'VE GOT TO GO.
NAKATSU...
BE STRONG.
I-I'LL...
I'LL GO TOO.
I've got to explain what happened...!

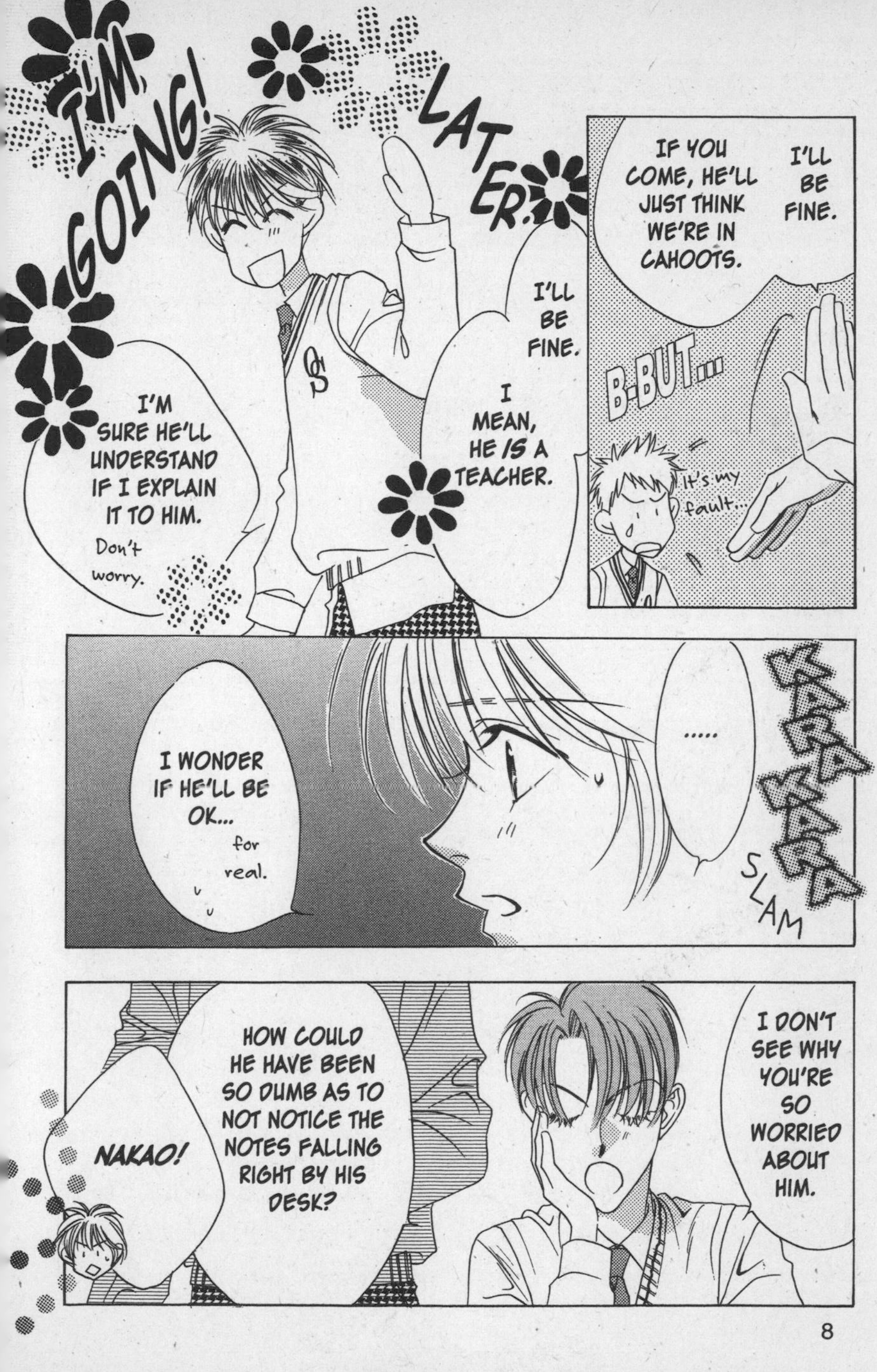
I'LL BE FINE.
IF YOU COME, HE'LL JUST THINK WE'RE IN CAHOOTS.
B-BUT...
It's my fault...
LATER.
I'M GOING!
I'LL BE FINE.
I MEAN, HE *IS* A TEACHER.
I'M SURE HE'LL UNDERSTAND IF I EXPLAIN IT TO HIM.
Don't worry.
KARA KARA
SLAM
.....
I WONDER IF HE'LL BE OK...
for real.
I DON'T SEE WHY YOU'RE SO WORRIED ABOUT HIM.
HOW COULD HE HAVE BEEN SO DUMB AS TO NOT NOTICE THE NOTES FALLING RIGHT BY HIS DESK?
NAKAO!

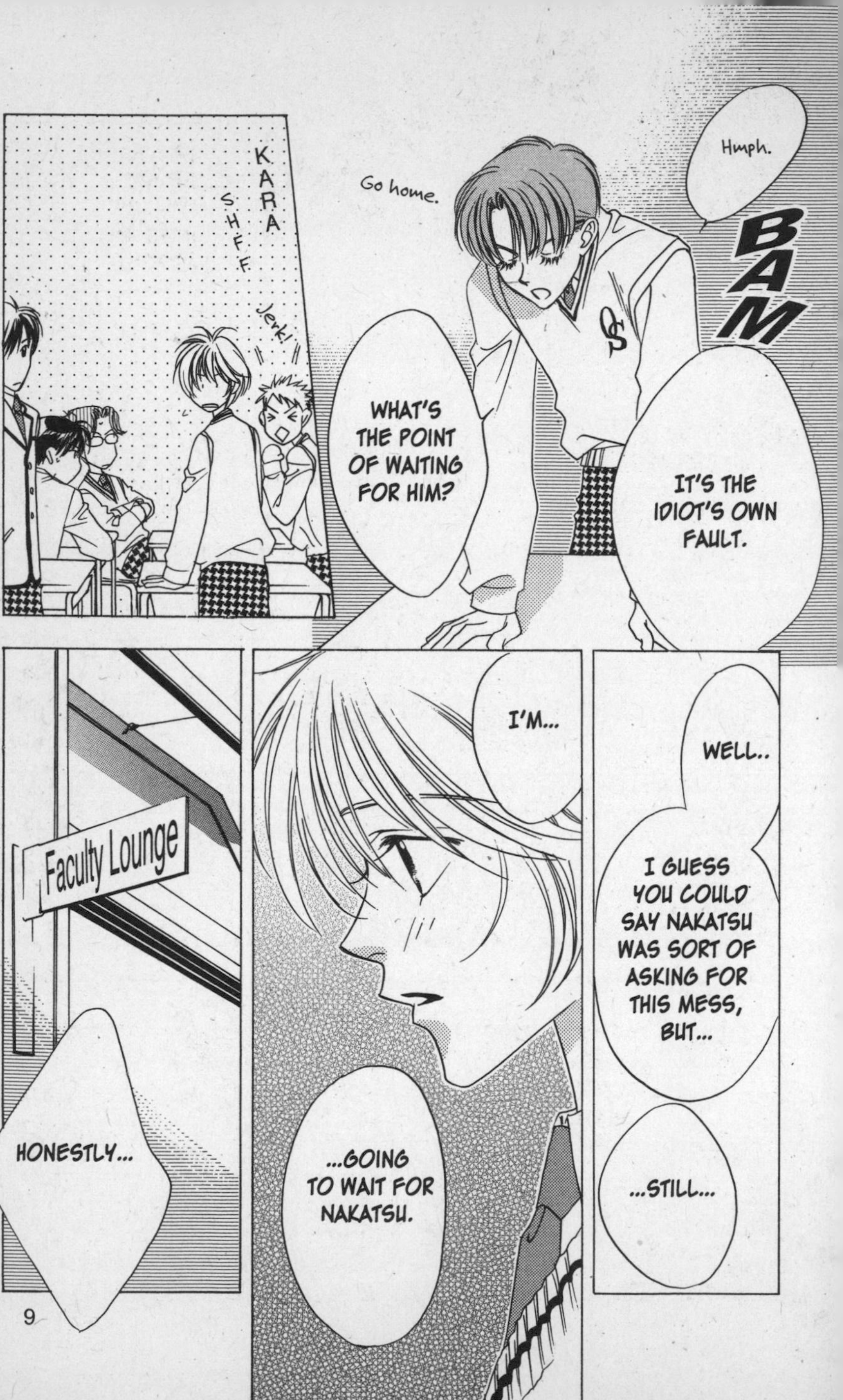
Hmph.
BAM
Go home.
IT'S THE IDIOT'S OWN FAULT.
WHAT'S THE POINT OF WAITING FOR HIM?
KARA
SHFF
Jerk!
WELL..
I GUESS YOU COULD SAY NAKATSU WAS SORT OF ASKING FOR THIS MESS, BUT...
...STILL...
I'M...
...GOING TO WAIT FOR NAKATSU.
Faculty Lounge
HONESTLY...

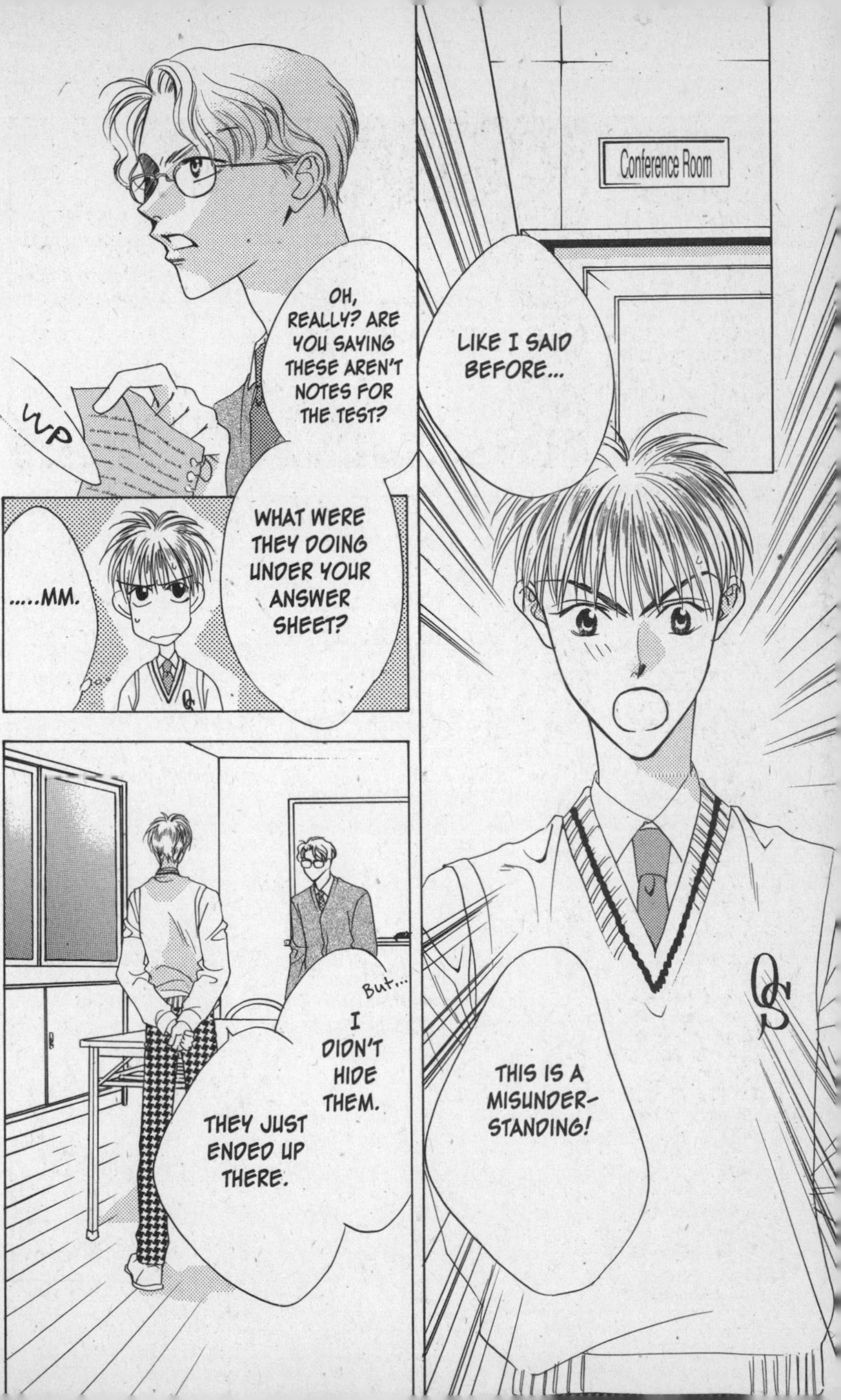
Conference Room
LIKE I SAID BEFORE...
THIS IS A MISUNDER-STANDING!
OH, REALLY? ARE YOU SAYING THESE AREN'T NOTES FOR THE TEST?
WP
WHAT WERE THEY DOING UNDER YOUR ANSWER SHEET?
.....MM.
But...
I DIDN'T HIDE THEM.
THEY JUST ENDED UP THERE.

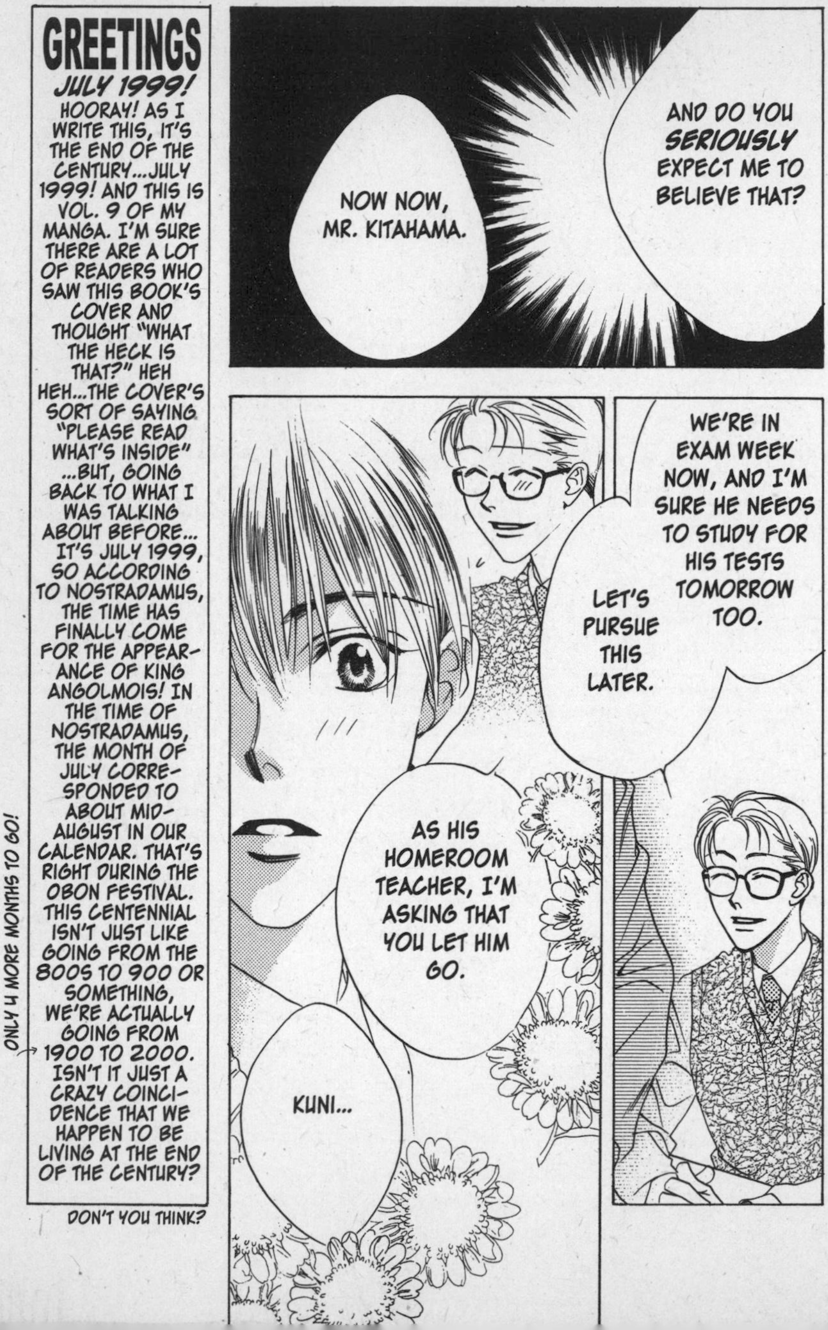
AND DO YOU SERIOUSLY EXPECT ME TO BELIEVE THAT?
NOW NOW, MR. KITAHAMA.
WE'RE IN EXAM WEEK NOW, AND I'M SURE HE NEEDS TO STUDY FOR HIS TESTS TOMORROW TOO.
LET'S PURSUE THIS LATER.
AS HIS HOMEROOM TEACHER, I'M ASKING THAT YOU LET HIM GO.
KUNI...

GREETINGS

JULY 1999!

HOORAY! AS I WRITE THIS, IT'S THE END OF THE CENTURY...JULY 1999! AND THIS IS VOL. 9 OF MY MANGA. I'M SURE THERE ARE A LOT OF READERS WHO SAW THIS BOOK'S COVER AND THOUGHT "WHAT THE HECK IS THAT?" HEH HEH...THE COVER'S SORT OF SAYING "PLEASE READ WHAT'S INSIDE" ...BUT, GOING BACK TO WHAT I WAS TALKING ABOUT BEFORE... IT'S JULY 1999, SO ACCORDING TO NOSTRADAMUS, THE TIME HAS FINALLY COME FOR THE APPEARANCE OF KING ANGOLMOIS! IN THE TIME OF NOSTRADAMUS, THE MONTH OF JULY CORRESPONDED TO ABOUT MID-AUGUST IN OUR CALENDAR. THAT'S RIGHT DURING THE OBON FESTIVAL. THIS CENTENNIAL ISN'T JUST LIKE GOING FROM THE 800S TO 900 OR SOMETHING, WE'RE ACTUALLY GOING FROM 1900 TO 2000. ISN'T IT JUST A CRAZY COINCIDENCE THAT WE HAPPEN TO BE LIVING AT THE END OF THE CENTURY?

ONLY 4 MORE MONTHS TO GO!

DON'T YOU THINK?

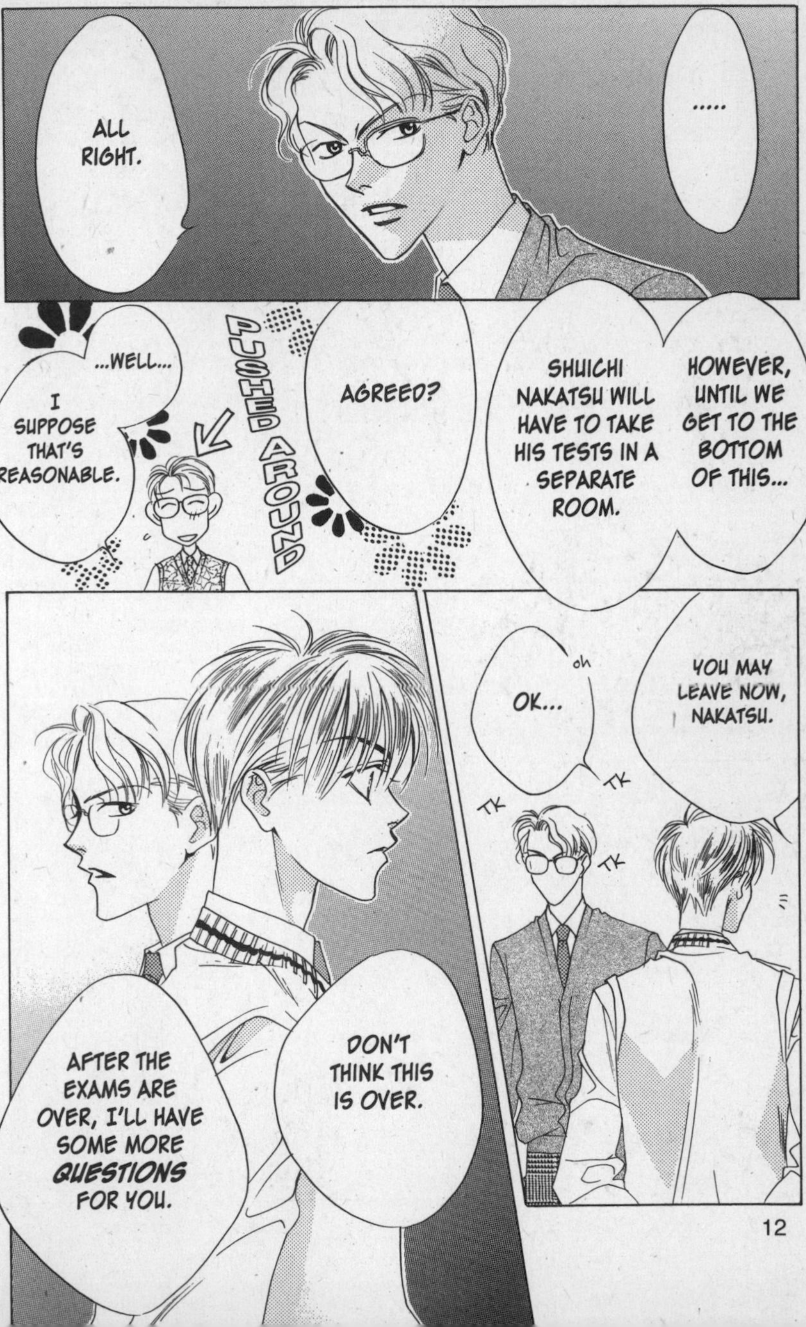
.....
ALL RIGHT.
HOWEVER, UNTIL WE GET TO THE BOTTOM OF THIS...
SHUICHI NAKATSU WILL HAVE TO TAKE HIS TESTS IN A SEPARATE ROOM.
AGREED?
PUSHED AROUND
...WELL...
I SUPPOSE THAT'S REASONABLE.
YOU MAY LEAVE NOW, NAKATSU.
oh
OK...
TK
TK
TK
DON'T THINK THIS IS OVER.
AFTER THE EXAMS ARE OVER, I'LL HAVE SOME MORE *QUESTIONS* FOR YOU.

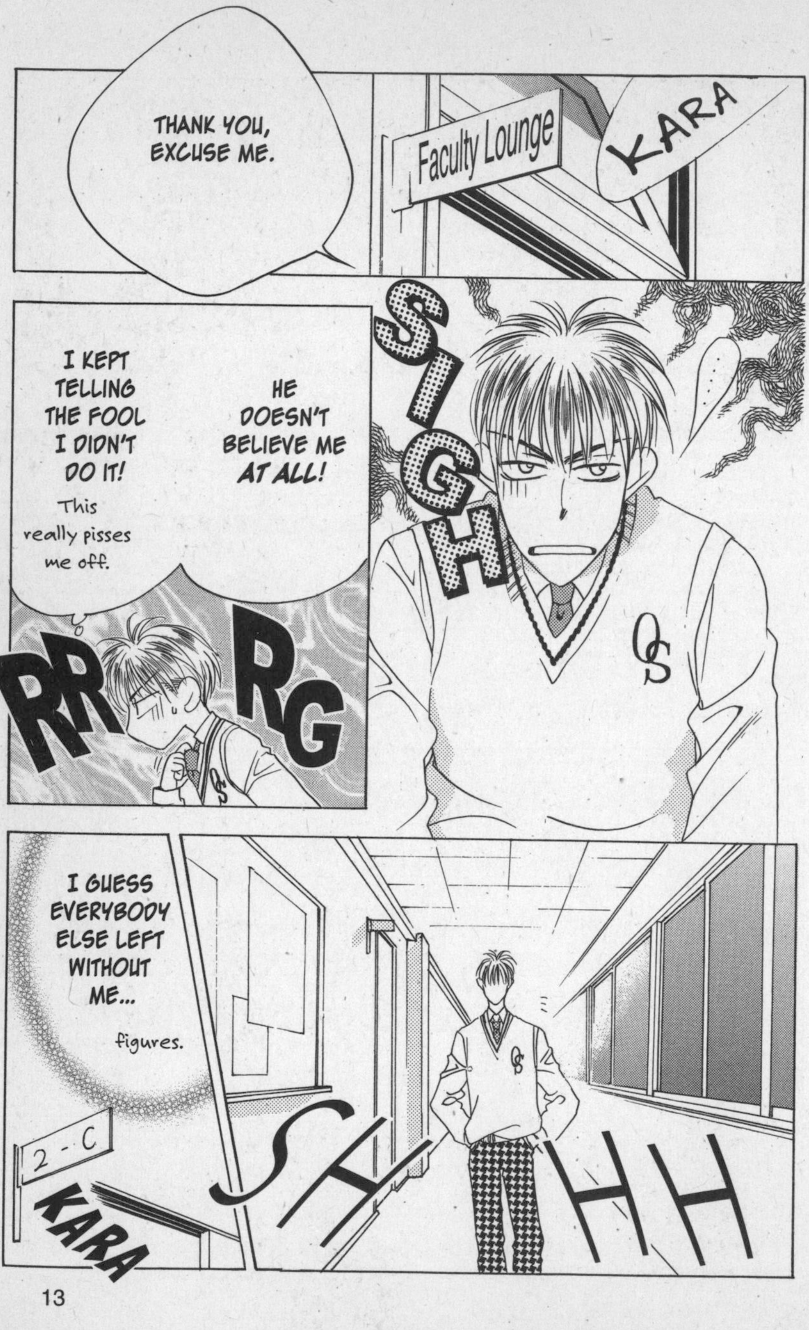
Faculty Lounge
KARA
THANK YOU, EXCUSE ME.
SIGH
I KEPT TELLING THE FOOL I DIDN'T DO IT!
HE DOESN'T BELIEVE ME AT ALL!
This really pisses me off.
RRRG
I GUESS EVERYBODY ELSE LEFT WITHOUT ME...
figures.
2 - C
KARA
SHHHH

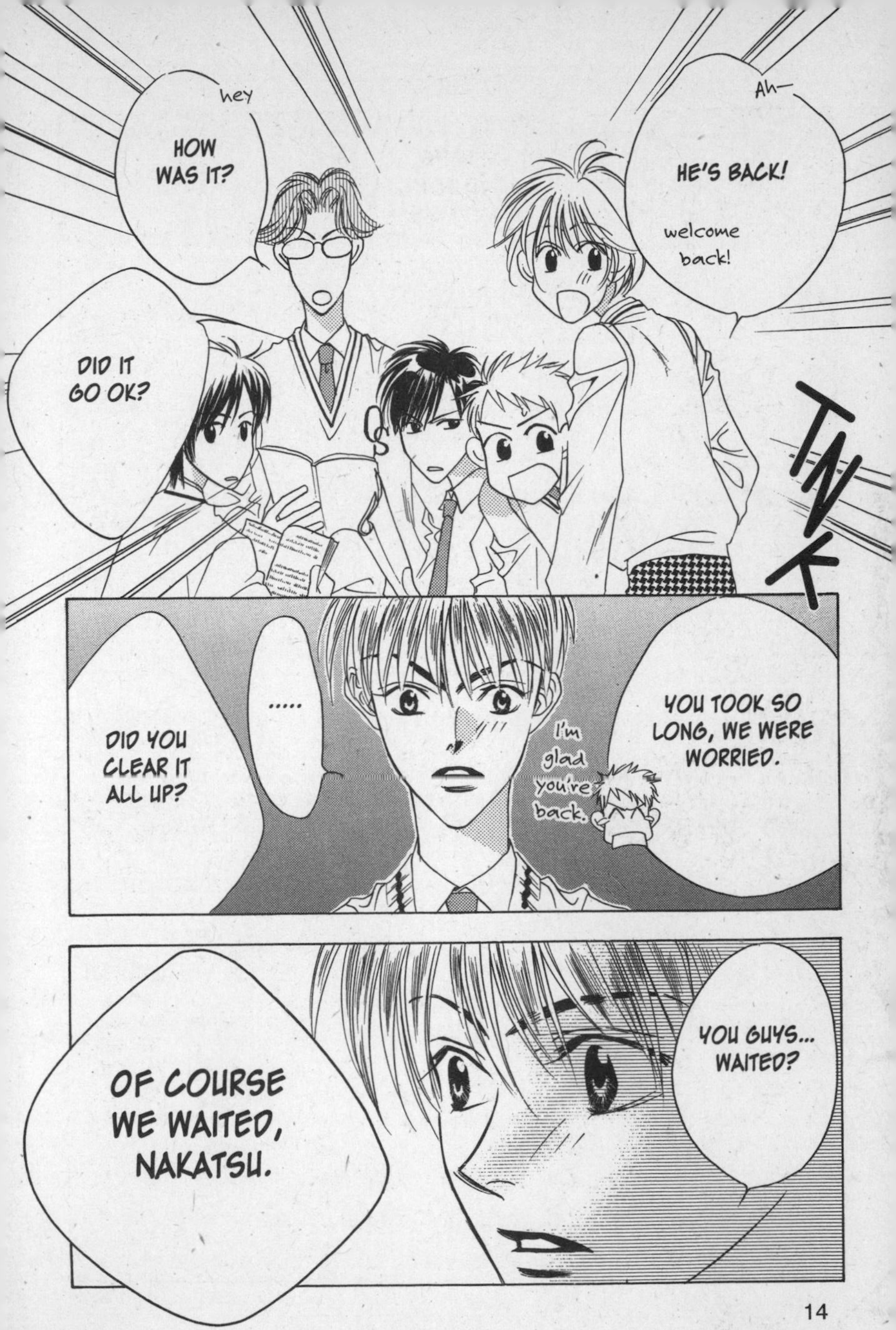
Ah—
HE'S BACK!
welcome back!
hey
HOW WAS IT?
DID IT GO OK?
TNK
YOU TOOK SO LONG, WE WERE WORRIED.
I'm glad you're back.
.....
DID YOU CLEAR IT ALL UP?
YOU GUYS... WAITED?
OF COURSE WE WAITED, NAKATSU.

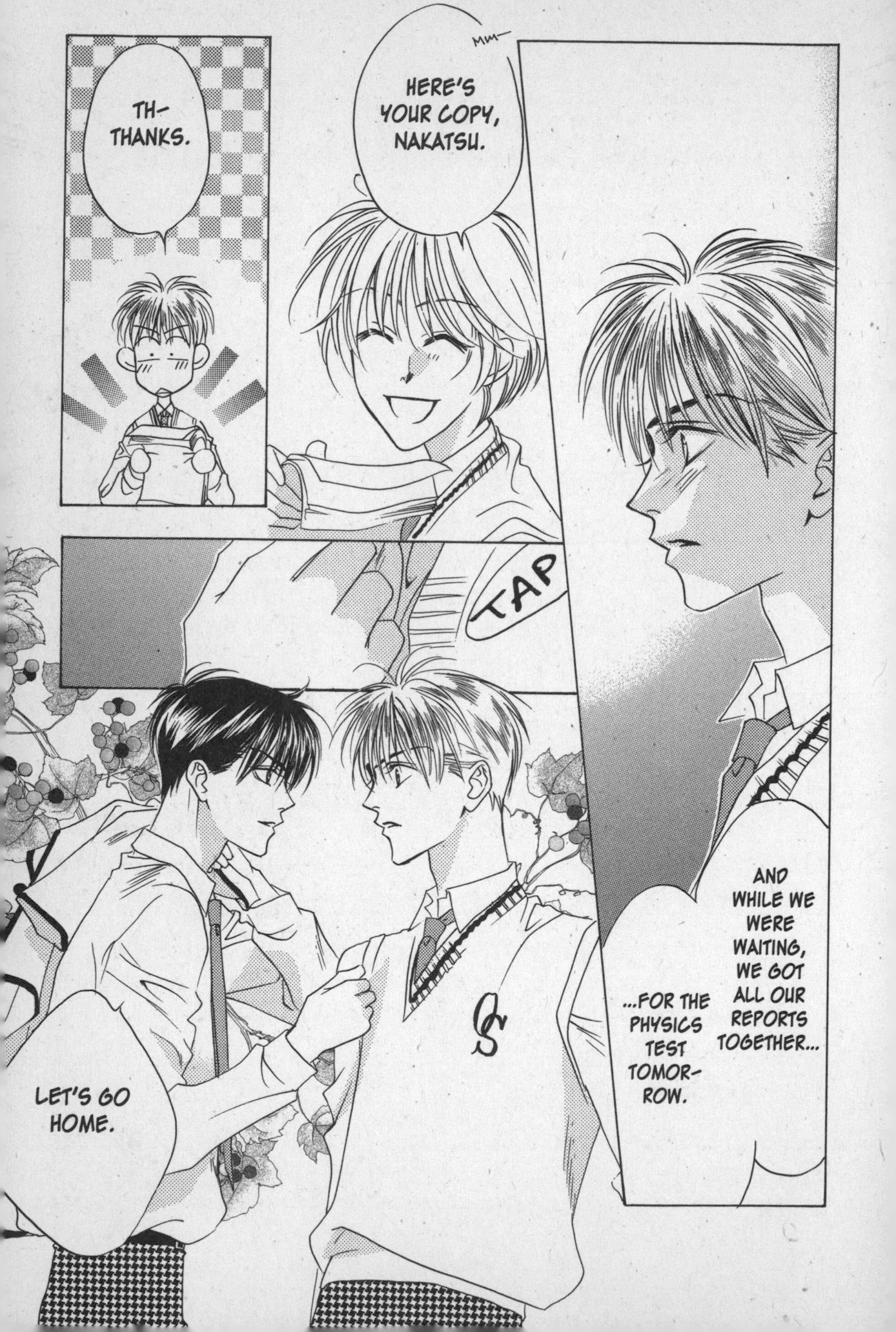
AND WHILE WE WERE WAITING, WE GOT ALL OUR REPORTS TOGETHER...
...FOR THE PHYSICS TEST TOMORROW.
MM—
HERE'S YOUR COPY, NAKATSU.
TH-THANKS.
TAP
LET'S GO HOME.

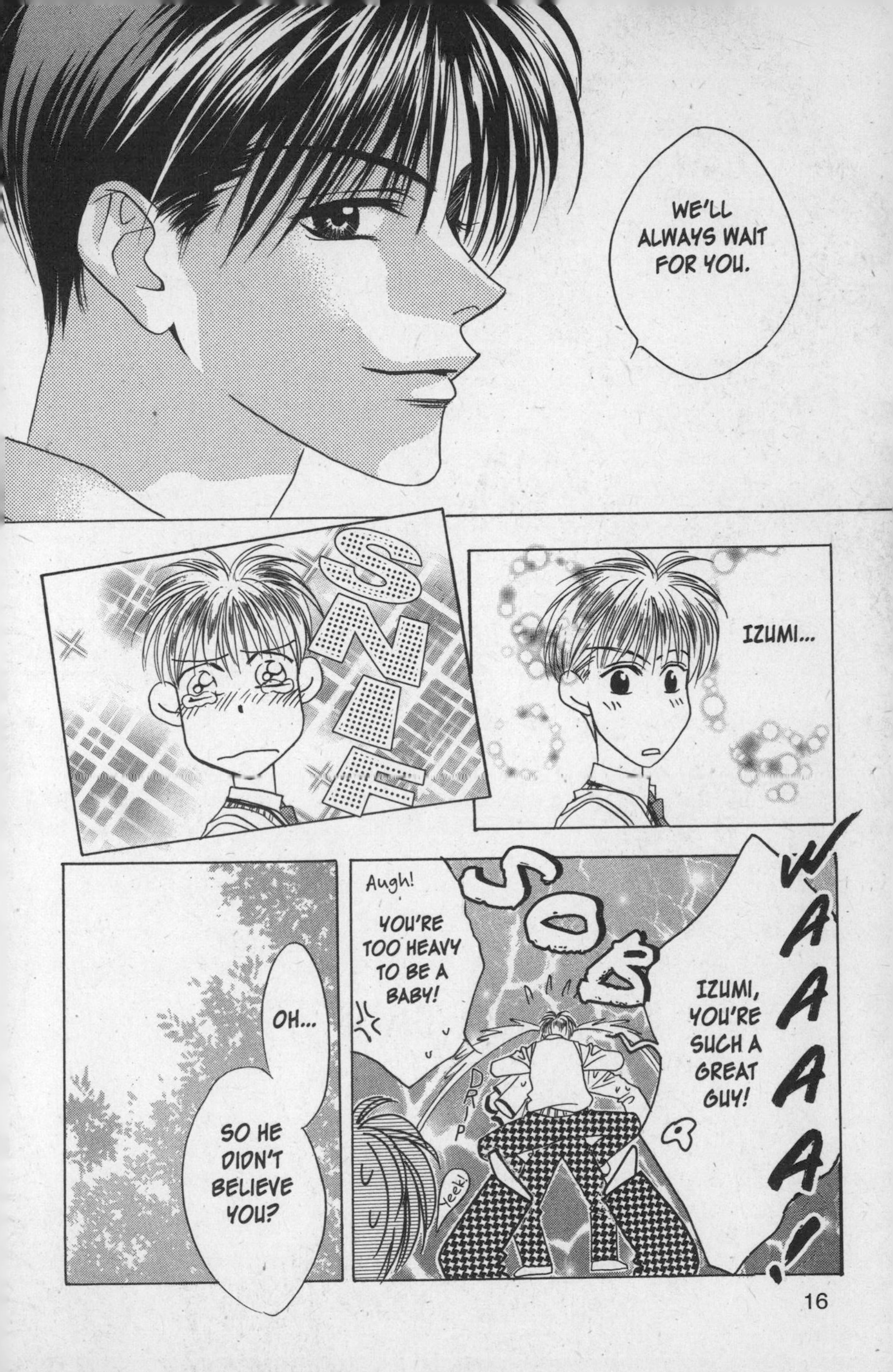
WE'LL ALWAYS WAIT FOR YOU.
IZUMI...
SNIFF
WAAAAA!!
IZUMI, YOU'RE SUCH A GREAT GUY!
SOB
Augh!
YOU'RE TOO HEAVY TO BE A BABY!
DRIP
Yeek!
OH...
SO HE DIDN'T BELIEVE YOU?

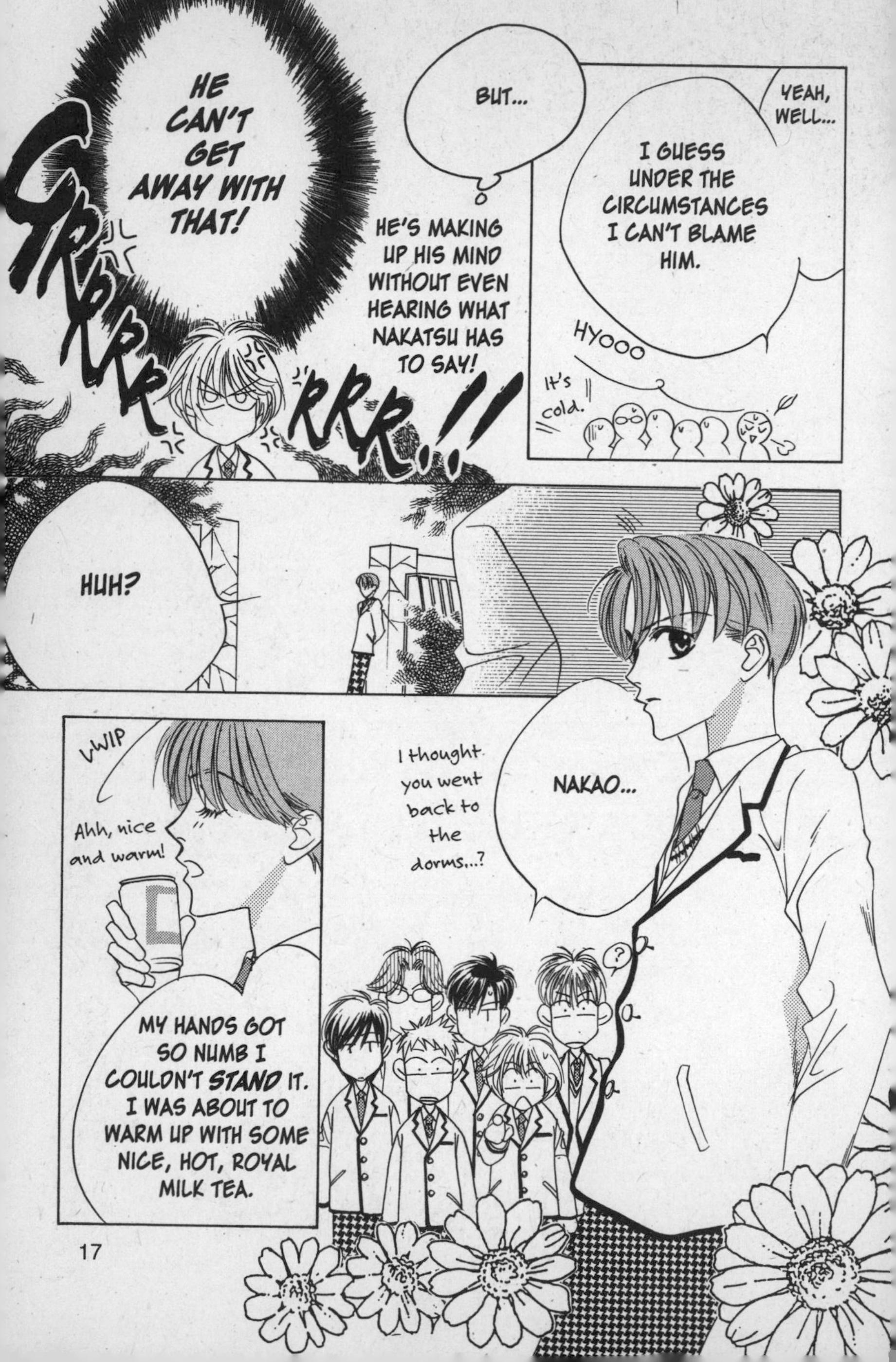
YEAH, WELL...
I GUESS UNDER THE CIRCUMSTANCES I CAN'T BLAME HIM.
HYOOO
It's cold.
BUT...
HE'S MAKING UP HIS MIND WITHOUT EVEN HEARING WHAT NAKATSU HAS TO SAY!
HE CAN'T GET AWAY WITH THAT!
GRRRRRRRR!!
HUH?
NAKAO...
I thought you went back to the dorms...?
WHIP
Ahh, nice and warm!
MY HANDS GOT SO NUMB I COULDN'T **STAND** IT. I WAS ABOUT TO WARM UP WITH SOME NICE, HOT, ROYAL MILK TEA.

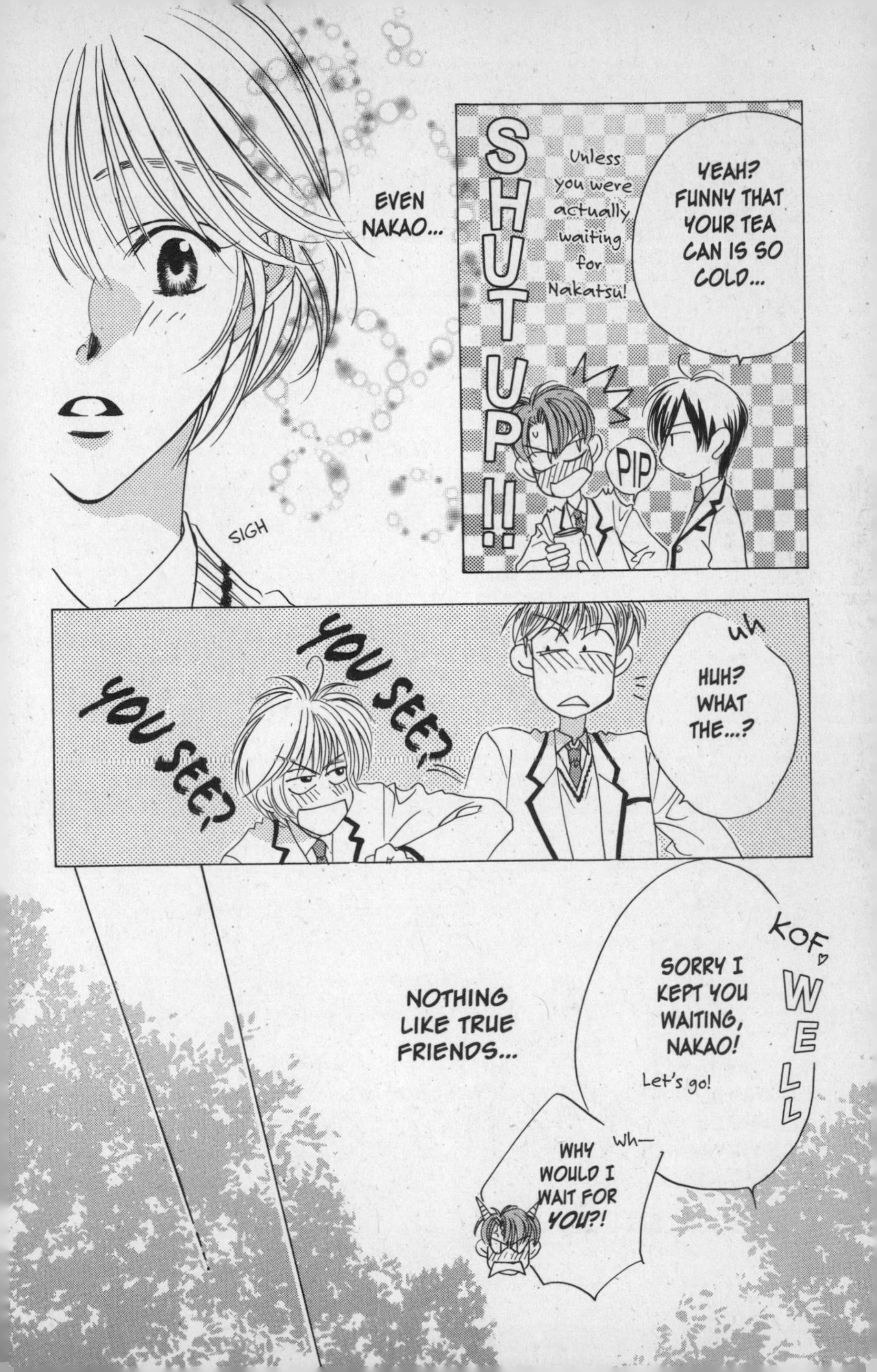
YEAH? FUNNY THAT YOUR TEA CAN IS SO COLD...
Unless you were actually waiting for Nakatsu!
SHUT UP!!
PIP
uh
HUH? WHAT THE...?
YOU SEE? YOU SEE?
EVEN NAKAO...
SIGH
KOF
WELL
SORRY I KEPT YOU WAITING, NAKAO!
Let's go!
NOTHING LIKE TRUE FRIENDS...
Wh—
WHY WOULD I WAIT FOR YOU?!

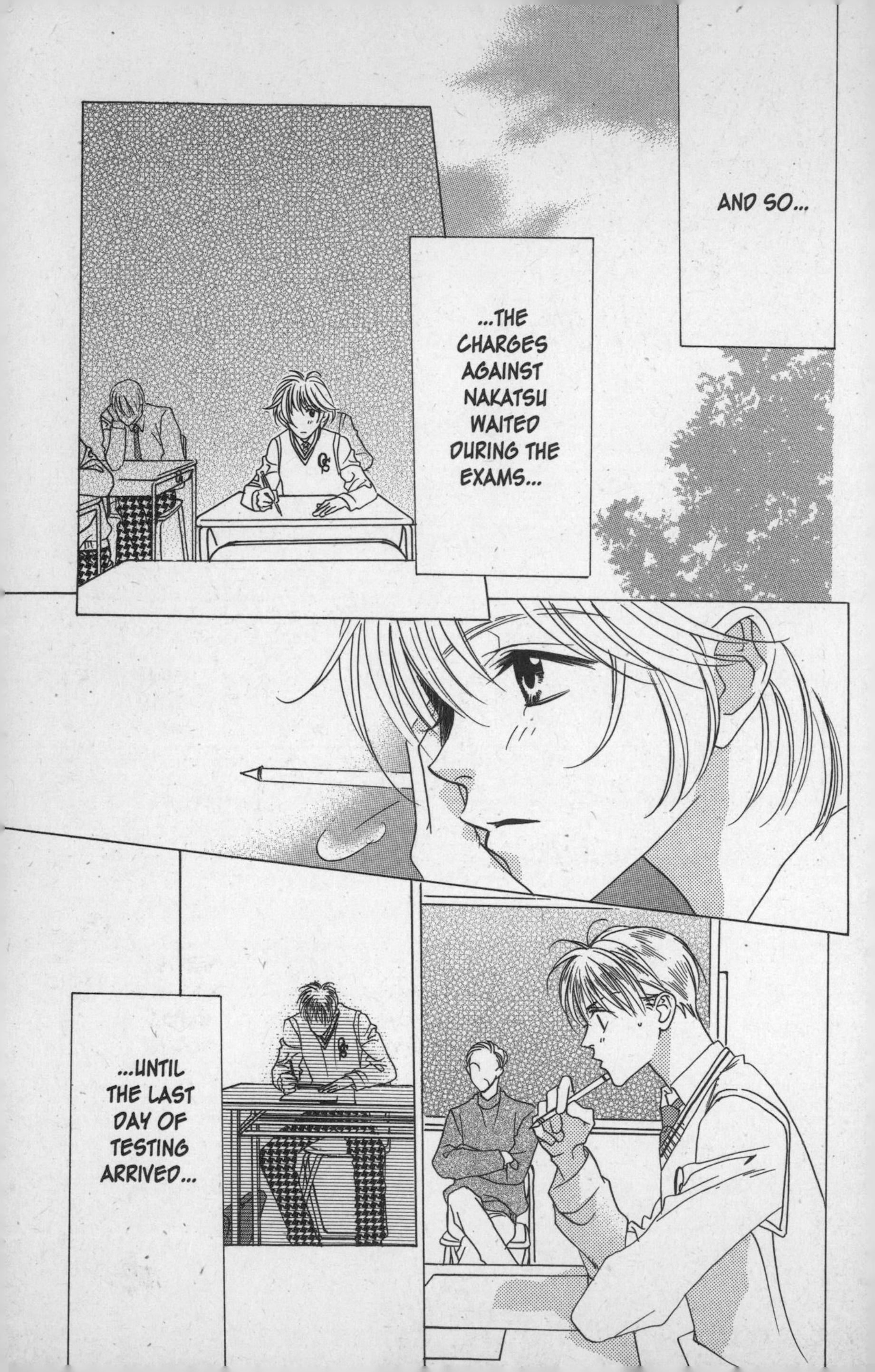
AND SO...
...THE CHARGES AGAINST NAKATSU WAITED DURING THE EXAMS...
...UNTIL THE LAST DAY OF TESTING ARRIVED...

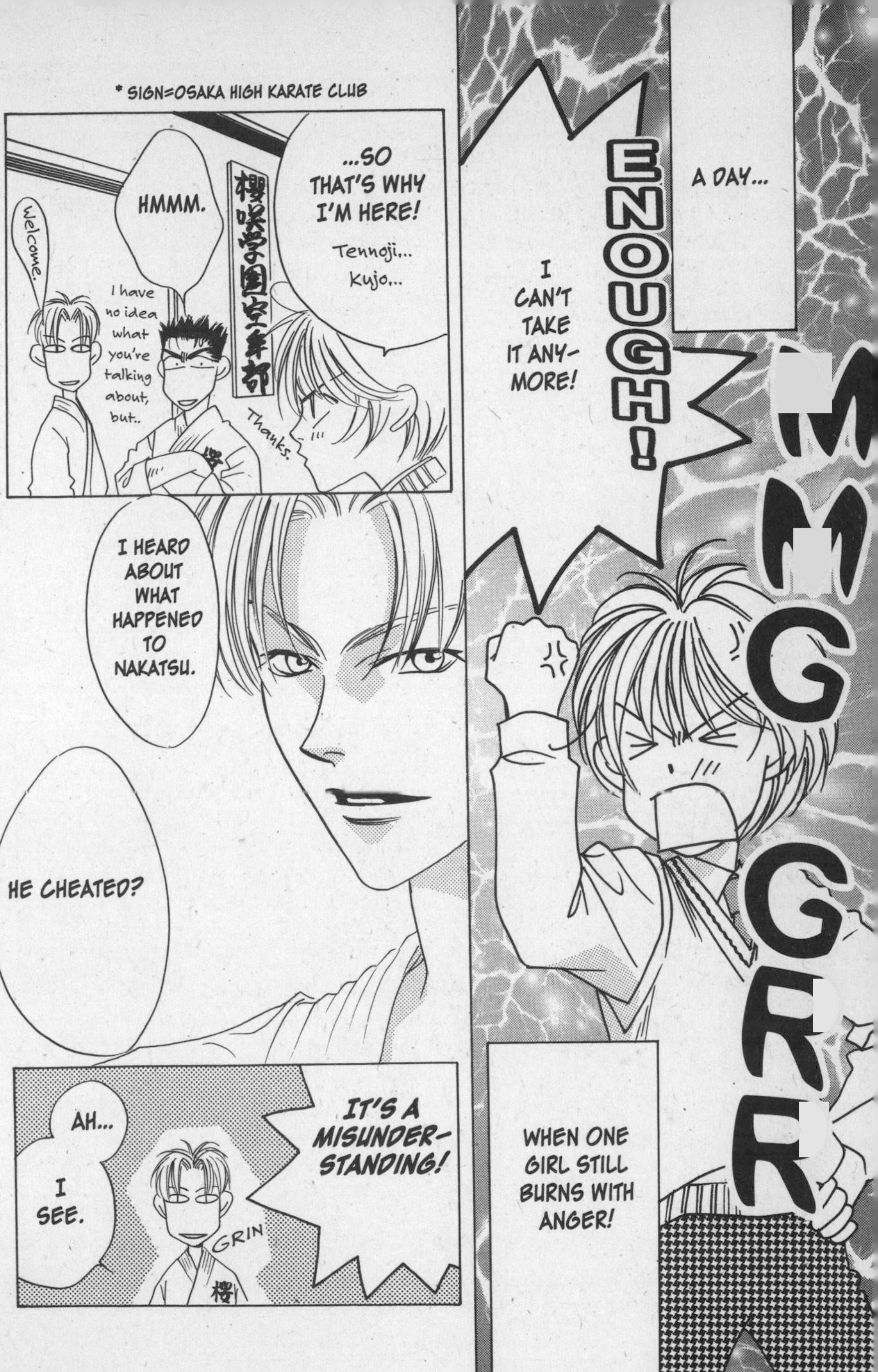
A DAY...
ENOUGH!
I CAN'T TAKE IT ANYMORE!
MMGGRR
WHEN ONE GIRL STILL BURNS WITH ANGER!
* SIGN=OSAKA HIGH KARATE CLUB
...SO THAT'S WHY I'M HERE!
Tennoji... Kujo...
櫻咲学園空手部
Thanks.
HMMM.
I have no idea what you're talking about, but..
Welcome.
I HEARD ABOUT WHAT HAPPENED TO NAKATSU.
HE CHEATED?
IT'S A MISUNDERSTANDING!
GRIN
AH...
I SEE.

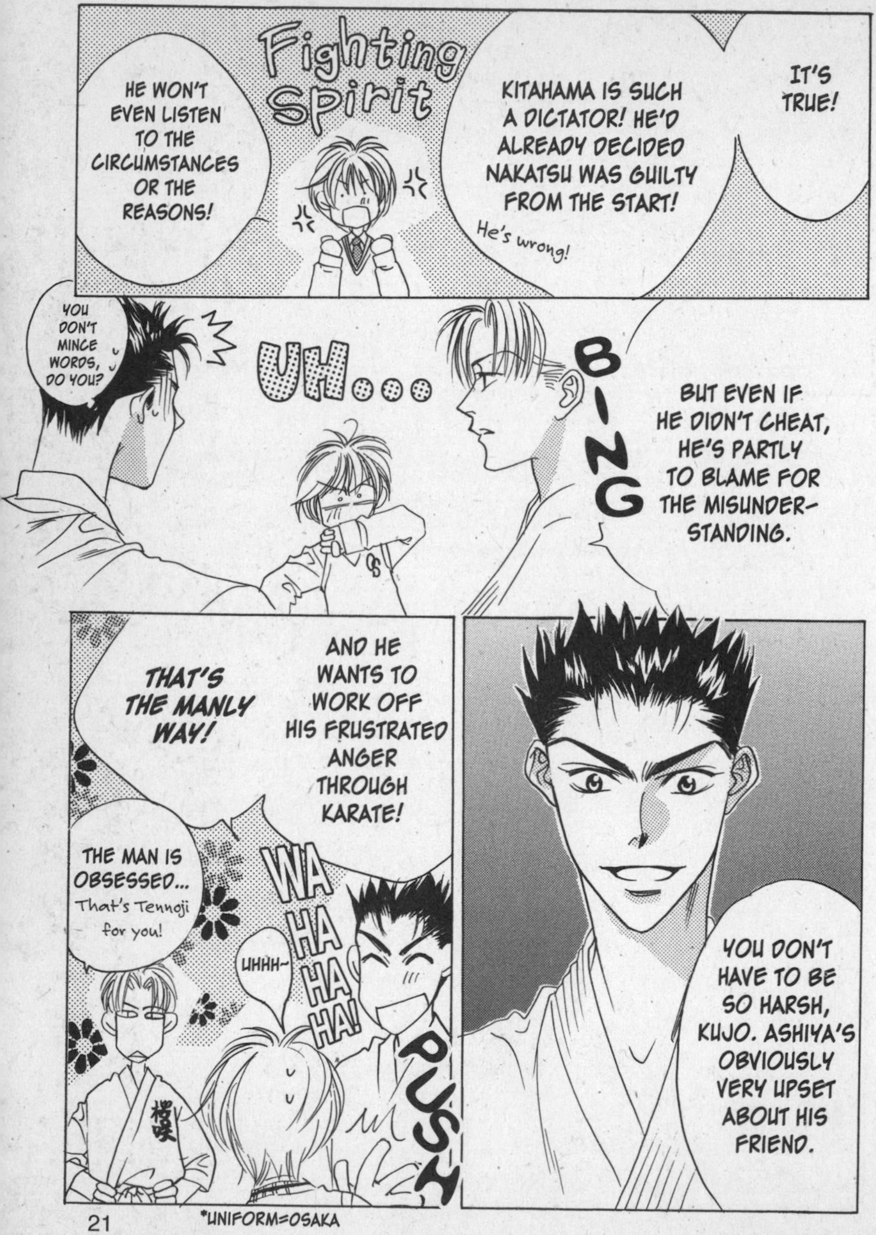
IT'S TRUE!
KITAHAMA IS SUCH A DICTATOR! HE'D ALREADY DECIDED NAKATSU WAS GUILTY FROM THE START!
He's wrong!
Fighting Spirit
HE WON'T EVEN LISTEN TO THE CIRCUMSTANCES OR THE REASONS!
BUT EVEN IF HE DIDN'T CHEAT, HE'S PARTLY TO BLAME FOR THE MISUNDER-STANDING.
BING
UH...
YOU DON'T MINCE WORDS, DO YOU?
YOU DON'T HAVE TO BE SO HARSH, KUJO. ASHIYA'S OBVIOUSLY VERY UPSET ABOUT HIS FRIEND.
AND HE WANTS TO WORK OFF HIS FRUSTRATED ANGER THROUGH KARATE!
THAT'S THE MANLY WAY!
WA HA HA HA!
PUSH
THE MAN IS OBSESSED...
That's Tennoji for you!
UHHH~

*UNIFORM=OSAKA

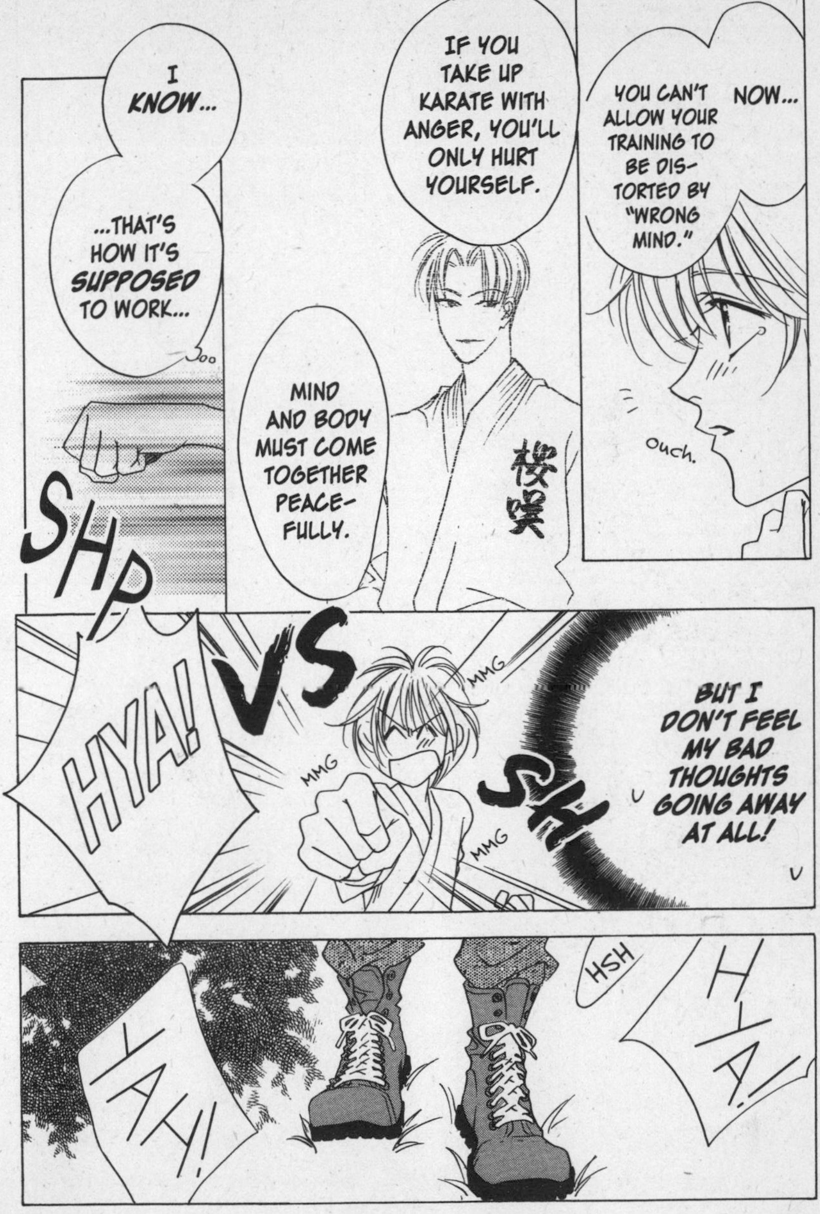
NOW...
YOU CAN'T ALLOW YOUR TRAINING TO BE DIS-TORTED BY "WRONG MIND."
Ouch.
IF YOU TAKE UP KARATE WITH ANGER, YOU'LL ONLY HURT YOURSELF.
MIND AND BODY MUST COME TOGETHER PEACE-FULLY.
I KNOW...
...THAT'S HOW IT'S SUPPOSED TO WORK...
SHP
BUT I DON'T FEEL MY BAD THOUGHTS GOING AWAY AT ALL!
SH
MMG
MMG
MMG
VS
HYA!
HYA!
HSH
YAH!

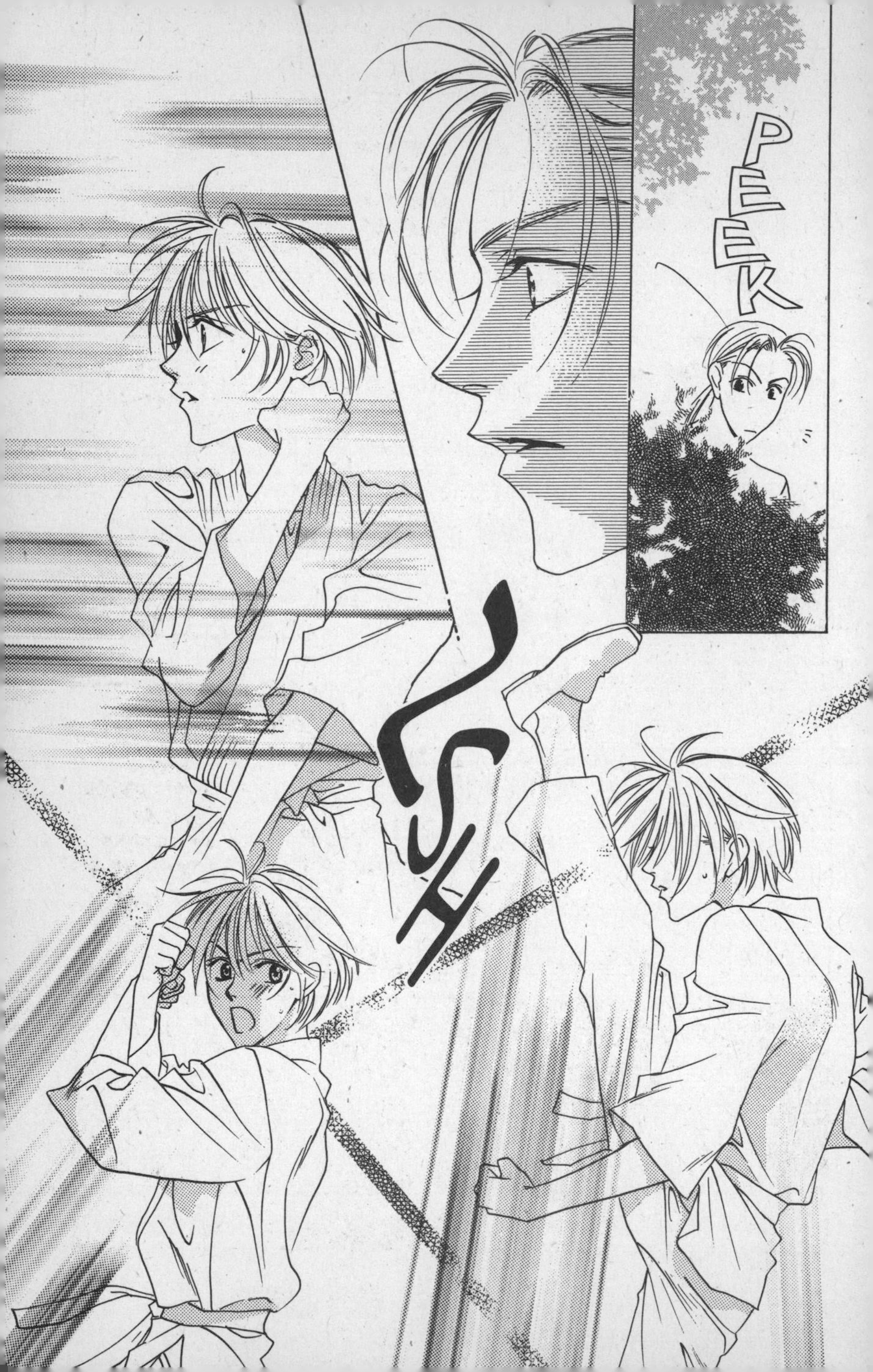
PEEK
SWISH

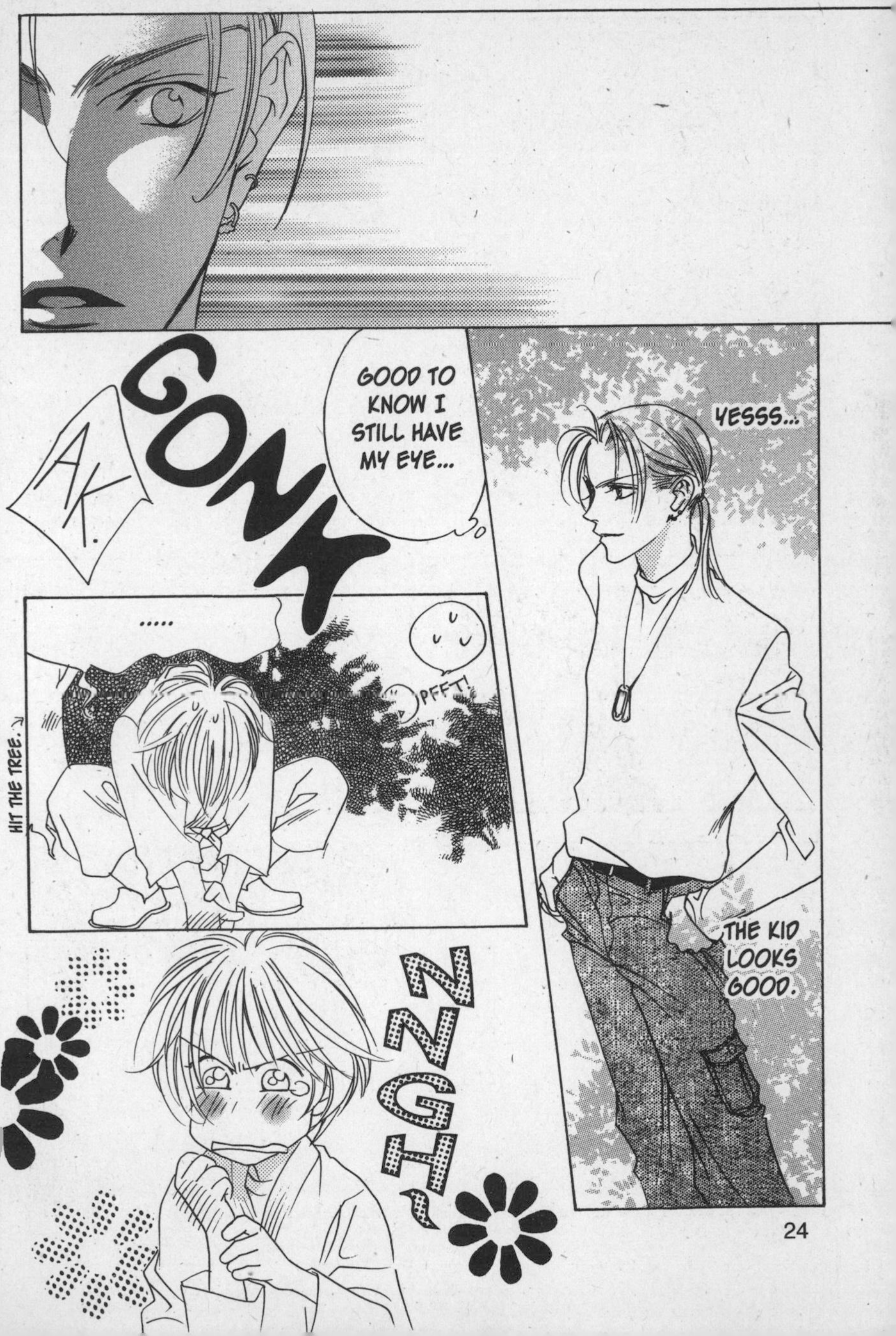
YESSS...
THE KID LOOKS GOOD.
GOOD TO KNOW I STILL HAVE MY EYE...
GONK
AK.
.....
PFFT!
HIT THE TREE.
NNGH,

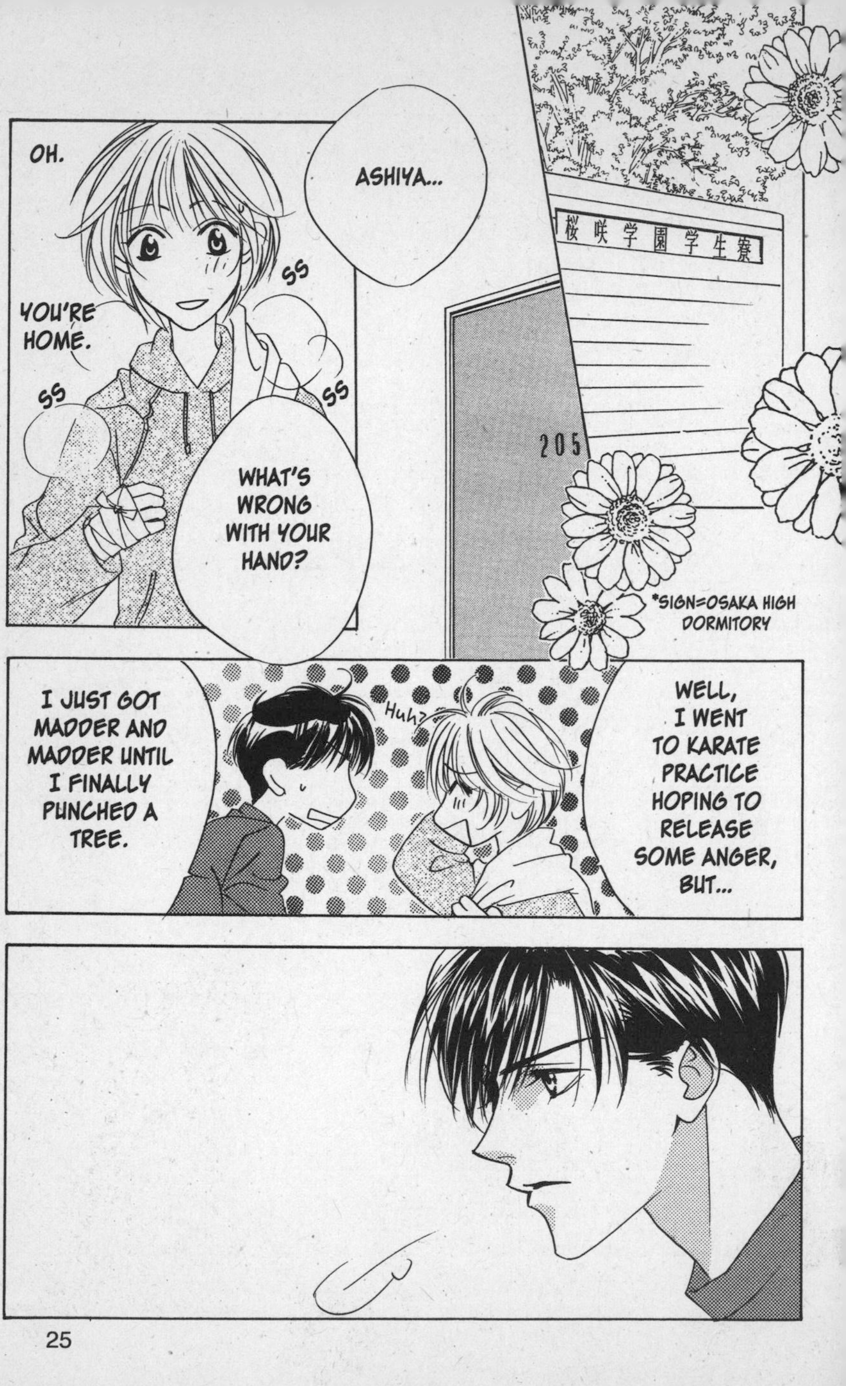
桜咲学園学生寮
205
*SIGN=OSAKA HIGH DORMITORY
OH.
ASHIYA...
YOU'RE HOME.
SS
SS
SS
WHAT'S WRONG WITH YOUR HAND?
WELL, I WENT TO KARATE PRACTICE HOPING TO RELEASE SOME ANGER, BUT...
Huh?
I JUST GOT MADDER AND MADDER UNTIL I FINALLY PUNCHED A TREE.

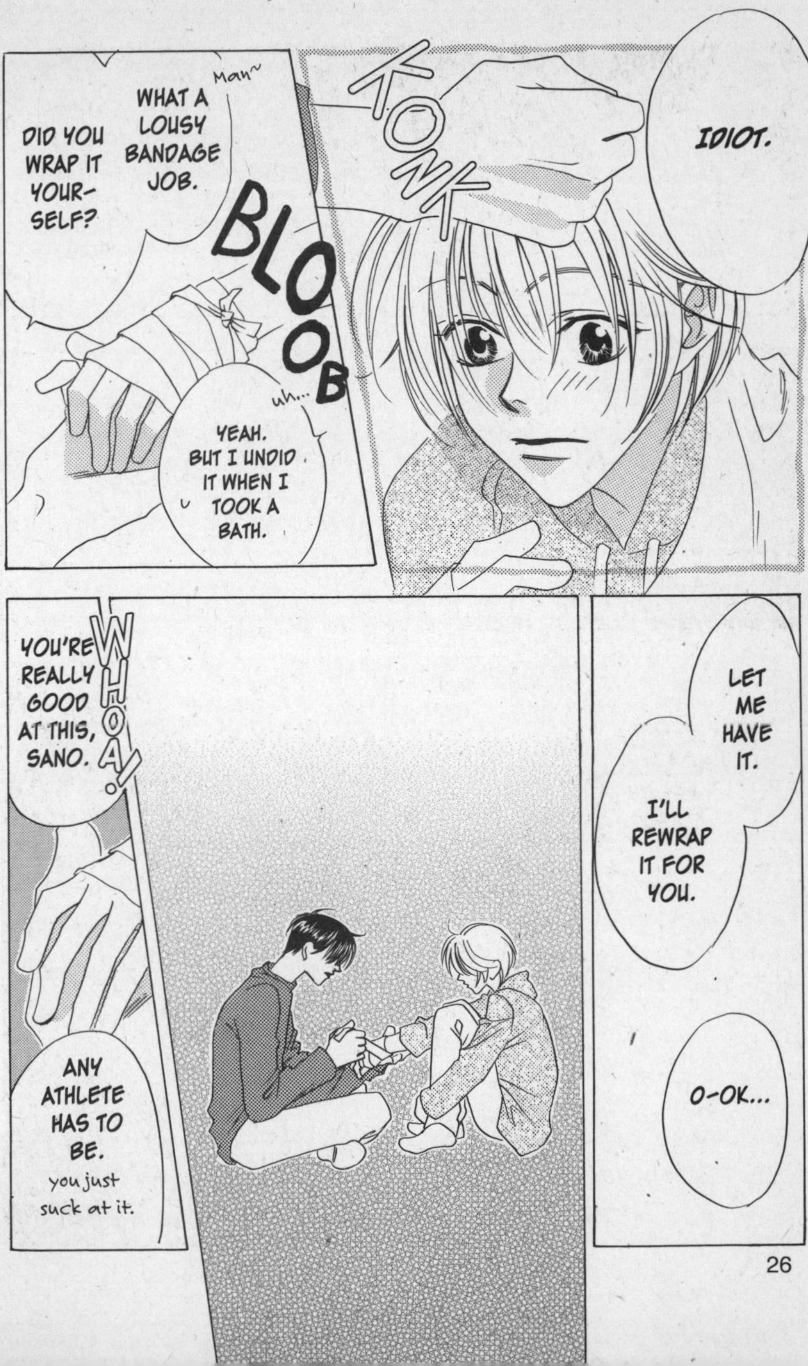
KONK
IDIOT.
Man~
WHAT A LOUSY BANDAGE JOB.
DID YOU WRAP IT YOURSELF?
BLOOB
uh...
YEAH. BUT I UNDID IT WHEN I TOOK A BATH.
LET ME HAVE IT.
I'LL REWRAP IT FOR YOU.
O-OK...
WHOA!
YOU'RE REALLY GOOD AT THIS, SANO.
ANY ATHLETE HAS TO BE.
you just suck at it.

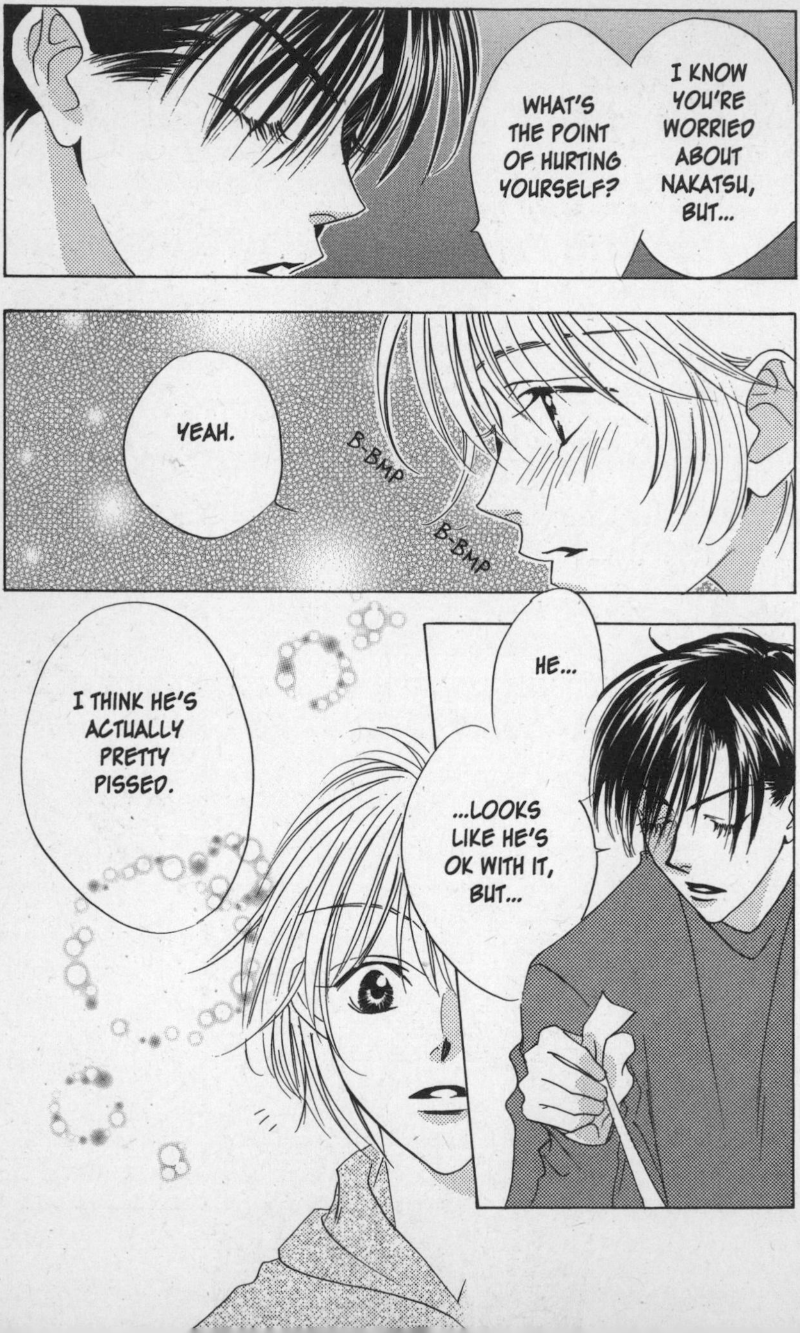
I KNOW YOU'RE WORRIED ABOUT NAKATSU, BUT...
WHAT'S THE POINT OF HURTING YOURSELF?
YEAH.
B-BMP
B-BMP
HE...
...LOOKS LIKE HE'S OK WITH IT, BUT...
I THINK HE'S ACTUALLY PRETTY PISSED.

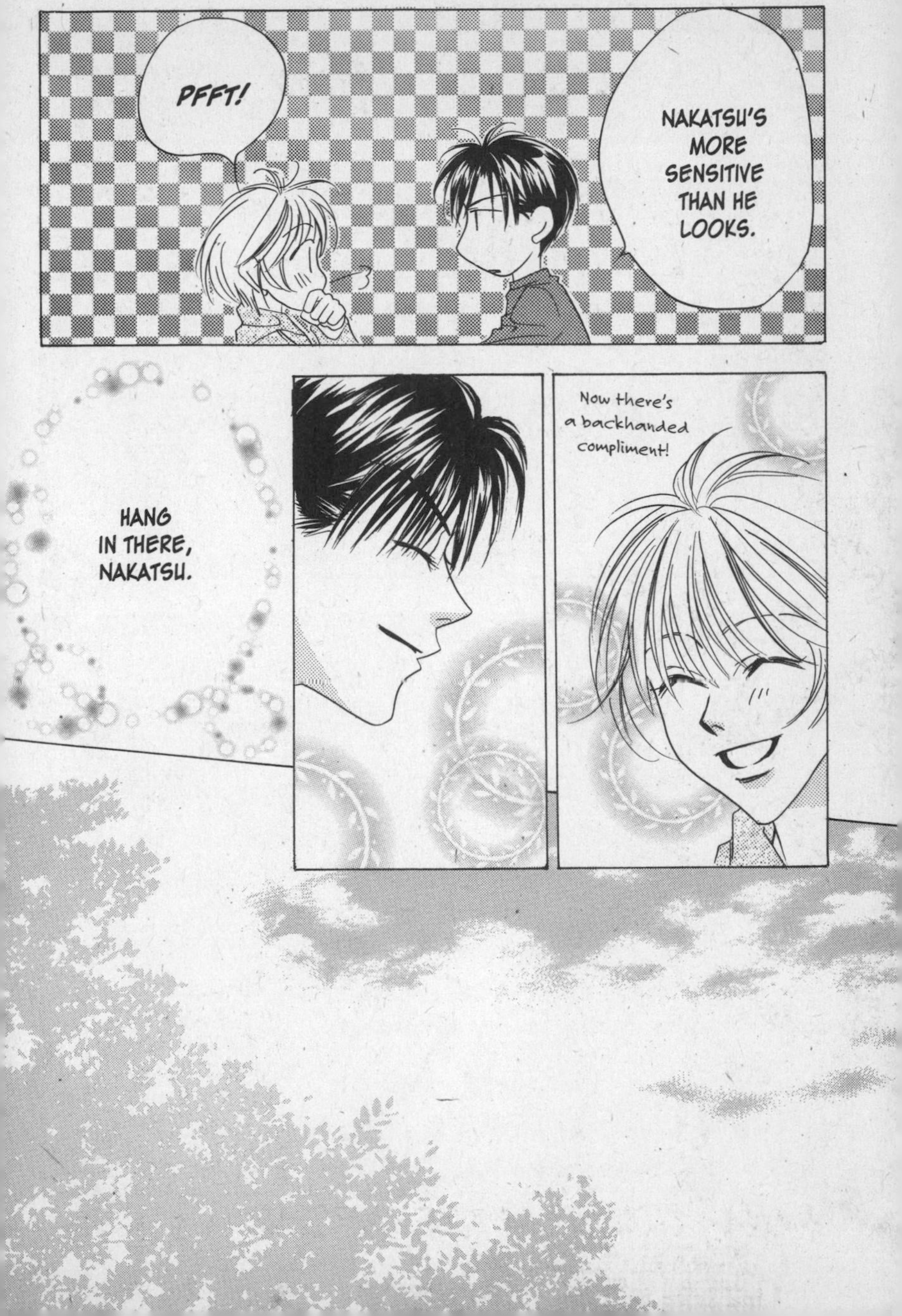
NAKATSU'S MORE SENSITIVE THAN HE LOOKS.
PFFT!
Now there's a backhanded compliment!
HANG IN THERE, NAKATSU.

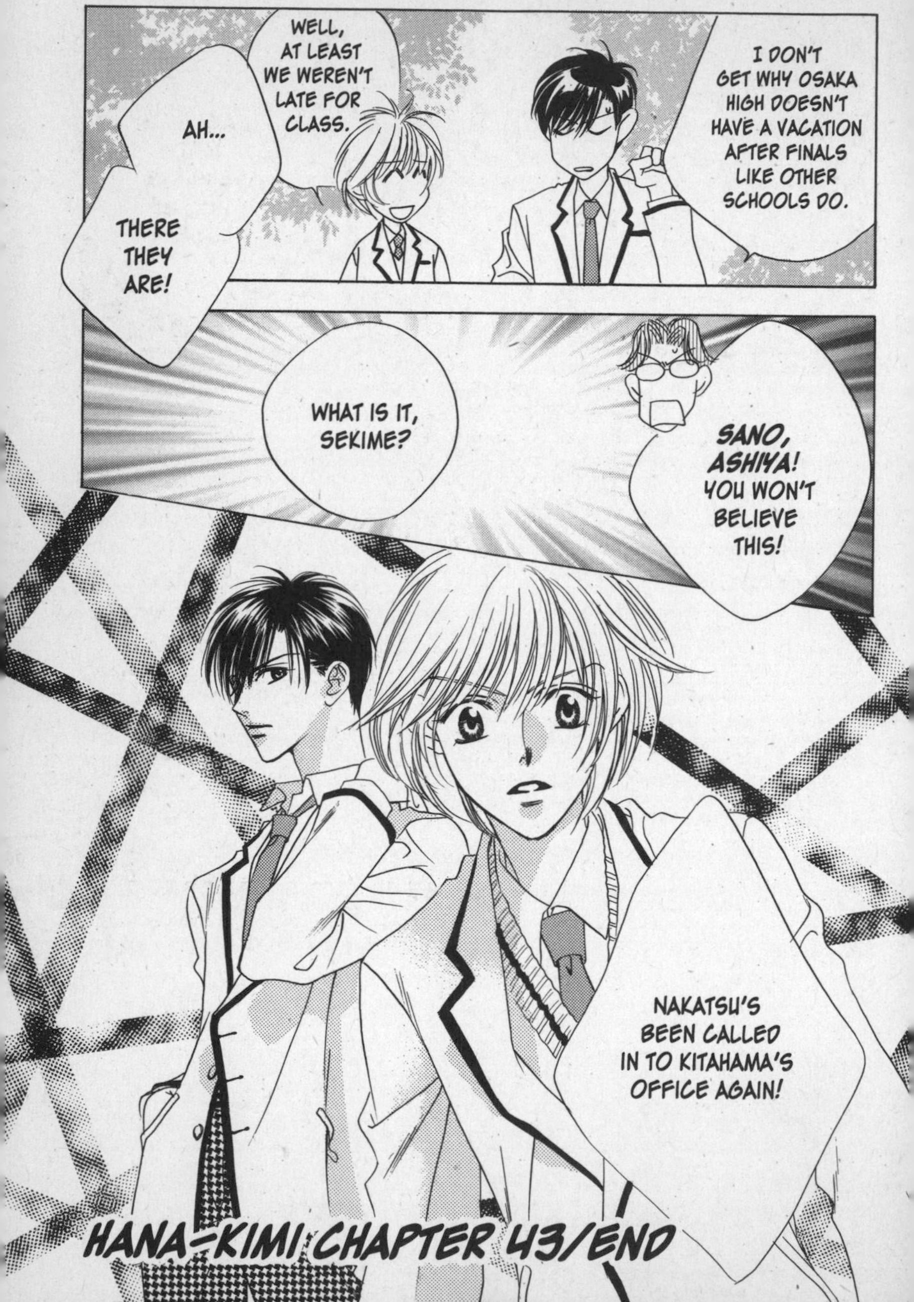
I DON'T GET WHY OSAKA HIGH DOESN'T HAVE A VACATION AFTER FINALS LIKE OTHER SCHOOLS DO.
WELL, AT LEAST WE WEREN'T LATE FOR CLASS.
AH... THERE THEY ARE!
SANO, ASHIYA! YOU WON'T BELIEVE THIS!
WHAT IS IT, SEKIME?
NAKATSU'S BEEN CALLED IN TO KITAHAMA'S OFFICE AGAIN!
HANA-KIMI CHAPTER 43/END

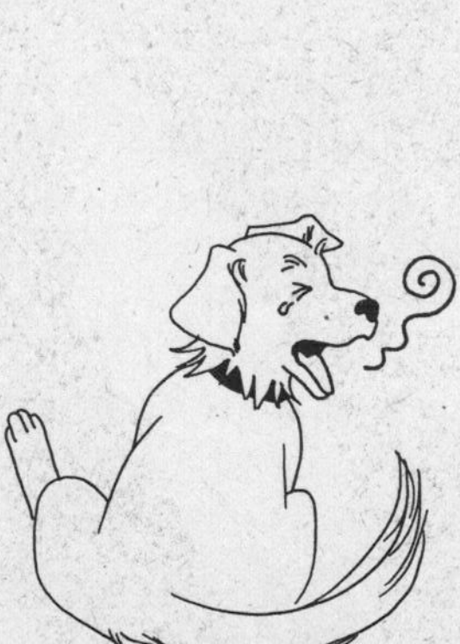

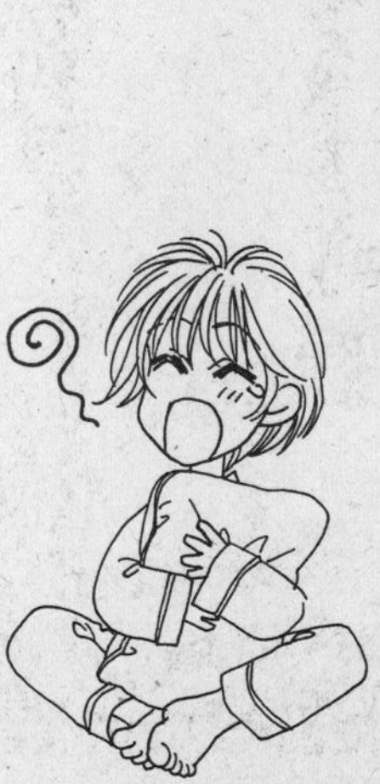

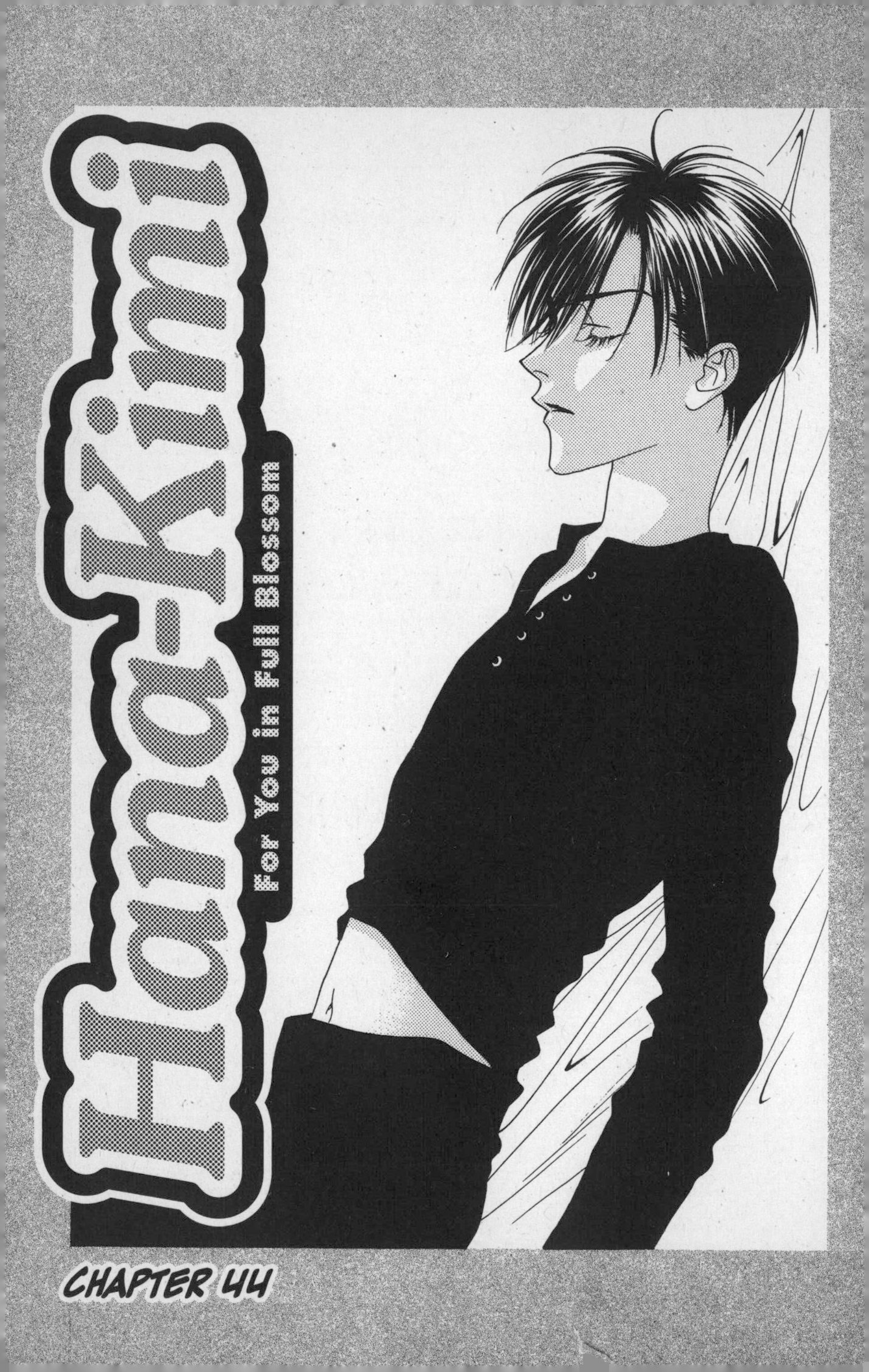
Hana-Kimi
For You in Full Blossom

CHAPTER 44

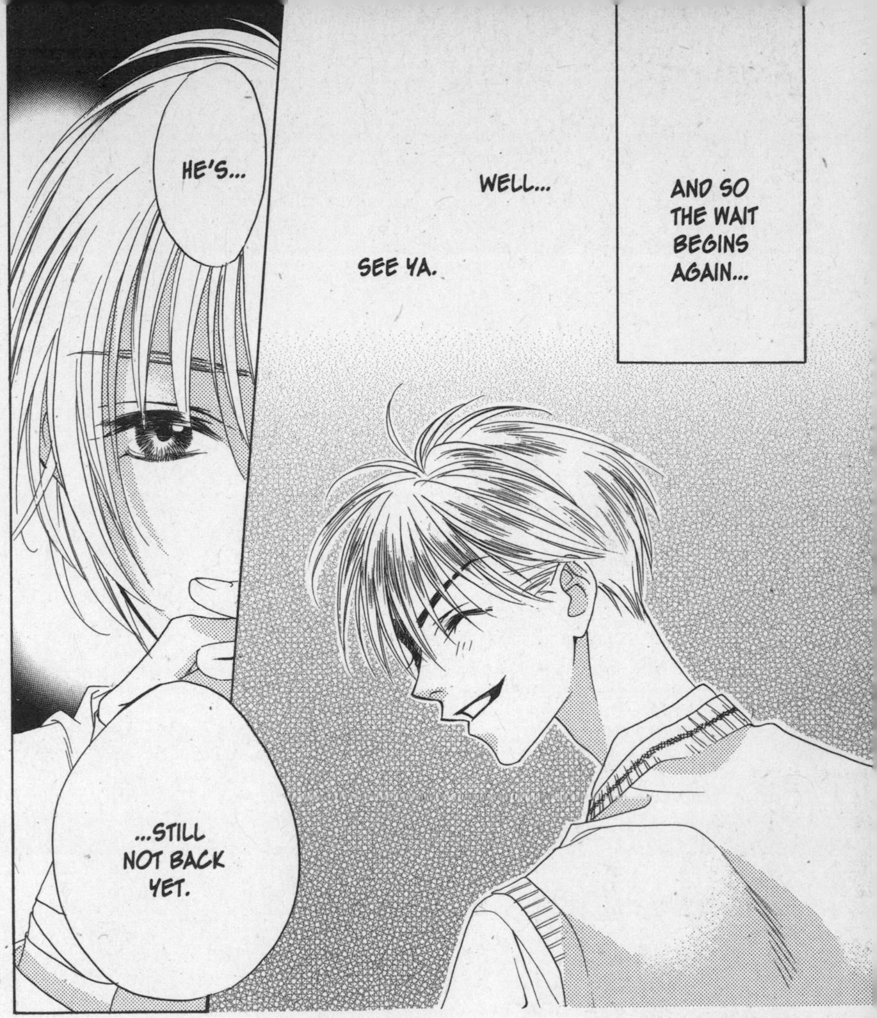
AND SO THE WAIT BEGINS AGAIN...
WELL...
SEE YA.
HE'S...
...STILL NOT BACK YET.

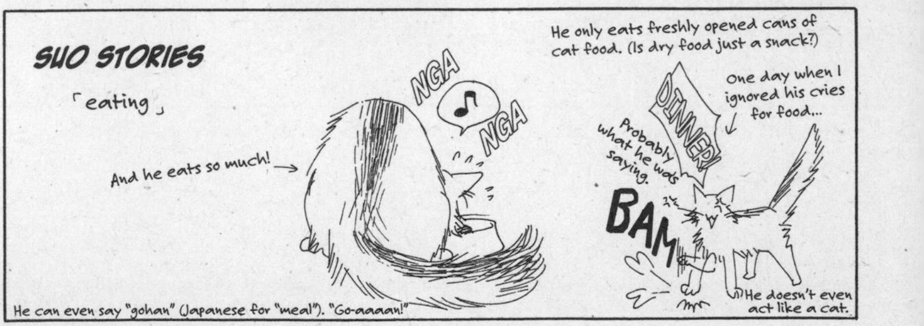
SUO STORIES
「eating」
He only eats freshly opened cans of cat food. (Is dry food just a snack?)
One day when I ignored his cries for food...
DINNER!
Probably what he was saying.
BAM
He doesn't even act like a cat.
NGA
♪
NGA
And he eats so much!
He can even say "gohan" (Japanese for "meal"). "Go-aaaaan!"

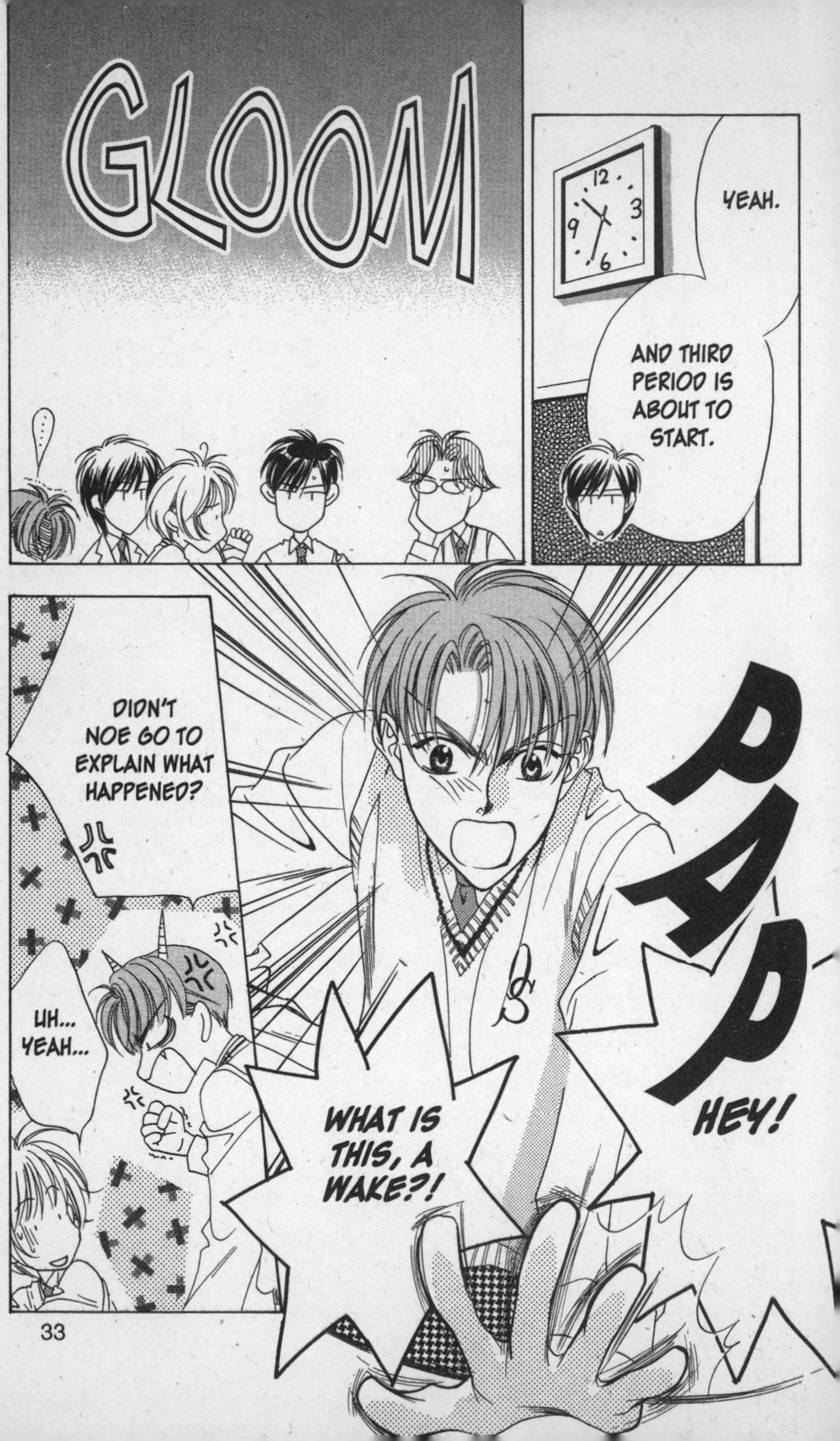
YEAH.
AND THIRD PERIOD IS ABOUT TO START.
GLOOM
PAP
HEY!
WHAT IS THIS, A WAKE?!
DIDN'T NOE GO TO EXPLAIN WHAT HAPPENED?
UH... YEAH...

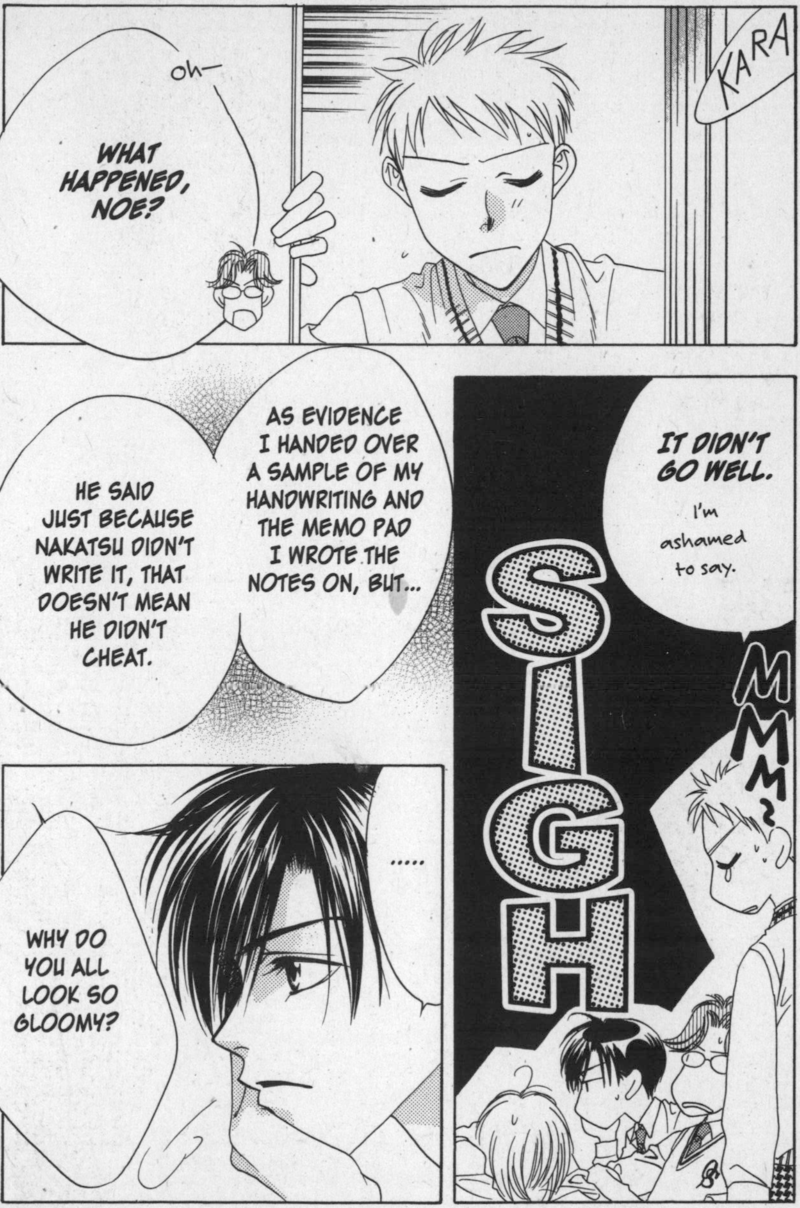
KARA
Oh—
WHAT HAPPENED, NOE?
IT DIDN'T GO WELL.
I'm ashamed to say.
SIGH
MMMM
AS EVIDENCE I HANDED OVER A SAMPLE OF MY HANDWRITING AND THE MEMO PAD I WROTE THE NOTES ON, BUT...
HE SAID JUST BECAUSE NAKATSU DIDN'T WRITE IT, THAT DOESN'T MEAN HE DIDN'T CHEAT.
.....
WHY DO YOU ALL LOOK SO GLOOMY?

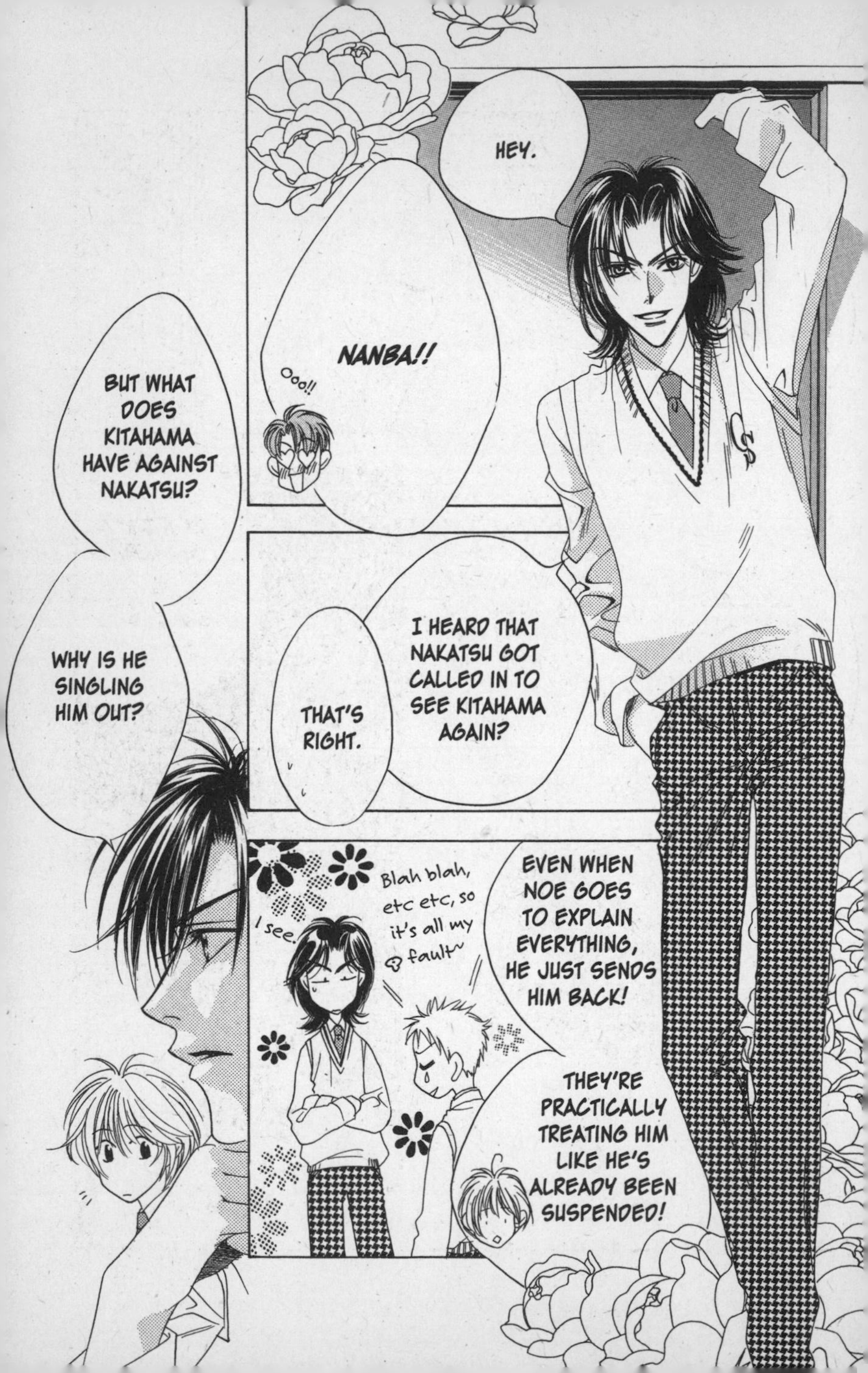
HEY.
NANBA!!
Ooo!!
I HEARD THAT NAKATSU GOT CALLED IN TO SEE KITAHAMA AGAIN?
THAT'S RIGHT.
EVEN WHEN NOE GOES TO EXPLAIN EVERYTHING, HE JUST SENDS HIM BACK!
THEY'RE PRACTICALLY TREATING HIM LIKE HE'S ALREADY BEEN SUSPENDED!
Blah blah, etc etc, so it's all my fault~
I see.
BUT WHAT DOES KITAHAMA HAVE AGAINST NAKATSU?
WHY IS HE SINGLING HIM OUT?

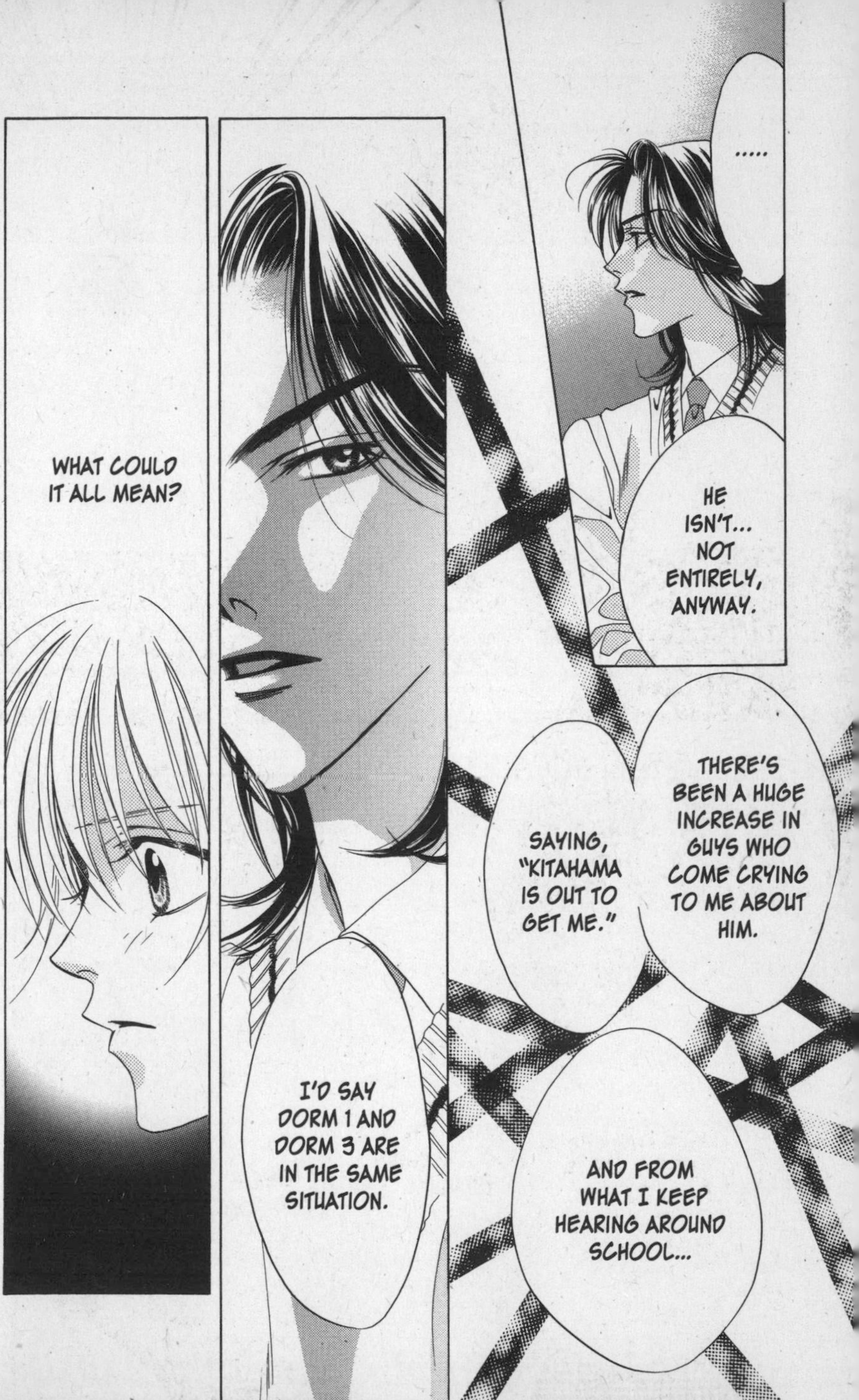
.....
HE ISN'T... NOT ENTIRELY, ANYWAY.
THERE'S BEEN A HUGE INCREASE IN GUYS WHO COME CRYING TO ME ABOUT HIM.
SAYING, "KITAHAMA IS OUT TO GET ME."
AND FROM WHAT I KEEP HEARING AROUND SCHOOL...
I'D SAY DORM 1 AND DORM 3 ARE IN THE SAME SITUATION.
WHAT COULD IT ALL MEAN?

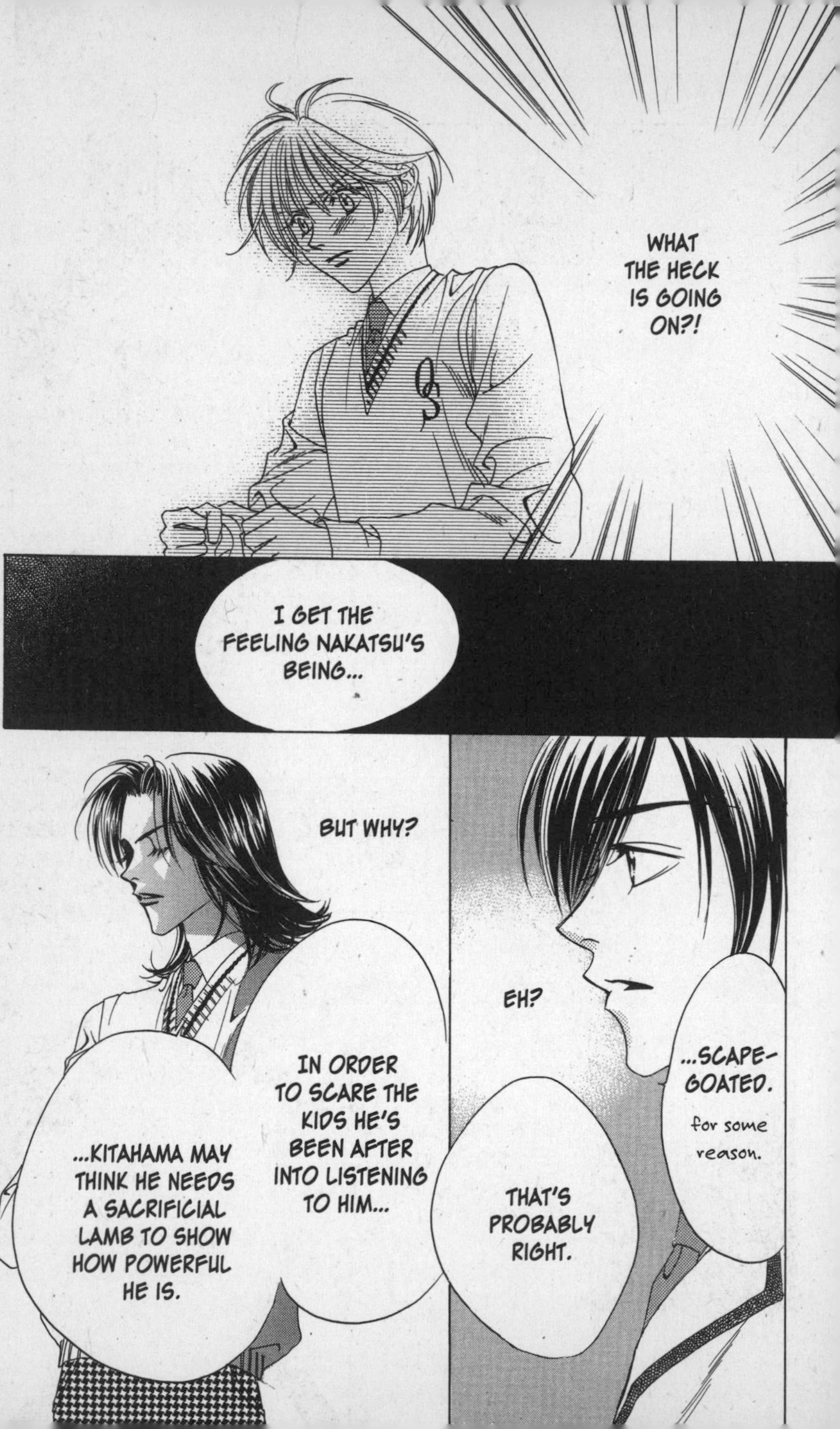
WHAT THE HECK IS GOING ON?!
I GET THE FEELING NAKATSU'S BEING...
...SCAPE-GOATED.
for some reason.
EH?
THAT'S PROBABLY RIGHT.
BUT WHY?
IN ORDER TO SCARE THE KIDS HE'S BEEN AFTER INTO LISTENING TO HIM...
...KITAHAMA MAY THINK HE NEEDS A SACRIFICIAL LAMB TO SHOW HOW POWERFUL HE IS.

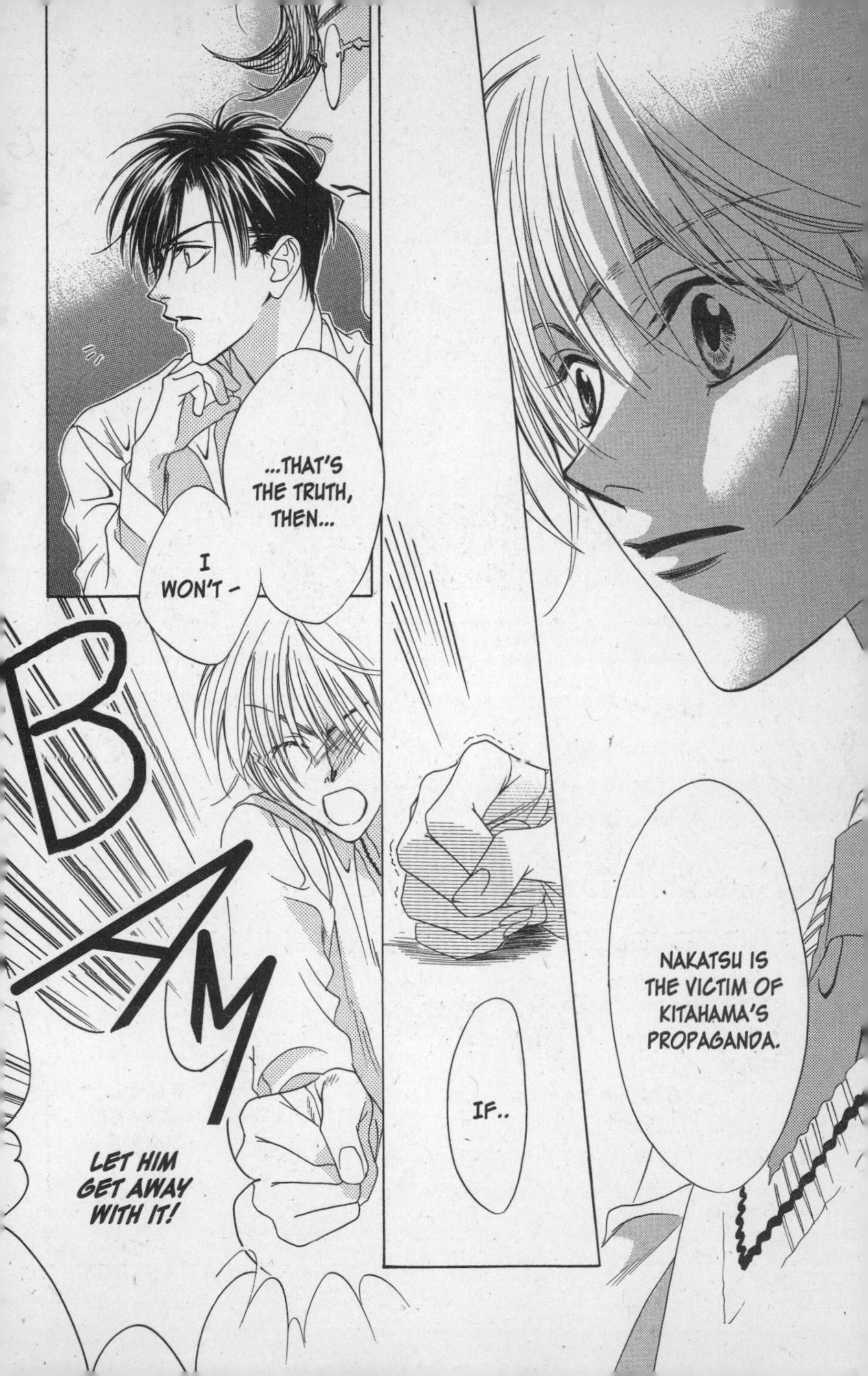
NAKATSU IS THE VICTIM OF KITAHAMA'S PROPAGANDA.
IF..
...THAT'S THE TRUTH, THEN...
I WON'T -
BAM
LET HIM GET AWAY WITH IT!

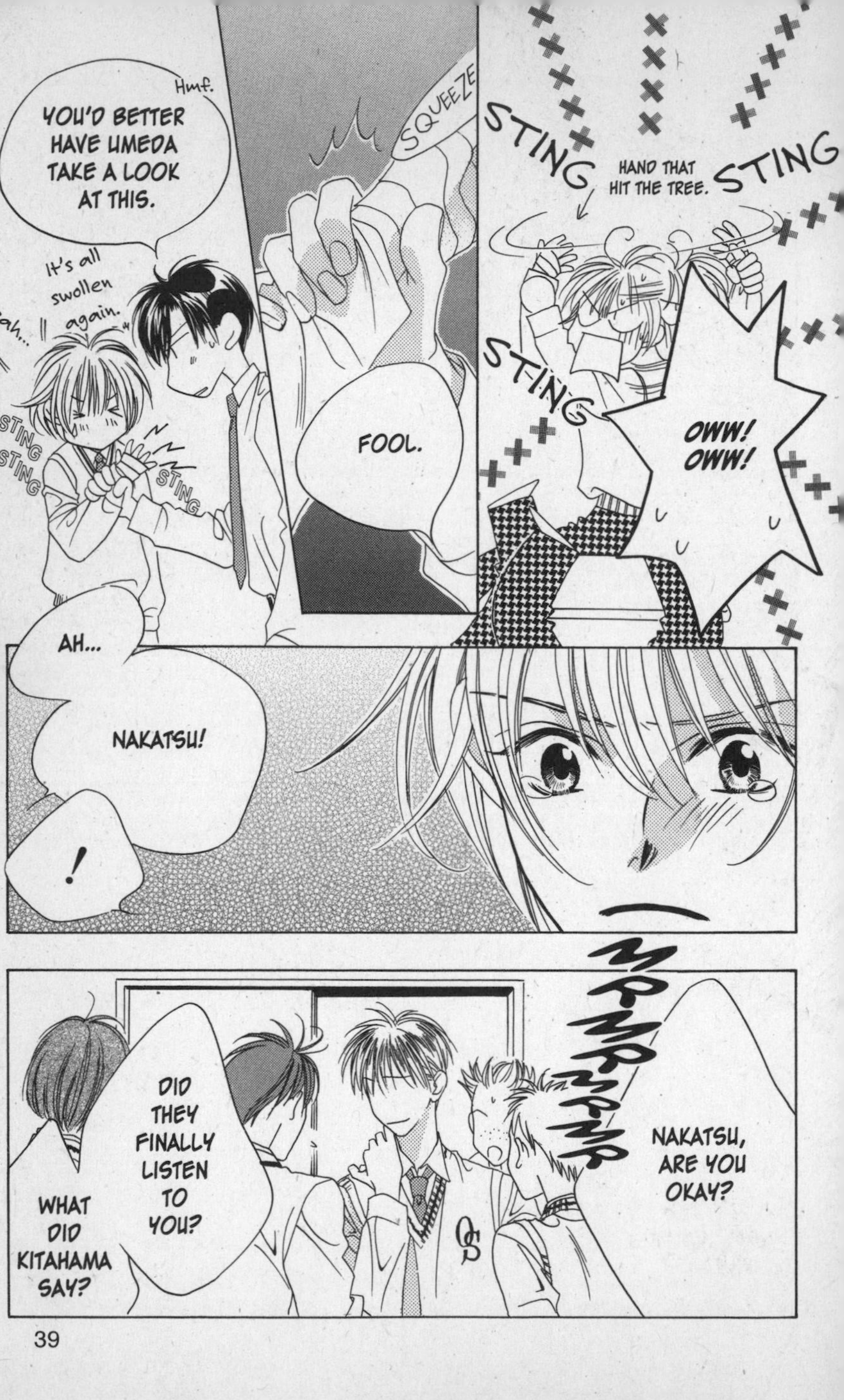
STING
HAND THAT HIT THE TREE.
STING
STING
OWW! OWW!
SQUEEZE
FOOL.
Hmf.
YOU'D BETTER HAVE UMEDA TAKE A LOOK AT THIS.
It's all swollen again.
Yeah...
STING STING
STING
AH...
NAKATSU!
!
NAKATSU, ARE YOU OKAY?
MRMRMRMR
DID THEY FINALLY LISTEN TO YOU?
WHAT DID KITAHAMA SAY?

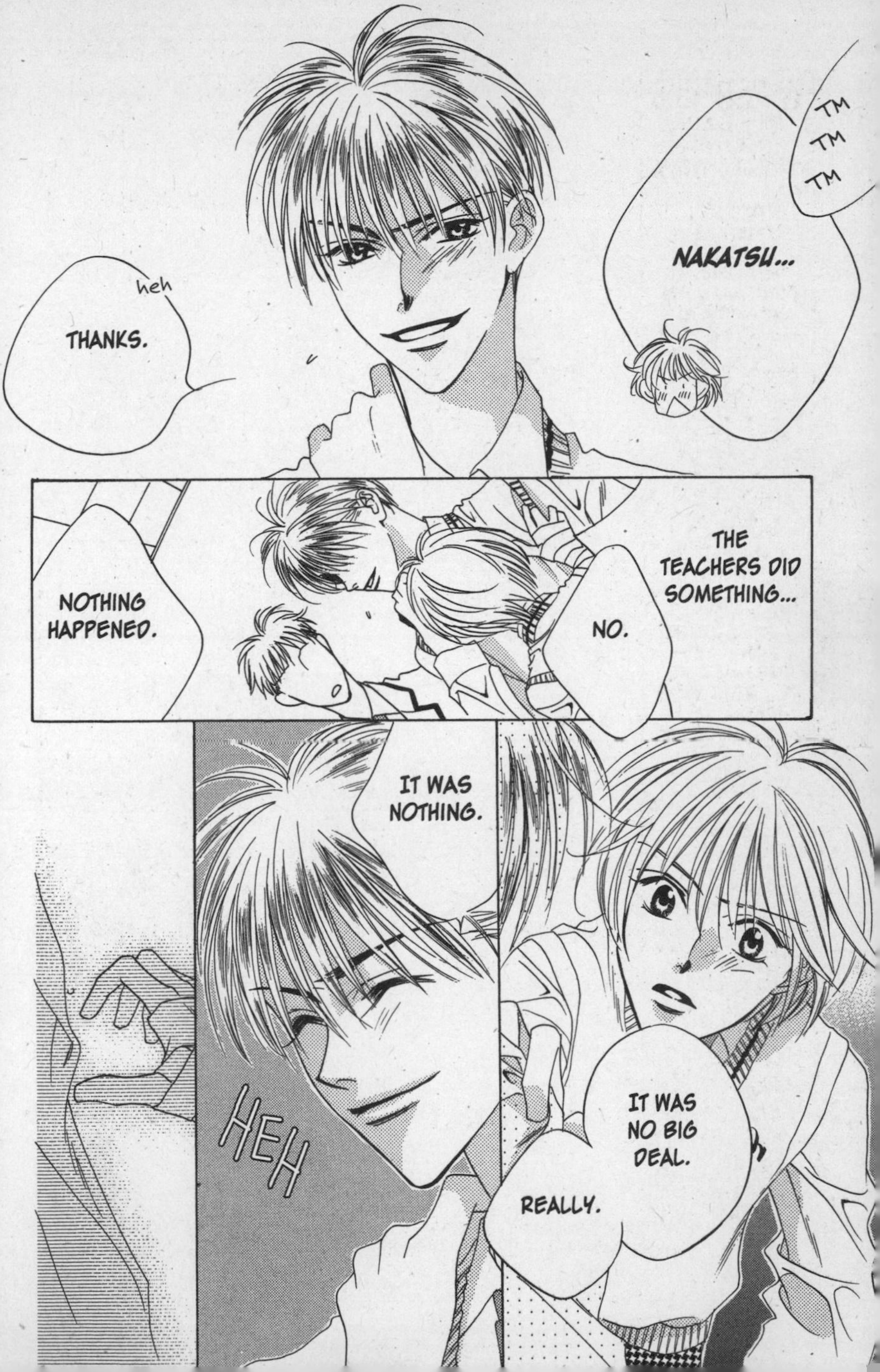
TM
TM
TM
NAKATSU...
heh
THANKS.
THE TEACHERS DID SOMETHING...
NO.
NOTHING HAPPENED.
IT WAS NOTHING.
HEH
IT WAS NO BIG DEAL.
REALLY.

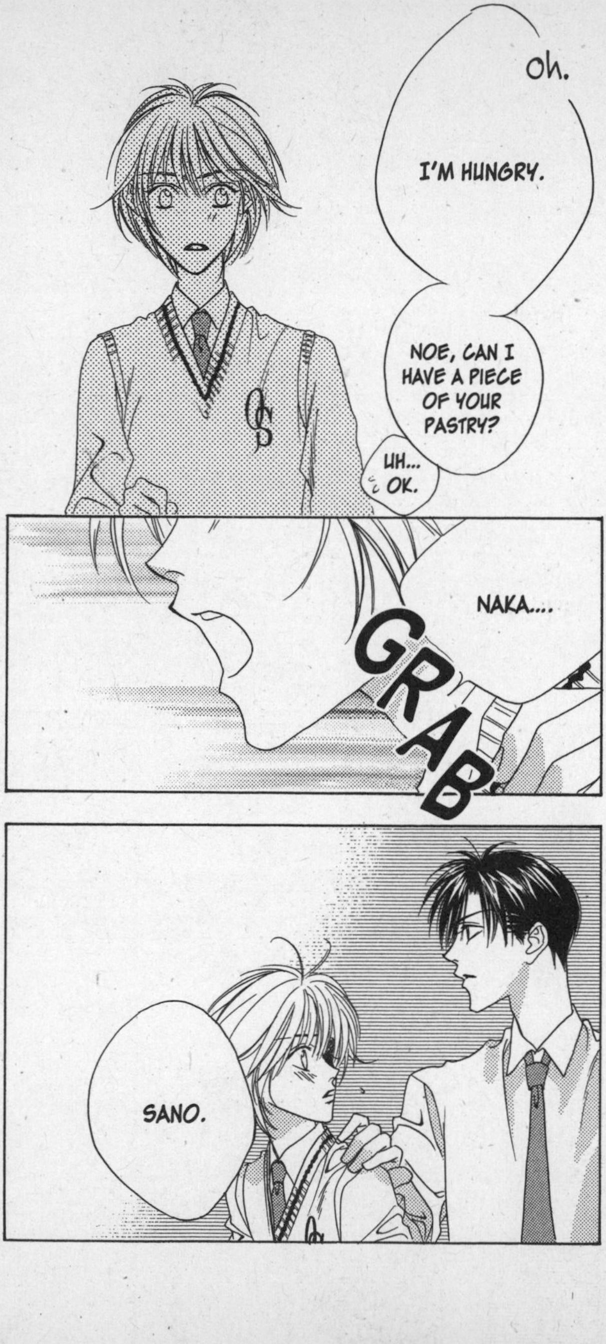
Oh.
I'M HUNGRY.
NOE, CAN I HAVE A PIECE OF YOUR PASTRY?
UH... OK.
NAKA....
GRAB
SANO.

WHISPERED SECRETS

PREMONITION

THIS CAN DEFINITELY BE CLASSIFIED AS "STRANGE." I DON'T HAVE ESP OR ANYTHING, BUT SOMETIMES I HAVE THESE WEIRD DREAMS. I HAD THE FIRST ONE WHEN I WAS IN 6TH GRADE. IN THE DREAM, IT WAS THE DAY BEFORE MY JUNIOR HIGH ENTRANCE EXAMS AND MY CLASSMATE "O" (WHO WAS SUPPOSED TO HAVE A BETTER CHANCE OF PASSING THAN ME) AND I WERE STANDING IN AN AREA WHERE THE FLOOR WAS COVERED WITH CHERRY BLOSSOMS. A BLACK PIT SUDDENLY OPENED UP AND "O" FELL IN. I THOUGHT IT WAS JUST A WEIRD DREAM, BUT ON THE DAY WE GOT OUR SCORES, I FOUND OUT THAT "O" HAD FAILED AND I HAD PASSED. AND I HAD THE SAME KIND OF DREAMS DURING MY HIGH SCHOOL AND COLLEGE ENTRANCE EXAMS. WHAT'S UP WITH THAT?

WE WERE TRYING TO GET INTO DIFFERENT SCHOOLS

AND THEY CAME TRUE!

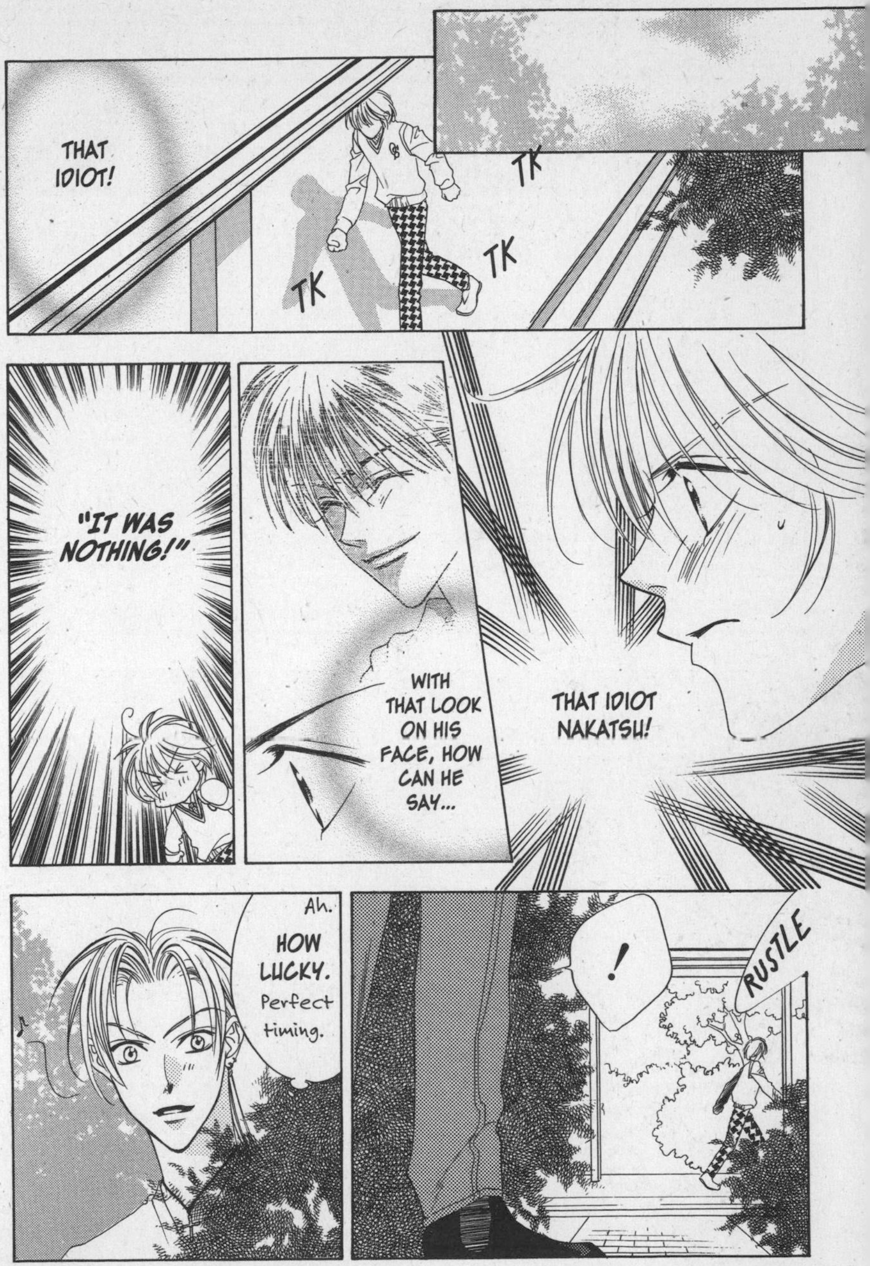
TK
TK
TK
THAT IDIOT!
THAT IDIOT NAKATSU!
WITH THAT LOOK ON HIS FACE, HOW CAN HE SAY...
"IT WAS NOTHING!"
RUSTLE
!
Ah.
HOW LUCKY.
Perfect timing.

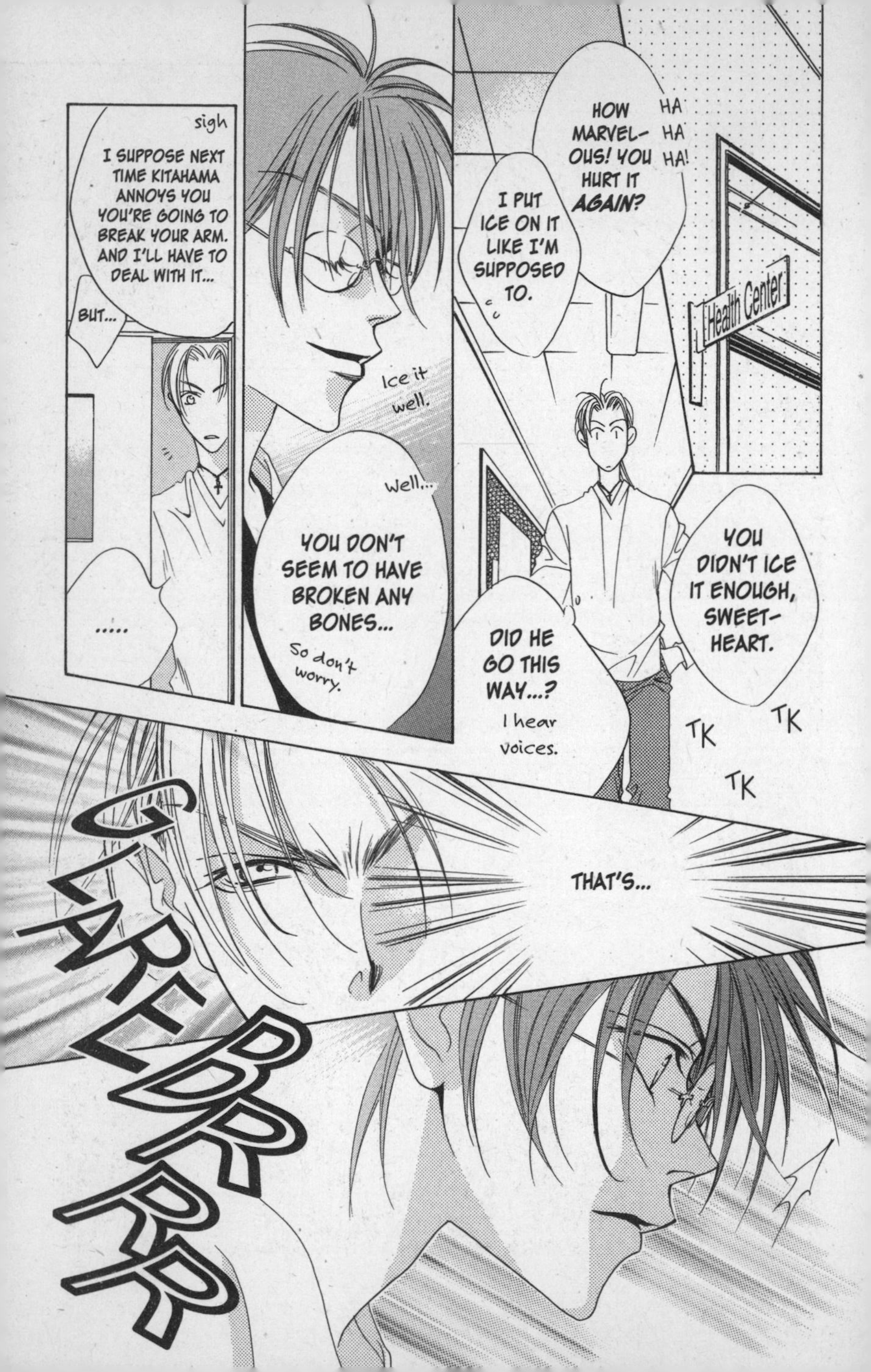
HOW MARVELOUS! YOU HURT IT AGAIN?
HA HA HA!
I PUT ICE ON IT LIKE I'M SUPPOSED TO.
Health Center
YOU DIDN'T ICE IT ENOUGH, SWEETHEART.
DID HE GO THIS WAY...?
I hear voices.
TK
TK
TK
Ice it well.
well...
YOU DON'T SEEM TO HAVE BROKEN ANY BONES...
So don't worry.
sigh
I SUPPOSE NEXT TIME KITAHAMA ANNOYS YOU YOU'RE GOING TO BREAK YOUR ARM. AND I'LL HAVE TO DEAL WITH IT...
BUT...
.....
THAT'S...
GLARE
BRRR

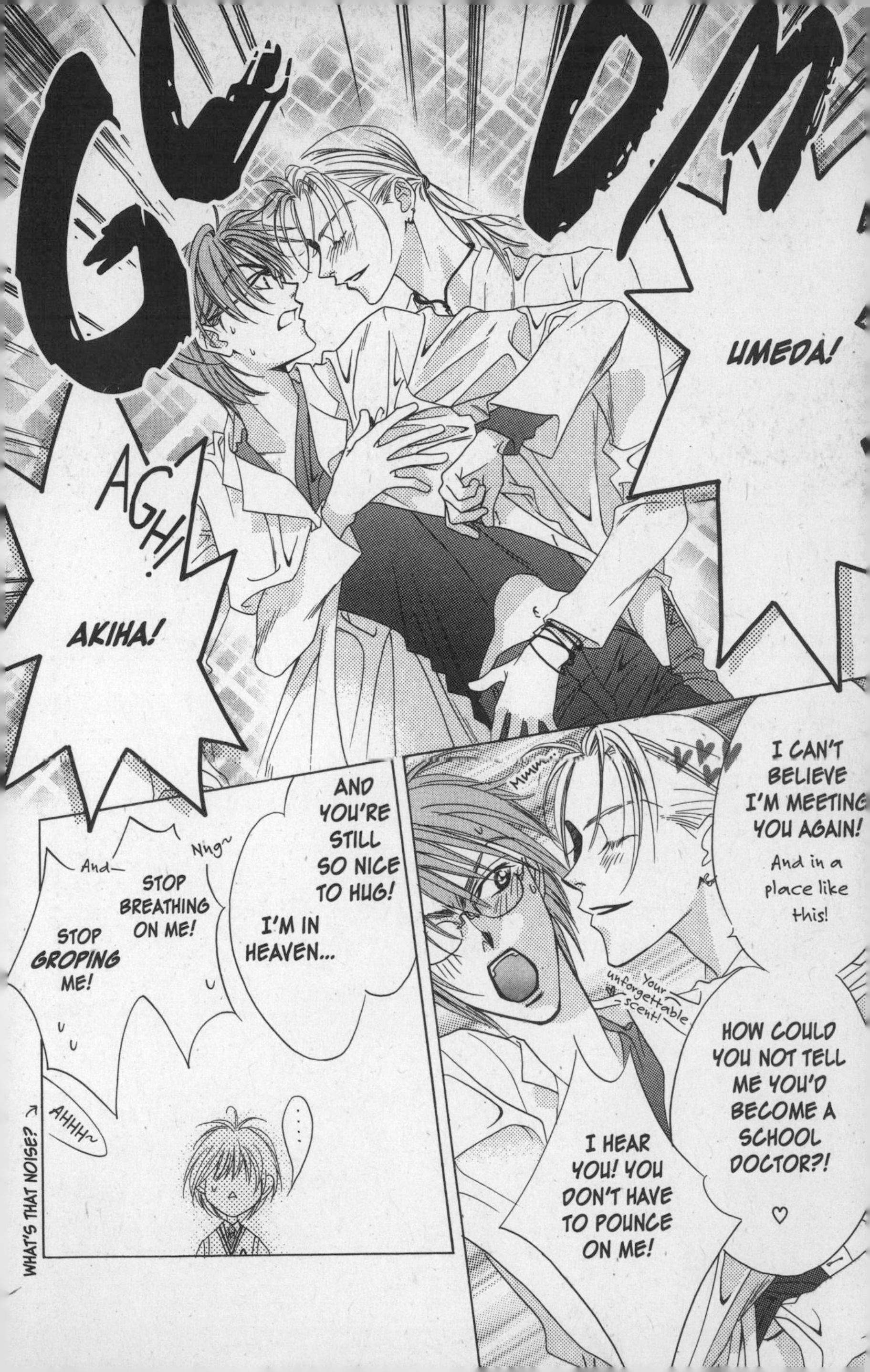
UMEDA!
AGH!
AKIHA!
I CAN'T BELIEVE I'M MEETING YOU AGAIN!
And in a place like this!
Your unforgettable scent!
HOW COULD YOU NOT TELL ME YOU'D BECOME A SCHOOL DOCTOR?! ♡
I HEAR YOU! YOU DON'T HAVE TO POUNCE ON ME!
AND YOU'RE STILL SO NICE TO HUG!
I'M IN HEAVEN...
Nng~
STOP BREATHING ON ME!
And—
STOP GROPING ME!
AHHH~
...
WHAT'S THAT NOISE?

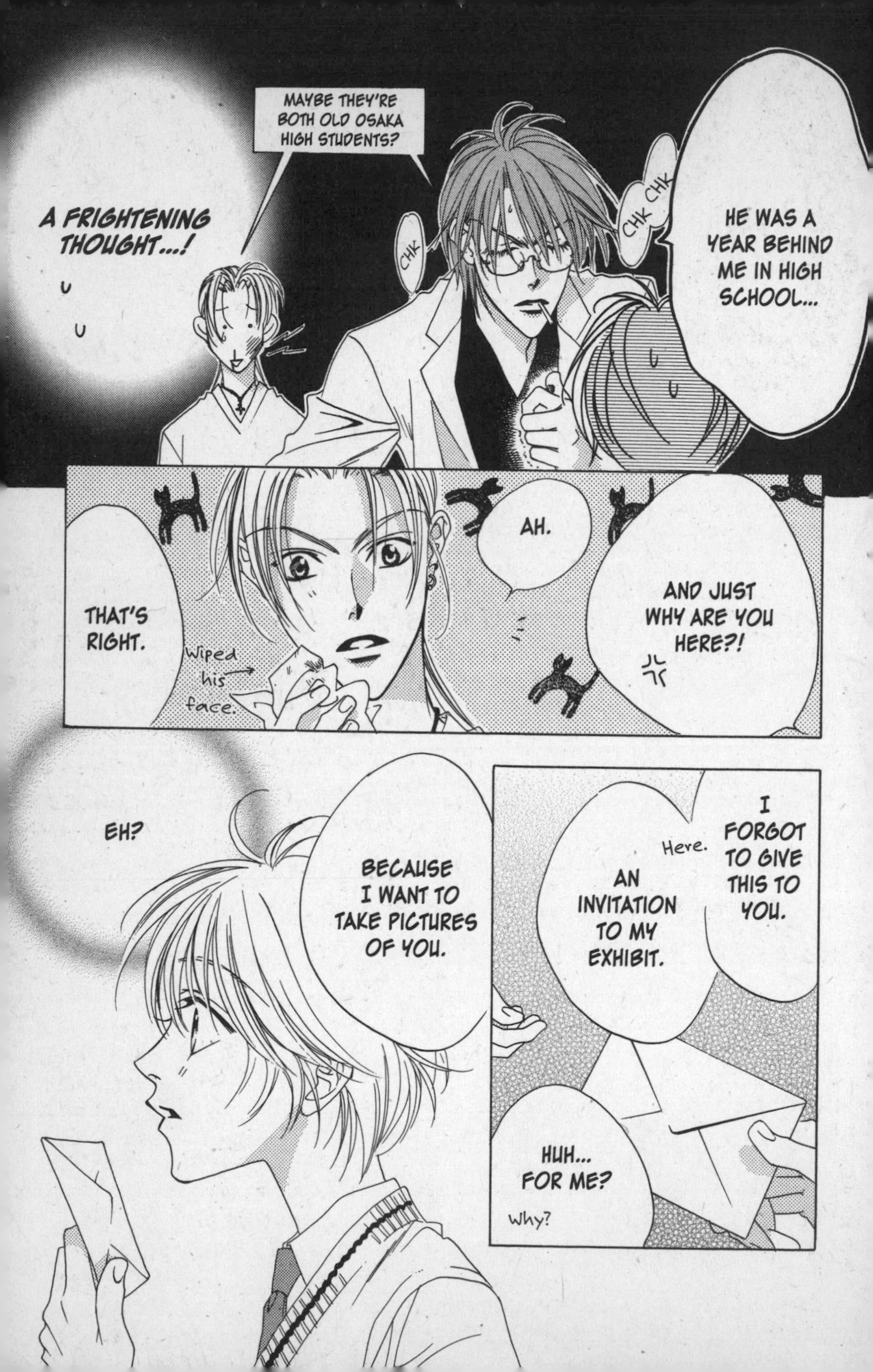
HE WAS A YEAR BEHIND ME IN HIGH SCHOOL...
CHK CHK
CHK
MAYBE THEY'RE BOTH OLD OSAKA HIGH STUDENTS?
A FRIGHTENING THOUGHT...!
AND JUST WHY ARE YOU HERE?!
AH.
THAT'S RIGHT.
Wiped his face.
I FORGOT TO GIVE THIS TO YOU.
Here.
AN INVITATION TO MY EXHIBIT.
HUH... FOR ME?
Why?
BECAUSE I WANT TO TAKE PICTURES OF YOU.
EH?

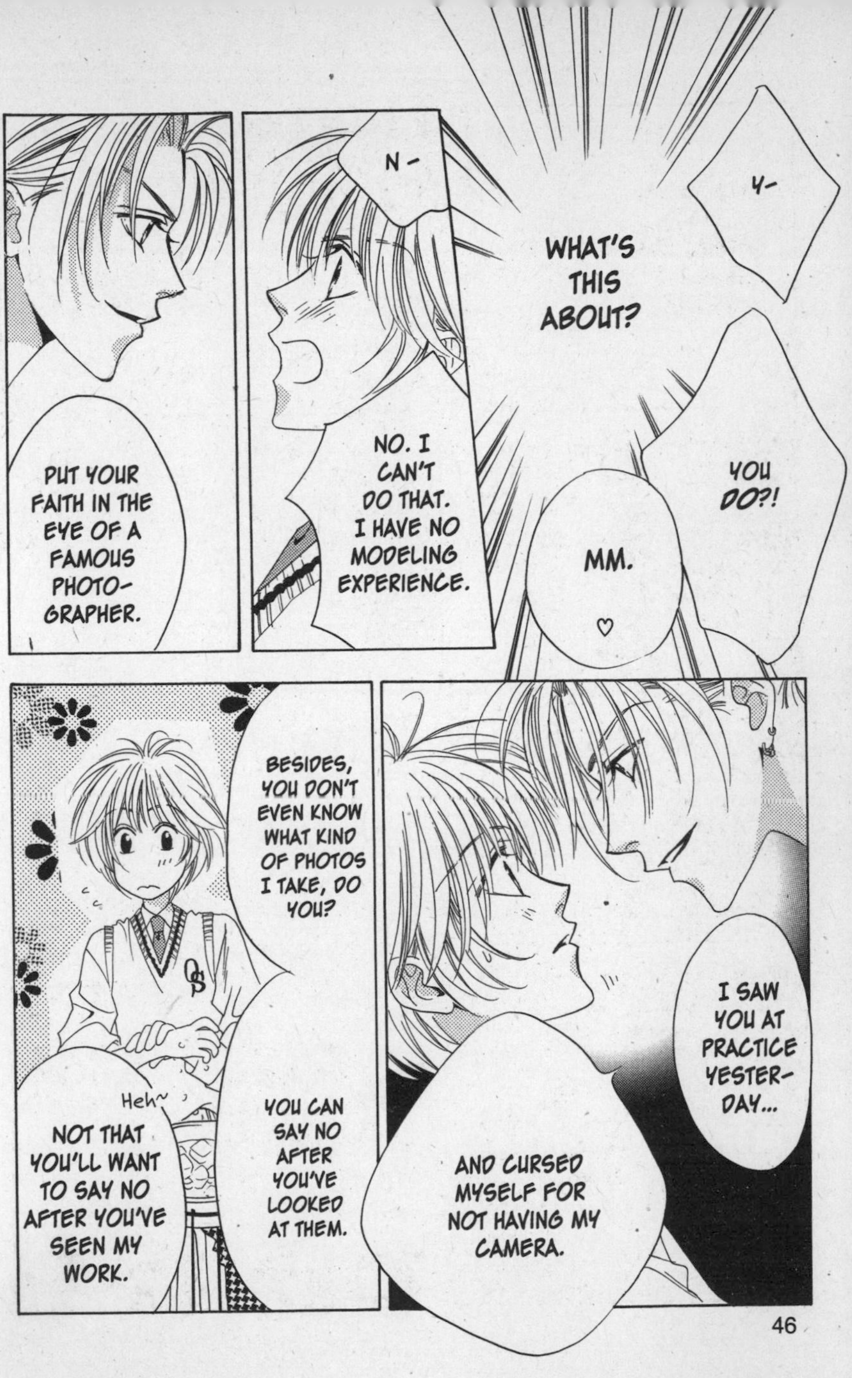
Y-
WHAT'S THIS ABOUT?
YOU DO?!
MM. ♡
N-
NO. I CAN'T DO THAT. I HAVE NO MODELING EXPERIENCE.
PUT YOUR FAITH IN THE EYE OF A FAMOUS PHOTO-GRAPHER.
I SAW YOU AT PRACTICE YESTER-DAY...
AND CURSED MYSELF FOR NOT HAVING MY CAMERA.
BESIDES, YOU DON'T EVEN KNOW WHAT KIND OF PHOTOS I TAKE, DO YOU?
YOU CAN SAY NO AFTER YOU'VE LOOKED AT THEM.
Heh~
NOT THAT YOU'LL WANT TO SAY NO AFTER YOU'VE SEEN MY WORK.

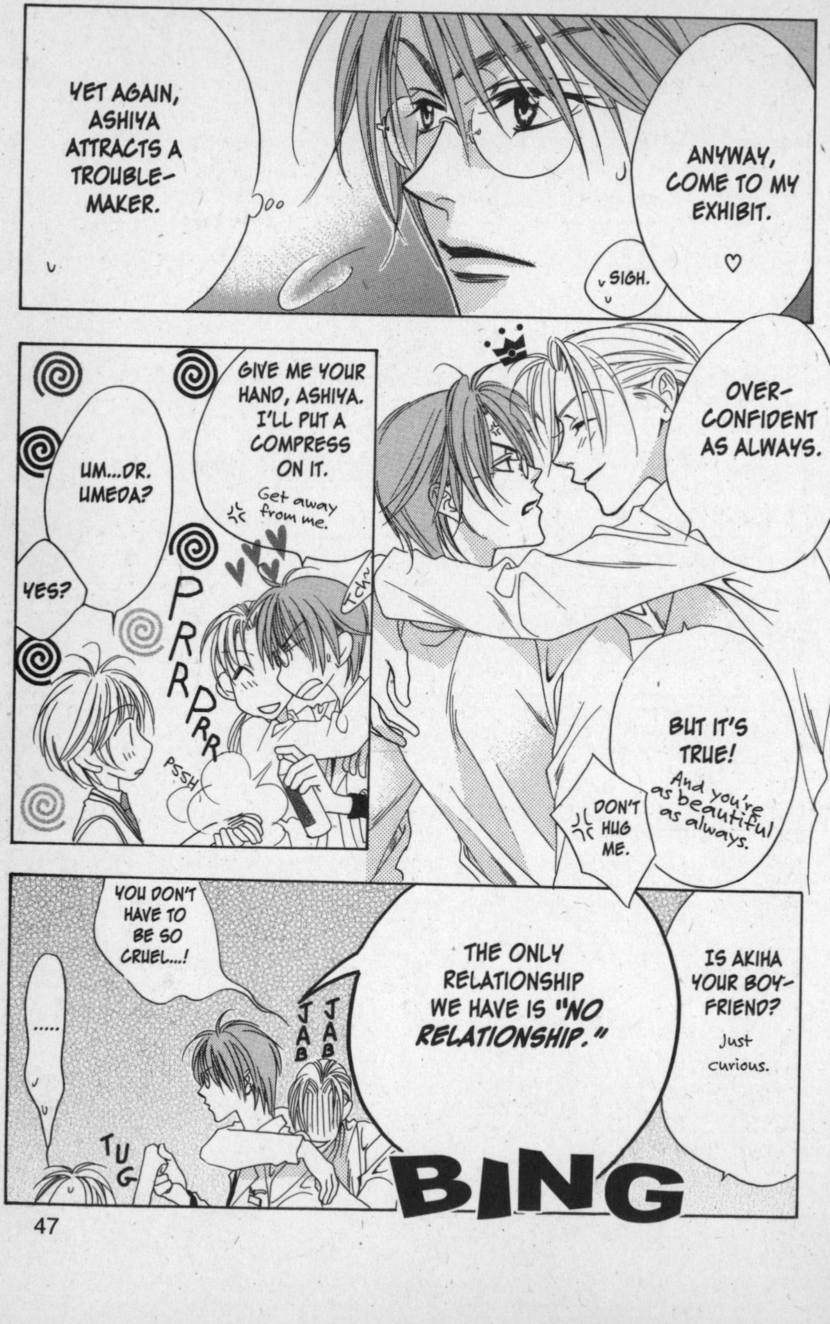
ANYWAY, COME TO MY EXHIBIT. ♥
SIGH.
YET AGAIN, ASHIYA ATTRACTS A TROUBLE-MAKER.
OVER-CONFIDENT AS ALWAYS.
Tch
BUT IT'S TRUE!
And you're as beautiful as always.
DON'T HUG ME.
GIVE ME YOUR HAND, ASHIYA. I'LL PUT A COMPRESS ON IT.
Get away from me.
UM...DR. UMEDA?
YES?
PRRPRR
PSSH
IS AKIHA YOUR BOY-FRIEND?
Just curious.
THE ONLY RELATIONSHIP WE HAVE IS "NO RELATIONSHIP."
BING
JAB JAB
YOU DON'T HAVE TO BE SO CRUEL...!
.....
TUG

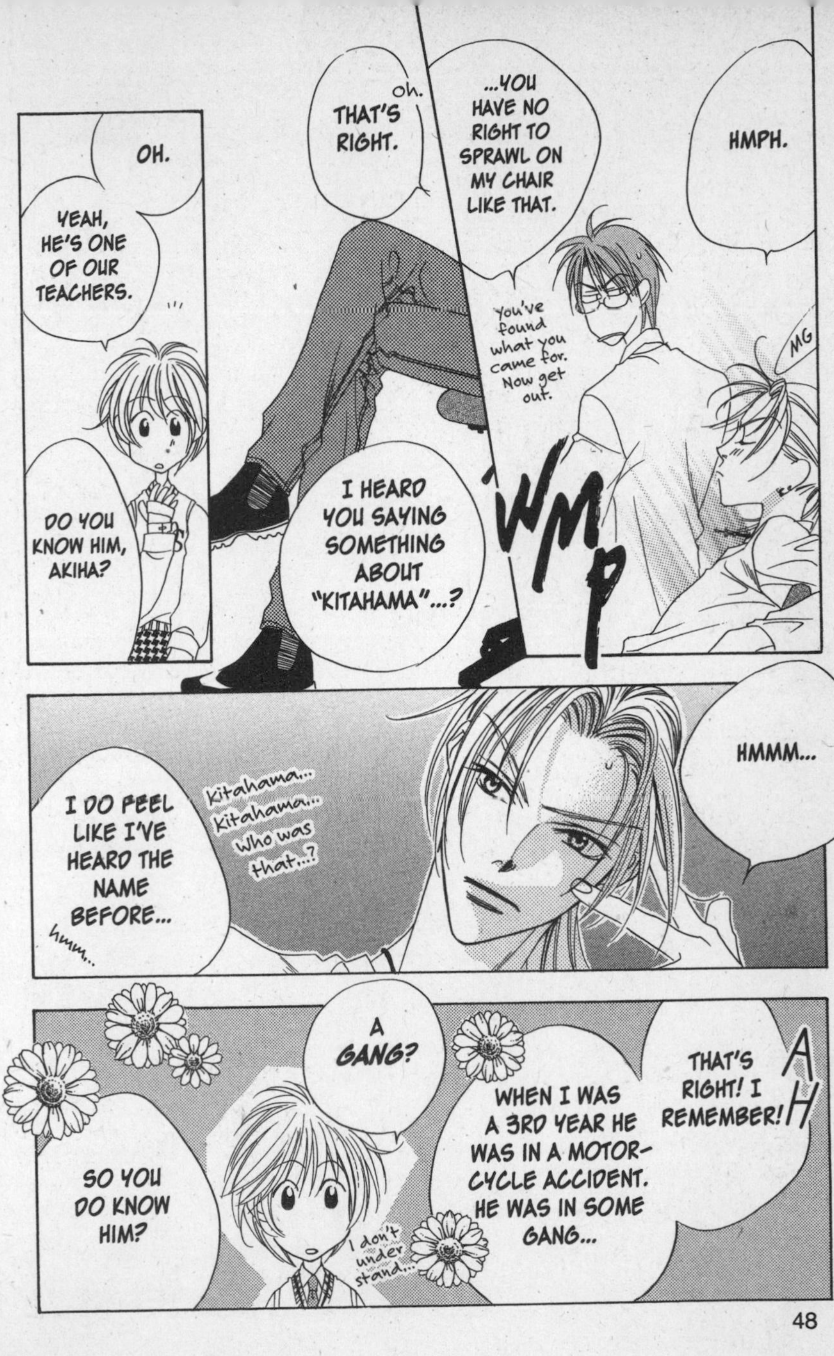
HMPH.
...YOU HAVE NO RIGHT TO SPRAWL ON MY CHAIR LIKE THAT.
You've found what you came for. Now get out.
MG
WMP
oh. THAT'S RIGHT.
I HEARD YOU SAYING SOMETHING ABOUT "KITAHAMA"...?
OH.
YEAH, HE'S ONE OF OUR TEACHERS.
DO YOU KNOW HIM, AKIHA?
HMMM...
Kitahama... Kitahama... Who was that...?
I DO FEEL LIKE I'VE HEARD THE NAME BEFORE...
hmm...
AH
THAT'S RIGHT! I REMEMBER!
WHEN I WAS A 3RD YEAR HE WAS IN A MOTOR-CYCLE ACCIDENT. HE WAS IN SOME GANG...
A GANG?
I don't understand...
SO YOU DO KNOW HIM?

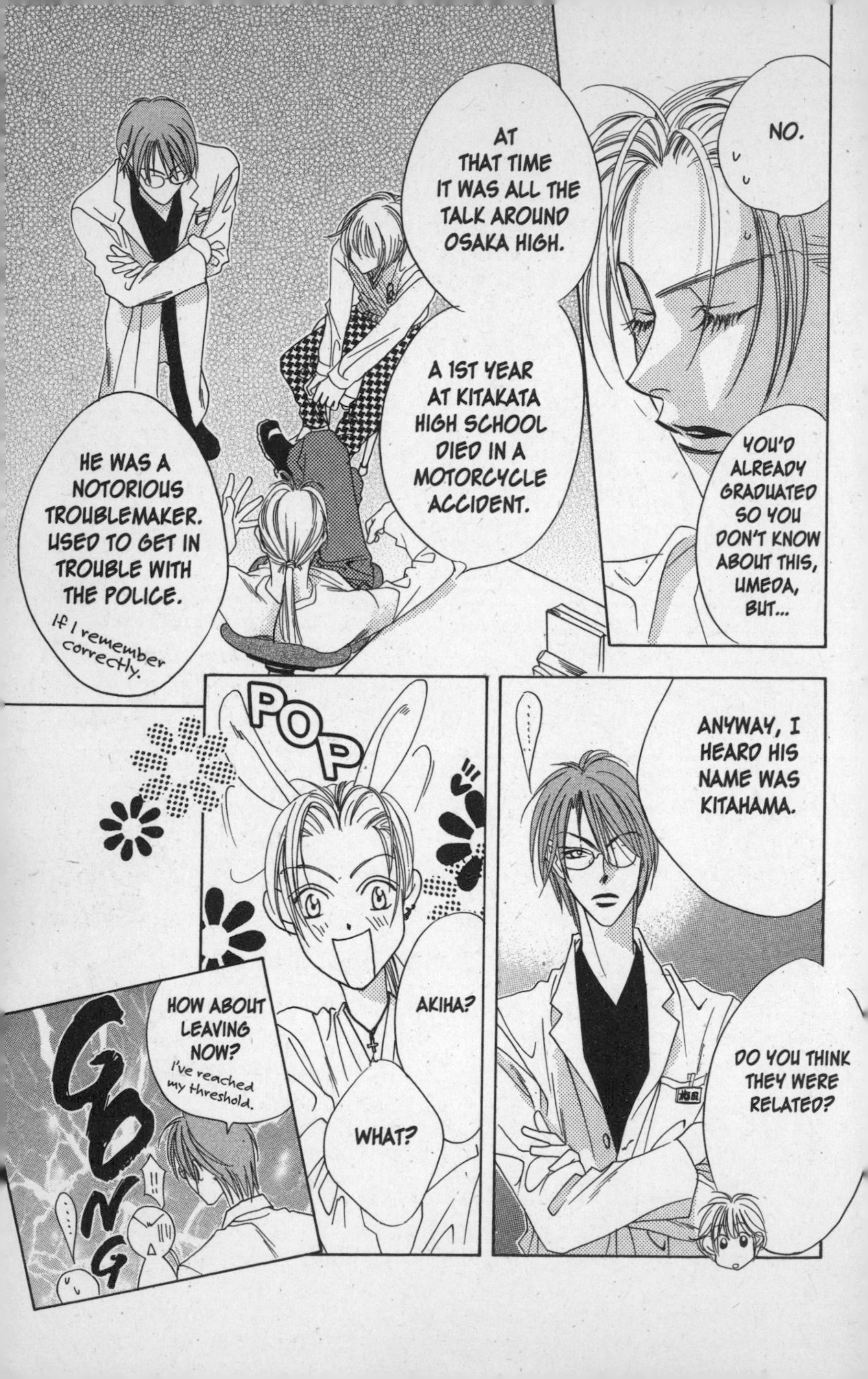
NO.
YOU'D ALREADY GRADUATED SO YOU DON'T KNOW ABOUT THIS, UMEDA, BUT...
AT THAT TIME IT WAS ALL THE TALK AROUND OSAKA HIGH.
A 1ST YEAR AT KITAKATA HIGH SCHOOL DIED IN A MOTORCYCLE ACCIDENT.
HE WAS A NOTORIOUS TROUBLEMAKER. USED TO GET IN TROUBLE WITH THE POLICE.
If I remember correctly.
ANYWAY, I HEARD HIS NAME WAS KITAHAMA.
DO YOU THINK THEY WERE RELATED?
POP
AKIHA?
WHAT?
HOW ABOUT LEAVING NOW?
I've reached my threshold.
GONG
!!

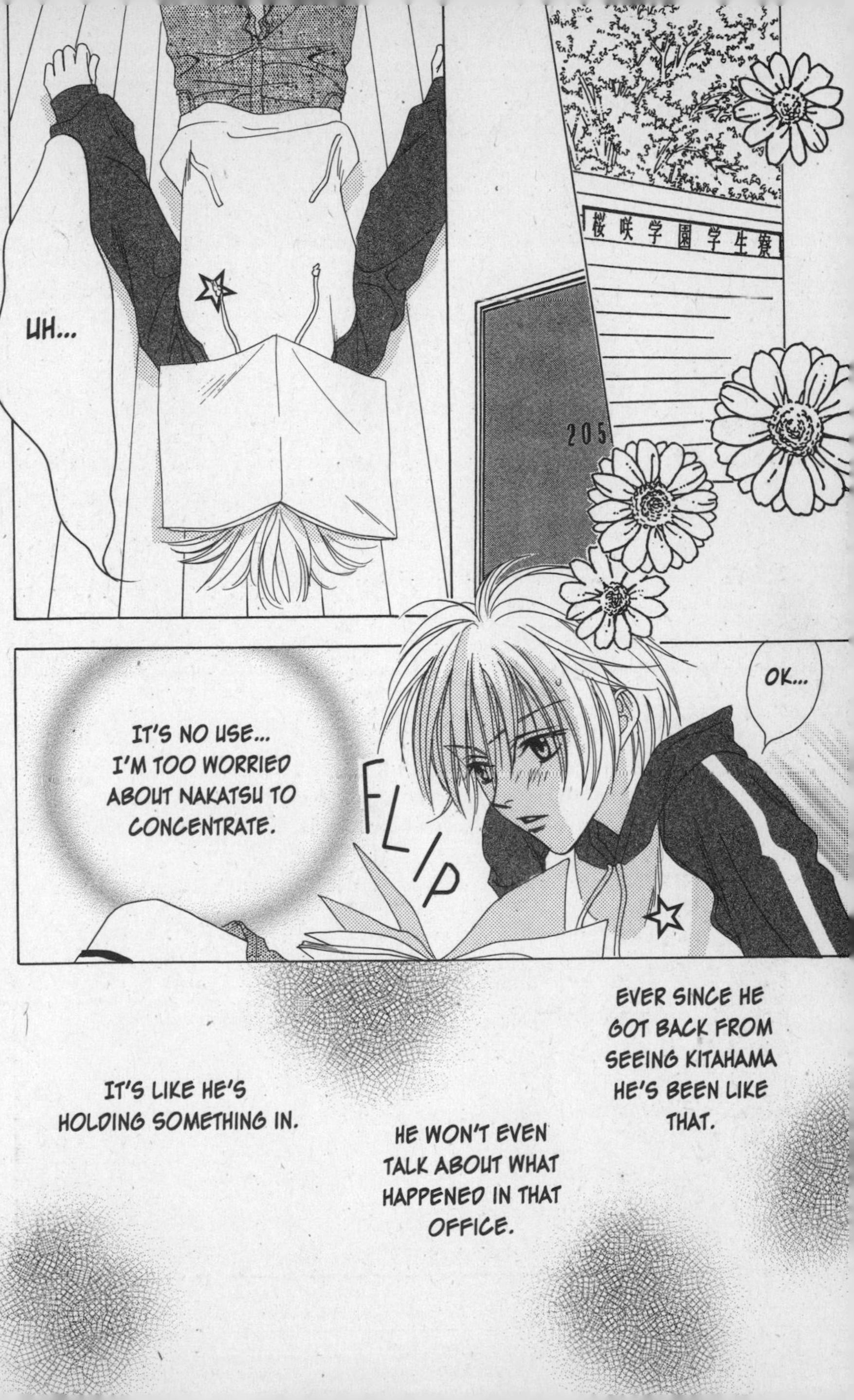
桜咲学園学生寮
205
UH...
OK...
IT'S NO USE... I'M TOO WORRIED ABOUT NAKATSU TO CONCENTRATE.
FLIP
EVER SINCE HE GOT BACK FROM SEEING KITAHAMA HE'S BEEN LIKE THAT.
HE WON'T EVEN TALK ABOUT WHAT HAPPENED IN THAT OFFICE.
IT'S LIKE HE'S HOLDING SOMETHING IN.

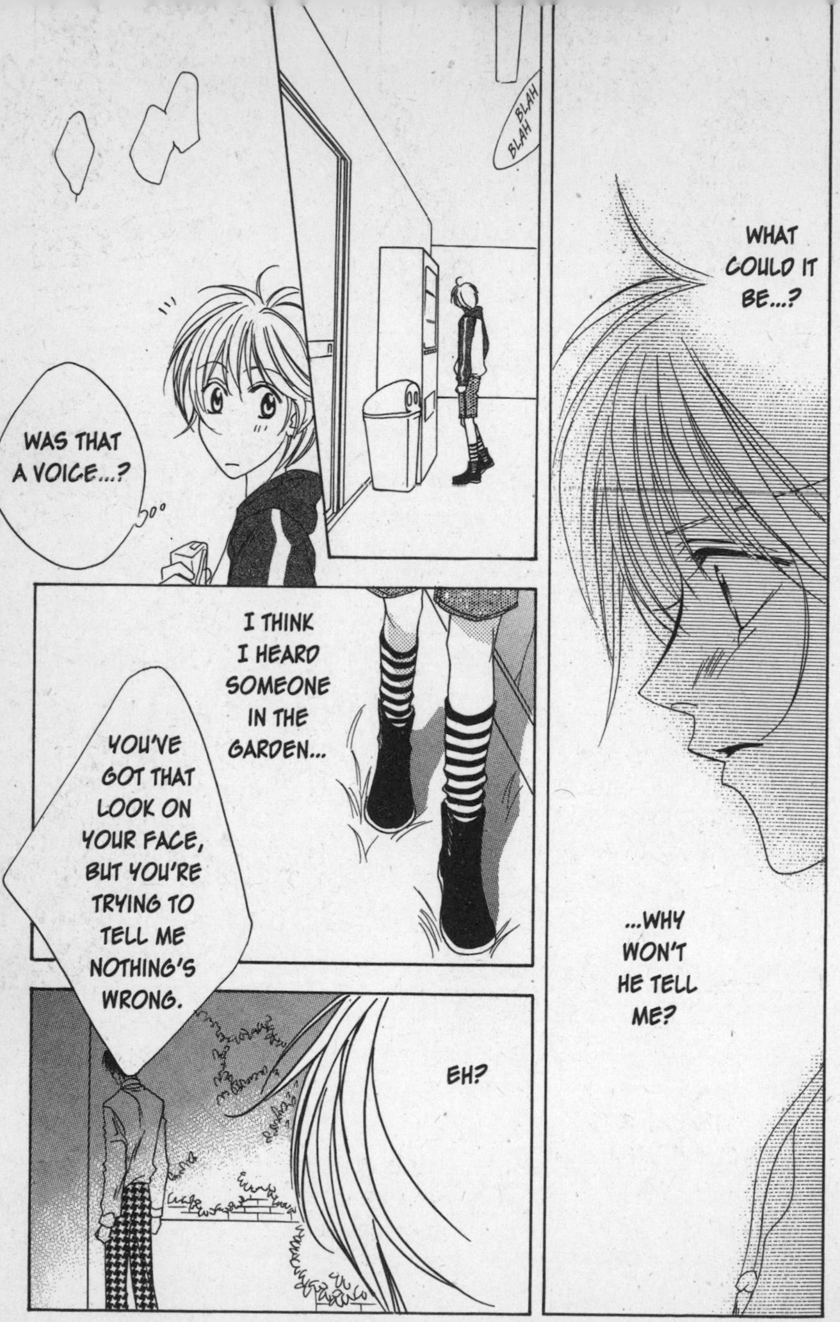
WHAT COULD IT BE...?
...WHY WON'T HE TELL ME?
BLAH BLAH
WAS THAT A VOICE...?
I THINK I HEARD SOMEONE IN THE GARDEN...
YOU'VE GOT THAT LOOK ON YOUR FACE, BUT YOU'RE TRYING TO TELL ME NOTHING'S WRONG.
EH?

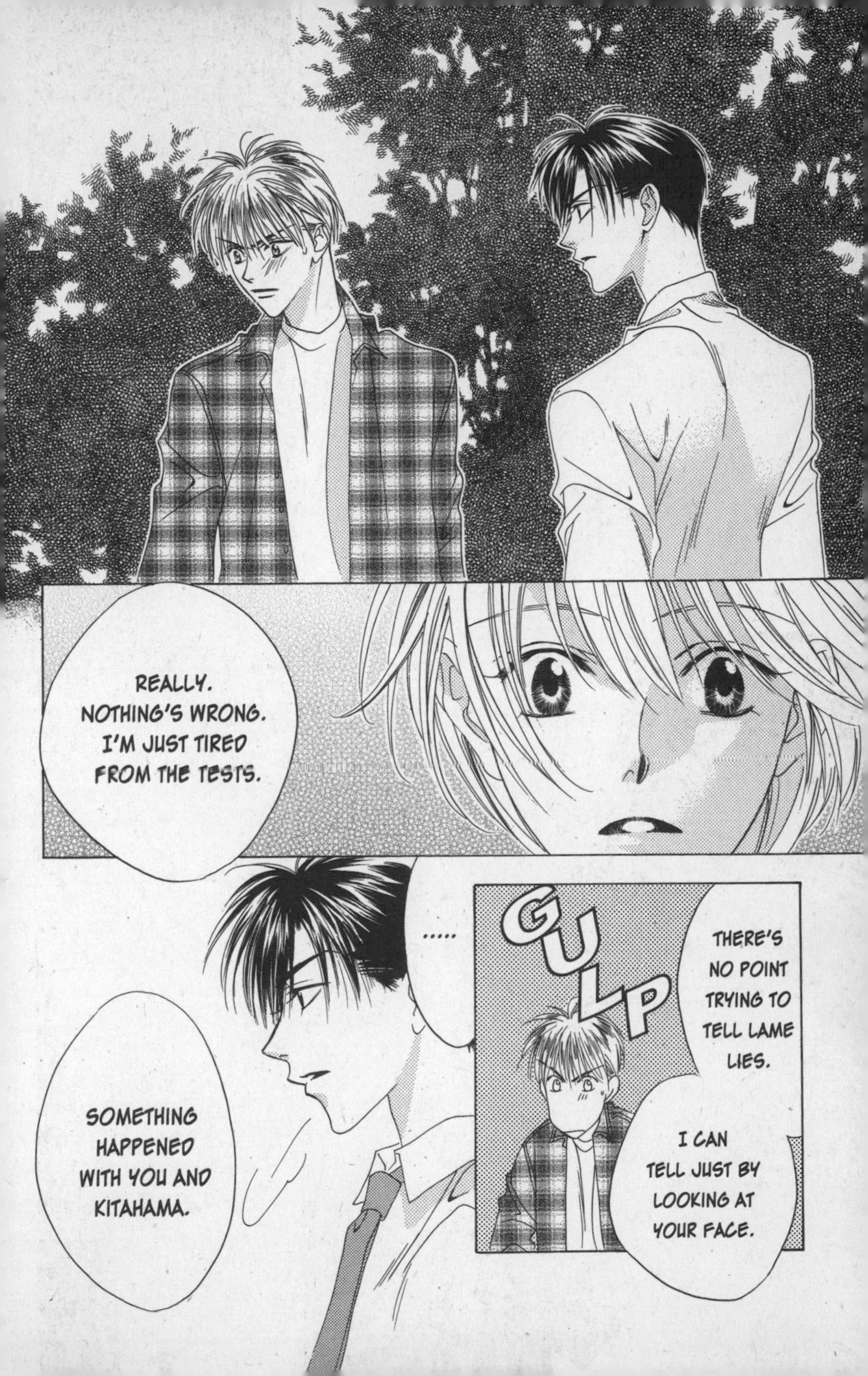
REALLY. NOTHING'S WRONG. I'M JUST TIRED FROM THE TESTS.
GULP
THERE'S NO POINT TRYING TO TELL LAME LIES.
I CAN TELL JUST BY LOOKING AT YOUR FACE.
.....
SOMETHING HAPPENED WITH YOU AND KITAHAMA.

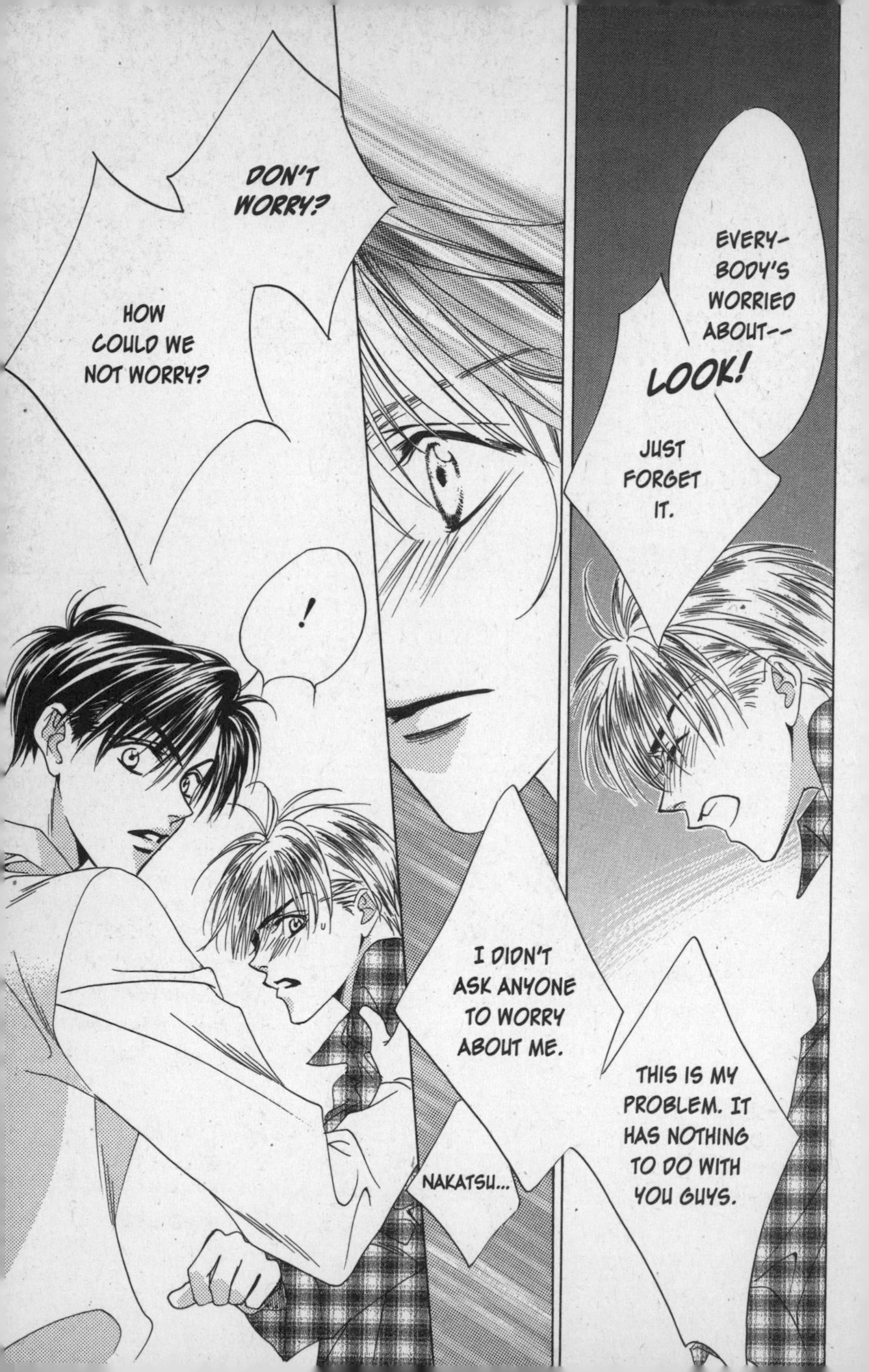
EVERY-BODY'S WORRIED ABOUT--
LOOK!
JUST FORGET IT.
THIS IS MY PROBLEM. IT HAS NOTHING TO DO WITH YOU GUYS.
I DIDN'T ASK ANYONE TO WORRY ABOUT ME.
DON'T WORRY?
HOW COULD WE NOT WORRY?
!
NAKATSU...

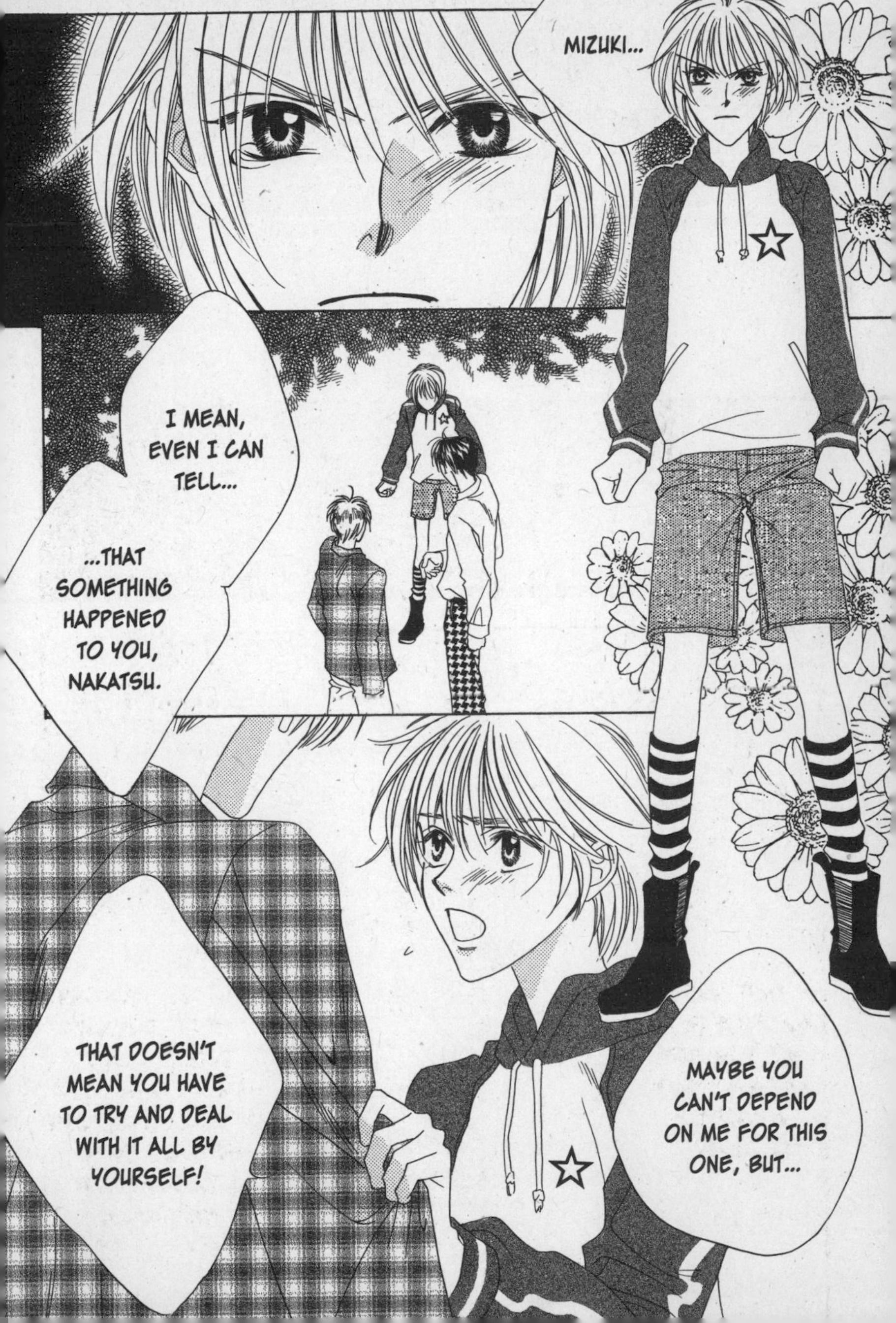
MIZUKI...
I MEAN, EVEN I CAN TELL...
...THAT SOMETHING HAPPENED TO YOU, NAKATSU.
MAYBE YOU CAN'T DEPEND ON ME FOR THIS ONE, BUT...
THAT DOESN'T MEAN YOU HAVE TO TRY AND DEAL WITH IT ALL BY YOURSELF!

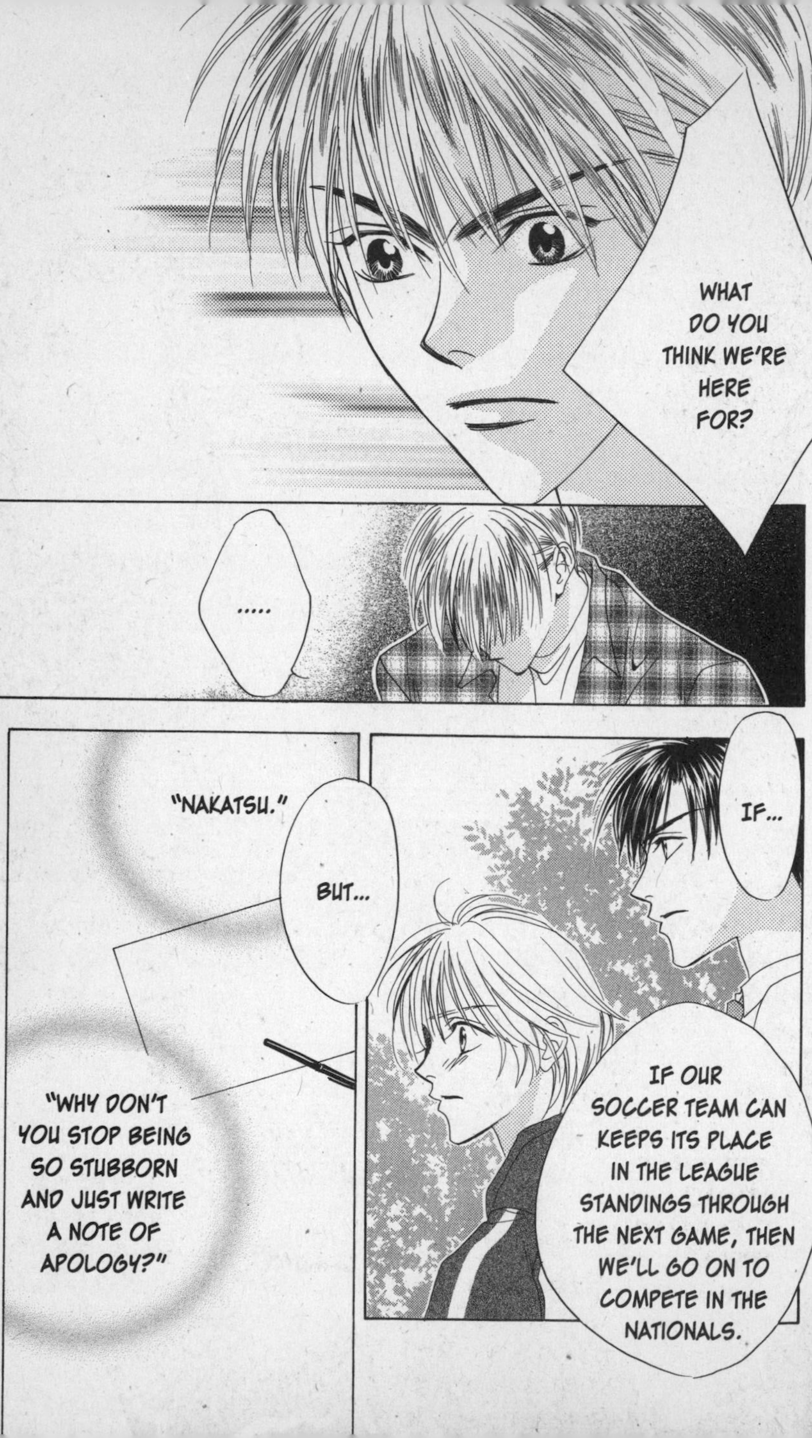
WHAT DO YOU THINK WE'RE HERE FOR?
.....
IF...
IF OUR SOCCER TEAM CAN KEEPS ITS PLACE IN THE LEAGUE STANDINGS THROUGH THE NEXT GAME, THEN WE'LL GO ON TO COMPETE IN THE NATIONALS.
BUT...
"NAKATSU."
"WHY DON'T YOU STOP BEING SO STUBBORN AND JUST WRITE A NOTE OF APOLOGY?"

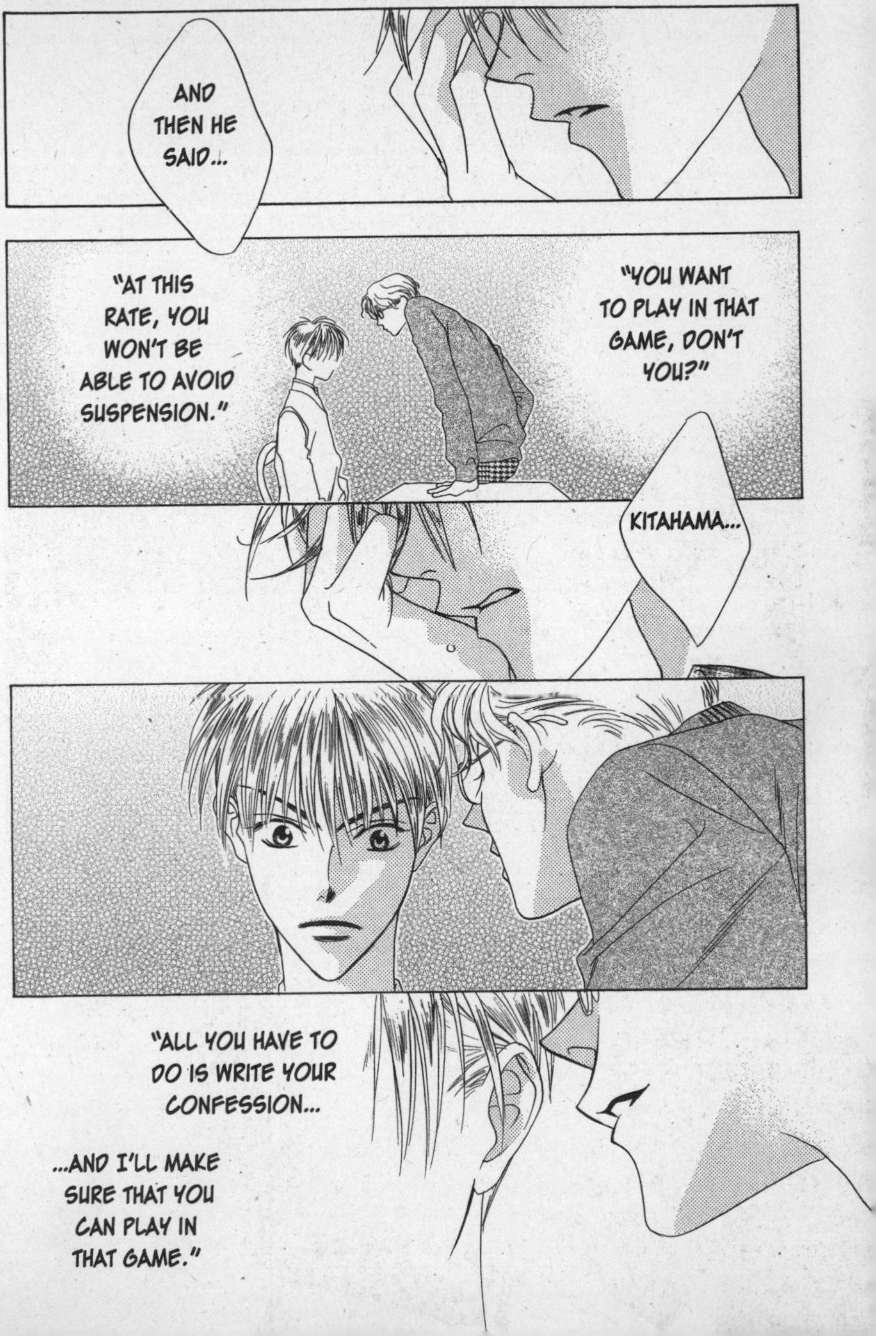
AND THEN HE SAID...
"YOU WANT TO PLAY IN THAT GAME, DON'T YOU?"
"AT THIS RATE, YOU WON'T BE ABLE TO AVOID SUSPENSION."
KITAHAMA...
"ALL YOU HAVE TO DO IS WRITE YOUR CONFESSION...
...AND I'LL MAKE SURE THAT YOU CAN PLAY IN THAT GAME."

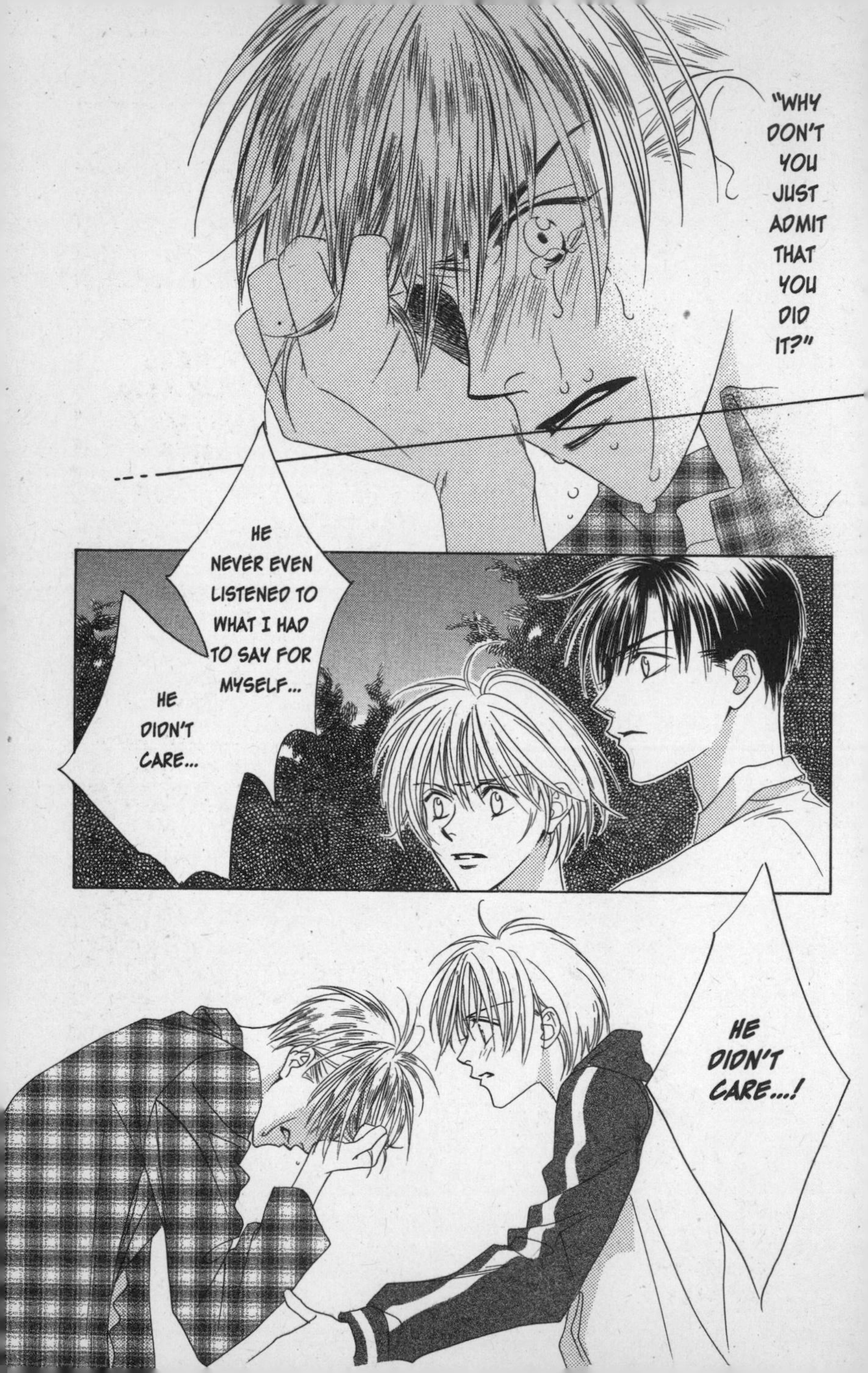
"WHY DON'T YOU JUST ADMIT THAT YOU DID IT?"
HE NEVER EVEN LISTENED TO WHAT I HAD TO SAY FOR MYSELF...
HE DIDN'T CARE...
HE DIDN'T CARE...!

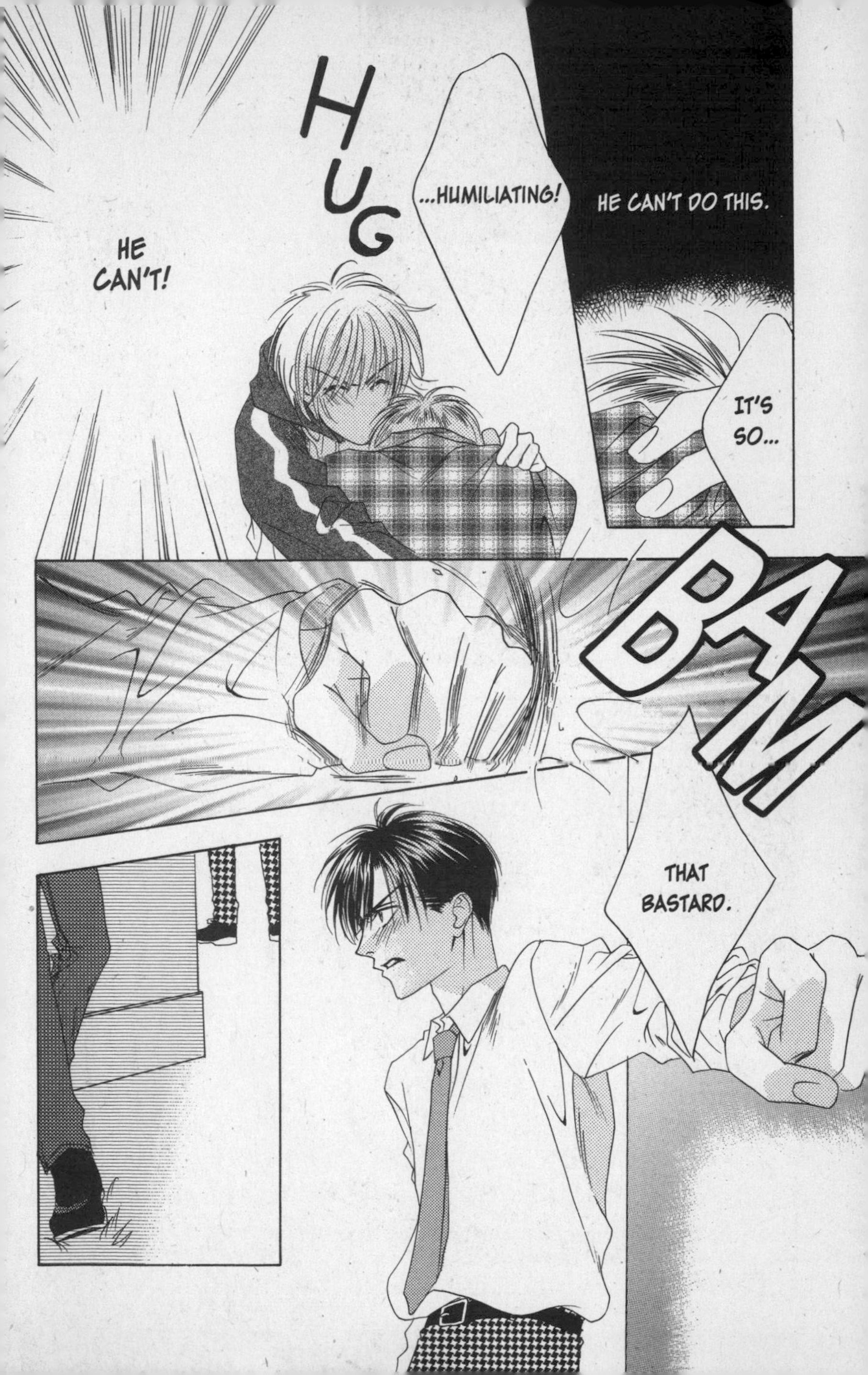
HE CAN'T DO THIS.
IT'S SO...
...HUMILIATING!
HUG
HE CAN'T!
BAM
THAT BASTARD.

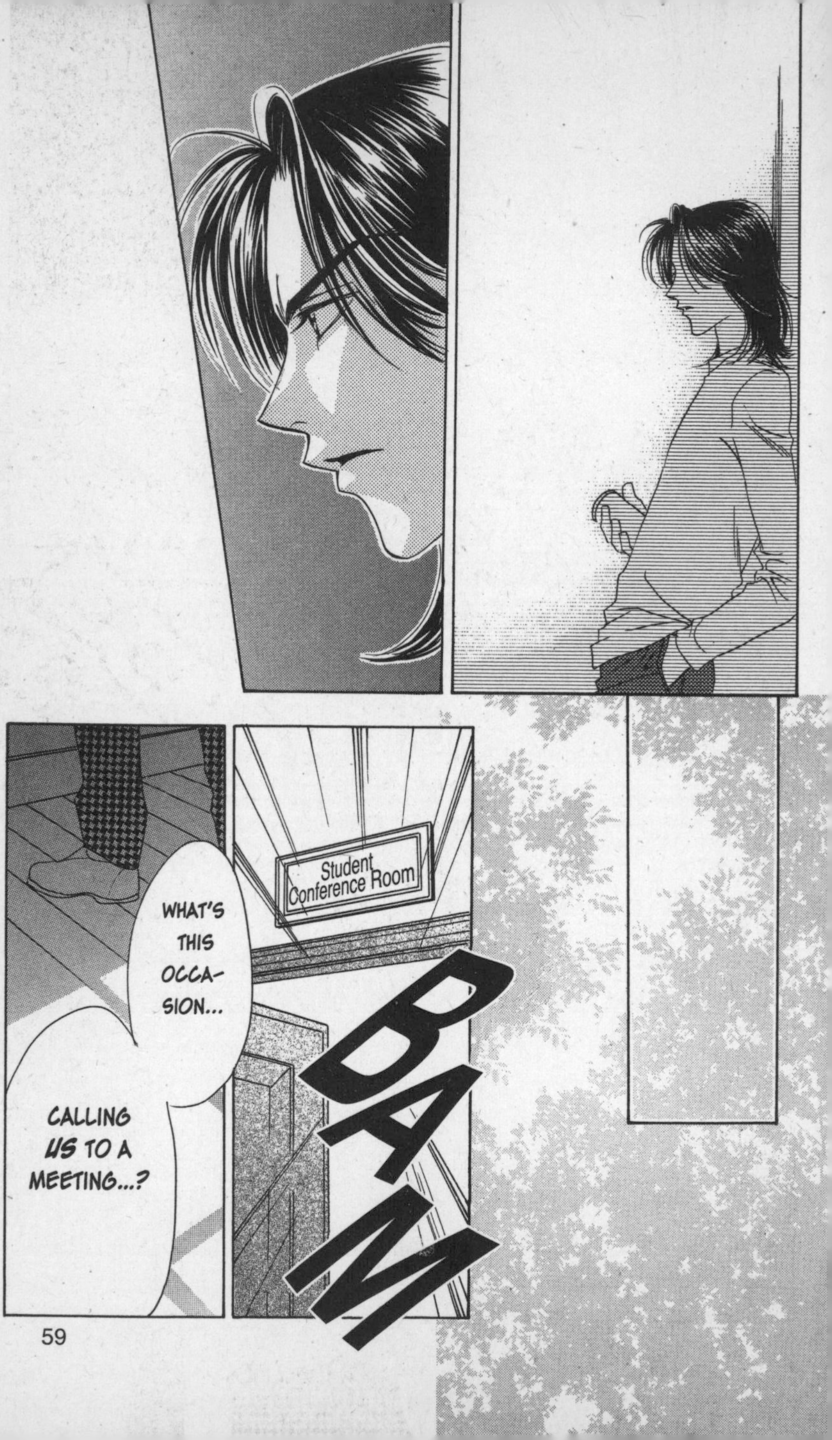
Student Conference Room
BAM
WHAT'S THIS OCCA-SION...
CALLING US TO A MEETING...?

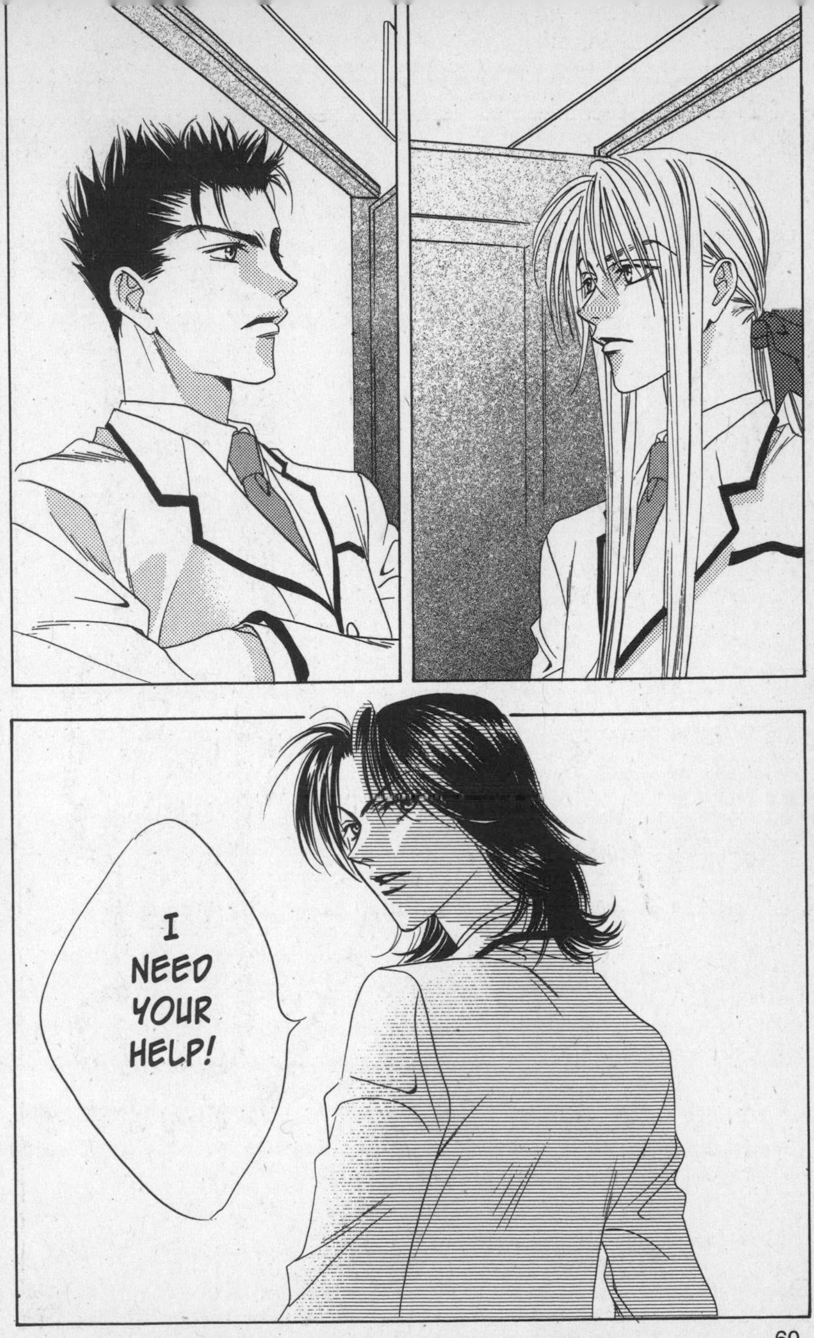
I NEED YOUR HELP!

HANA-KIMI CHAPTER 44/END

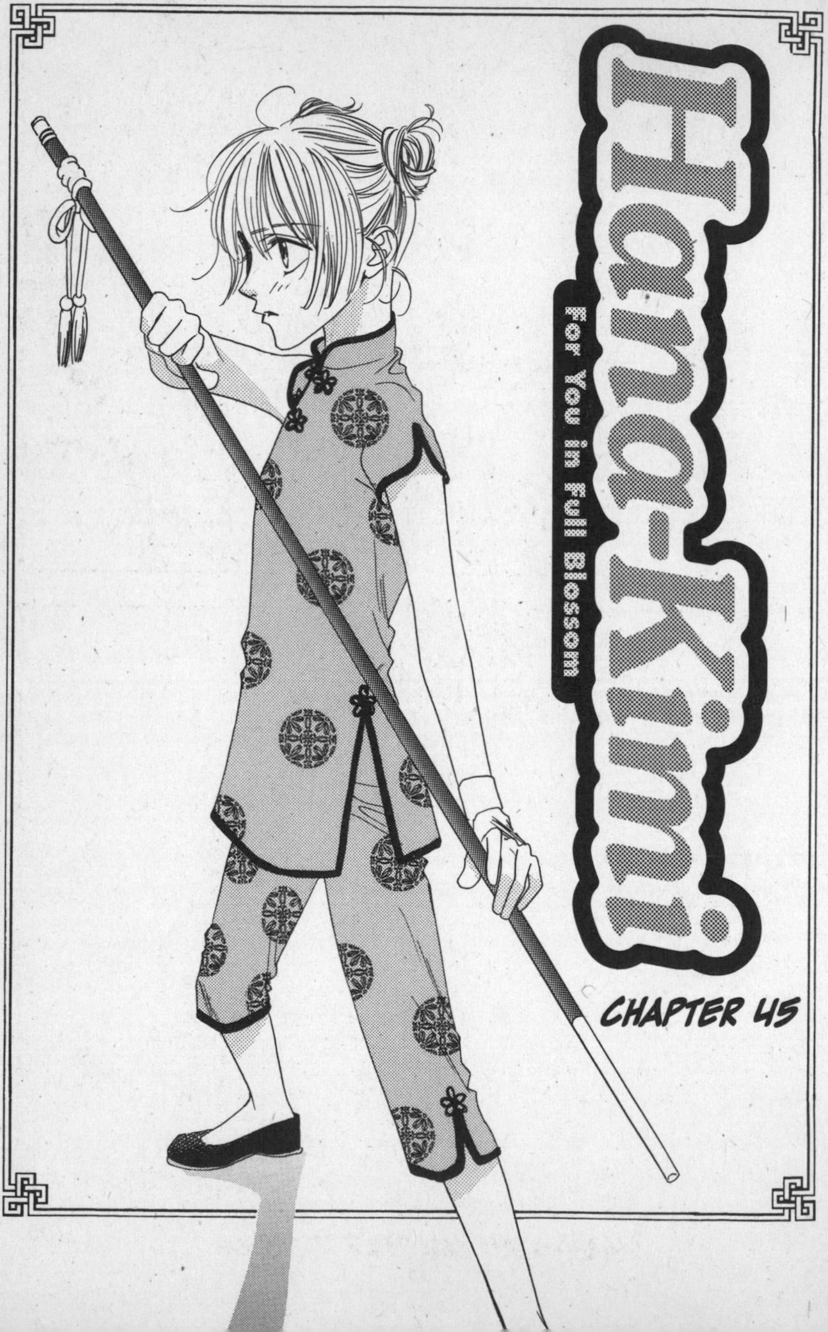
Hana-Kimi
For You in Full Blossom
CHAPTER 45

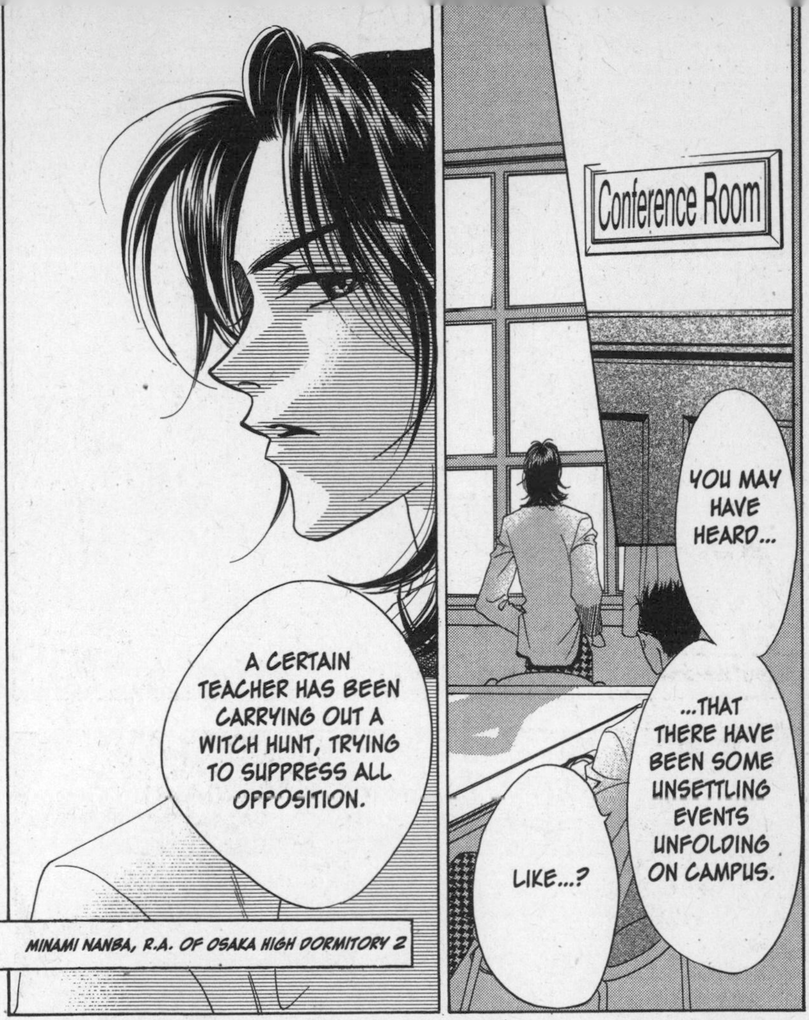
Conference Room
YOU MAY HAVE HEARD...
...THAT THERE HAVE BEEN SOME UNSETTLING EVENTS UNFOLDING ON CAMPUS.
LIKE...?
A CERTAIN TEACHER HAS BEEN CARRYING OUT A WITCH HUNT, TRYING TO SUPPRESS ALL OPPOSITION.
MINAMI NANBA, R.A. OF OSAKA HIGH DORMITORY 2

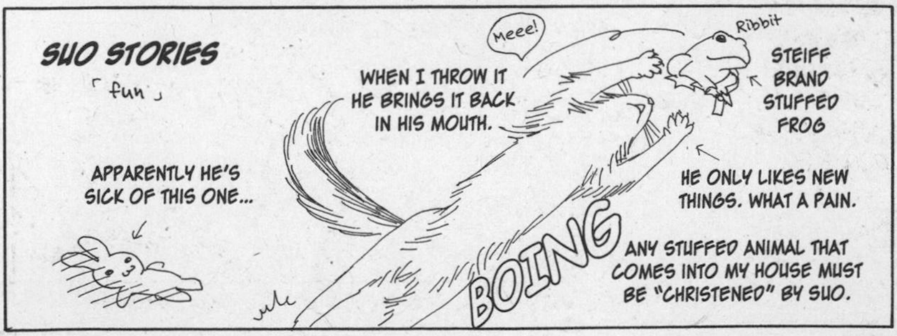
SUO STORIES
「fun」
Meee!
Ribbit
STEIFF BRAND STUFFED FROG
WHEN I THROW IT HE BRINGS IT BACK IN HIS MOUTH.
HE ONLY LIKES NEW THINGS. WHAT A PAIN.
APPARENTLY HE'S SICK OF THIS ONE...
ANY STUFFED ANIMAL THAT COMES INTO MY HOUSE MUST BE "CHRISTENED" BY SUO.
BOING

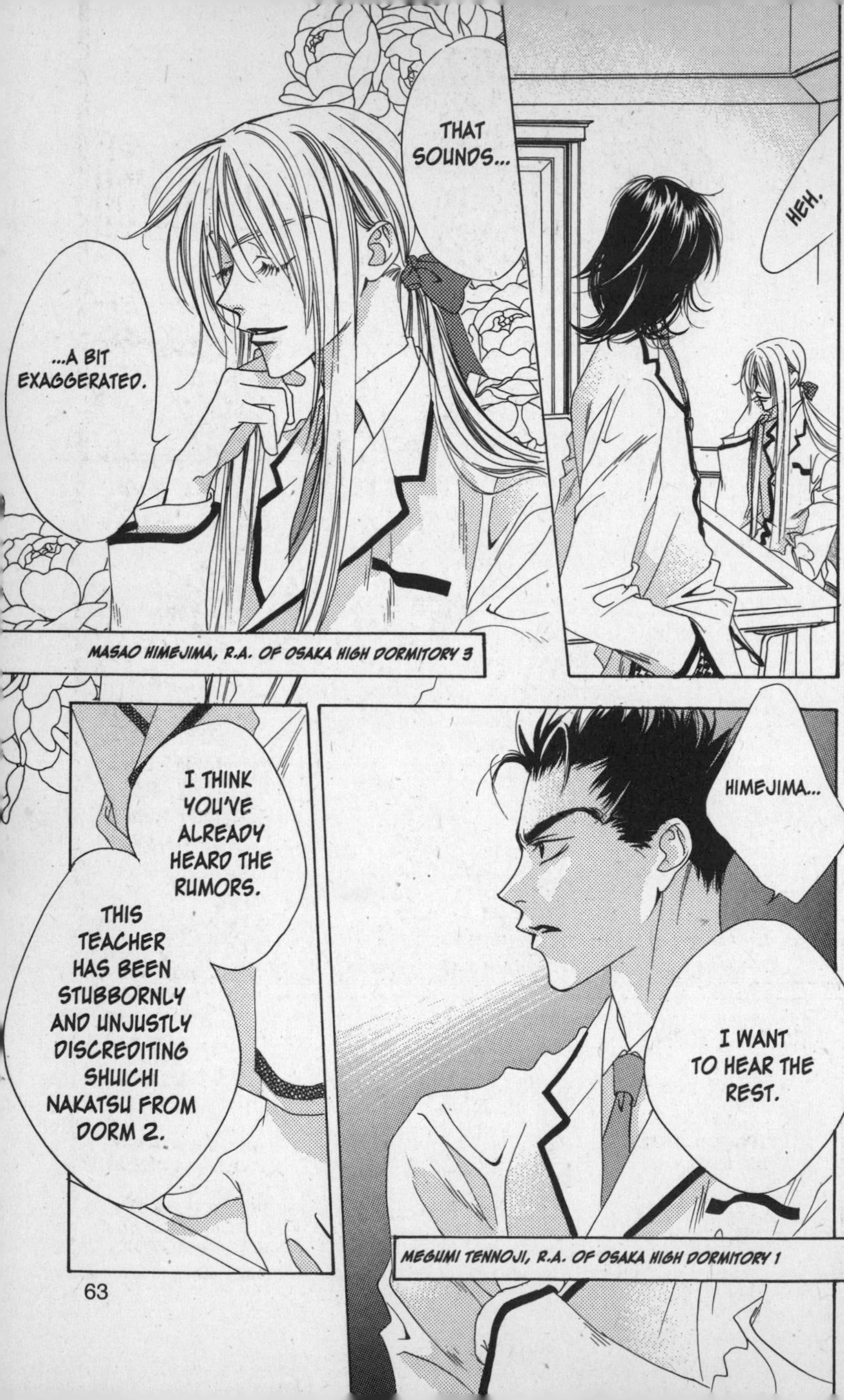
HEH.
THAT SOUNDS...
...A BIT EXAGGERATED.
MASAO HIMEJIMA, R.A. OF OSAKA HIGH DORMITORY 3
HIMEJIMA...
I WANT TO HEAR THE REST.
MEGUMI TENNOJI, R.A. OF OSAKA HIGH DORMITORY 1
I THINK YOU'VE ALREADY HEARD THE RUMORS.
THIS TEACHER HAS BEEN STUBBORNLY AND UNJUSTLY DISCREDITING SHUICHI NAKATSU FROM DORM 2.

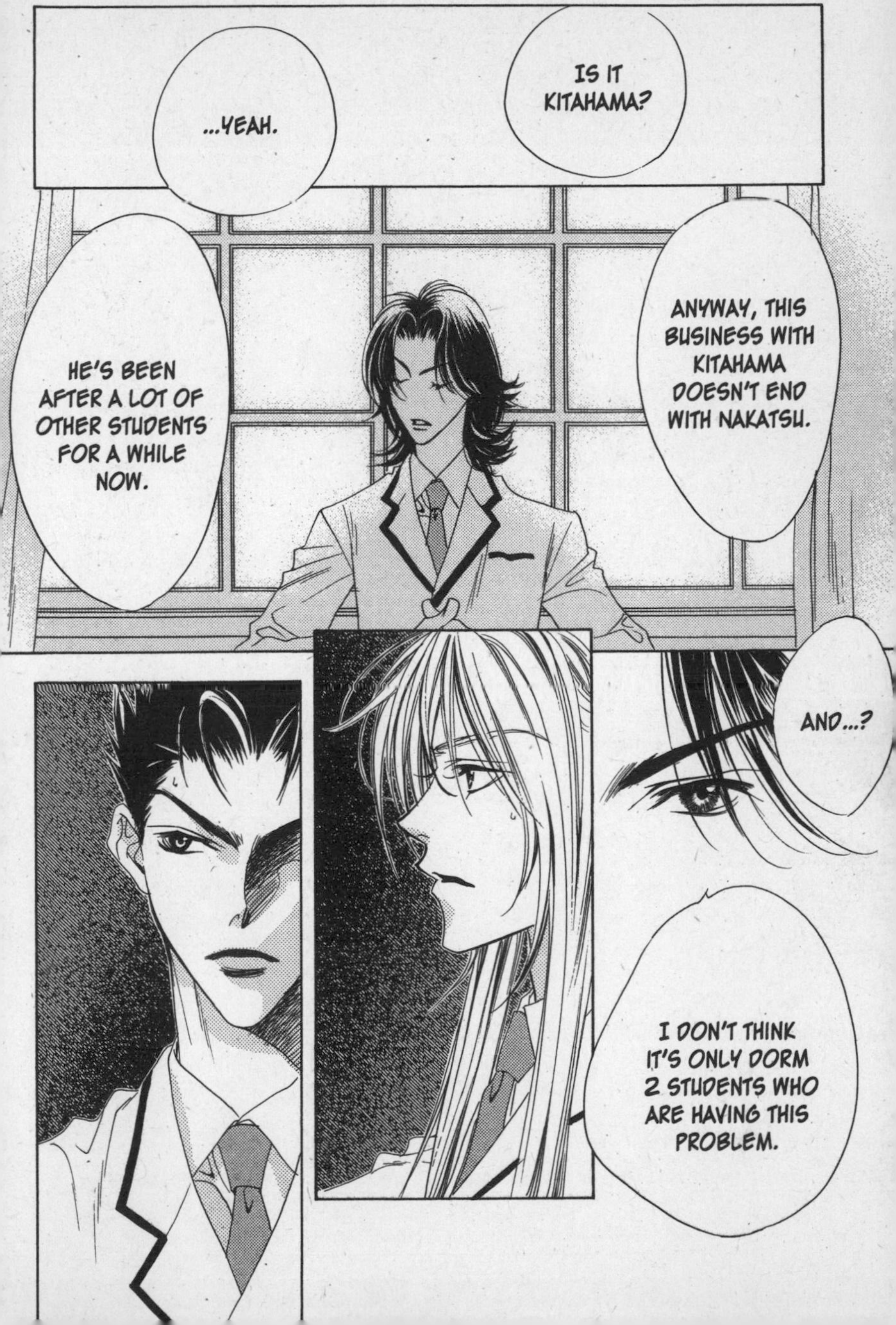
IS IT KITAHAMA?
...YEAH.
ANYWAY, THIS BUSINESS WITH KITAHAMA DOESN'T END WITH NAKATSU.
HE'S BEEN AFTER A LOT OF OTHER STUDENTS FOR A WHILE NOW.
AND...?
I DON'T THINK IT'S ONLY DORM 2 STUDENTS WHO ARE HAVING THIS PROBLEM.

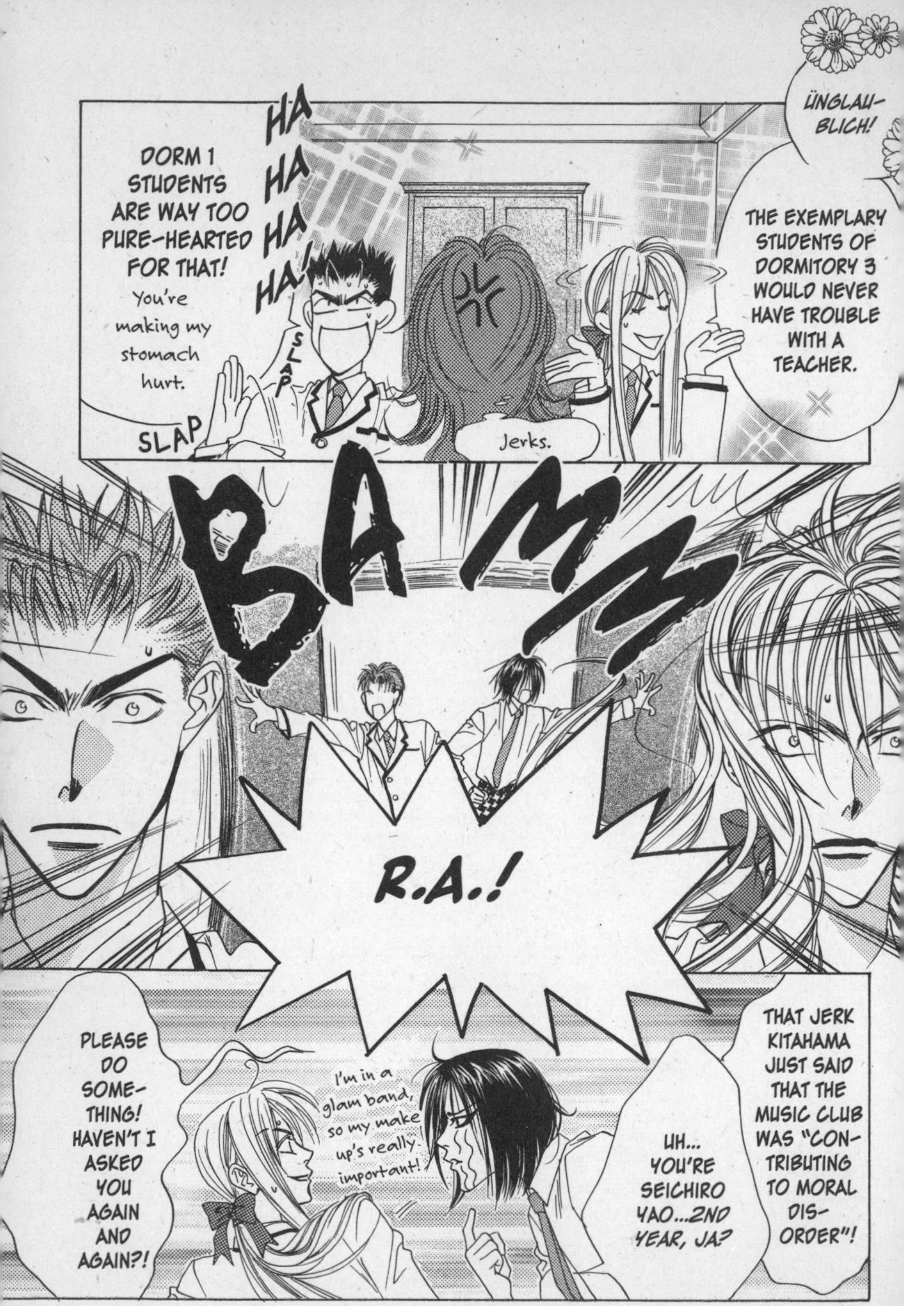

ÜNGLAU-BLICH!
THE EXEMPLARY STUDENTS OF DORMITORY 3 WOULD NEVER HAVE TROUBLE WITH A TEACHER.
Jerks.
HA HA HA HA!
DORM 1 STUDENTS ARE WAY TOO PURE-HEARTED FOR THAT!
You're making my stomach hurt.
SLAP
SLAP
BAMM
R.A.!
THAT JERK KITAHAMA JUST SAID THAT THE MUSIC CLUB WAS "CON-TRIBUTING TO MORAL DIS-ORDER"!
UH... YOU'RE SEICHIRO YAO...2ND YEAR, JA?
I'm in a glam band, so my make up's really important!
PLEASE DO SOME-THING! HAVEN'T I ASKED YOU AGAIN AND AGAIN?!

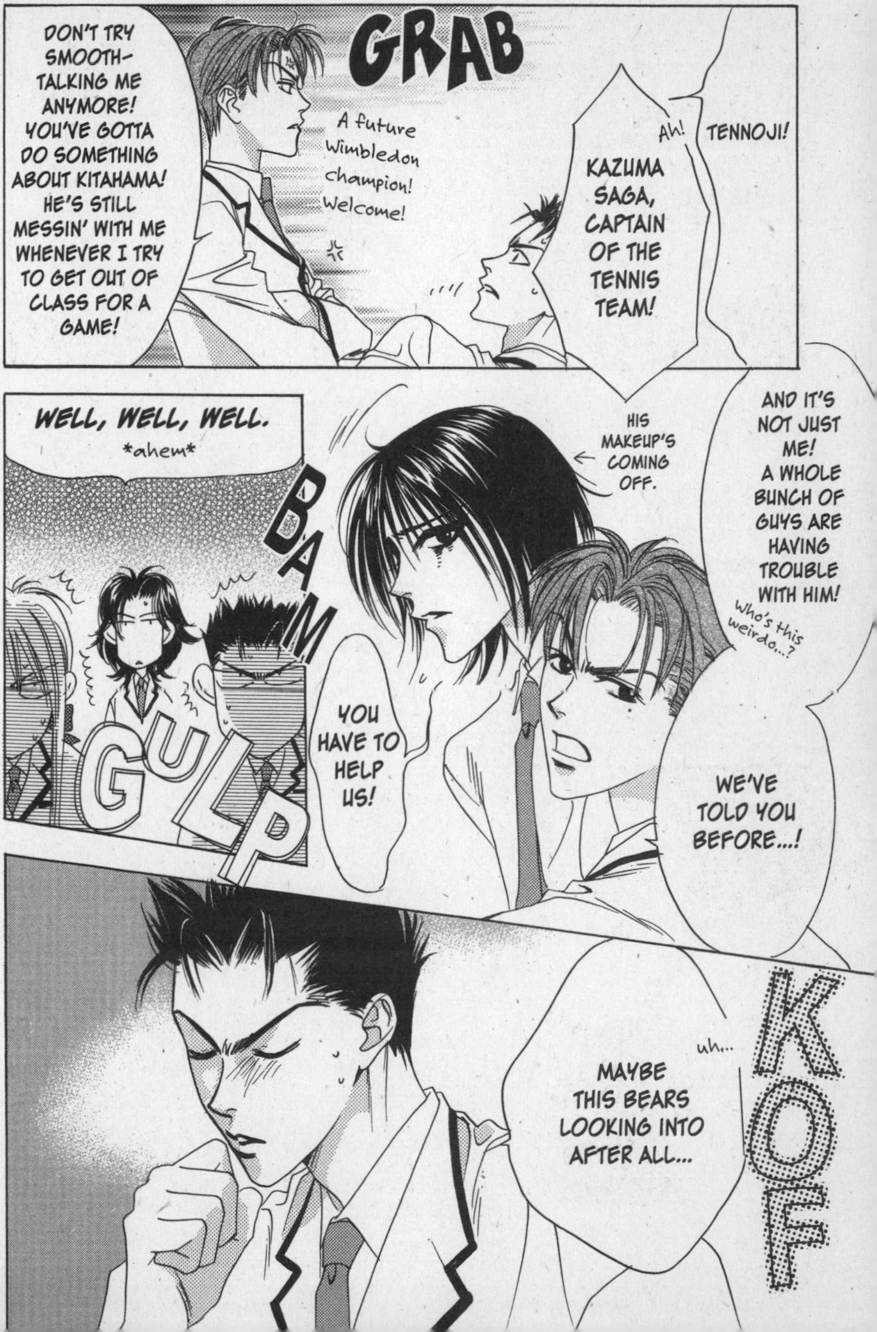
TENNOJI!
Ah!
KAZUMA SAGA, CAPTAIN OF THE TENNIS TEAM!
GRAB
A future Wimbledon champion! Welcome!
DON'T TRY SMOOTH-TALKING ME ANYMORE! YOU'VE GOTTA DO SOMETHING ABOUT KITAHAMA! HE'S STILL MESSIN' WITH ME WHENEVER I TRY TO GET OUT OF CLASS FOR A GAME!
AND IT'S NOT JUST ME! A WHOLE BUNCH OF GUYS ARE HAVING TROUBLE WITH HIM!
Who's this weirdo...?
HIS MAKEUP'S COMING OFF.
WE'VE TOLD YOU BEFORE...!
YOU HAVE TO HELP US!
BAM
WELL, WELL, WELL.
ahem
GULP
KOFF
uh...
MAYBE THIS BEARS LOOKING INTO AFTER ALL...

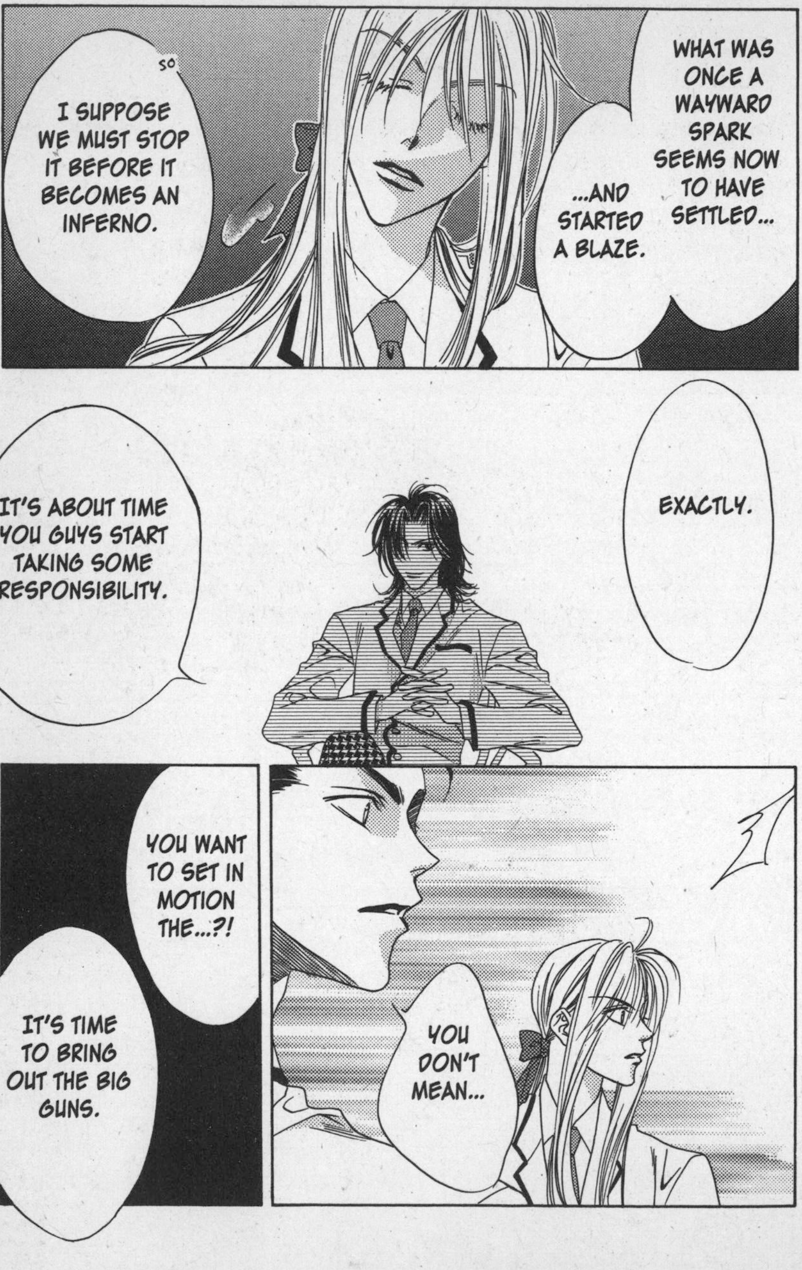
WHAT WAS ONCE A WAYWARD SPARK SEEMS NOW TO HAVE SETTLED...
...AND STARTED A BLAZE.
SO
I SUPPOSE WE MUST STOP IT BEFORE IT BECOMES AN INFERNO.
EXACTLY.
IT'S ABOUT TIME YOU GUYS START TAKING SOME RESPONSIBILITY.
YOU DON'T MEAN...
YOU WANT TO SET IN MOTION THE...?!
IT'S TIME TO BRING OUT THE BIG GUNS.

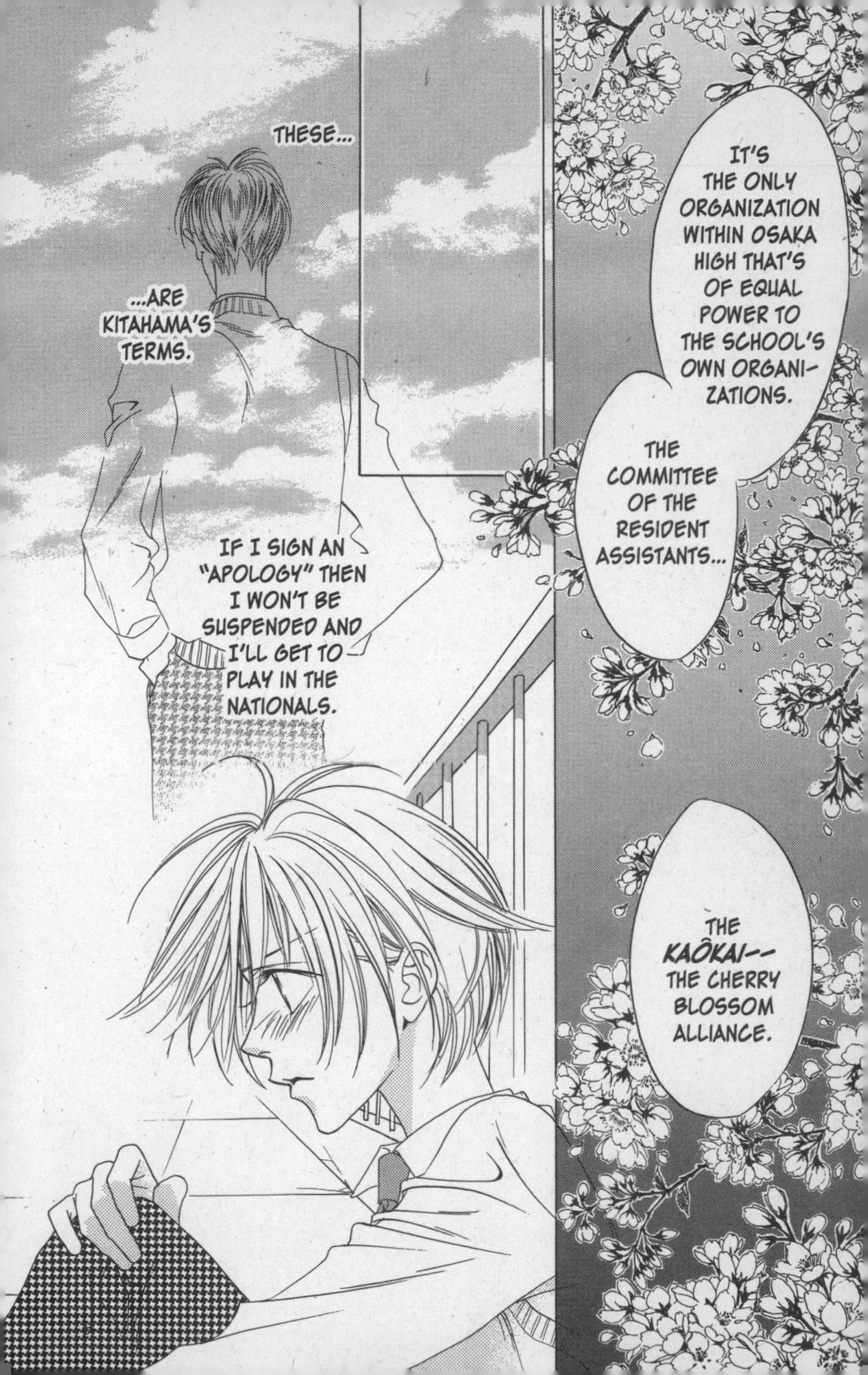
IT'S THE ONLY ORGANIZATION WITHIN OSAKA HIGH THAT'S OF EQUAL POWER TO THE SCHOOL'S OWN ORGANI-ZATIONS.
THE COMMITTEE OF THE RESIDENT ASSISTANTS...
THE *KAÔKAI*-- THE CHERRY BLOSSOM ALLIANCE.
THESE...
...ARE KITAHAMA'S TERMS.
IF I SIGN AN "APOLOGY" THEN I WON'T BE SUSPENDED AND I'LL GET TO PLAY IN THE NATIONALS.

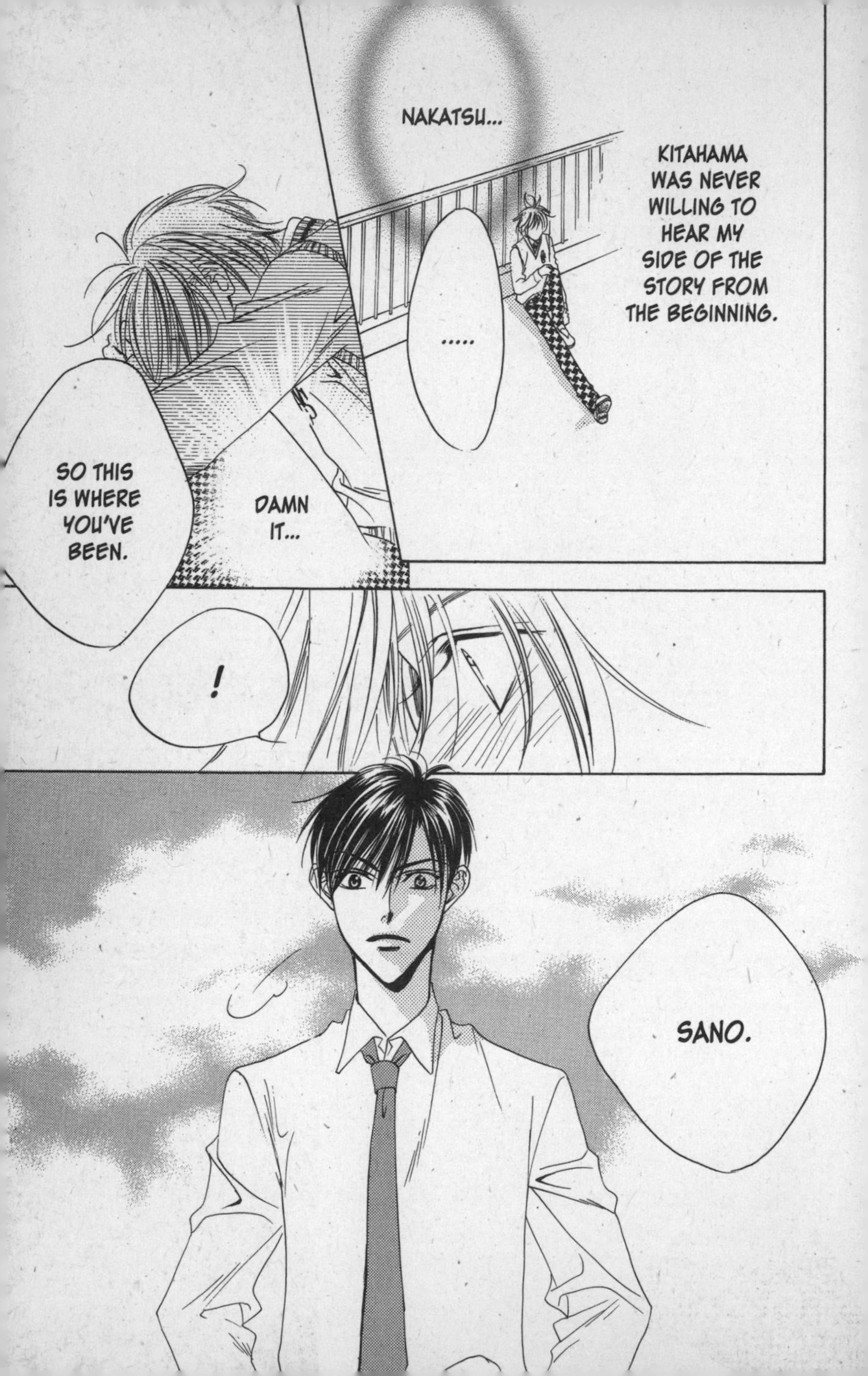
KITAHAMA WAS NEVER WILLING TO HEAR MY SIDE OF THE STORY FROM THE BEGINNING.
NAKATSU...
.....
DAMN IT...
SO THIS IS WHERE YOU'VE BEEN.
!
SANO.

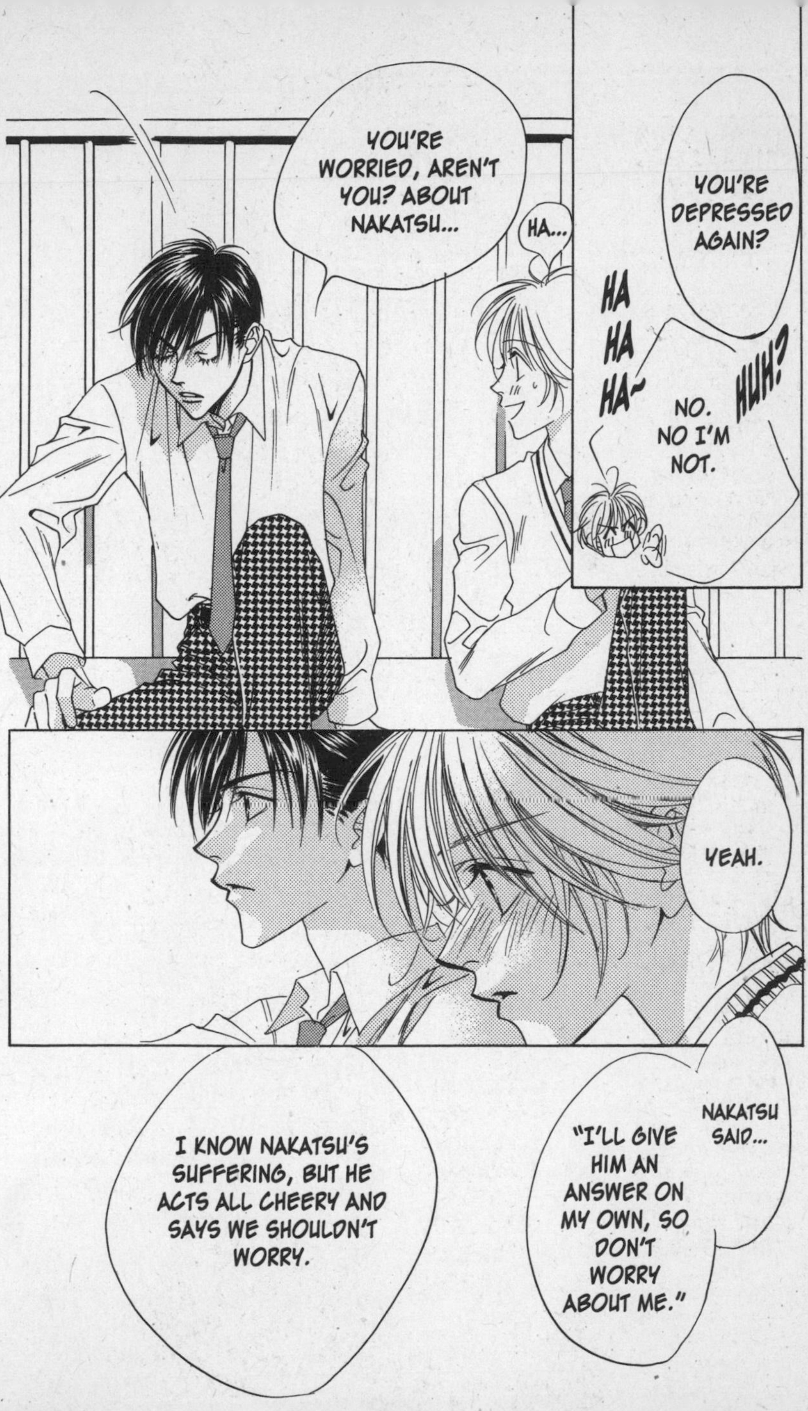
YOU'RE DEPRESSED AGAIN?
HUH?
NO. NO I'M NOT.
HA HA HA~
HA...
YOU'RE WORRIED, AREN'T YOU? ABOUT NAKATSU...
YEAH.
NAKATSU SAID...
"I'LL GIVE HIM AN ANSWER ON MY OWN, SO DON'T WORRY ABOUT ME."
I KNOW NAKATSU'S SUFFERING, BUT HE ACTS ALL CHEERY AND SAYS WE SHOULDN'T WORRY.

WHISPERED SECRETS

「Injury」

JUST BEFORE THE DEADLINE FOR CHAPTER 47, MY CAT (SUO, MALE, 11 MONTHS OLD AT THE TIME) BIT MY RIGHT HAND REALLY HARD AND LEFT SIX RICE-GRAIN SIZED HOLES!!!

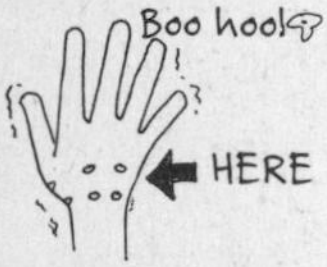
Boo hoo!
HERE

DURING HIS MATING SEASON, A PERSON HE HATES CAME OVER FOR A VISIT AND HE GOT ALL RILED UP, APPARENTLY. MORE THAN PAIN, I FELT SHOCK AND FOR A WHILE I JUST STARED AT THE HOLES AND THE WHITE MEAT THEY REVEALED. AFTER THAT IT HURT LIKE CRAZY. A WEEK EARLIER MY FRIEND "S" HAD SPENT THE NIGHT AND FELL PREY TO SUO, TOO.

LUCKILY THE NERVES IN MY HAND WEREN'T DAMAGED.

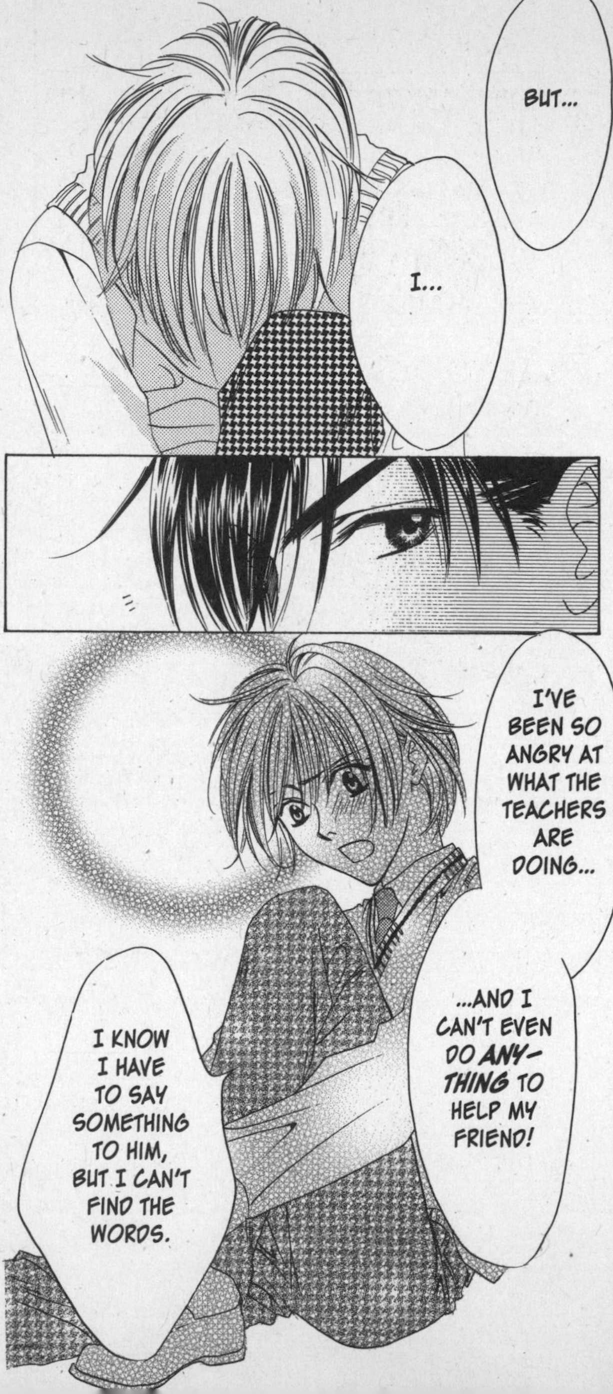
BUT...
I...
I'VE BEEN SO ANGRY AT WHAT THE TEACHERS ARE DOING...
...AND I CAN'T EVEN DO ***ANYTHING*** TO HELP MY FRIEND!
I KNOW I HAVE TO SAY SOMETHING TO HIM, BUT I CAN'T FIND THE WORDS.

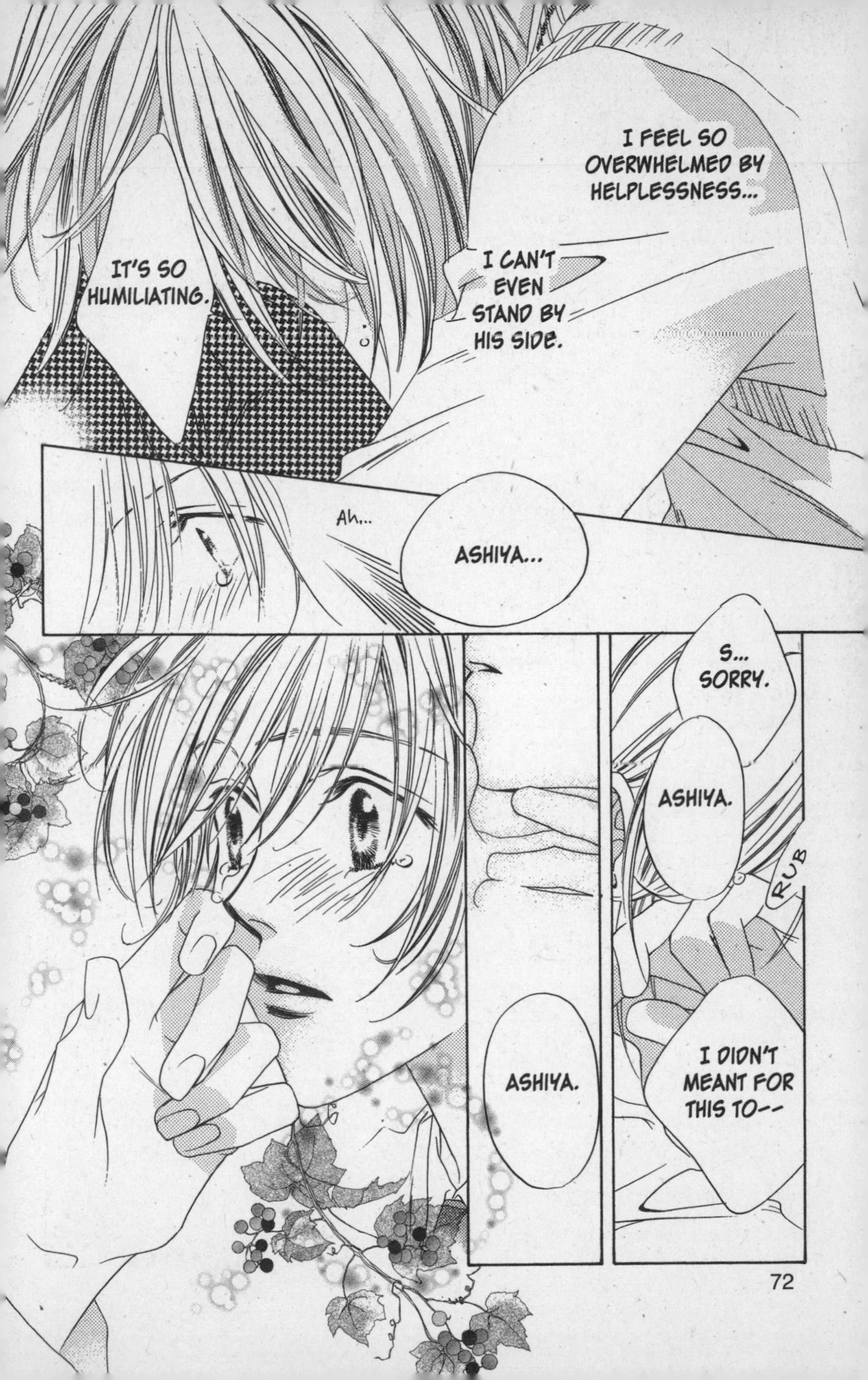
I FEEL SO OVERWHELMED BY HELPLESSNESS...
I CAN'T EVEN STAND BY HIS SIDE.
IT'S SO HUMILIATING.
ASHIYA...
Ah...
S... SORRY.
ASHIYA.
RUB
I DIDN'T MEANT FOR THIS TO--
ASHIYA.

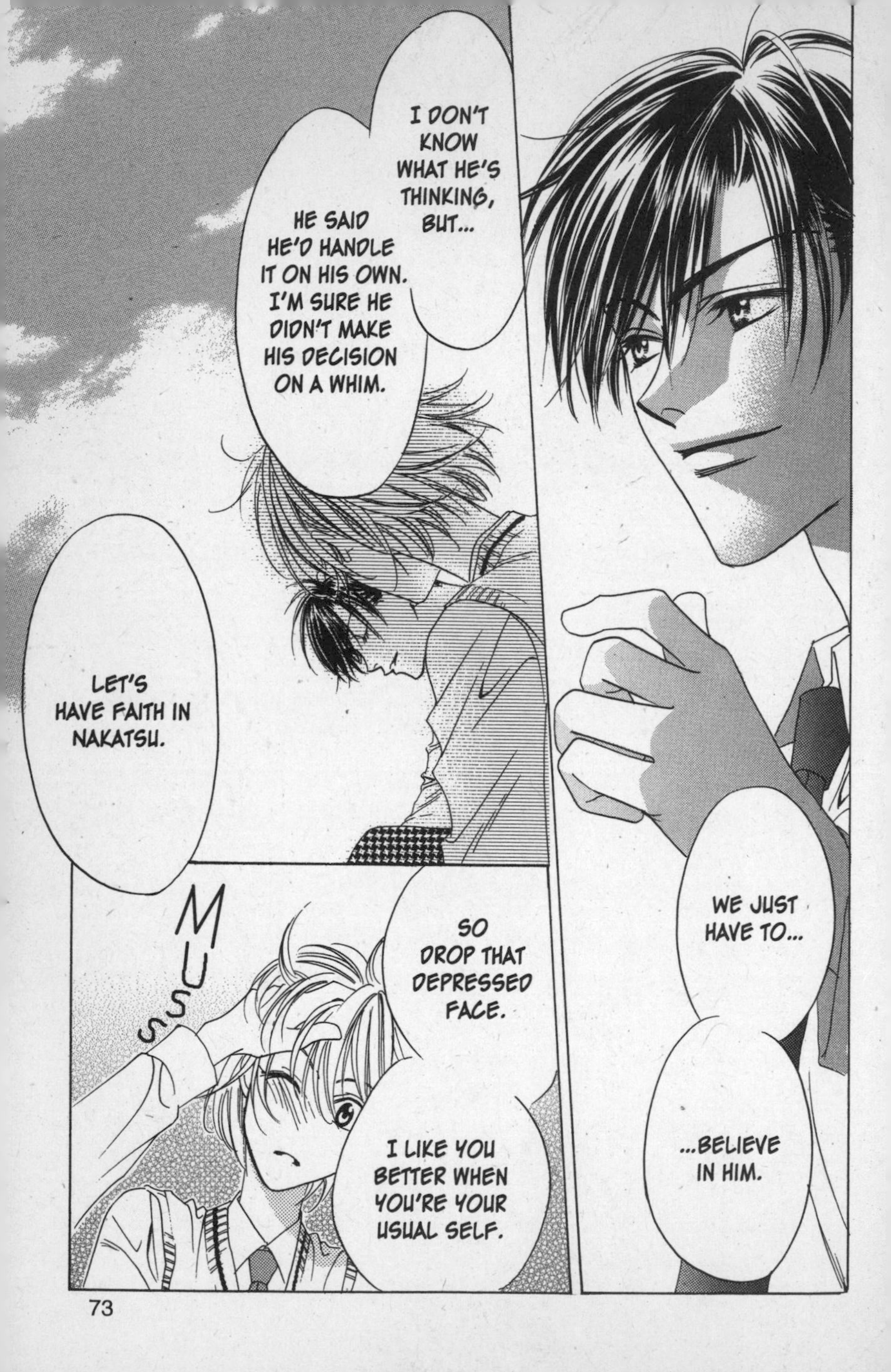
WE JUST HAVE TO...
...BELIEVE IN HIM.
I DON'T KNOW WHAT HE'S THINKING, BUT...
HE SAID HE'D HANDLE IT ON HIS OWN. I'M SURE HE DIDN'T MAKE HIS DECISION ON A WHIM.
LET'S HAVE FAITH IN NAKATSU.
MUSS
SO DROP THAT DEPRESSED FACE.
I LIKE YOU BETTER WHEN YOU'RE YOUR USUAL SELF.

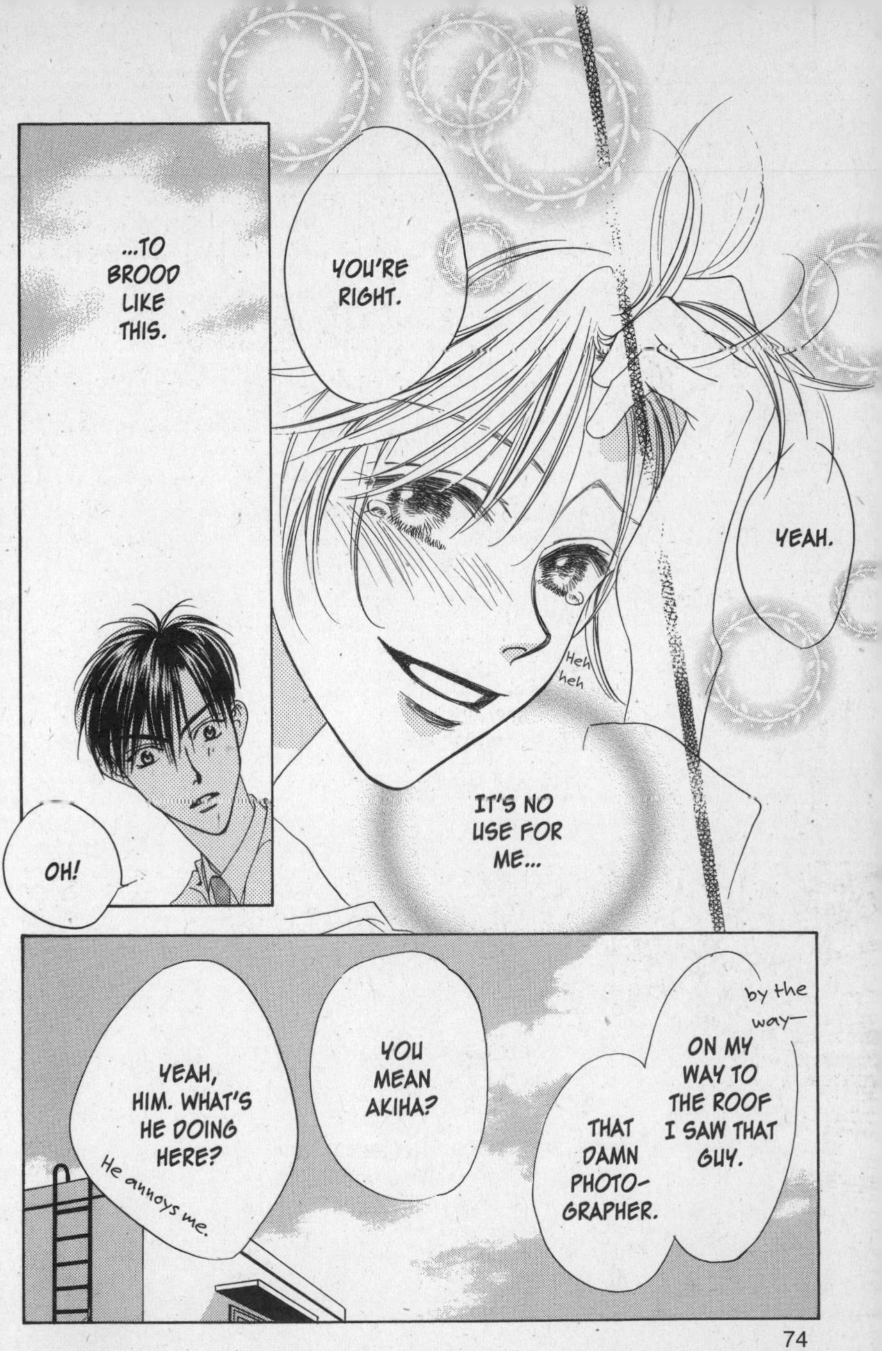
YEAH.
YOU'RE RIGHT.
Heh heh
IT'S NO USE FOR ME...
...TO BROOD LIKE THIS.
OH!
by the way—
ON MY WAY TO THE ROOF I SAW THAT GUY.
THAT DAMN PHOTOGRAPHER.
YOU MEAN AKIHA?
YEAH, HIM. WHAT'S HE DOING HERE?
He annoys me.

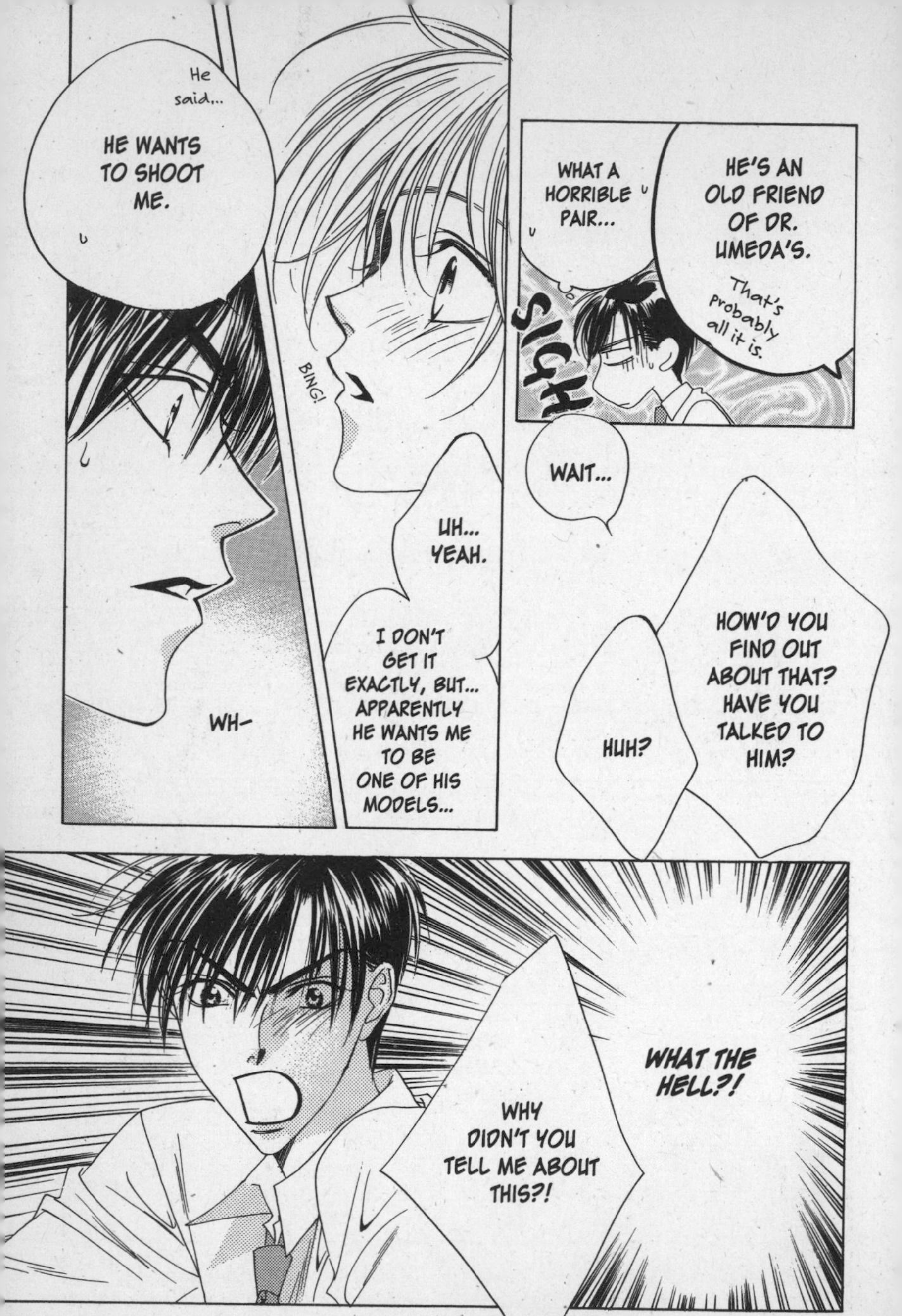
HE'S AN OLD FRIEND OF DR. UMEDA'S.
That's probably all it is.
WHAT A HORRIBLE PAIR...
SIGH
WAIT...
HOW'D YOU FIND OUT ABOUT THAT? HAVE YOU TALKED TO HIM?
HUH?
BING!
UH... YEAH.
I DON'T GET IT EXACTLY, BUT... APPARENTLY HE WANTS ME TO BE ONE OF HIS MODELS...
He said...
HE WANTS TO SHOOT ME.
WH-
WHAT THE HELL?!
WHY DIDN'T YOU TELL ME ABOUT THIS?!

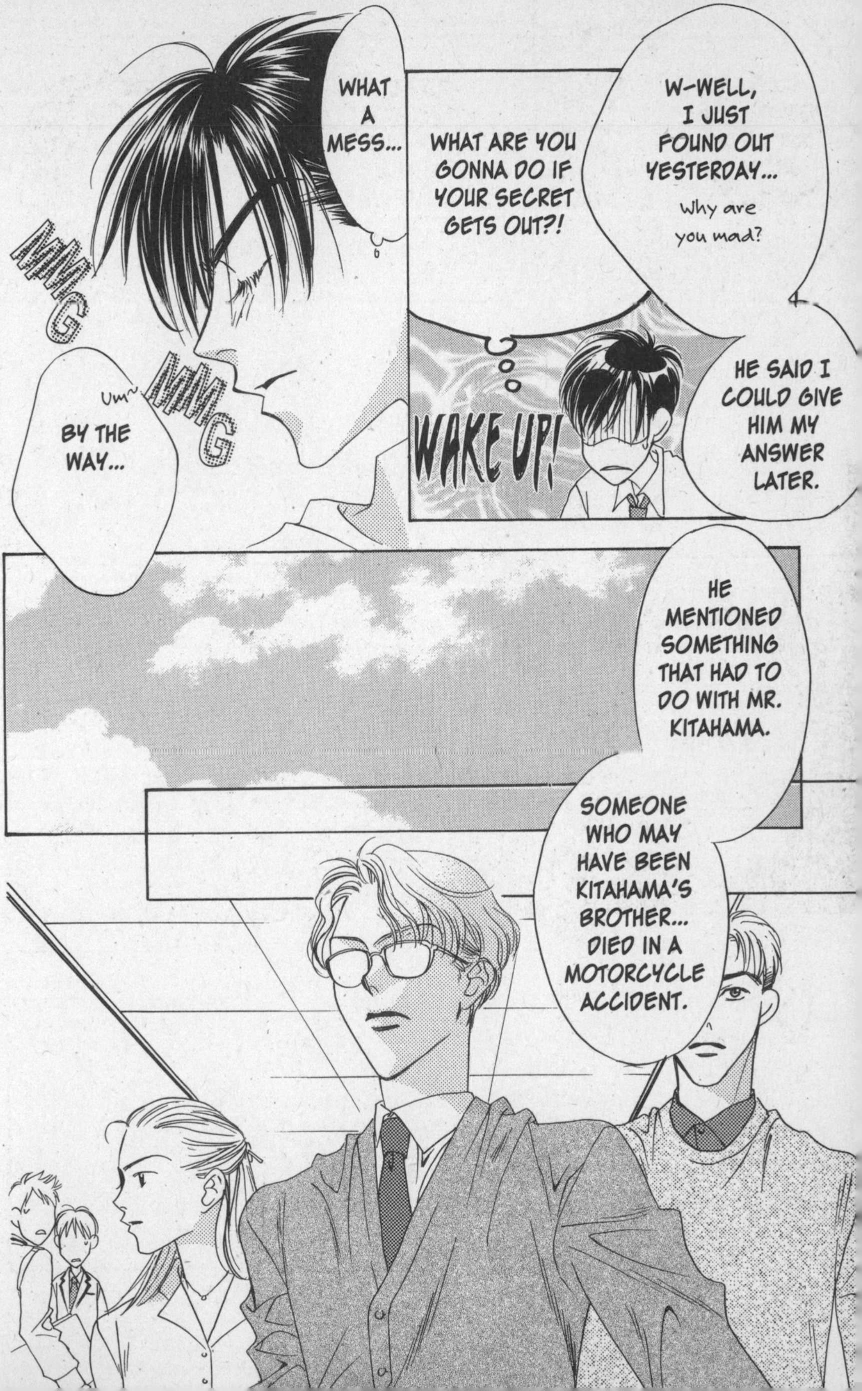
W-WELL, I JUST FOUND OUT YESTERDAY...
Why are you mad?
WHAT ARE YOU GONNA DO IF YOUR SECRET GETS OUT?!
HE SAID I COULD GIVE HIM MY ANSWER LATER.
WAKE UP!
WHAT A MESS...
MMG
MMG
Um~ BY THE WAY...
HE MENTIONED SOMETHING THAT HAD TO DO WITH MR. KITAHAMA.
SOMEONE WHO MAY HAVE BEEN KITAHAMA'S BROTHER... DIED IN A MOTORCYCLE ACCIDENT.

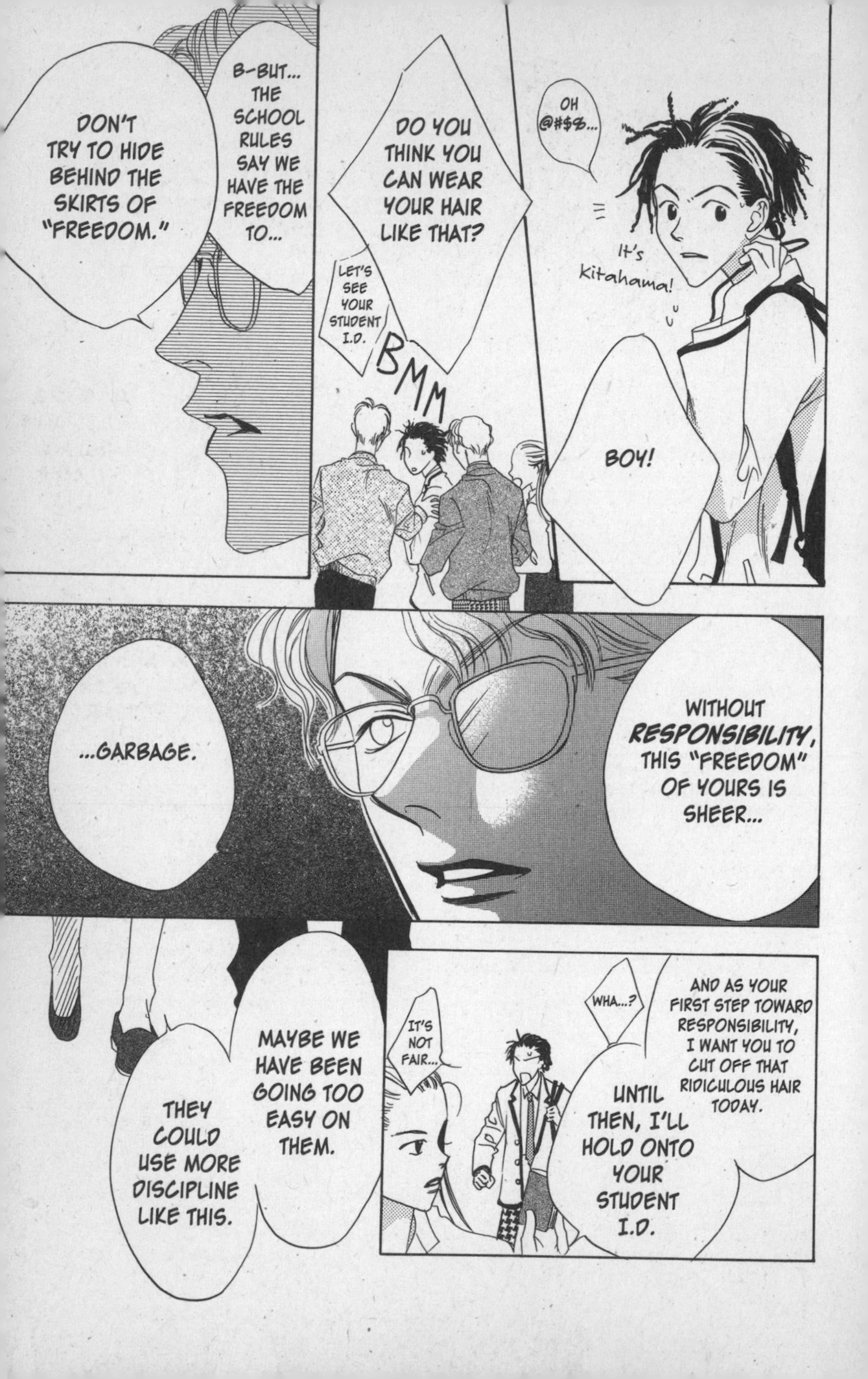
OH @#$&...
It's Kitahama!
BOY!
DO YOU THINK YOU CAN WEAR YOUR HAIR LIKE THAT?
LET'S SEE YOUR STUDENT I.D.
BMM
B-BUT... THE SCHOOL RULES SAY WE HAVE THE FREEDOM TO...
DON'T TRY TO HIDE BEHIND THE SKIRTS OF "FREEDOM."
WITHOUT *RESPONSIBILITY*, THIS "FREEDOM" OF YOURS IS SHEER...
...GARBAGE.
AND AS YOUR FIRST STEP TOWARD RESPONSIBILITY, I WANT YOU TO CUT OFF THAT RIDICULOUS HAIR TODAY.
WHA...?
UNTIL THEN, I'LL HOLD ONTO YOUR STUDENT I.D.
IT'S NOT FAIR...
MAYBE WE HAVE BEEN GOING TOO EASY ON THEM.
THEY COULD USE MORE DISCIPLINE LIKE THIS.

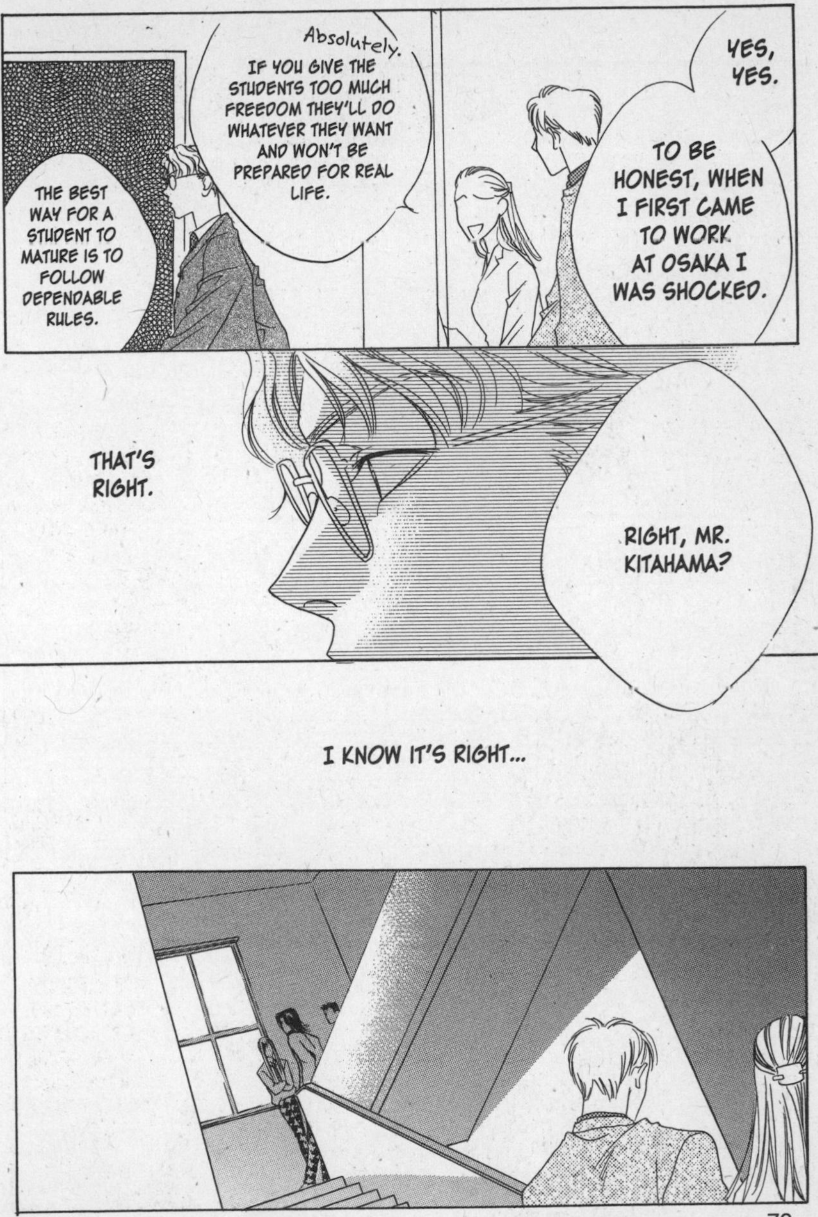
YES, YES.
TO BE HONEST, WHEN I FIRST CAME TO WORK AT OSAKA I WAS SHOCKED.
Absolutely.
IF YOU GIVE THE STUDENTS TOO MUCH FREEDOM THEY'LL DO WHATEVER THEY WANT AND WON'T BE PREPARED FOR REAL LIFE.
THE BEST WAY FOR A STUDENT TO MATURE IS TO FOLLOW DEPENDABLE RULES.
RIGHT, MR. KITAHAMA?
THAT'S RIGHT.
I KNOW IT'S RIGHT...

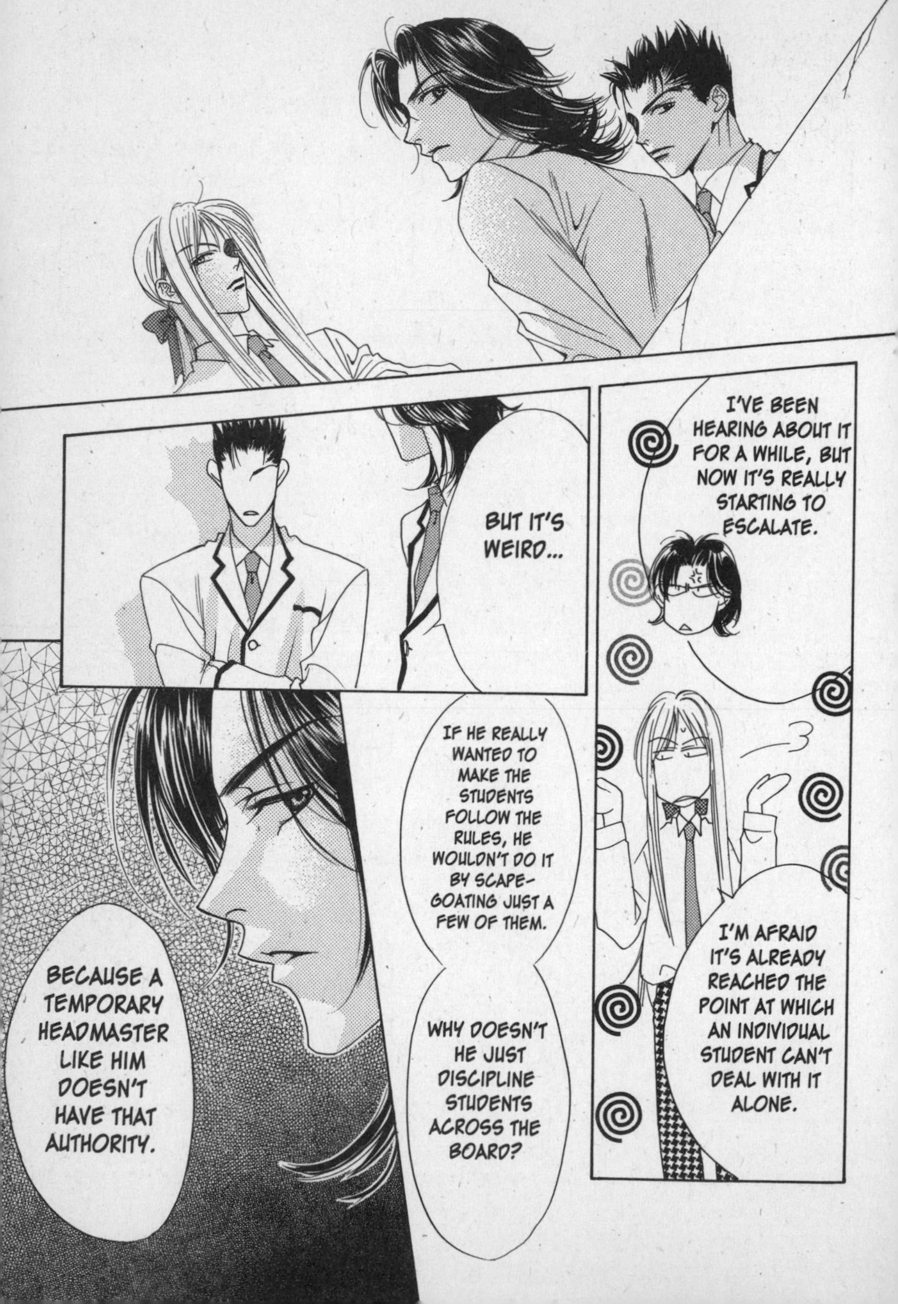
I'VE BEEN HEARING ABOUT IT FOR A WHILE, BUT NOW IT'S REALLY STARTING TO ESCALATE.
I'M AFRAID IT'S ALREADY REACHED THE POINT AT WHICH AN INDIVIDUAL STUDENT CAN'T DEAL WITH IT ALONE.
BUT IT'S WEIRD...
IF HE REALLY WANTED TO MAKE THE STUDENTS FOLLOW THE RULES, HE WOULDN'T DO IT BY SCAPE-GOATING JUST A FEW OF THEM.
WHY DOESN'T HE JUST DISCIPLINE STUDENTS ACROSS THE BOARD?
BECAUSE A TEMPORARY HEADMASTER LIKE HIM DOESN'T HAVE THAT AUTHORITY.

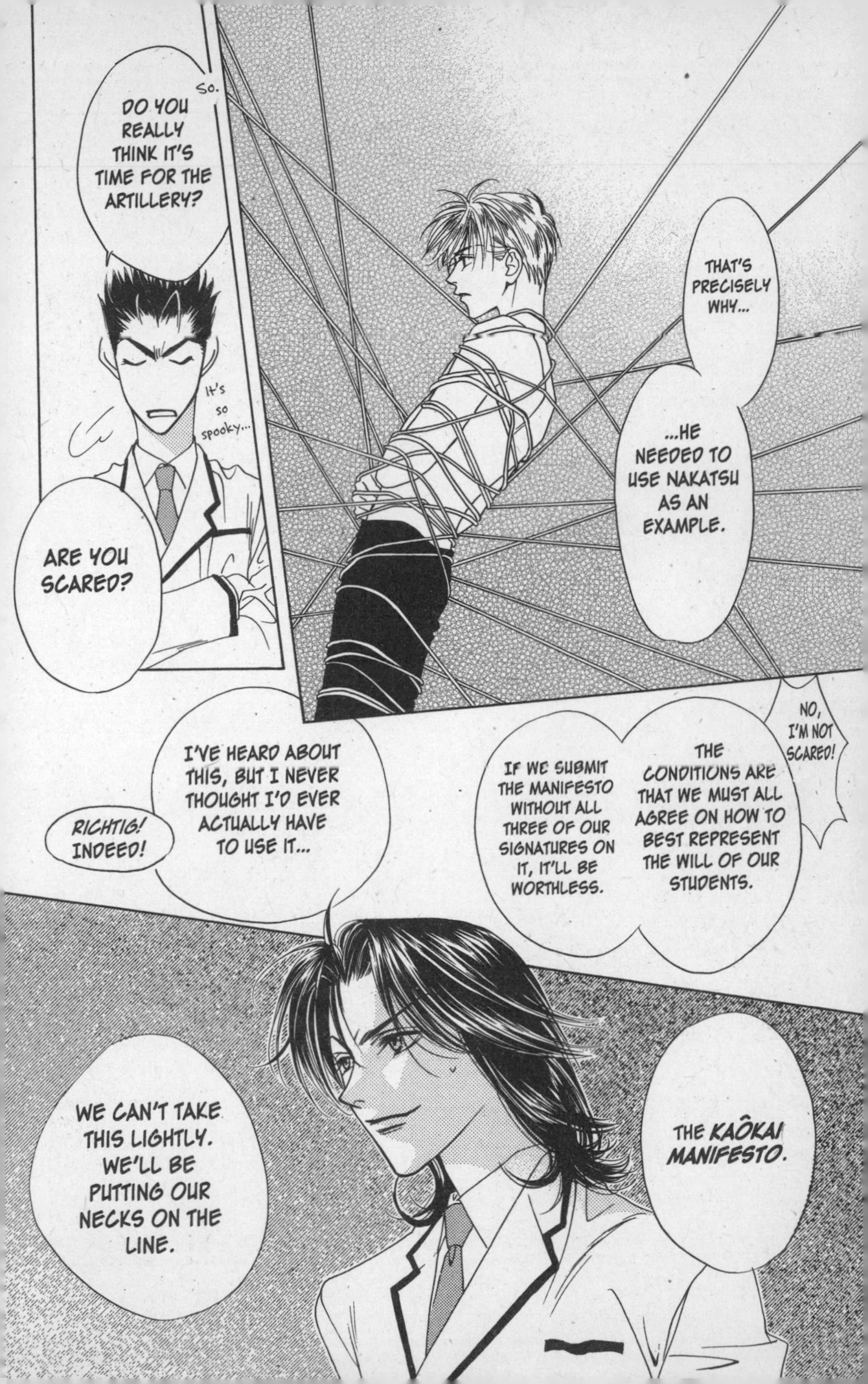
THAT'S PRECISELY WHY...
...HE NEEDED TO USE NAKATSU AS AN EXAMPLE.
So.
DO YOU REALLY THINK IT'S TIME FOR THE ARTILLERY?
It's so spooky...
ARE YOU SCARED?
NO, I'M NOT SCARED!
THE CONDITIONS ARE THAT WE MUST ALL AGREE ON HOW TO BEST REPRESENT THE WILL OF OUR STUDENTS.
IF WE SUBMIT THE MANIFESTO WITHOUT ALL THREE OF OUR SIGNATURES ON IT, IT'LL BE WORTHLESS.
I'VE HEARD ABOUT THIS, BUT I NEVER THOUGHT I'D EVER ACTUALLY HAVE TO USE IT...
RICHTIG! INDEED!
THE *KAÔKAI MANIFESTO*.
WE CAN'T TAKE THIS LIGHTLY. WE'LL BE PUTTING OUR NECKS ON THE LINE.

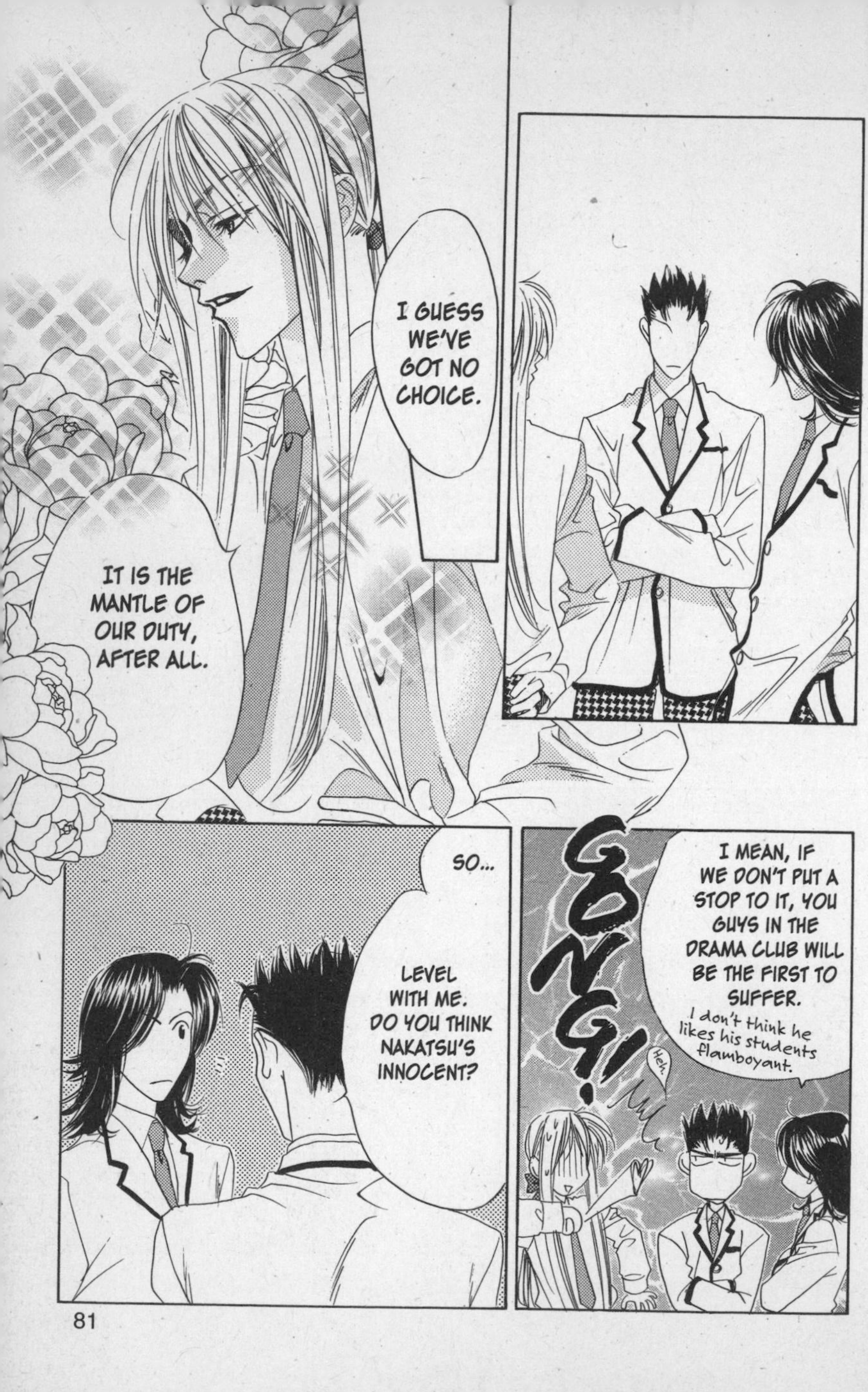
I GUESS WE'VE GOT NO CHOICE.
IT IS THE MANTLE OF OUR DUTY, AFTER ALL.
I MEAN, IF WE DON'T PUT A STOP TO IT, YOU GUYS IN THE DRAMA CLUB WILL BE THE FIRST TO SUFFER.
I don't think he likes his students flamboyant.
GONG!
Heh.
SO...
LEVEL WITH ME. DO YOU THINK NAKATSU'S INNOCENT?

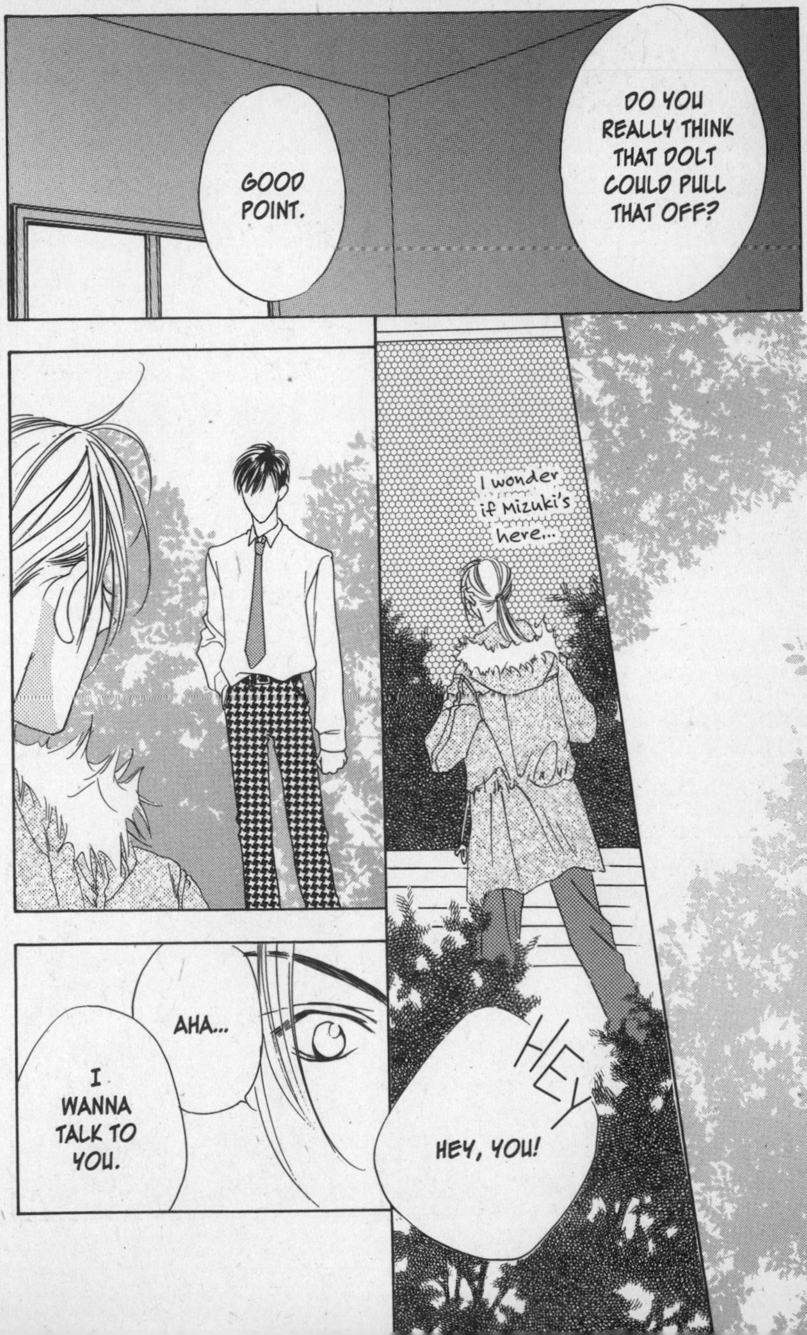
DO YOU REALLY THINK THAT DOLT COULD PULL THAT OFF?
GOOD POINT.
I wonder if Mizuki's here...
HEY
HEY, YOU!
AHA...
I WANNA TALK TO YOU.

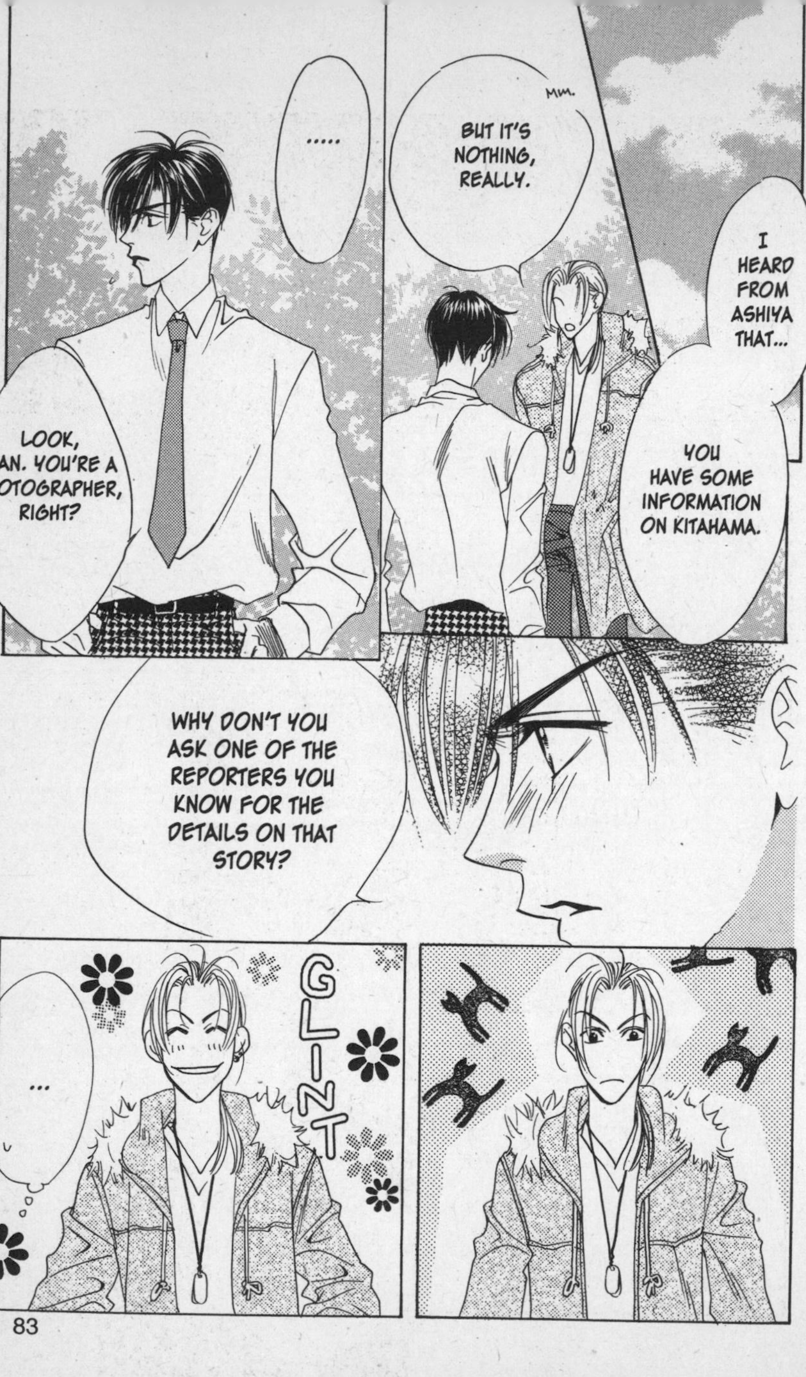
I HEARD FROM ASHIYA THAT...
YOU HAVE SOME INFORMATION ON KITAHAMA.
MM.
BUT IT'S NOTHING, REALLY.
.....
LOOK, MAN. YOU'RE A PHOTOGRAPHER, RIGHT?
WHY DON'T YOU ASK ONE OF THE REPORTERS YOU KNOW FOR THE DETAILS ON THAT STORY?
GLINT
...

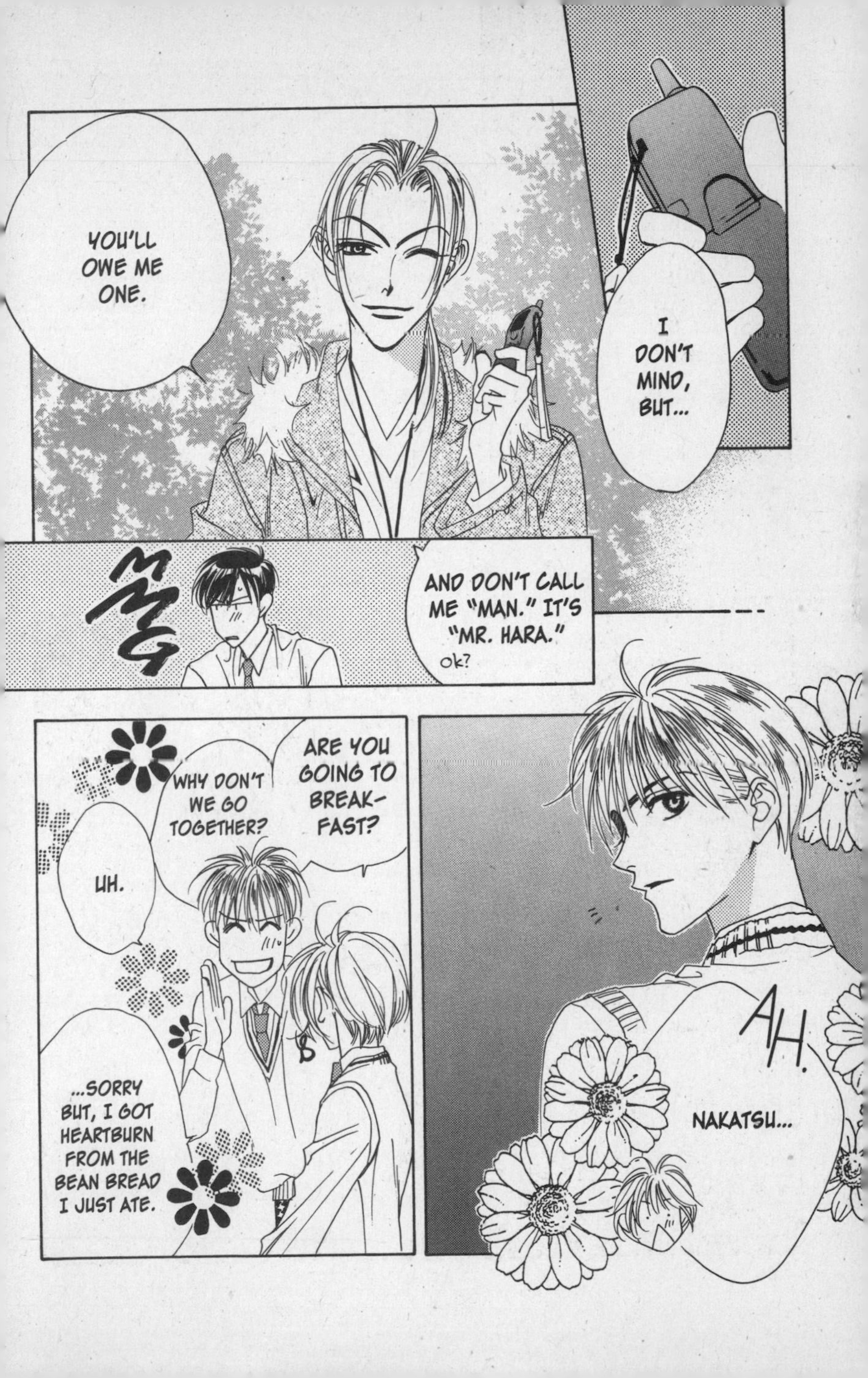
I DON'T MIND, BUT...
YOU'LL OWE ME ONE.
MMG
AND DON'T CALL ME "MAN." IT'S "MR. HARA."
ok?
AH.
NAKATSU...
ARE YOU GOING TO BREAK-FAST?
WHY DON'T WE GO TOGETHER?
UH.
...SORRY BUT, I GOT HEARTBURN FROM THE BEAN BREAD I JUST ATE.

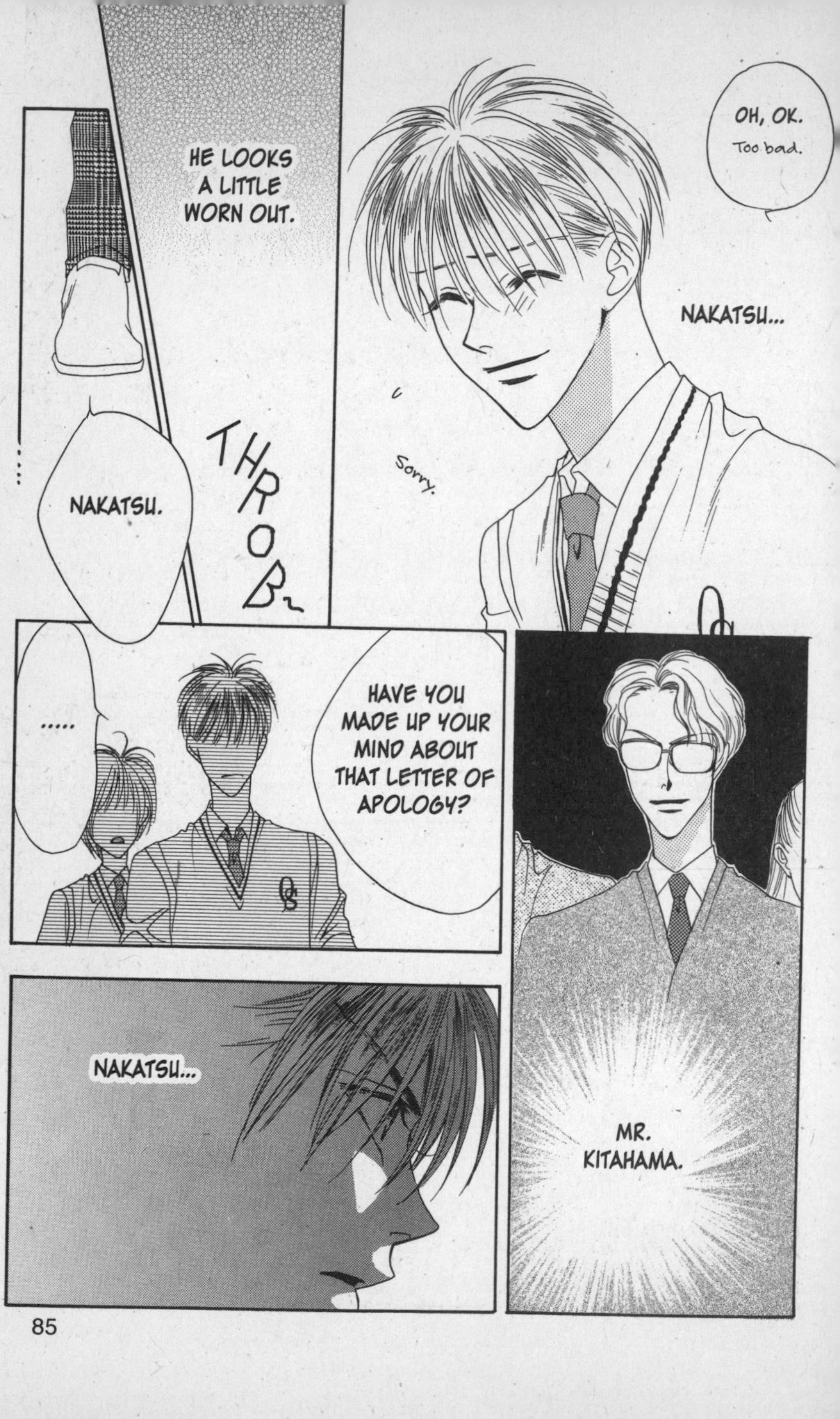
OH, OK.
Too bad.
NAKATSU...
Sorry.
HE LOOKS A LITTLE WORN OUT.
...
NAKATSU.
THROB
MR. KITAHAMA.
HAVE YOU MADE UP YOUR MIND ABOUT THAT LETTER OF APOLOGY?
.....
NAKATSU...

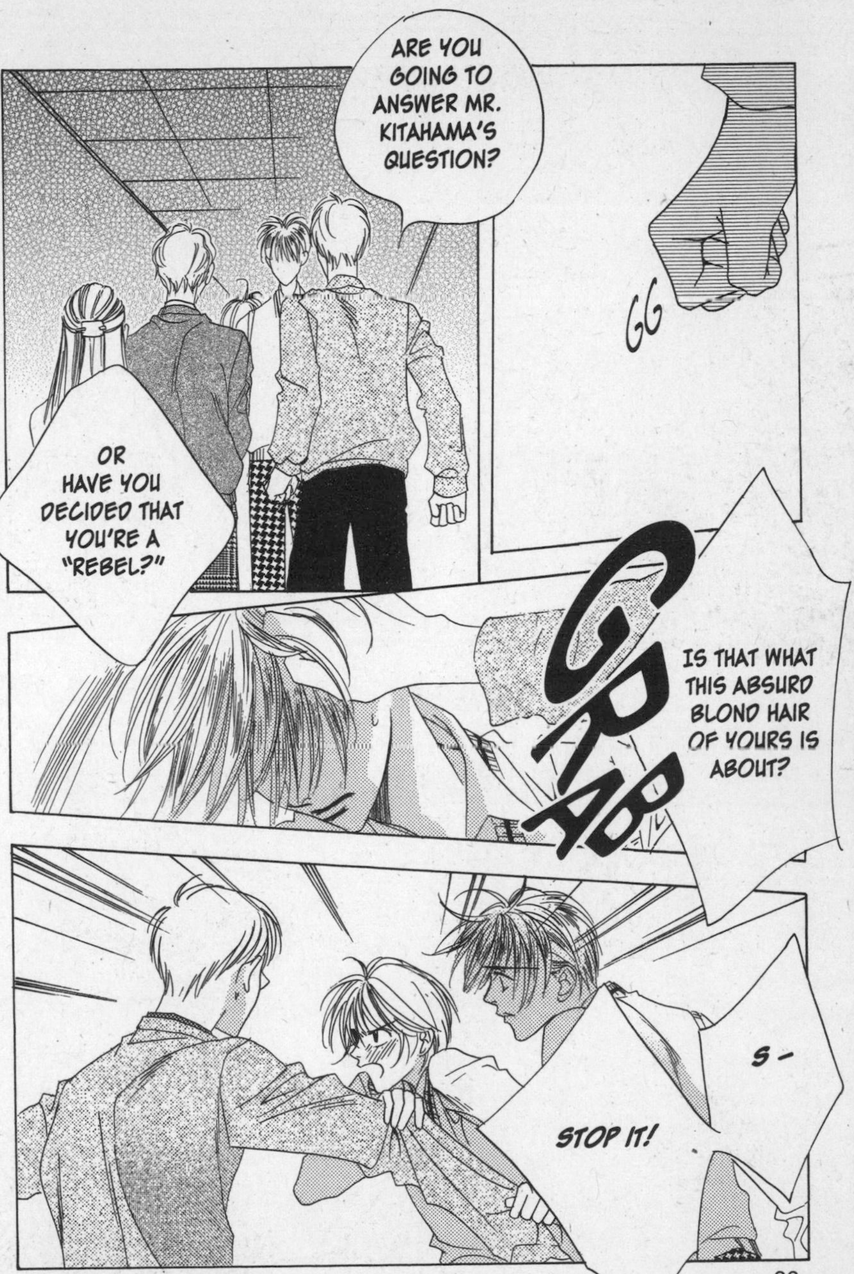
GG
ARE YOU GOING TO ANSWER MR. KITAHAMA'S QUESTION?
OR HAVE YOU DECIDED THAT YOU'RE A "REBEL?"
GRAB
IS THAT WHAT THIS ABSURD BLOND HAIR OF YOURS IS ABOUT?
S –
STOP IT!

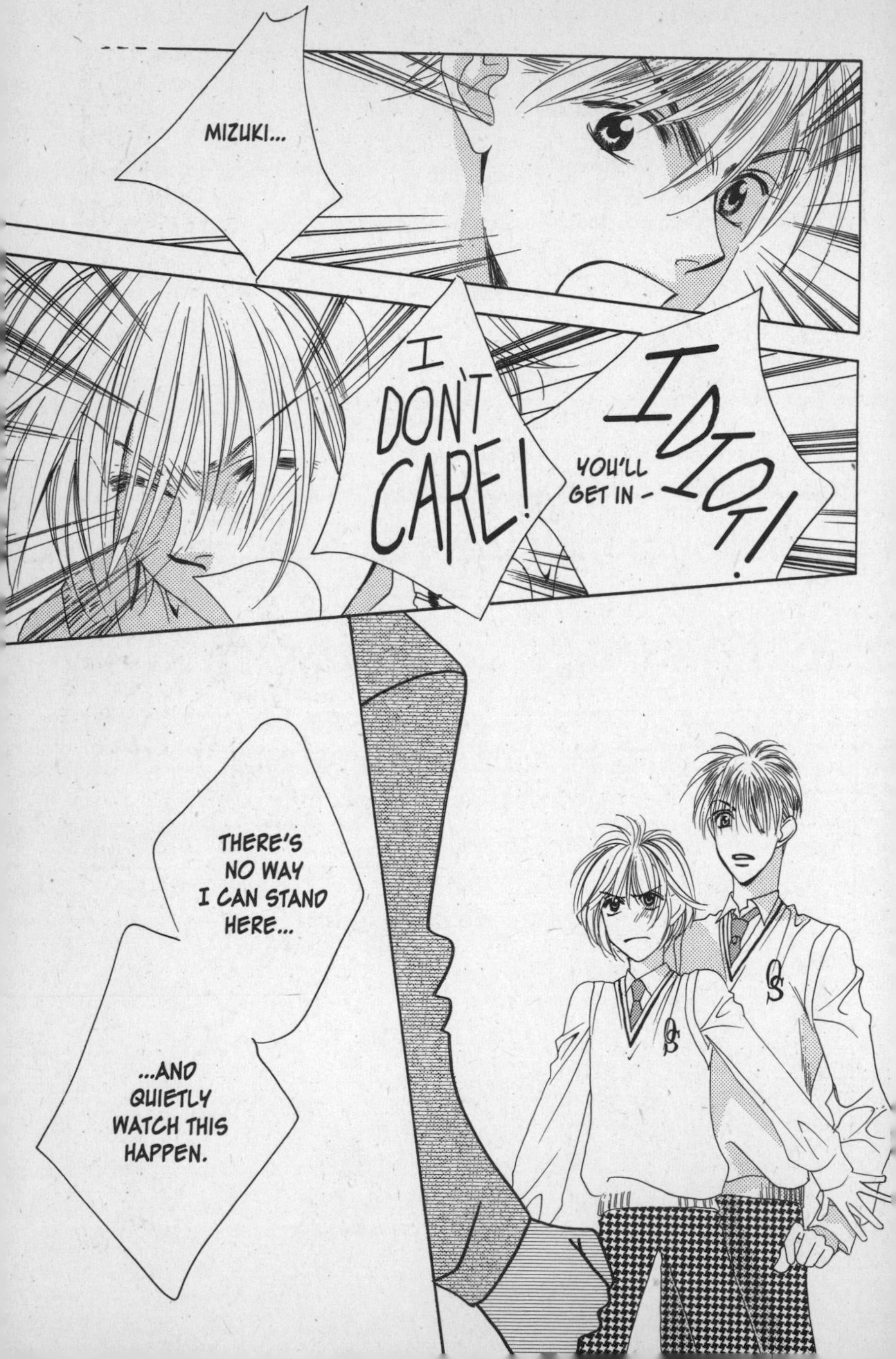
MIZUKI...
IDIOT! YOU'LL GET IN-
I DON'T CARE!
THERE'S NO WAY I CAN STAND HERE...
...AND QUIETLY WATCH THIS HAPPEN.

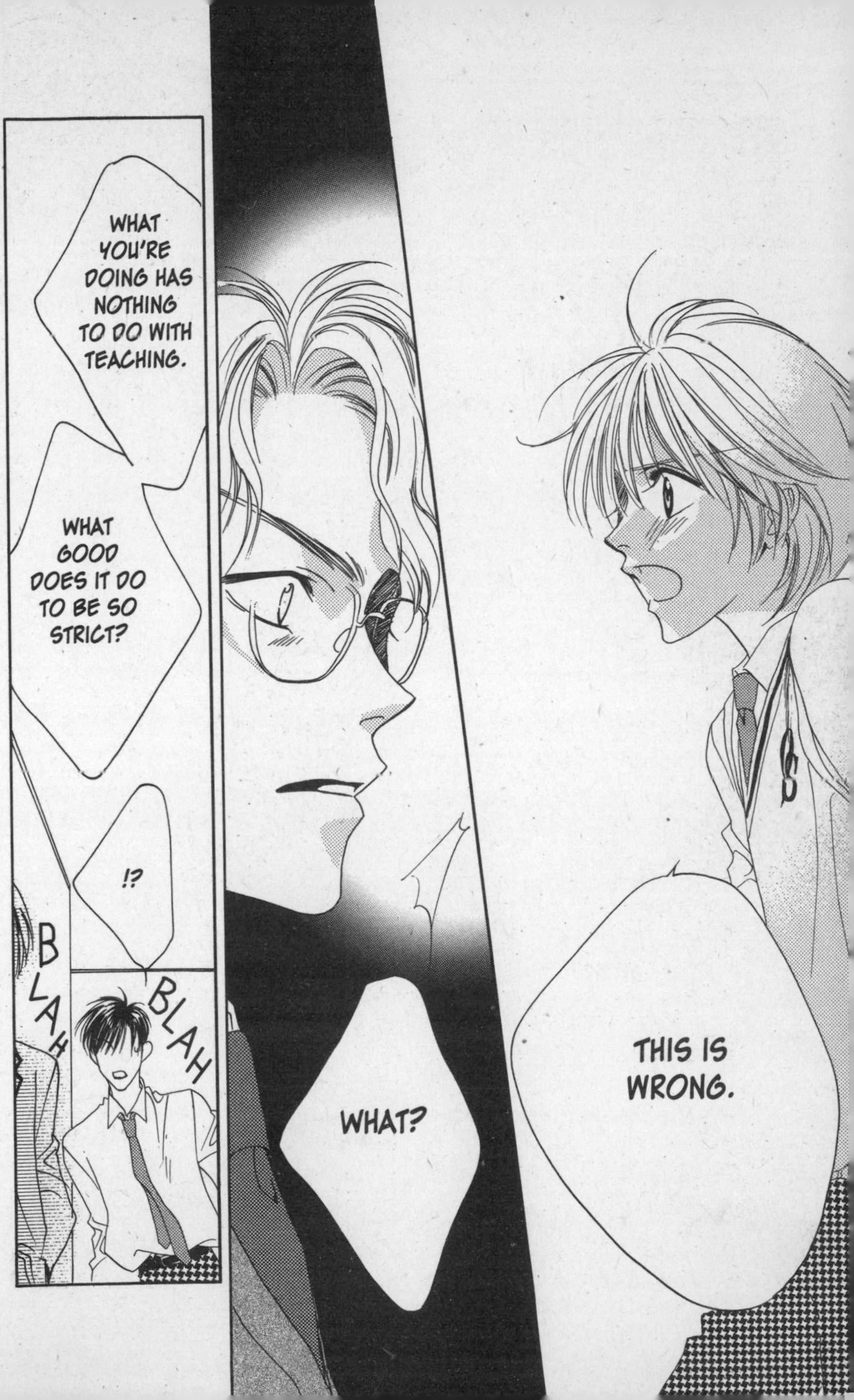
THIS IS WRONG.
WHAT?
WHAT YOU'RE DOING HAS NOTHING TO DO WITH TEACHING.
WHAT GOOD DOES IT DO TO BE SO STRICT?
!?
BLAH
BLAH

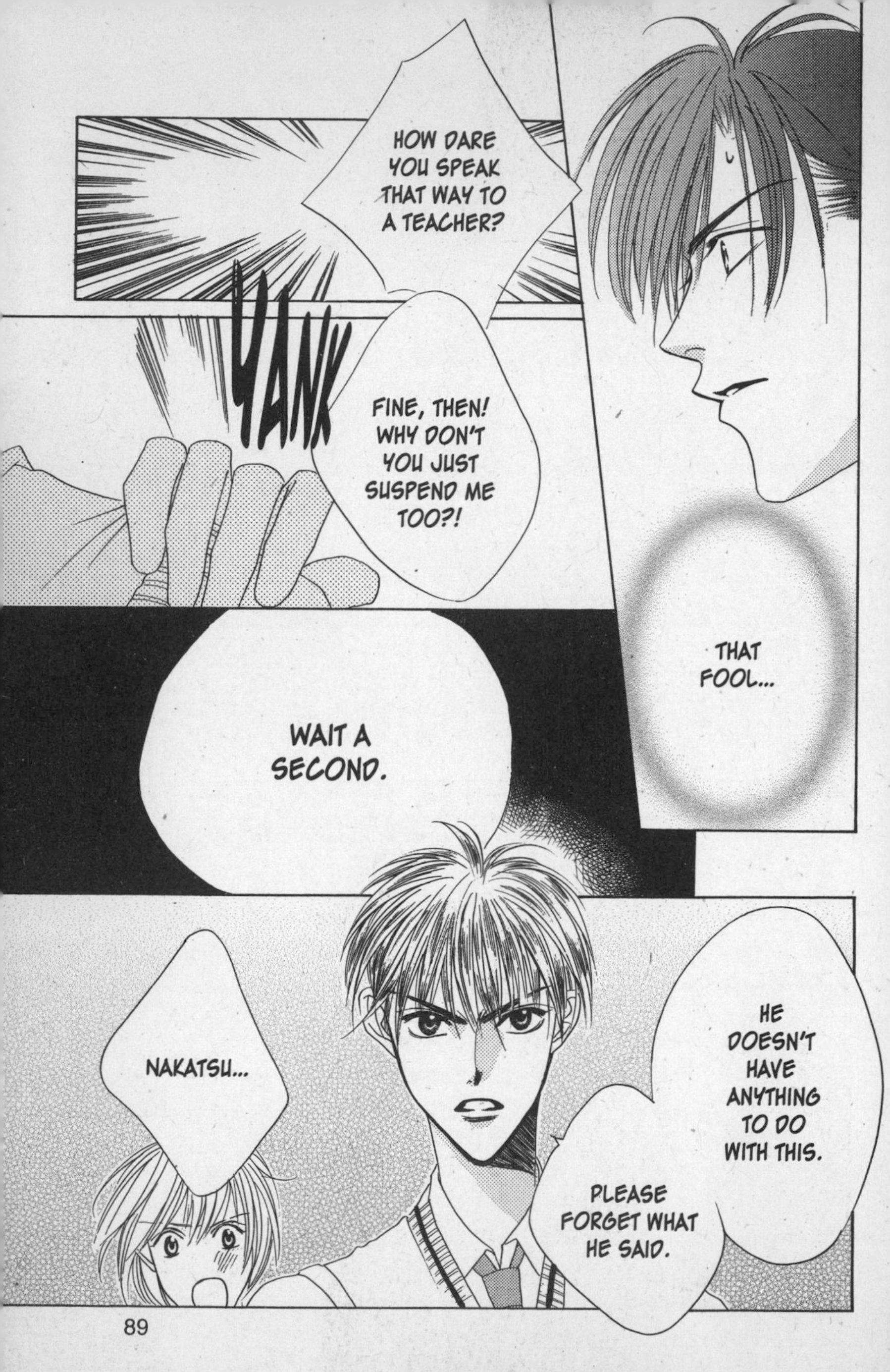
HOW DARE YOU SPEAK THAT WAY TO A TEACHER?
YANK
FINE, THEN! WHY DON'T YOU JUST SUSPEND ME TOO?!
THAT FOOL...
WAIT A SECOND.
HE DOESN'T HAVE ANYTHING TO DO WITH THIS.
PLEASE FORGET WHAT HE SAID.
NAKATSU...

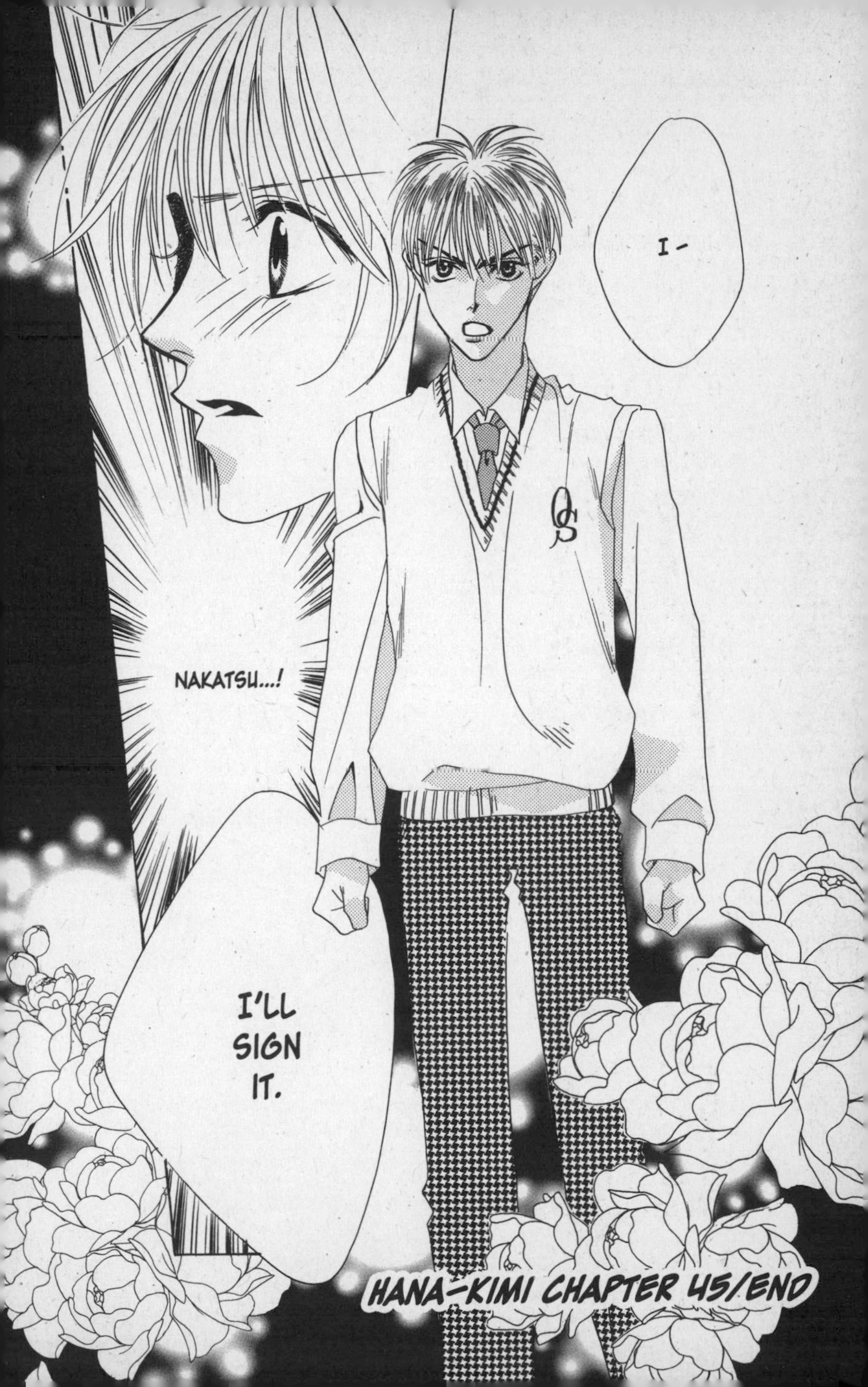
I-
NAKATSU...!
I'LL SIGN IT.
HANA-KIMI CHAPTER 45/END

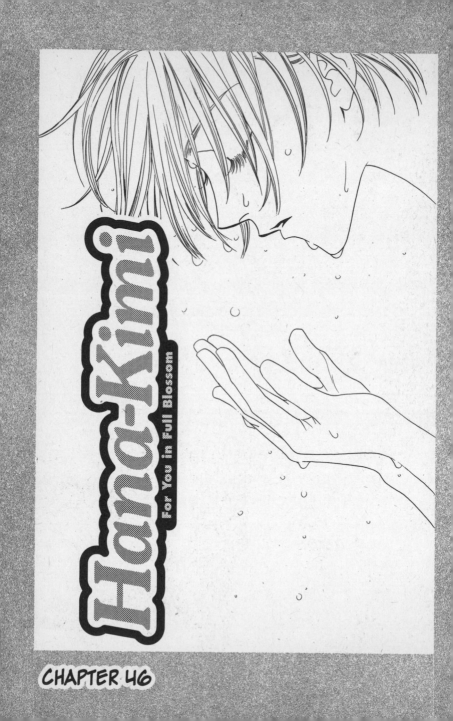

Hana-Kimi
For You in Full Blossom

CHAPTER 46

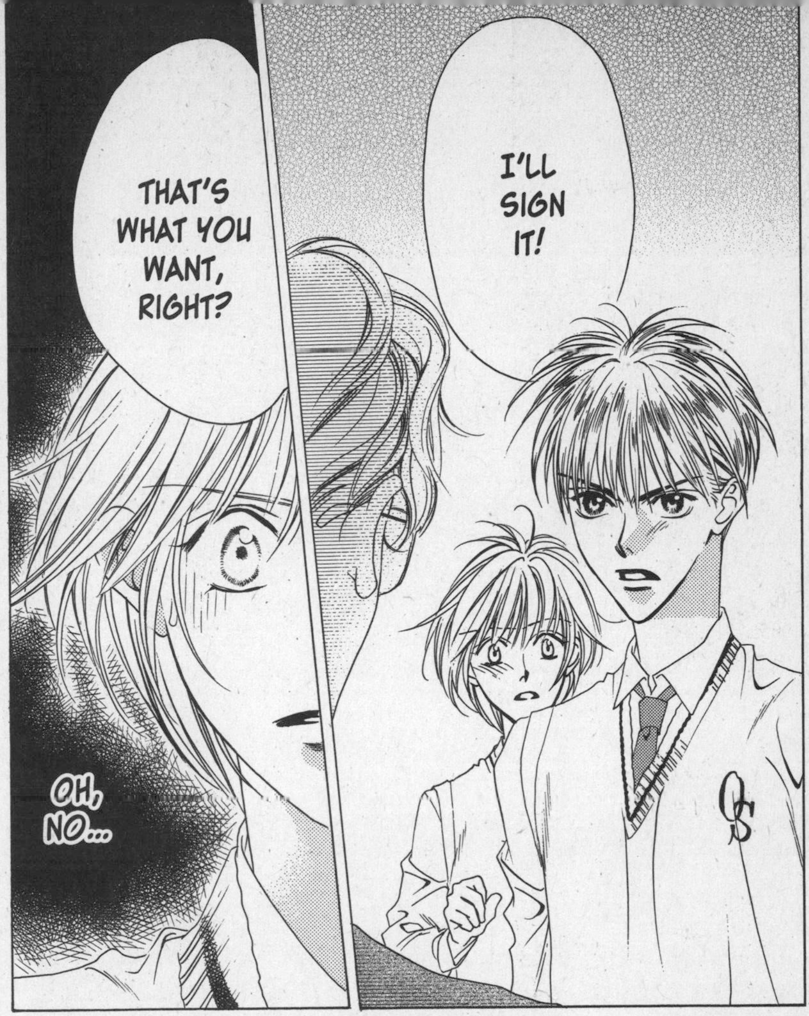
I'LL SIGN IT!
THAT'S WHAT YOU WANT, RIGHT?
OH, NO...

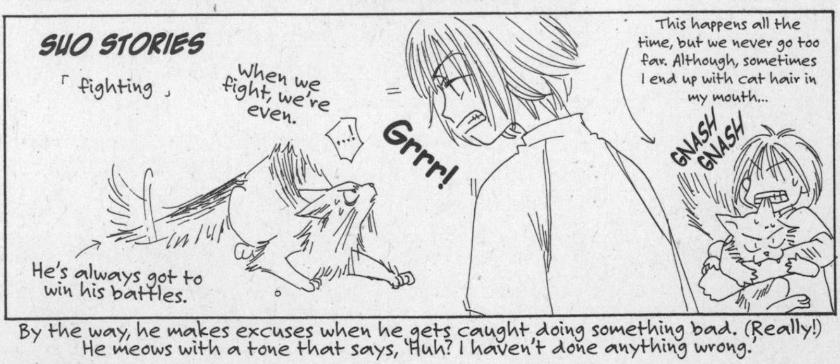
SUO STORIES
「fighting」
When we fight, we're even.
...!
Grrr!
He's always got to win his battles.
This happens all the time, but we never go too far. Although, sometimes I end up with cat hair in my mouth...
GNASH GNASH

By the way, he makes excuses when he gets caught doing something bad. (Really!) He meows with a tone that says, 'Huh? I haven't done anything wrong.'

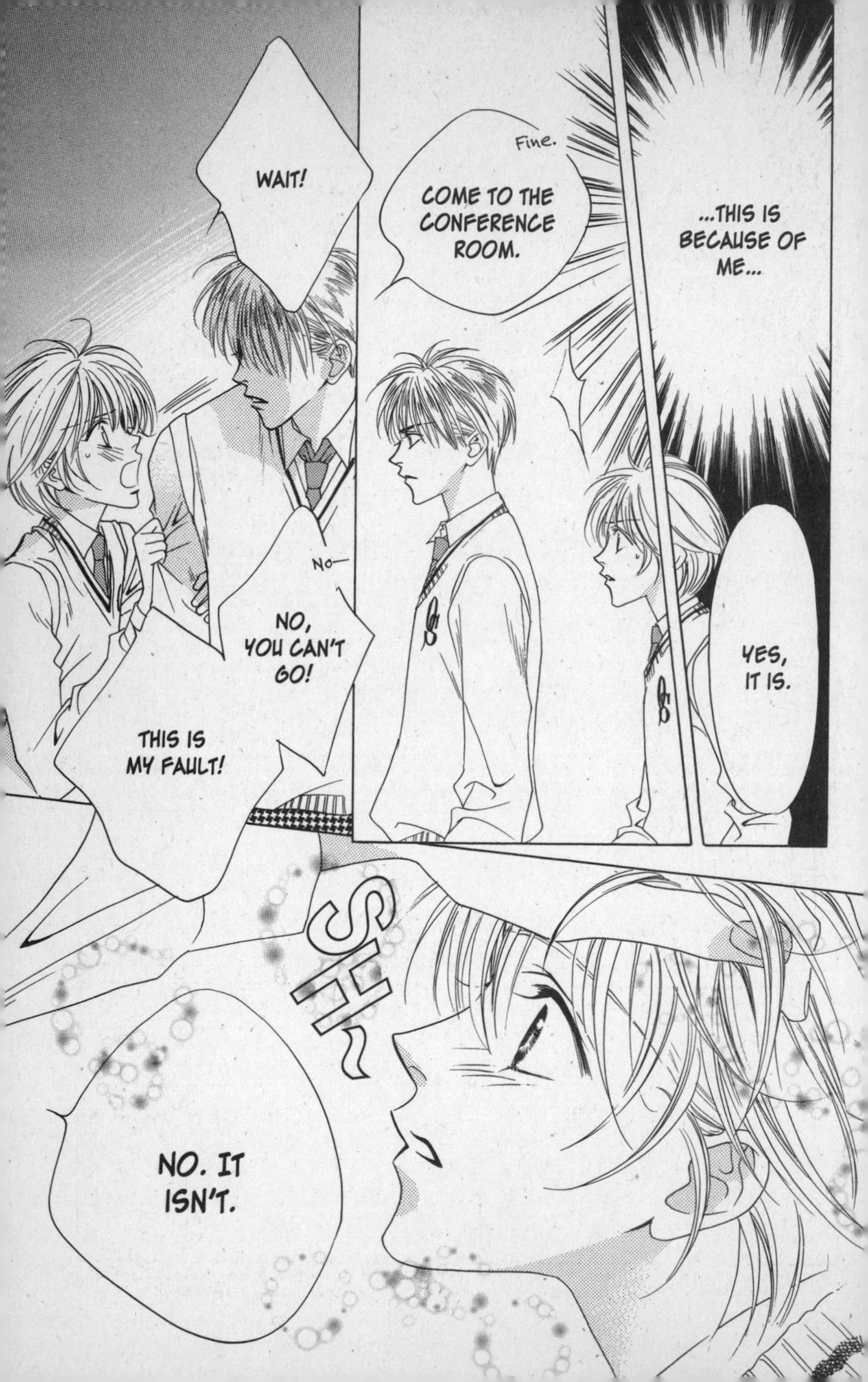
...THIS IS BECAUSE OF ME...
YES, IT IS.
Fine.
COME TO THE CONFERENCE ROOM.
WAIT!
No—
NO, YOU CAN'T GO!
THIS IS MY FAULT!
SH~
NO. IT ISN'T.

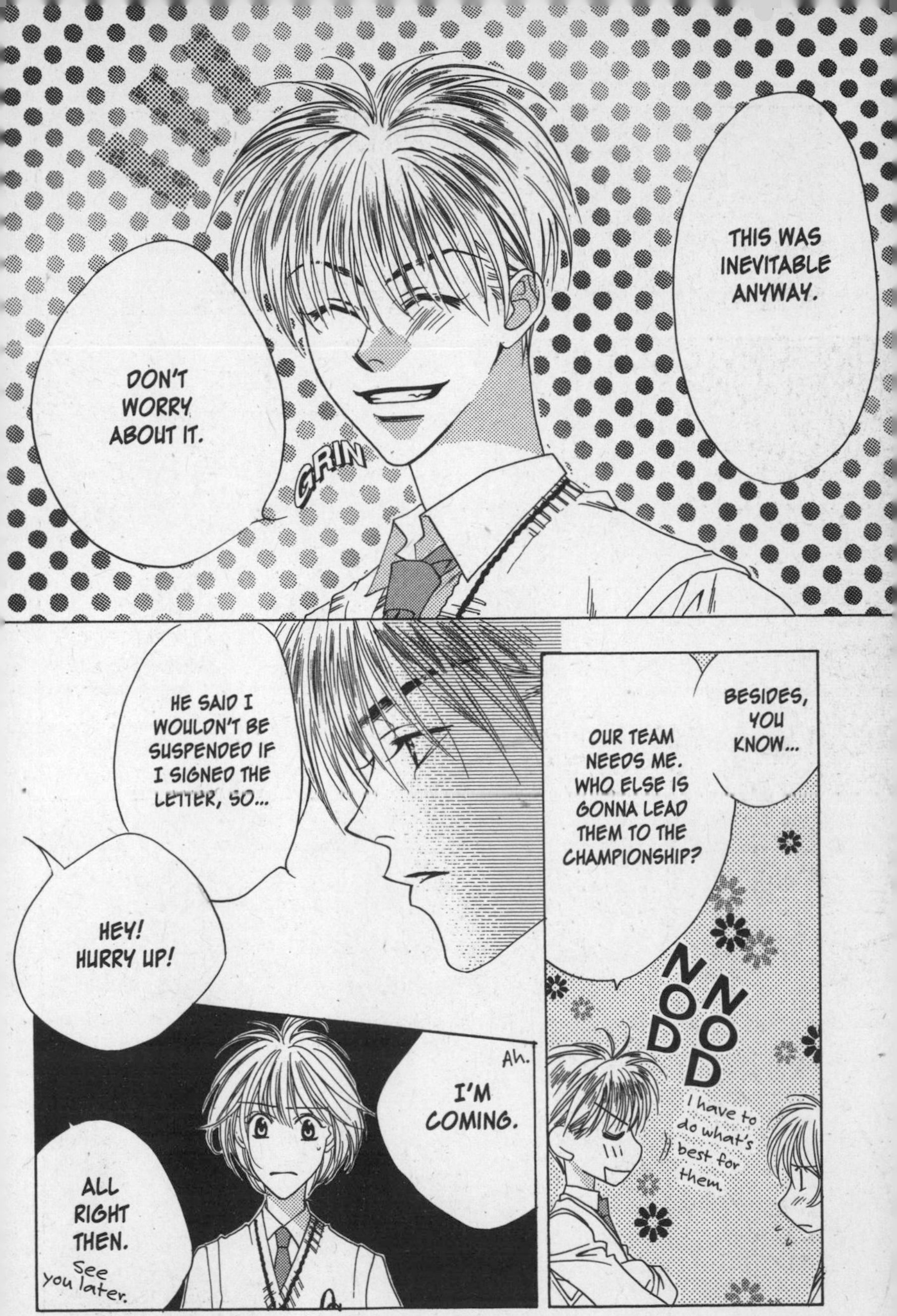
THIS WAS INEVITABLE ANYWAY.
DON'T WORRY ABOUT IT.
GRIN
BESIDES, YOU KNOW...
OUR TEAM NEEDS ME. WHO ELSE IS GONNA LEAD THEM TO THE CHAMPIONSHIP?
NOD NOD
I have to do what's best for them.
HE SAID I WOULDN'T BE SUSPENDED IF I SIGNED THE LETTER, SO...
HEY! HURRY UP!
Ah.
I'M COMING.
ALL RIGHT THEN.
See you later.

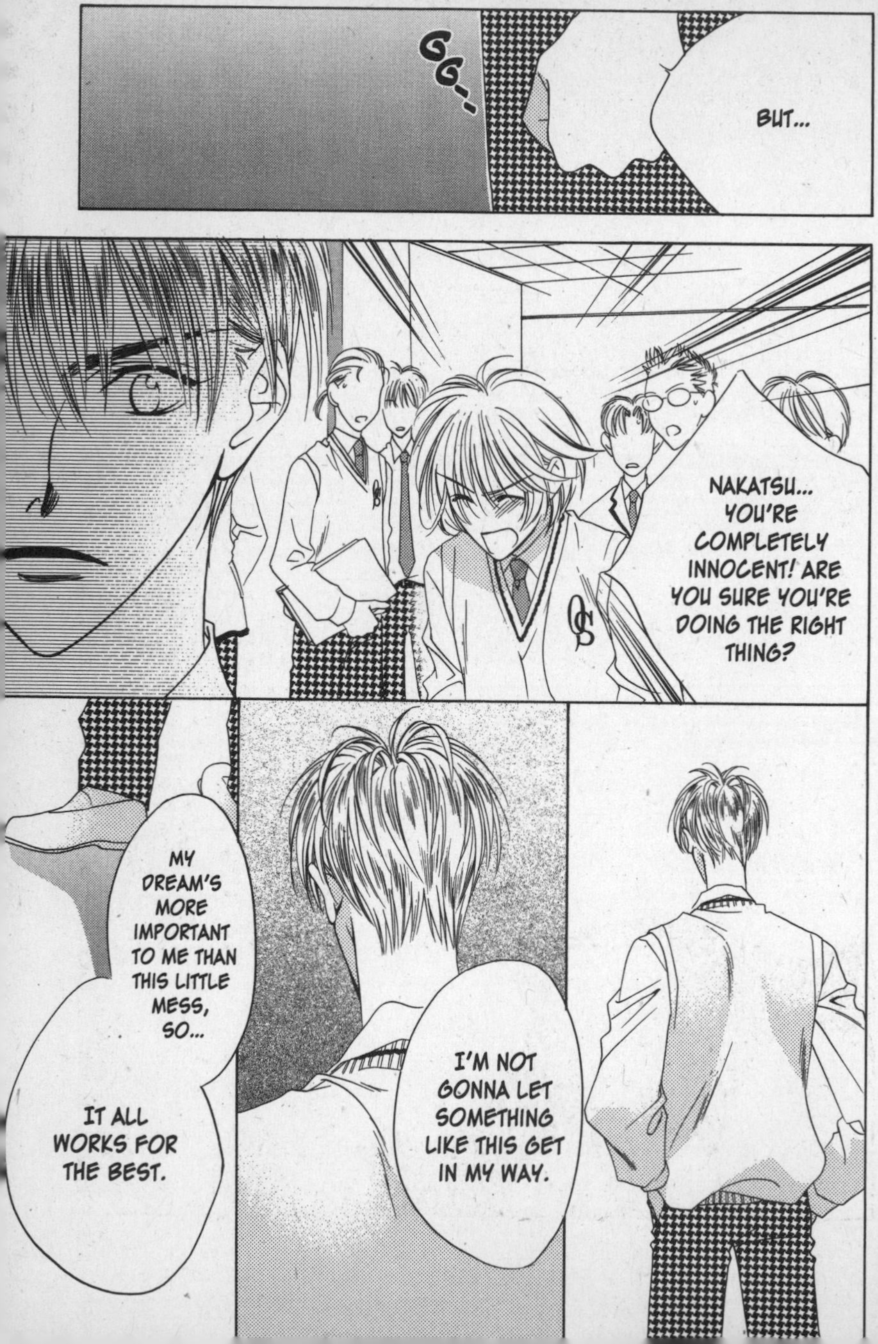
BUT...
GG...
NAKATSU... YOU'RE COMPLETELY INNOCENT! ARE YOU SURE YOU'RE DOING THE RIGHT THING?
I'M NOT GONNA LET SOMETHING LIKE THIS GET IN MY WAY.
MY DREAM'S MORE IMPORTANT TO ME THAN THIS LITTLE MESS, SO...
IT ALL WORKS FOR THE BEST.

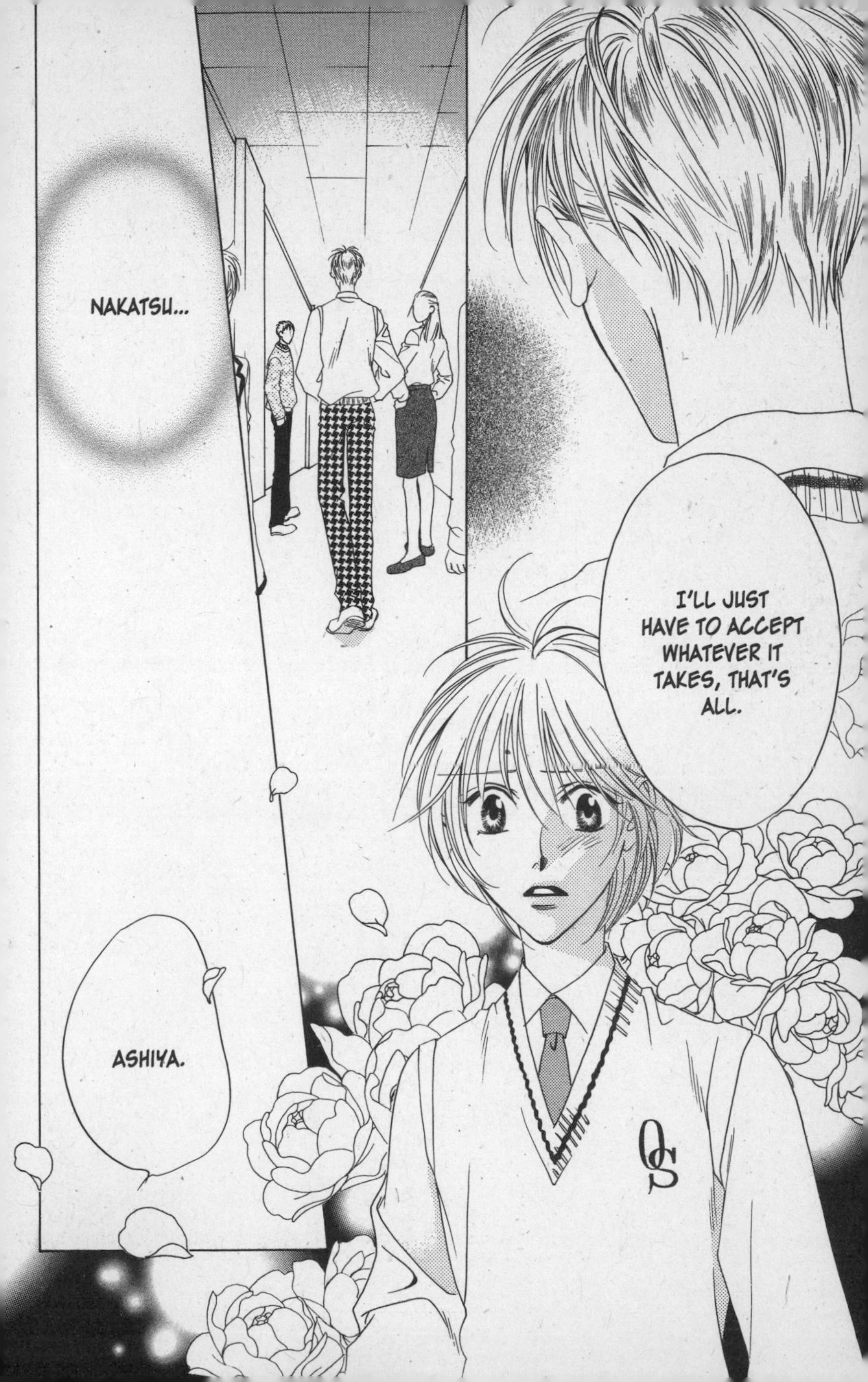
I'LL JUST HAVE TO ACCEPT WHATEVER IT TAKES, THAT'S ALL.
NAKATSU...
ASHIYA.

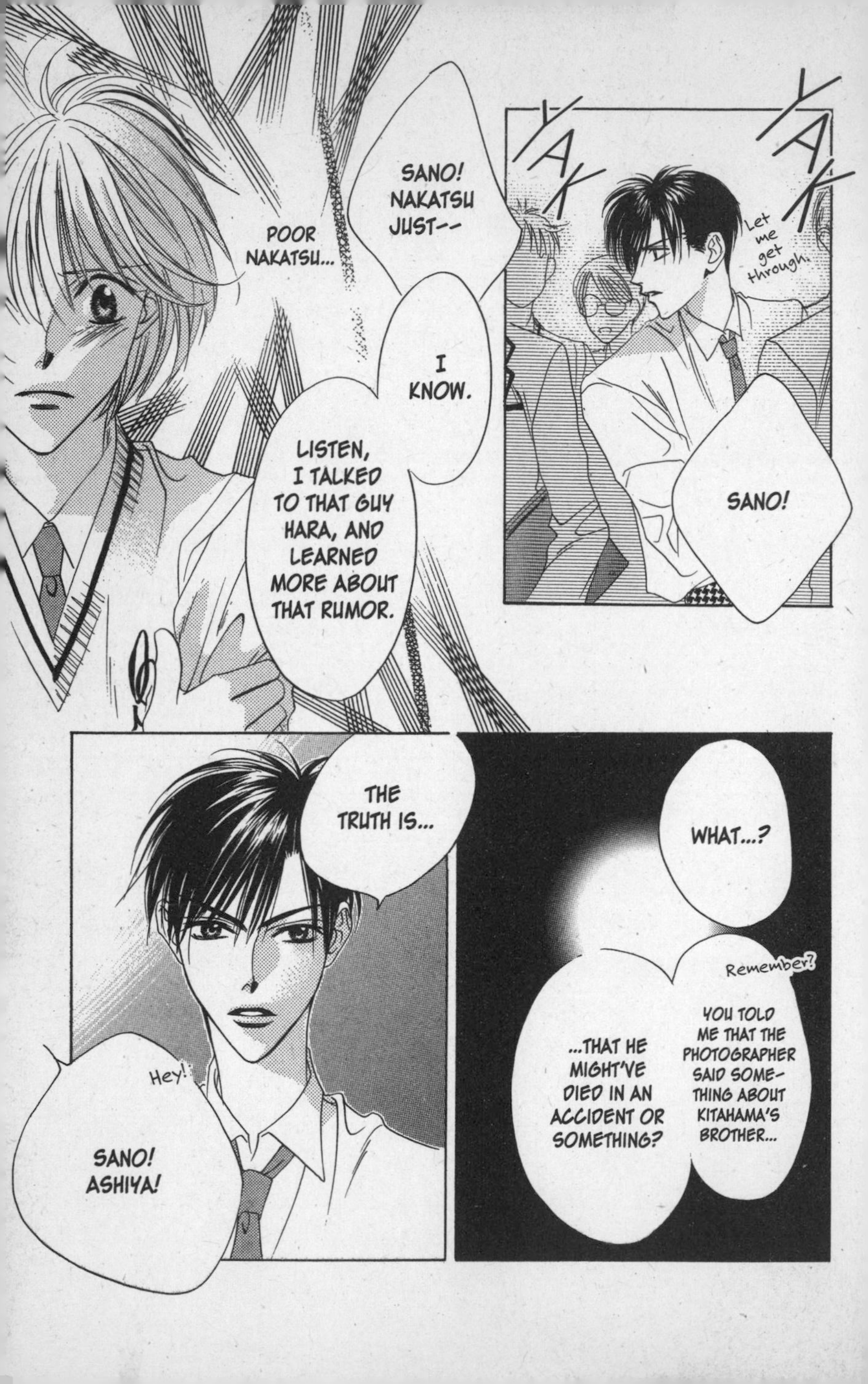
YAK
Let me get through.
YAK
SANO!
SANO! NAKATSU JUST--
POOR NAKATSU...
I KNOW.
LISTEN, I TALKED TO THAT GUY HARA, AND LEARNED MORE ABOUT THAT RUMOR.
WHAT...?
Remember?
YOU TOLD ME THAT THE PHOTOGRAPHER SAID SOME-THING ABOUT KITAHAMA'S BROTHER...
...THAT HE MIGHT'VE DIED IN AN ACCIDENT OR SOMETHING?
THE TRUTH IS...
Hey!
SANO! ASHIYA!

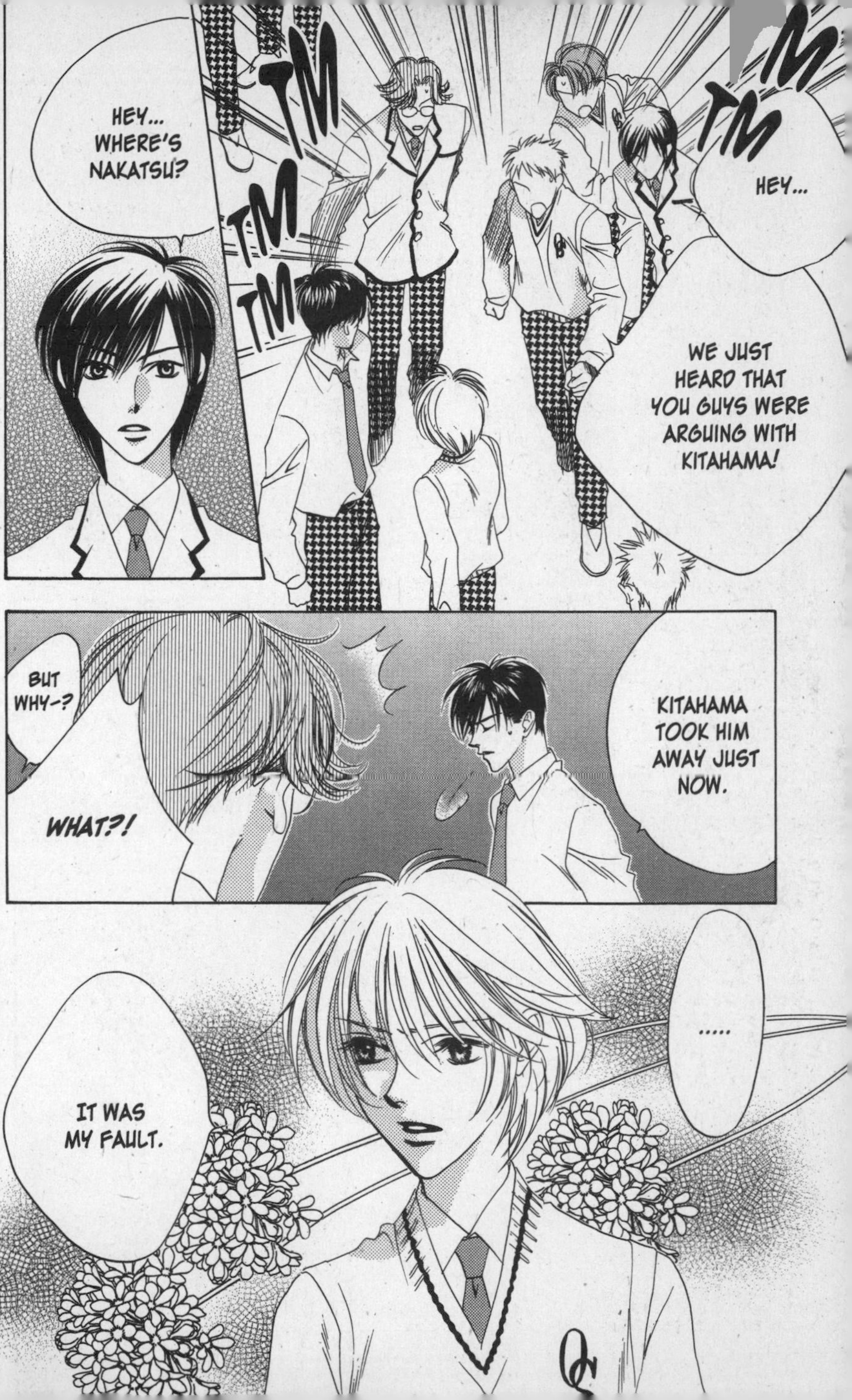
TM TM
HEY...
WE JUST HEARD THAT YOU GUYS WERE ARGUING WITH KITAHAMA!
TM TM TM TM
HEY... WHERE'S NAKATSU?
KITAHAMA TOOK HIM AWAY JUST NOW.
BUT WHY-?
WHAT?!
.....
IT WAS MY FAULT.

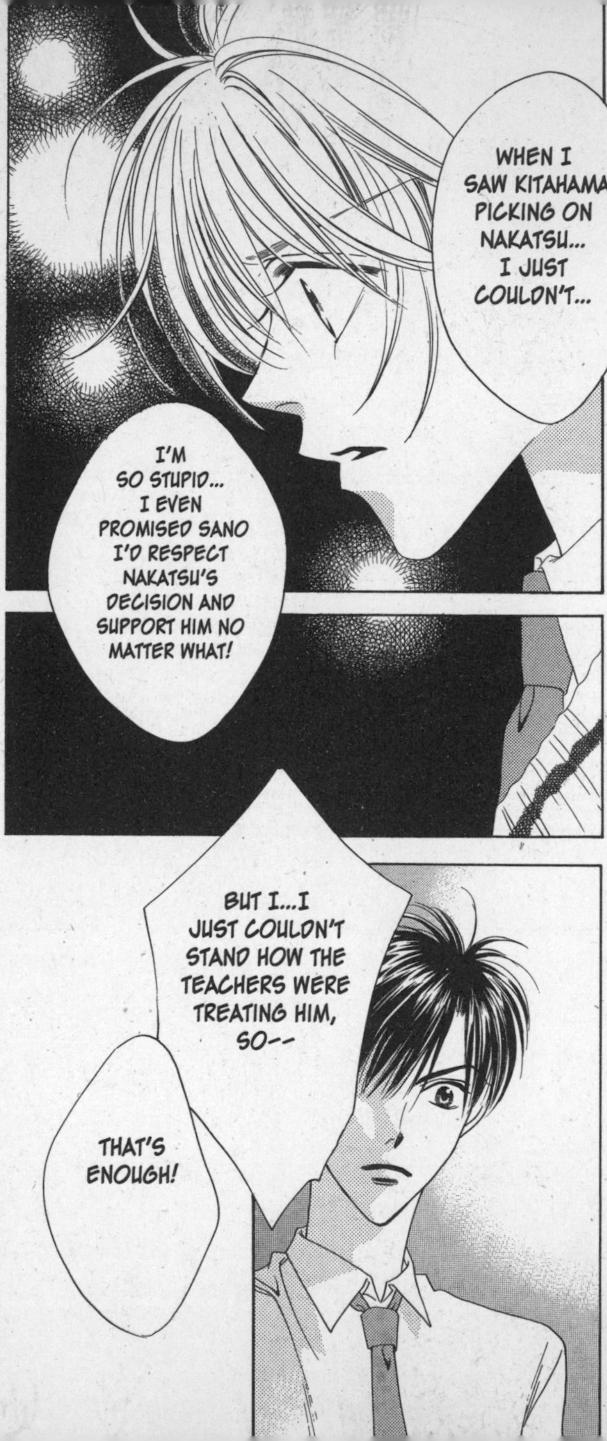
WHEN I SAW KITAHAMA PICKING ON NAKATSU... I JUST COULDN'T...
I'M SO STUPID... I EVEN PROMISED SANO I'D RESPECT NAKATSU'S DECISION AND SUPPORT HIM NO MATTER WHAT!
BUT I...I JUST COULDN'T STAND HOW THE TEACHERS WERE TREATING HIM, SO--
THAT'S ENOUGH!

WHISPERED SECRETS

INJURY: PART 2

HERE'S THE REST OF THE STORY. MY FRIEND WHO GOT BITTEN TOLD ME WHAT SHE HAD TO GO THROUGH AT THE HOSPITAL, SO I RUSHED TO ONE MYSELF. BUT THEN ! ALL THEY DID WAS DISINFECT MY WOUNDS AND GIVE ME AN ANTIBIOTIC SHOT! I WAS KIND OF EMBARRASSED BY THE FACT THAT I GOT BITTEN BY MY CAT...NO, NOT MY DOG...SO, I DIDN'T COMPLAIN, AND JUST WENT HOME THAT DAY...ALTHOUGH MY INNER VOICE WAS SCREAMING, "THEY CAN'T BE SERIOUS!" BUT LATER THAT NIGHT, JUST AS I EXPECTED, MY HAND STARTED SWELLING AND I CAME DOWN WITH A FEVER. WHAT A QUACK DOCTOR! UNFORTUNATELY, MY DEADLINE WAS APPROACHING, AND I HAD NO CHOICE BUT TO WORK...I WAS SUFFERING FROM PAIN IN MY FINGERS AND A FEVER, SO IT TOOK ME FIVE DAYS TO FINISH EVERYTHING ARRRGH!

I HEARD THAT WHEN YOU'RE BITTEN BY AN ANIMAL, THERE'S A RISK OF GETTING AN INFECTION, AND WORST CASE, YOU MIGHT HAVE TO AMPUTATE!! OH, MY GOD...THAT'S SO SCARY!

AT LEAST I GOT A CHANCE TO WORK SLOWLY AND PAY ATTENTION TO DETAILS...

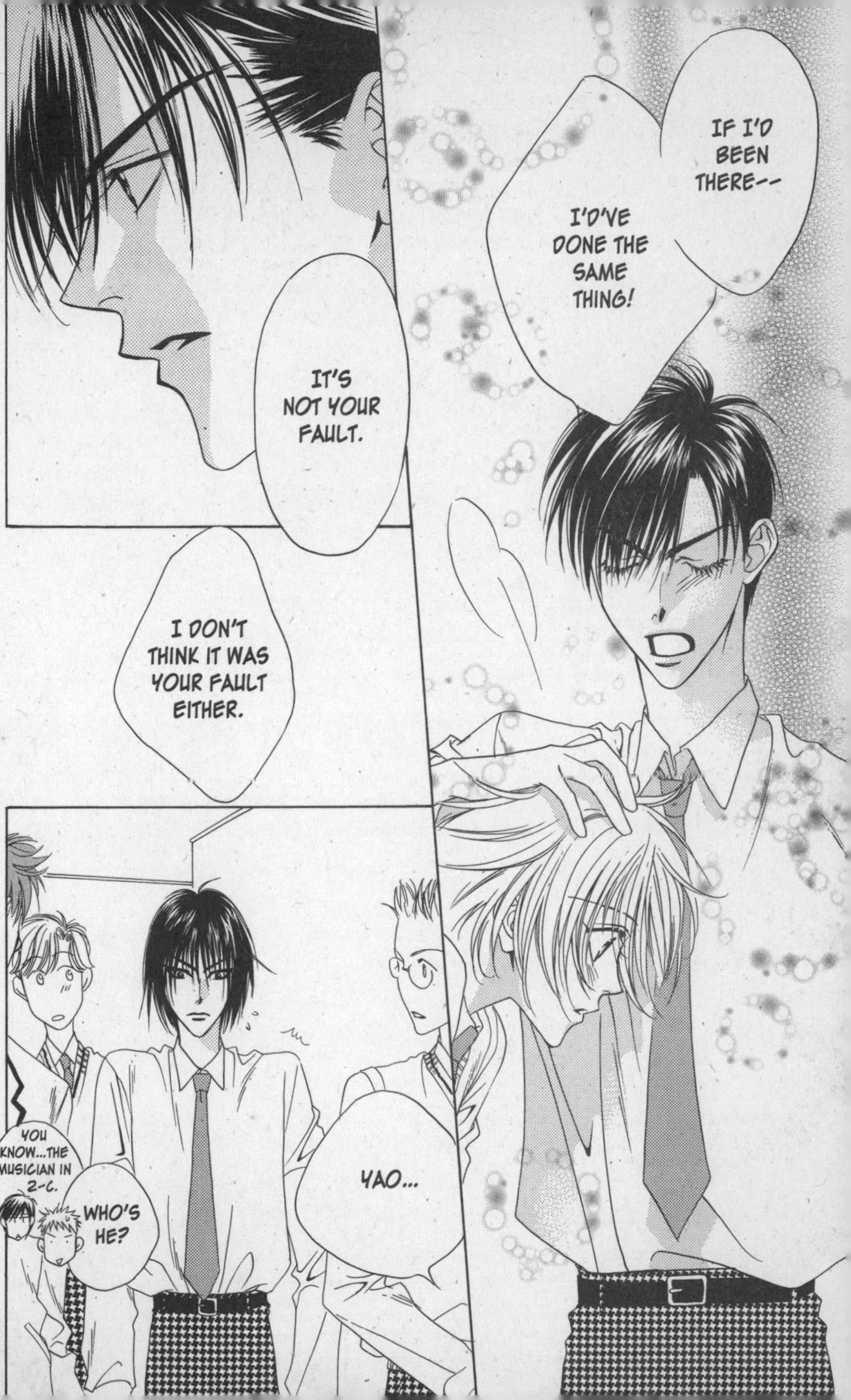
IF I'D BEEN THERE--
I'D'VE DONE THE SAME THING!
IT'S NOT YOUR FAULT.
I DON'T THINK IT WAS YOUR FAULT EITHER.
YAO...
WHO'S HE?
YOU KNOW...THE MUSICIAN IN 2-C.

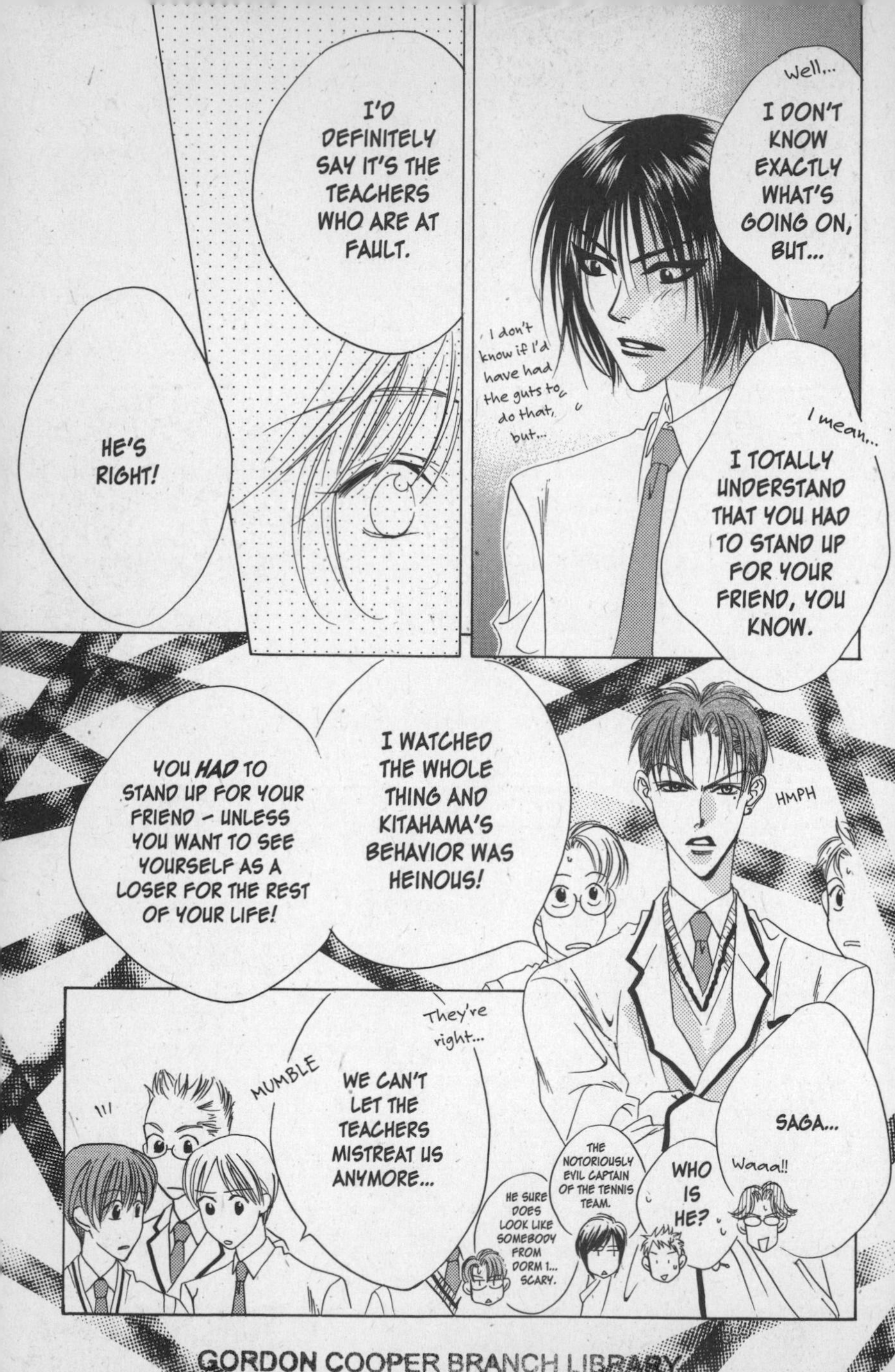
Well...
I DON'T KNOW EXACTLY WHAT'S GOING ON, BUT...
I mean...
I TOTALLY UNDERSTAND THAT YOU HAD TO STAND UP FOR YOUR FRIEND, YOU KNOW.
I don't know if I'd have had the guts to do that, but...
I'D DEFINITELY SAY IT'S THE TEACHERS WHO ARE AT FAULT.
HE'S RIGHT!
HMPH
I WATCHED THE WHOLE THING AND KITAHAMA'S BEHAVIOR WAS HEINOUS!
YOU *HAD* TO STAND UP FOR YOUR FRIEND - UNLESS YOU WANT TO SEE YOURSELF AS A LOSER FOR THE REST OF YOUR LIFE!
SAGA...
Waaa!!
WHO IS HE?
THE NOTORIOUSLY EVIL CAPTAIN OF THE TENNIS TEAM.
HE SURE DOES LOOK LIKE SOMEBODY FROM DORM 1... SCARY.
They're right...
WE CAN'T LET THE TEACHERS MISTREAT US ANYMORE...
MUMBLE

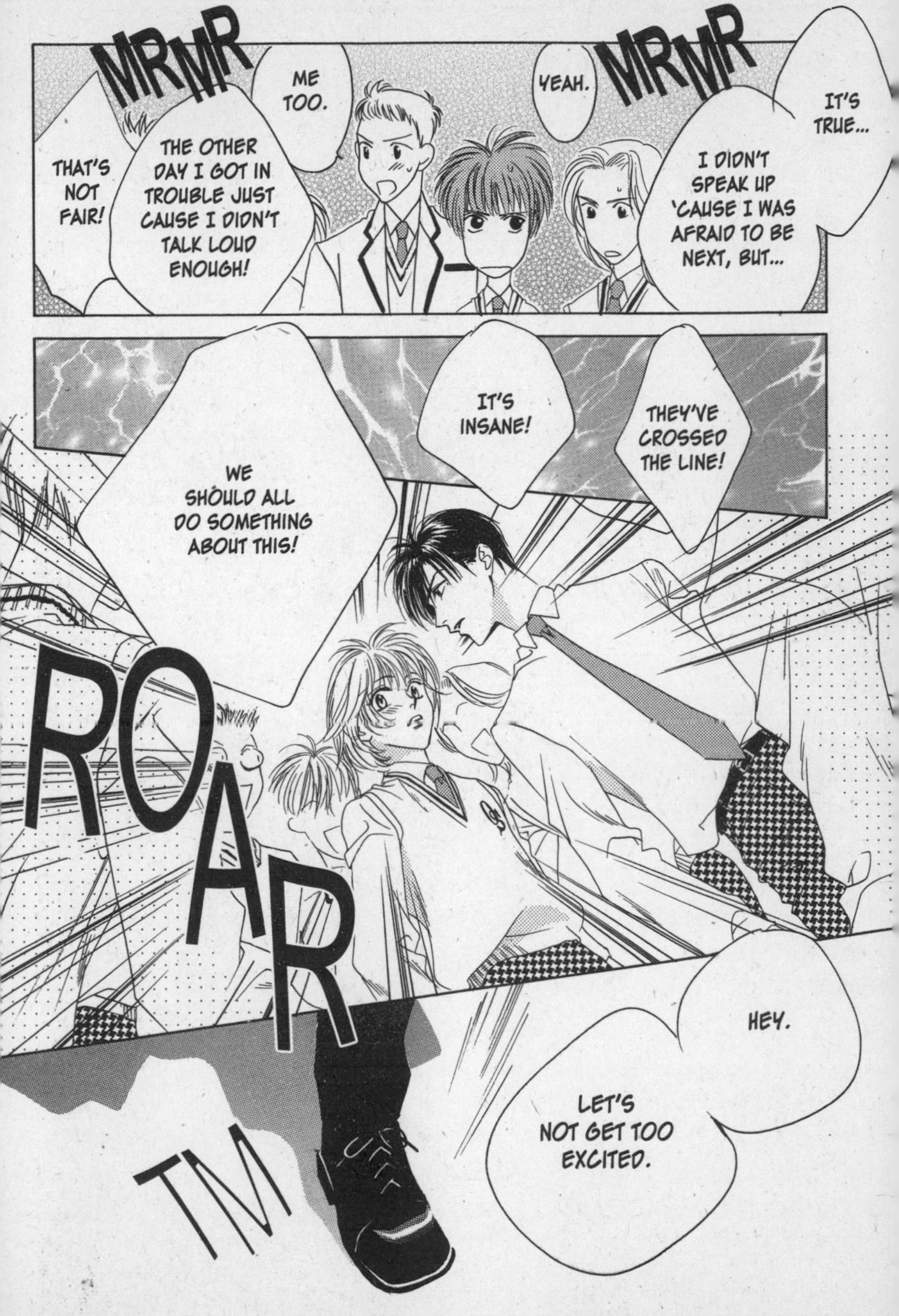
IT'S TRUE...
MRMR
I DIDN'T SPEAK UP 'CAUSE I WAS AFRAID TO BE NEXT, BUT...
YEAH.
ME TOO.
MRMR
THE OTHER DAY I GOT IN TROUBLE JUST CAUSE I DIDN'T TALK LOUD ENOUGH!
THAT'S NOT FAIR!
THEY'VE CROSSED THE LINE!
IT'S INSANE!
WE SHOULD ALL DO SOMETHING ABOUT THIS!
ROAR
HEY.
LET'S NOT GET TOO EXCITED.
TM

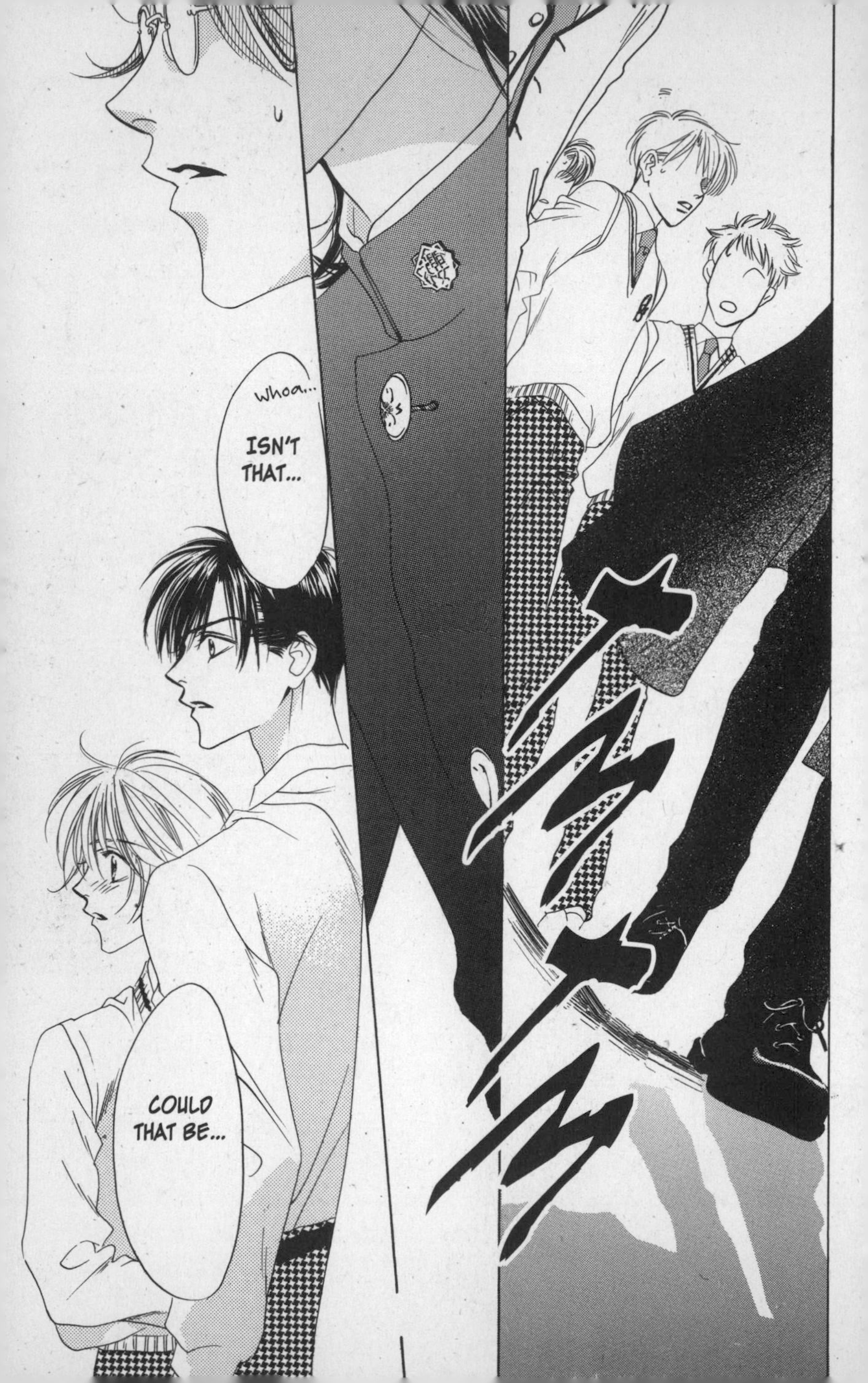
Whoa... ISN'T THAT...
COULD THAT BE...

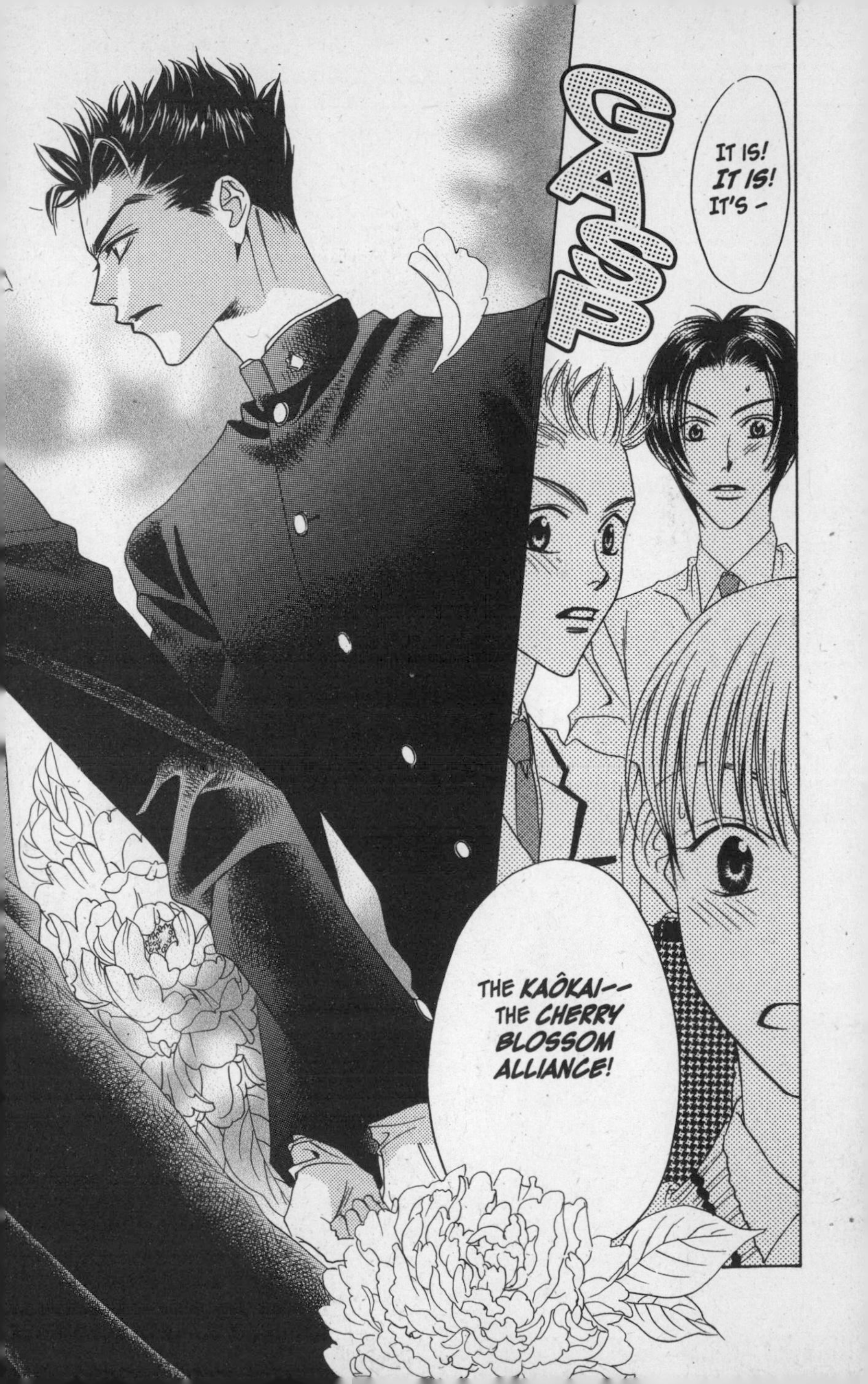
IT IS! IT IS! IT'S -
GASP
THE KAÔKAI-- THE CHERRY BLOSSOM ALLIANCE!

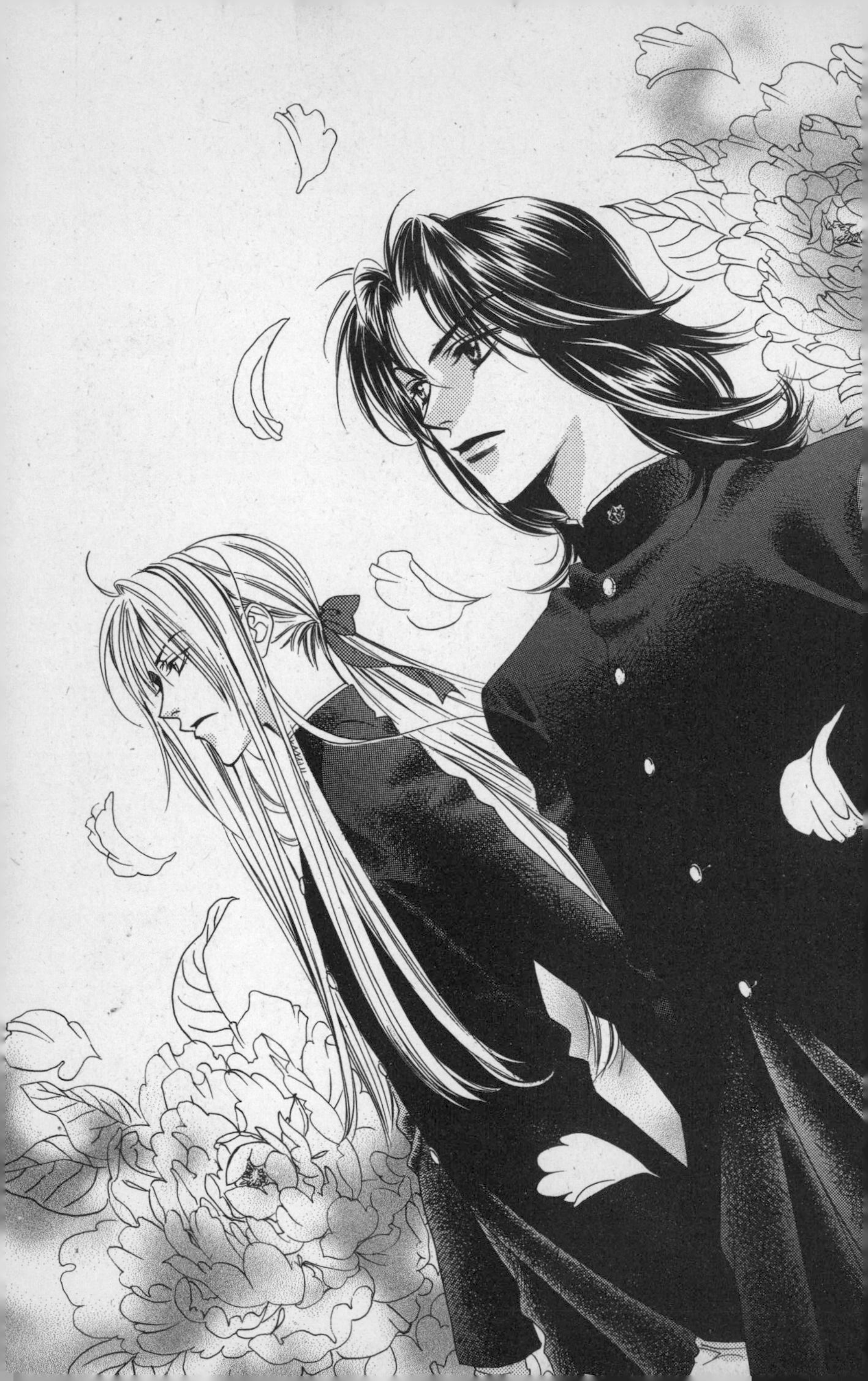

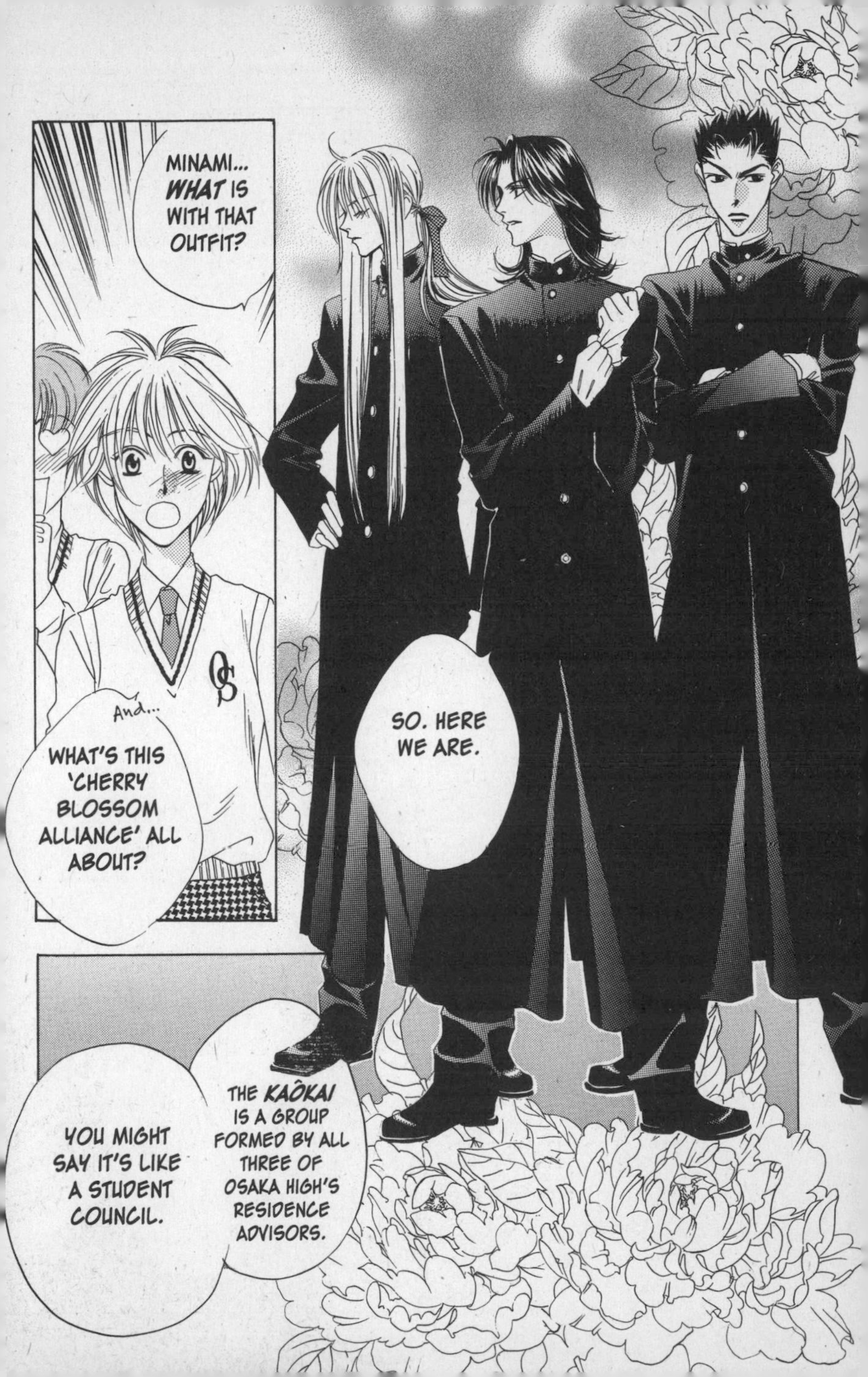
SO. HERE WE ARE.
MINAMI... WHAT IS WITH THAT OUTFIT?
And...
WHAT'S THIS 'CHERRY BLOSSOM ALLIANCE' ALL ABOUT?
THE KAÔKAI IS A GROUP FORMED BY ALL THREE OF OSAKA HIGH'S RESIDENCE ADVISORS.
YOU MIGHT SAY IT'S LIKE A STUDENT COUNCIL.

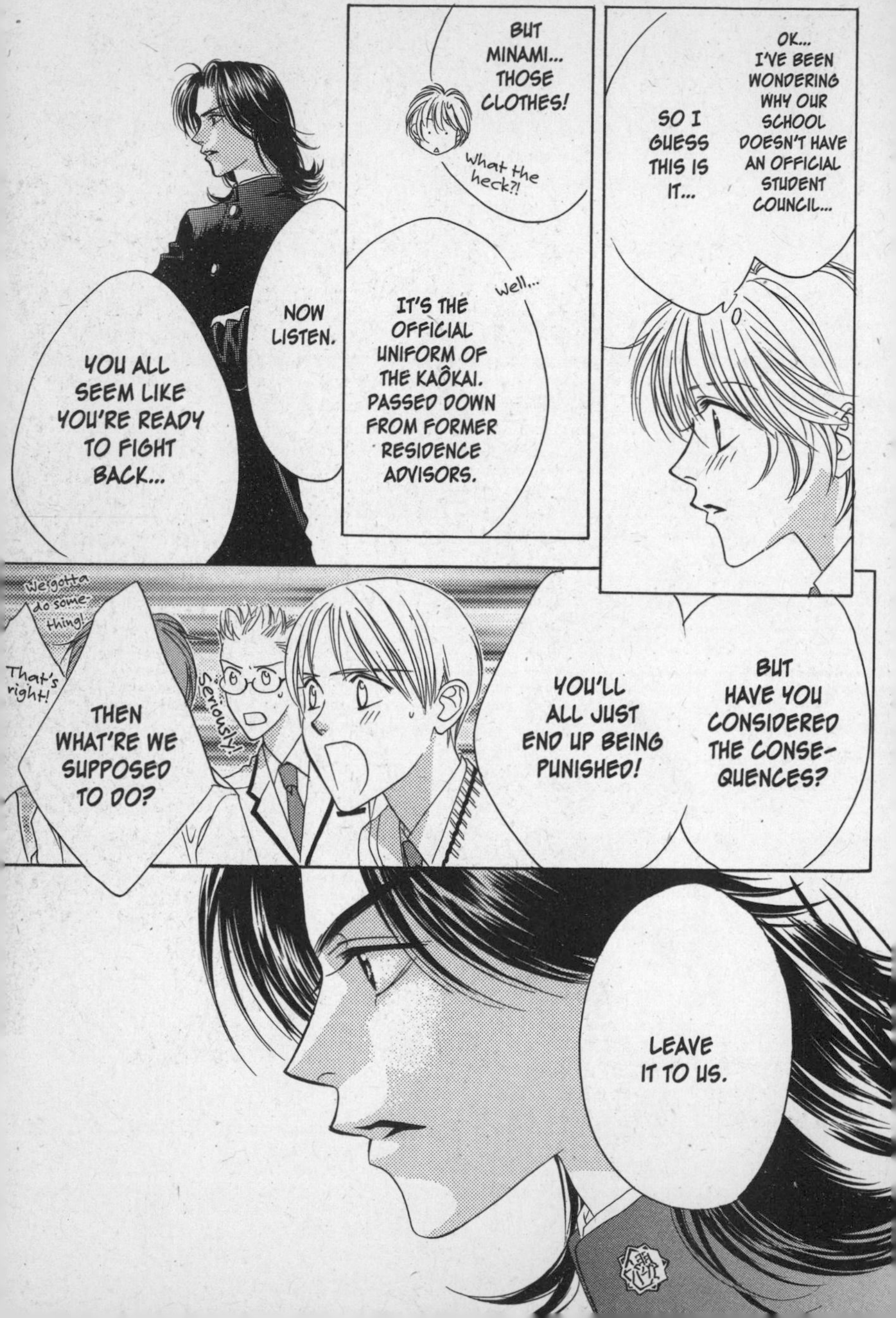
OK... I'VE BEEN WONDERING WHY OUR SCHOOL DOESN'T HAVE AN OFFICIAL STUDENT COUNCIL...
SO I GUESS THIS IS IT...
BUT MINAMI... THOSE CLOTHES!
What the heck?!
Well...
IT'S THE OFFICIAL UNIFORM OF THE KAÔKAI. PASSED DOWN FROM FORMER RESIDENCE ADVISORS.
NOW LISTEN.
YOU ALL SEEM LIKE YOU'RE READY TO FIGHT BACK...
BUT HAVE YOU CONSIDERED THE CONSE-QUENCES?
YOU'LL ALL JUST END UP BEING PUNISHED!
Seriously!
THEN WHAT'RE WE SUPPOSED TO DO?
We gotta do some-thing!
That's right!
LEAVE IT TO US.

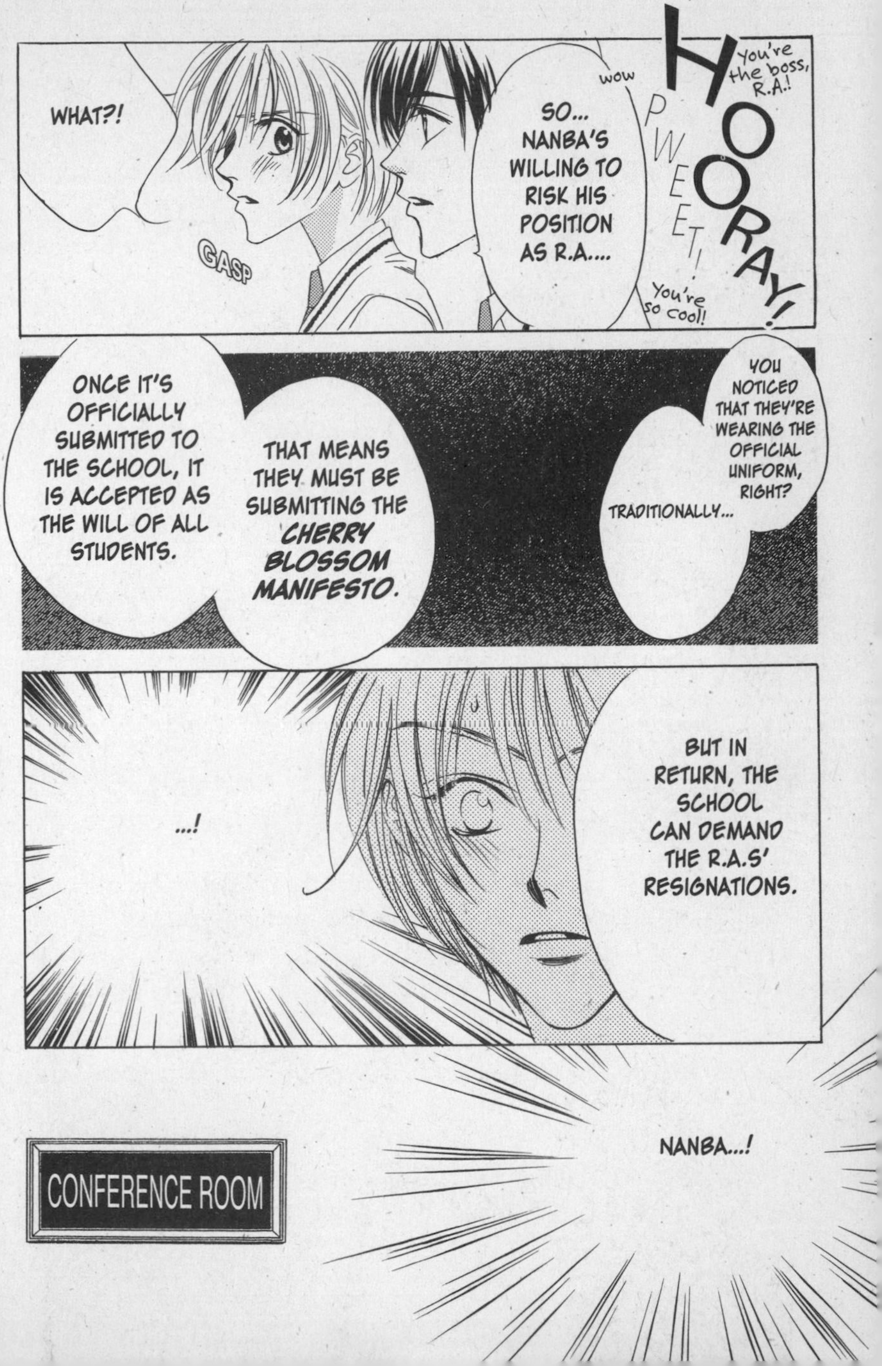
HOORAY!
You're the boss, R.A.!
PWEET!
You're so cool!
wow
SO... NANBA'S WILLING TO RISK HIS POSITION AS R.A....
GASP
WHAT?!
YOU NOTICED THAT THEY'RE WEARING THE OFFICIAL UNIFORM, RIGHT?
TRADITIONALLY...
THAT MEANS THEY MUST BE SUBMITTING THE *CHERRY BLOSSOM MANIFESTO*.
ONCE IT'S OFFICIALLY SUBMITTED TO THE SCHOOL, IT IS ACCEPTED AS THE WILL OF ALL STUDENTS.
BUT IN RETURN, THE SCHOOL CAN DEMAND THE R.A.S' RESIGNATIONS.
...!
NANBA...!
CONFERENCE ROOM

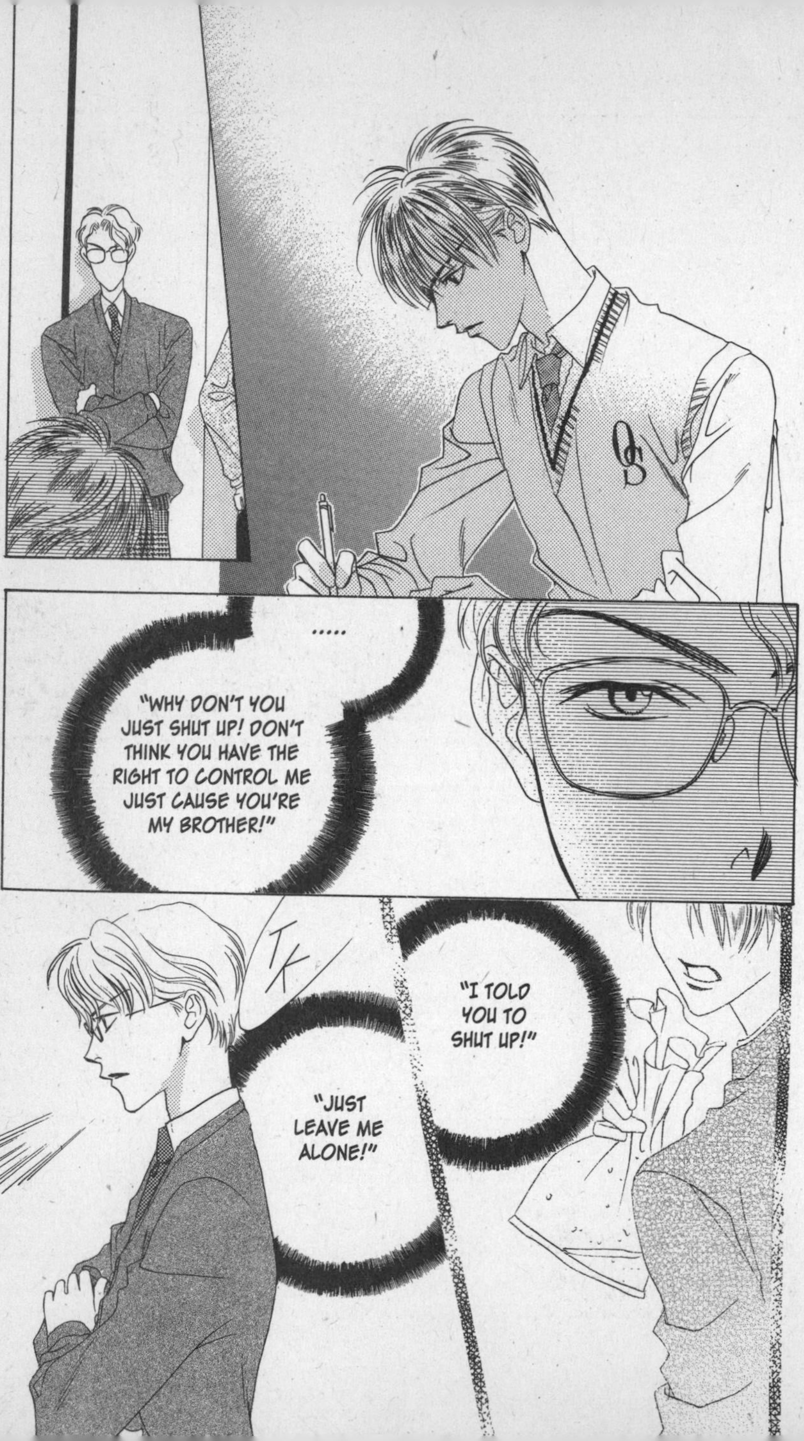
.....
"WHY DON'T YOU JUST SHUT UP! DON'T THINK YOU HAVE THE RIGHT TO CONTROL ME JUST CAUSE YOU'RE MY BROTHER!"
"I TOLD YOU TO SHUT UP!"
TK
"JUST LEAVE ME ALONE!"

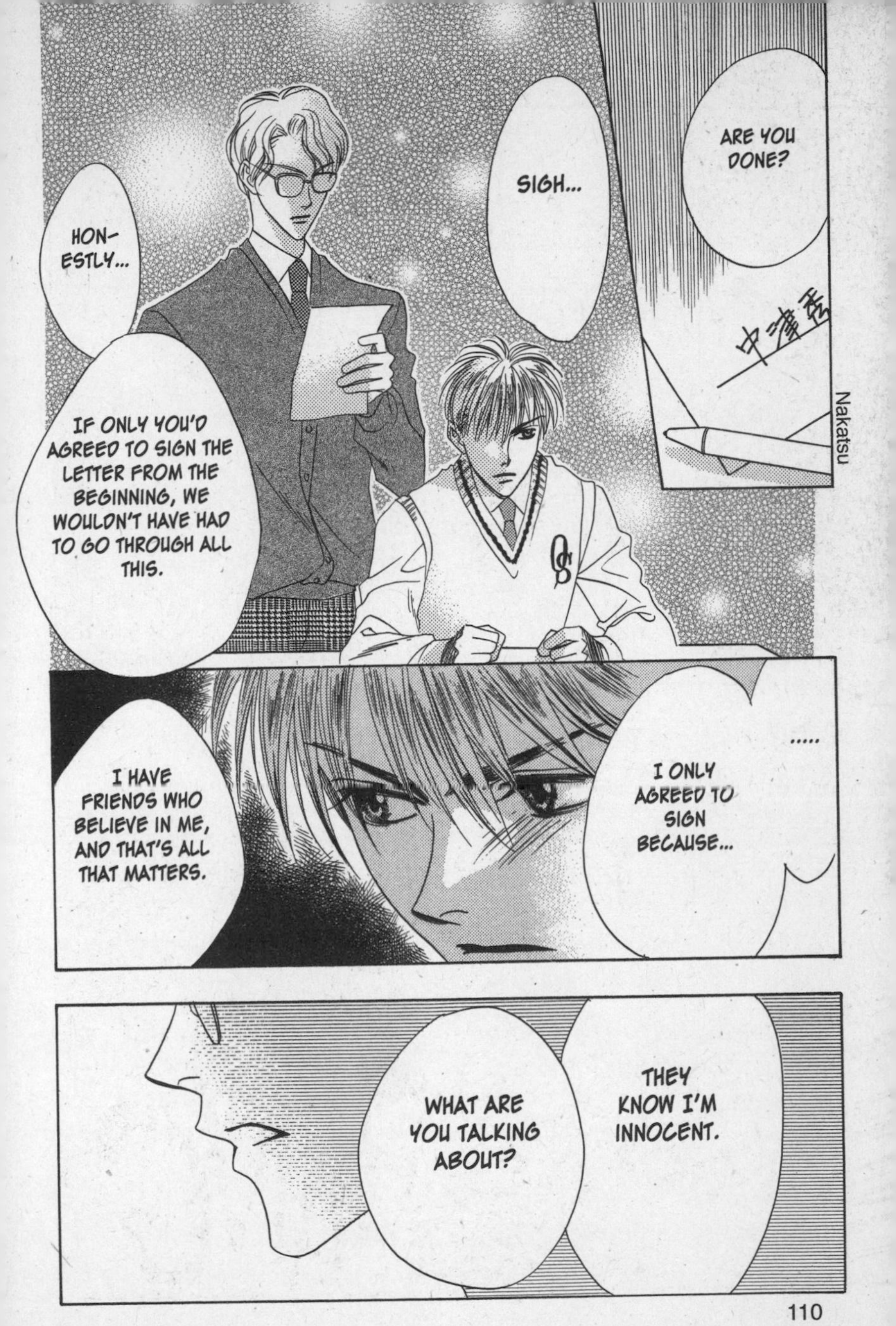
ARE YOU DONE?
中津秀
Nakatsu
SIGH...
HON-ESTLY...
IF ONLY YOU'D AGREED TO SIGN THE LETTER FROM THE BEGINNING, WE WOULDN'T HAVE HAD TO GO THROUGH ALL THIS.
.....
I ONLY AGREED TO SIGN BECAUSE...
I HAVE FRIENDS WHO BELIEVE IN ME, AND THAT'S ALL THAT MATTERS.
THEY KNOW I'M INNOCENT.
WHAT ARE YOU TALKING ABOUT?

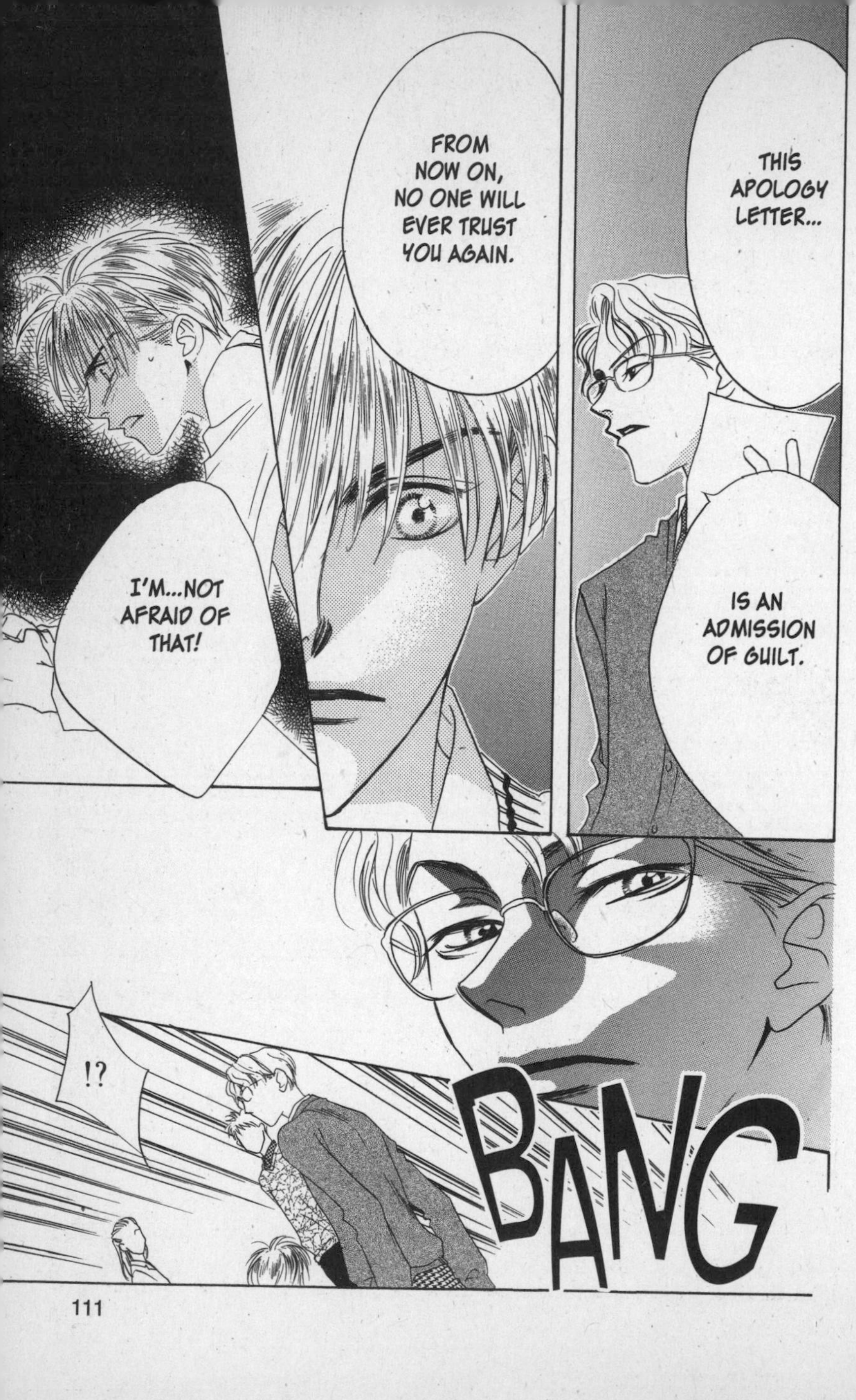
THIS APOLOGY LETTER...
IS AN ADMISSION OF GUILT.
FROM NOW ON, NO ONE WILL EVER TRUST YOU AGAIN.
I'M...NOT AFRAID OF THAT!
BANG
!?

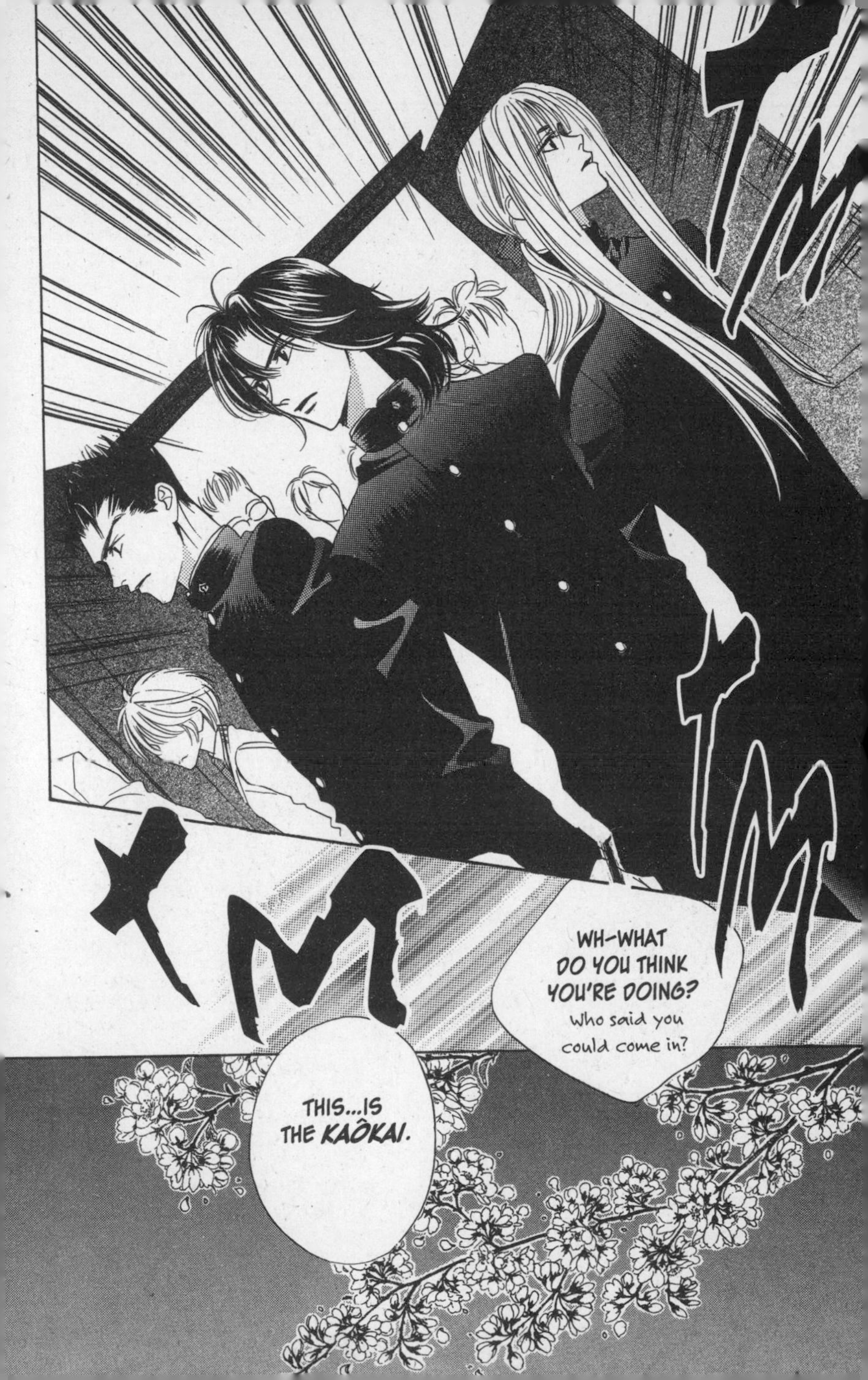
WH-WHAT DO YOU THINK YOU'RE DOING? Who said you could come in?
THIS...IS THE *KAÔKAI*.

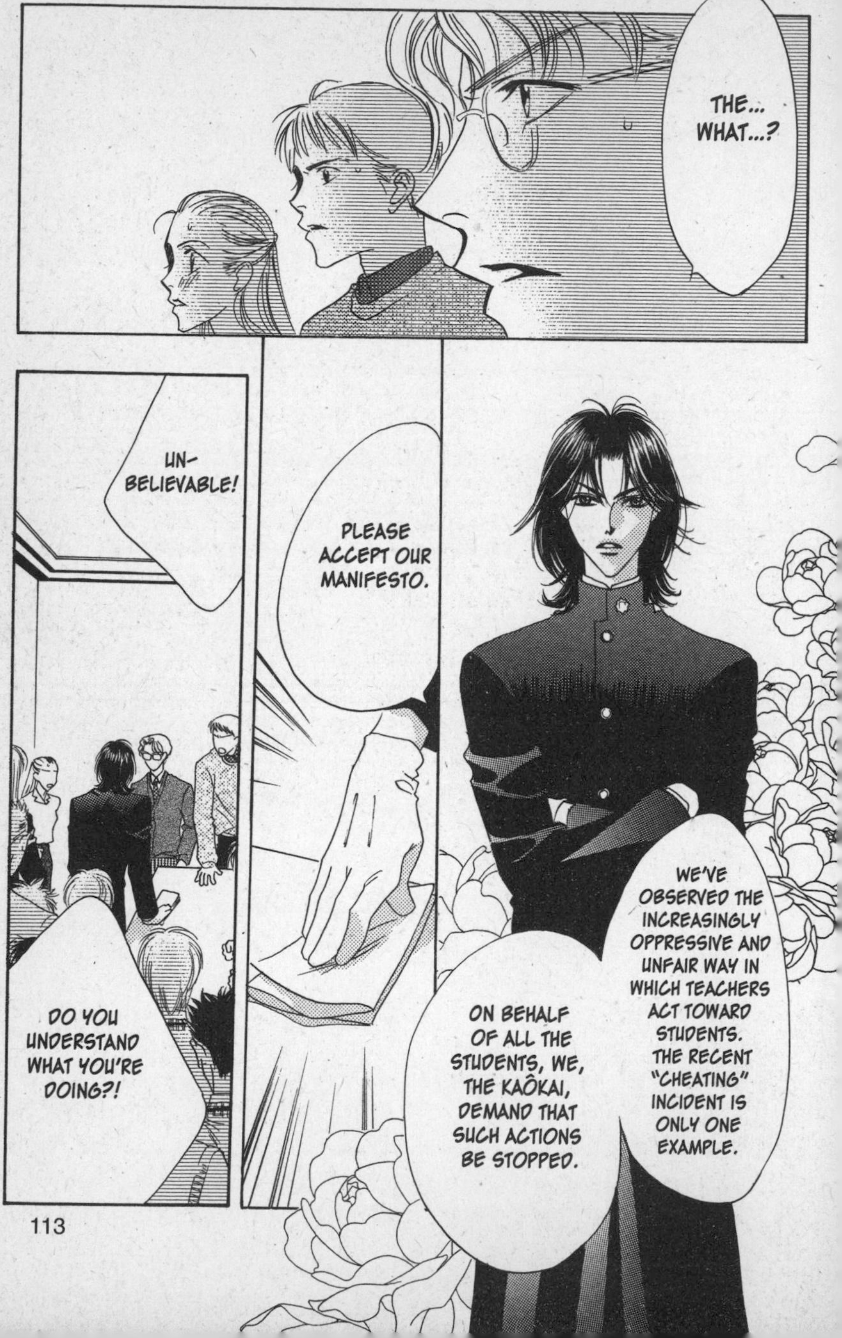
THE... WHAT...?
WE'VE OBSERVED THE INCREASINGLY OPPRESSIVE AND UNFAIR WAY IN WHICH TEACHERS ACT TOWARD STUDENTS. THE RECENT "CHEATING" INCIDENT IS ONLY ONE EXAMPLE.
ON BEHALF OF ALL THE STUDENTS, WE, THE KAÔKAI, DEMAND THAT SUCH ACTIONS BE STOPPED.
PLEASE ACCEPT OUR MANIFESTO.
UN-BELIEVABLE!
DO YOU UNDERSTAND WHAT YOU'RE DOING?!

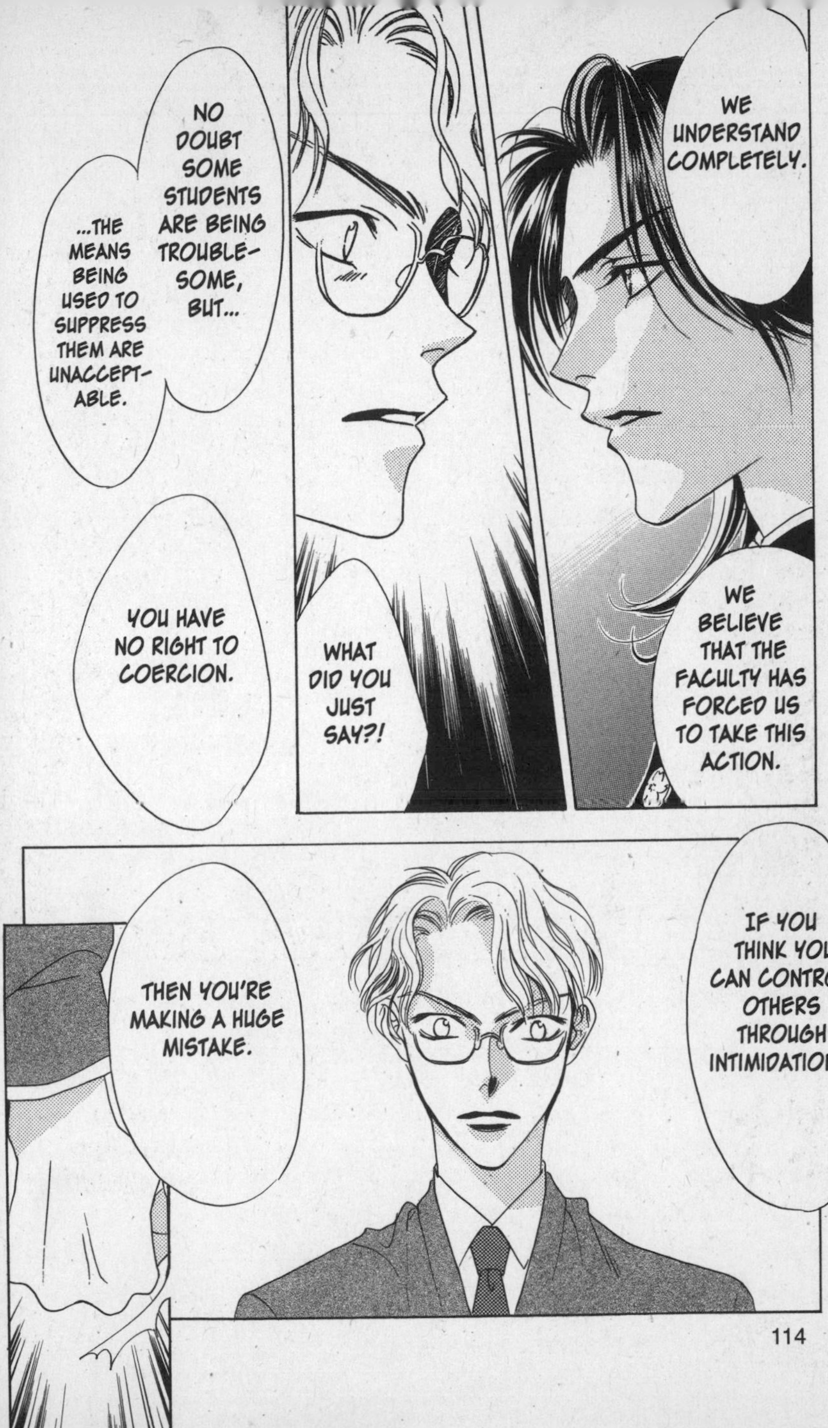
WE UNDERSTAND COMPLETELY.
WE BELIEVE THAT THE FACULTY HAS FORCED US TO TAKE THIS ACTION.
WHAT DID YOU JUST SAY?!
NO DOUBT SOME STUDENTS ARE BEING TROUBLE-SOME, BUT...
...THE MEANS BEING USED TO SUPPRESS THEM ARE UNACCEPT-ABLE.
YOU HAVE NO RIGHT TO COERCION.
IF YOU THINK YOU CAN CONTROL OTHERS THROUGH INTIMIDATION...
THEN YOU'RE MAKING A HUGE MISTAKE.

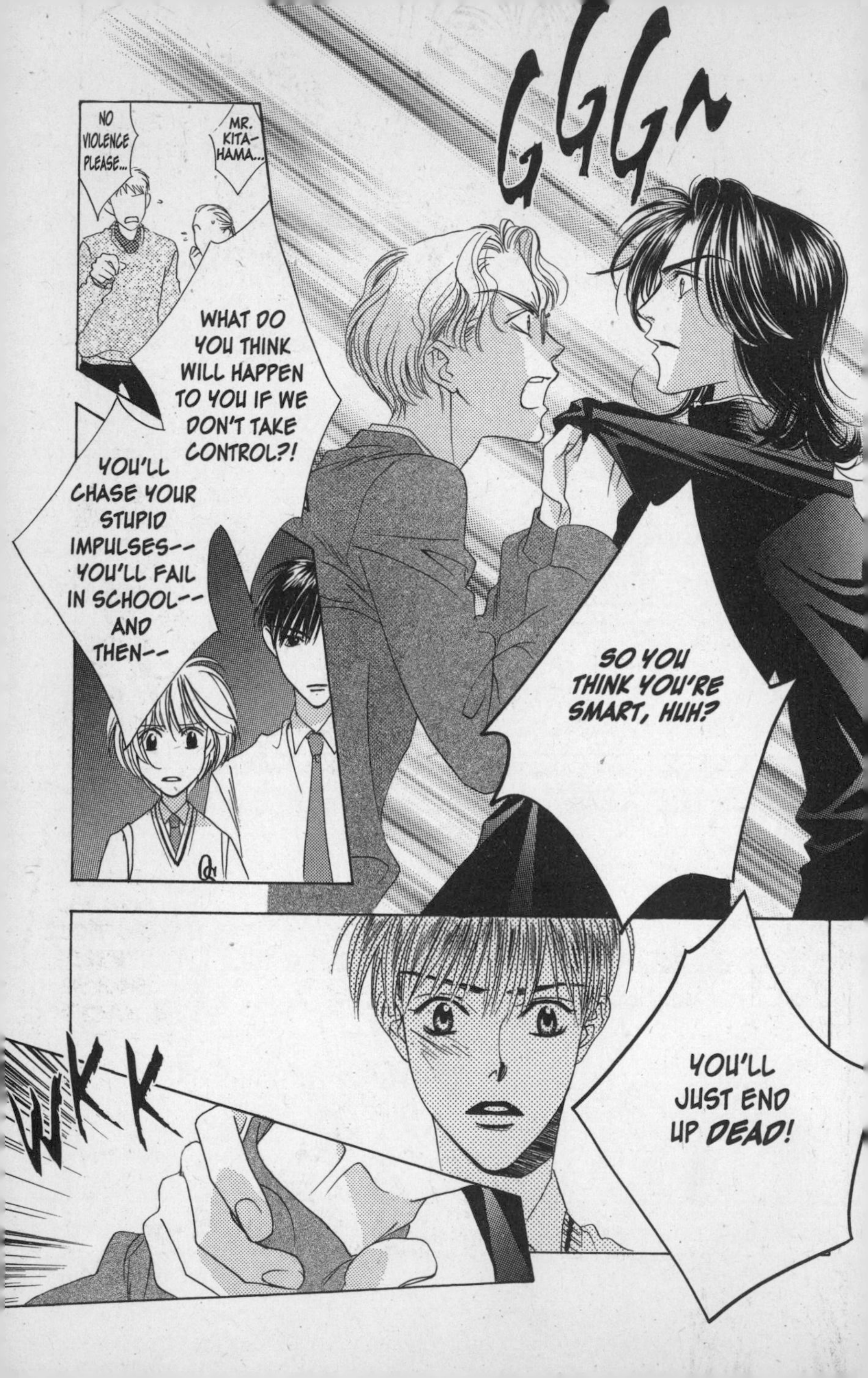
GGGN
SO YOU THINK YOU'RE SMART, HUH?
MR. KITA-HAMA...
NO VIOLENCE PLEASE...
WHAT DO YOU THINK WILL HAPPEN TO YOU IF WE DON'T TAKE CONTROL?!
YOU'LL CHASE YOUR STUPID IMPULSES-- YOU'LL FAIL IN SCHOOL-- AND THEN--
YOU'LL JUST END UP DEAD!
WKK

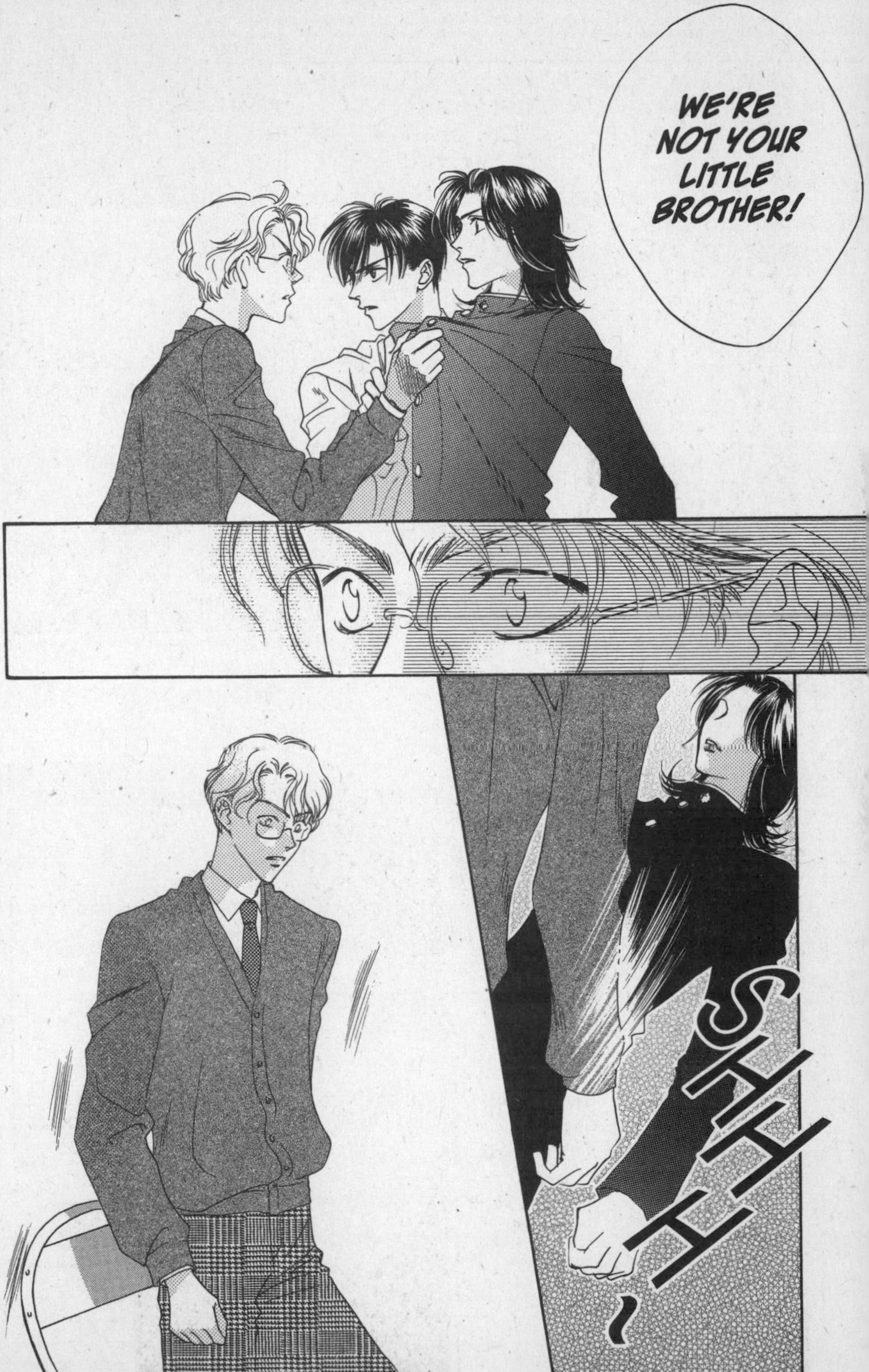
WE'RE NOT YOUR LITTLE BROTHER!
SHHH,

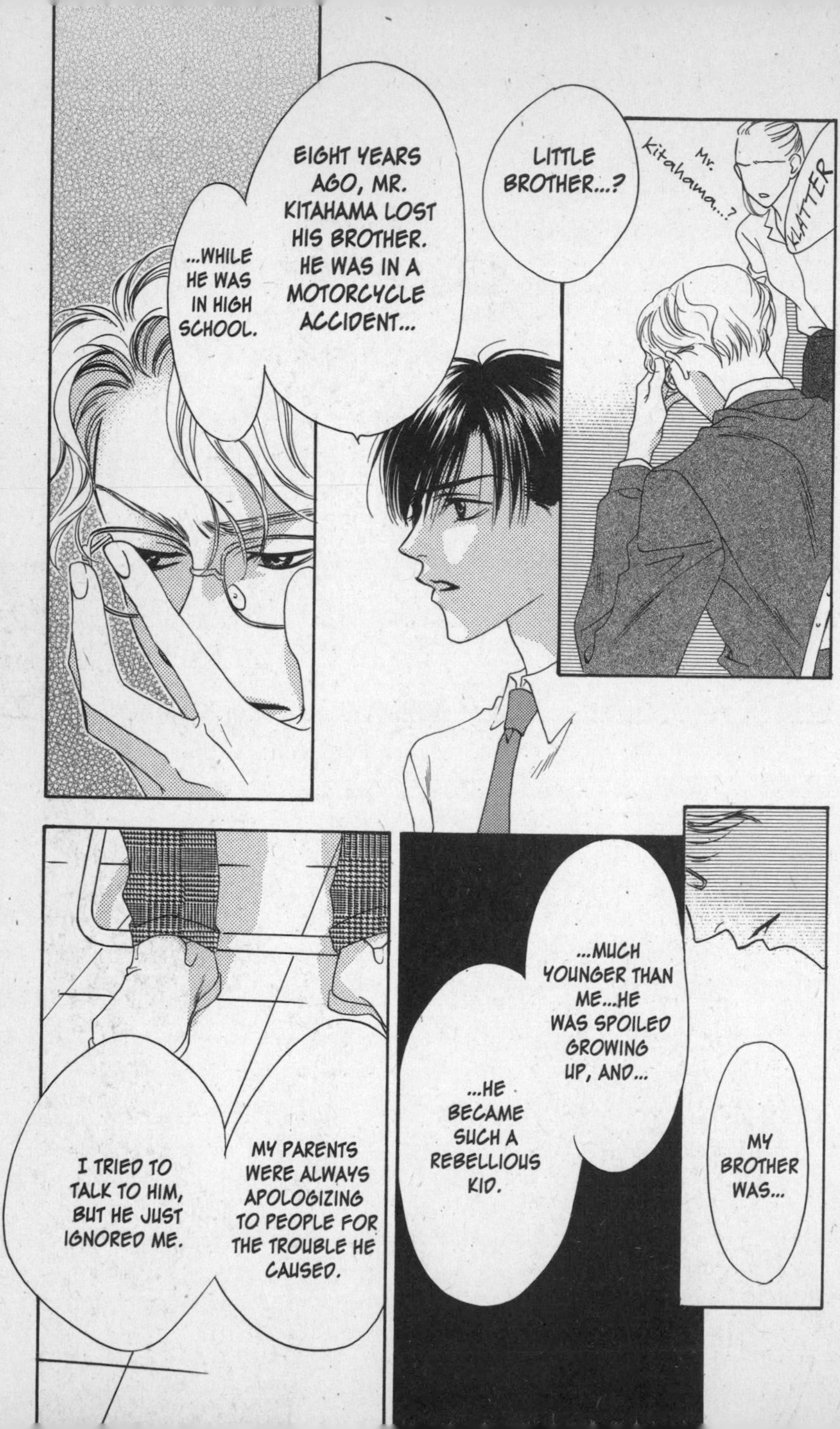
Mr. Kitahama...?
KLATTER
LITTLE BROTHER...?
EIGHT YEARS AGO, MR. KITAHAMA LOST HIS BROTHER. HE WAS IN A MOTORCYCLE ACCIDENT...
...WHILE HE WAS IN HIGH SCHOOL.
MY BROTHER WAS...
...MUCH YOUNGER THAN ME...HE WAS SPOILED GROWING UP, AND...
...HE BECAME SUCH A REBELLIOUS KID.
MY PARENTS WERE ALWAYS APOLOGIZING TO PEOPLE FOR THE TROUBLE HE CAUSED.
I TRIED TO TALK TO HIM, BUT HE JUST IGNORED ME.

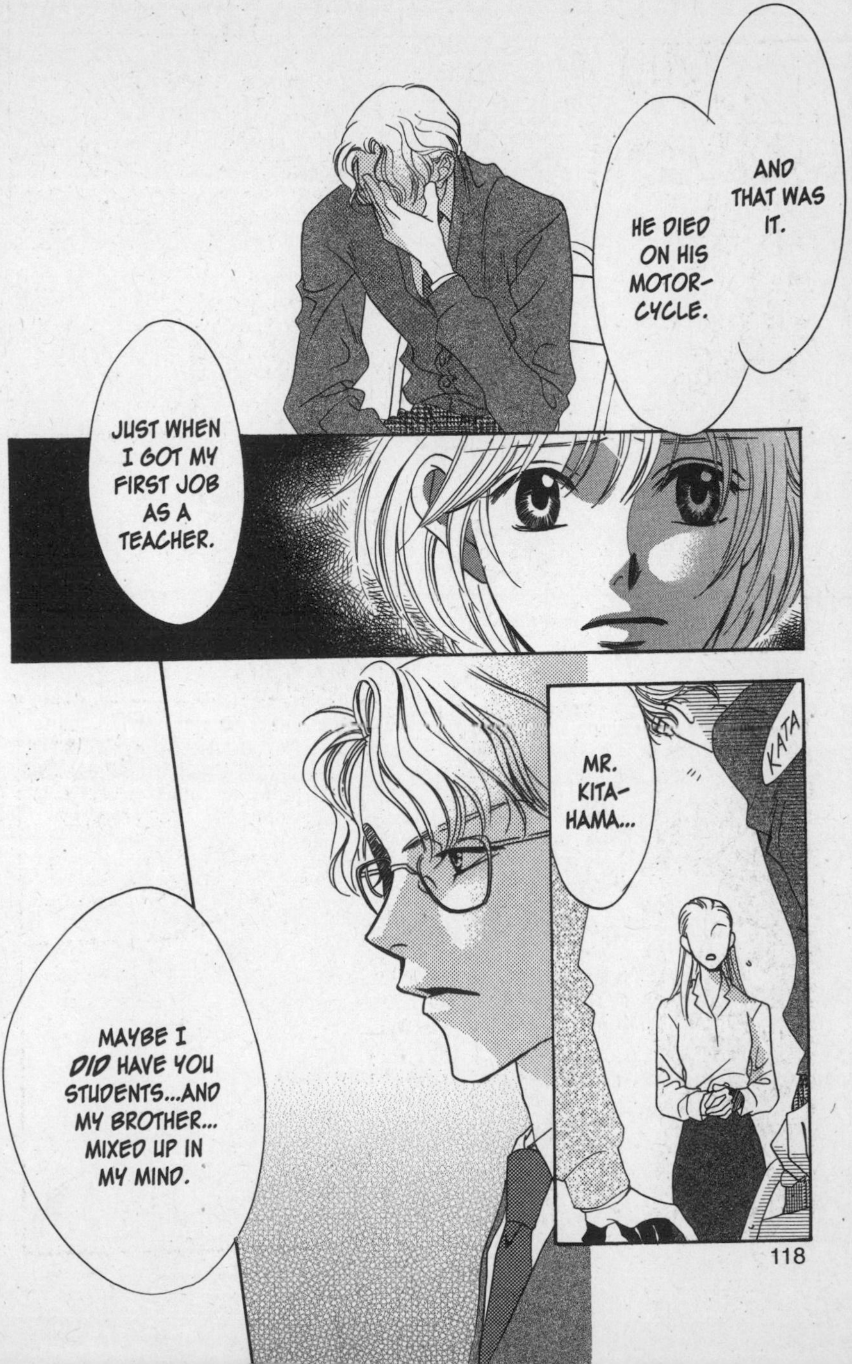
AND THAT WAS IT.
HE DIED ON HIS MOTOR-CYCLE.
JUST WHEN I GOT MY FIRST JOB AS A TEACHER.
KATA
MR. KITA-HAMA...
MAYBE I *DID* HAVE YOU STUDENTS...AND MY BROTHER... MIXED UP IN MY MIND.

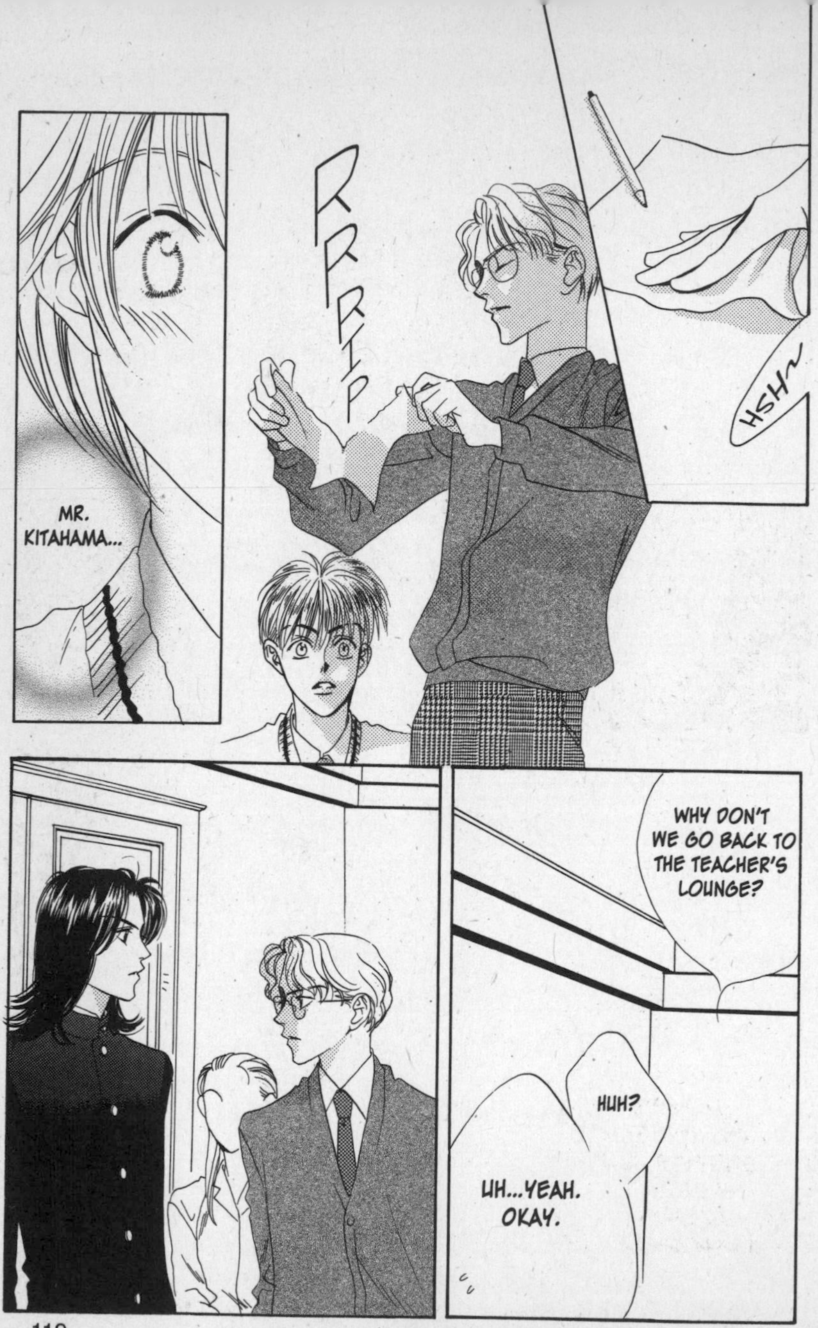
HSH~
RRRIP
MR. KITAHAMA...
WHY DON'T WE GO BACK TO THE TEACHER'S LOUNGE?
HUH?
UH...YEAH. OKAY.

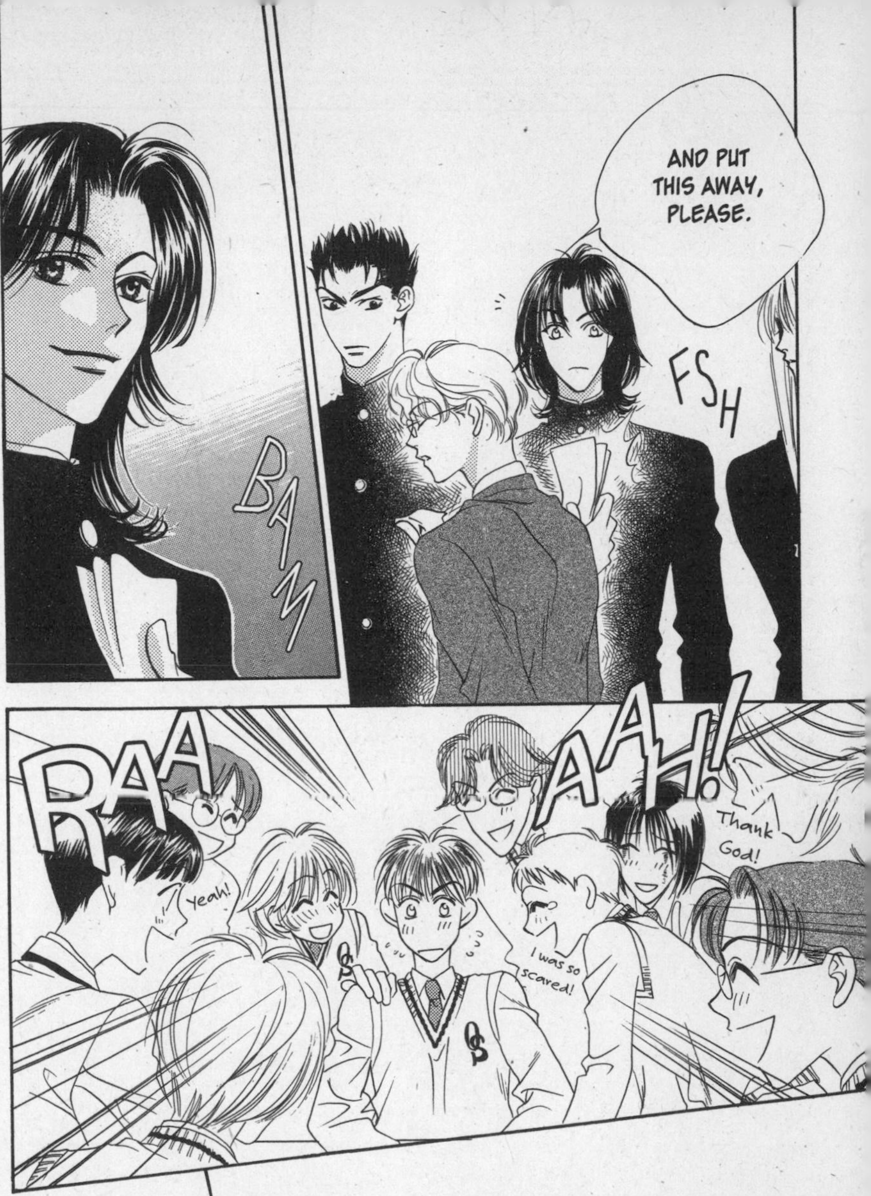
AND PUT THIS AWAY, PLEASE.
FSH
BAM
RAAAAH!
Thank God!
I was so scared!
Yeah!

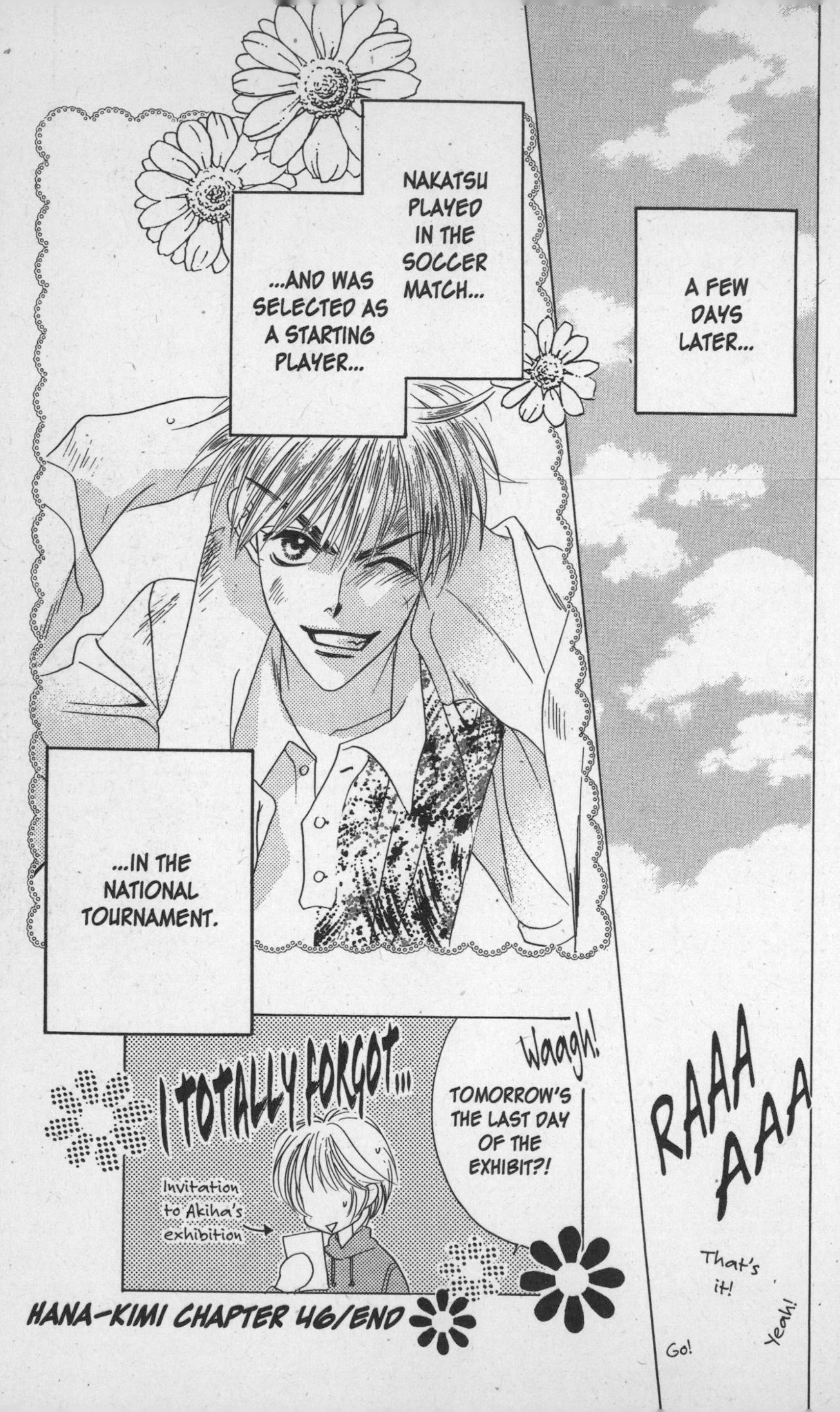
A FEW DAYS LATER...
RAAA AAA
That's it!
Yeah!
Go!
NAKATSU PLAYED IN THE SOCCER MATCH...
...AND WAS SELECTED AS A STARTING PLAYER...
...IN THE NATIONAL TOURNAMENT.
Waagh!
TOMORROW'S THE LAST DAY OF THE EXHIBIT?!
I TOTALLY FORGOT...
Invitation to Akiha's exhibition

HANA-KIMI CHAPTER 46/END

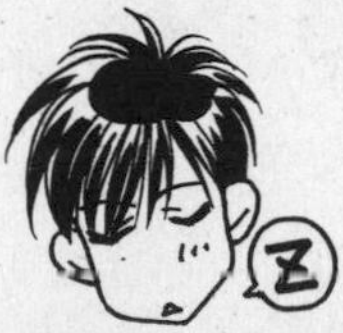
Z
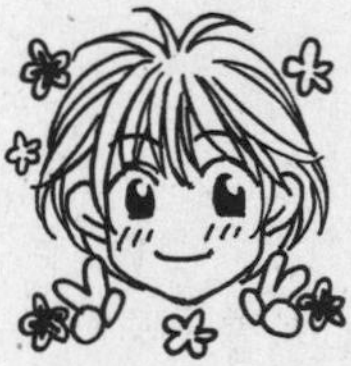
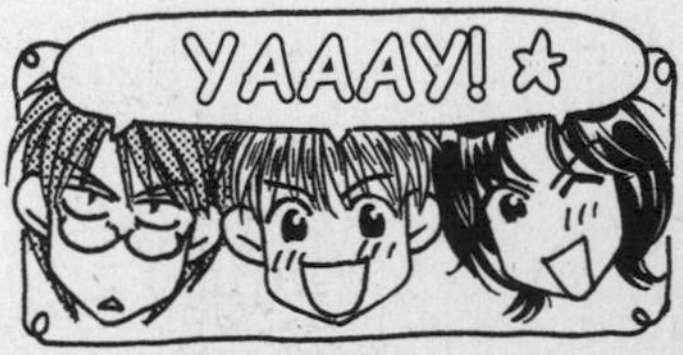
YAAAY! ☆

Hana-Kimi!

For You in Full Blossom

CHAPTER 47

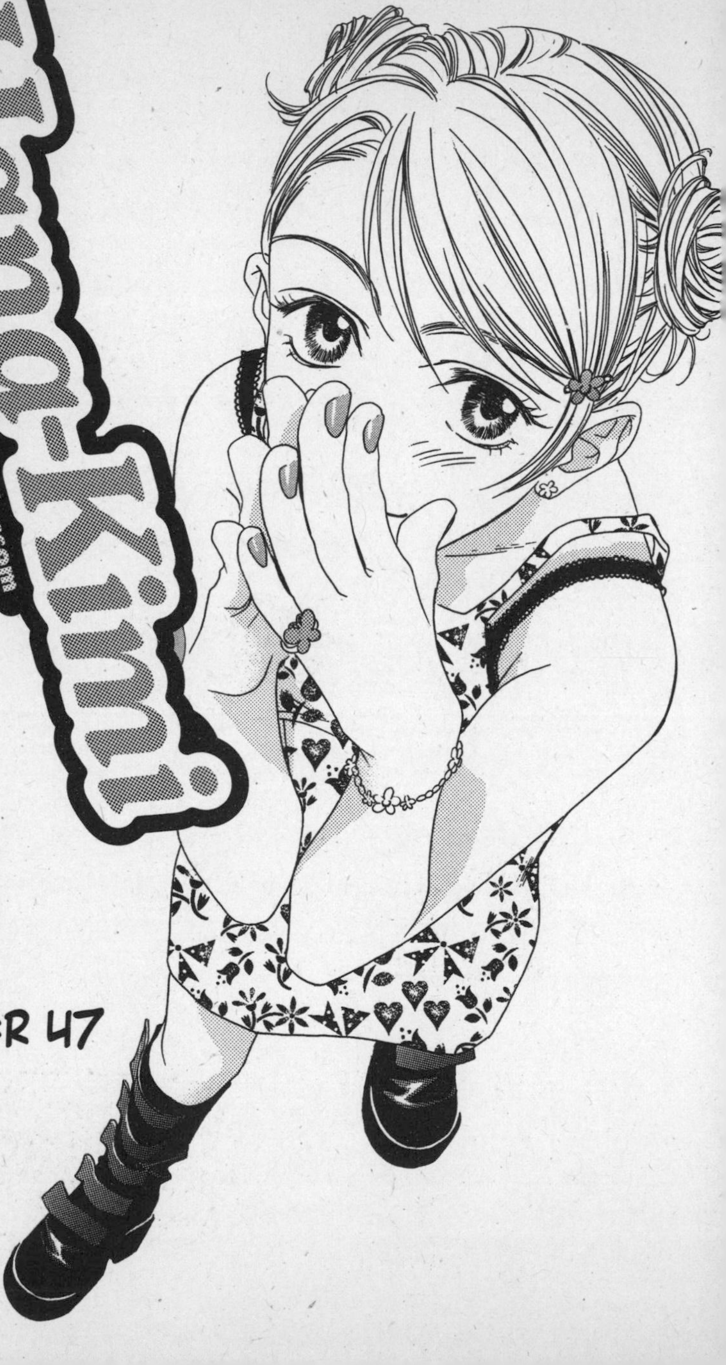

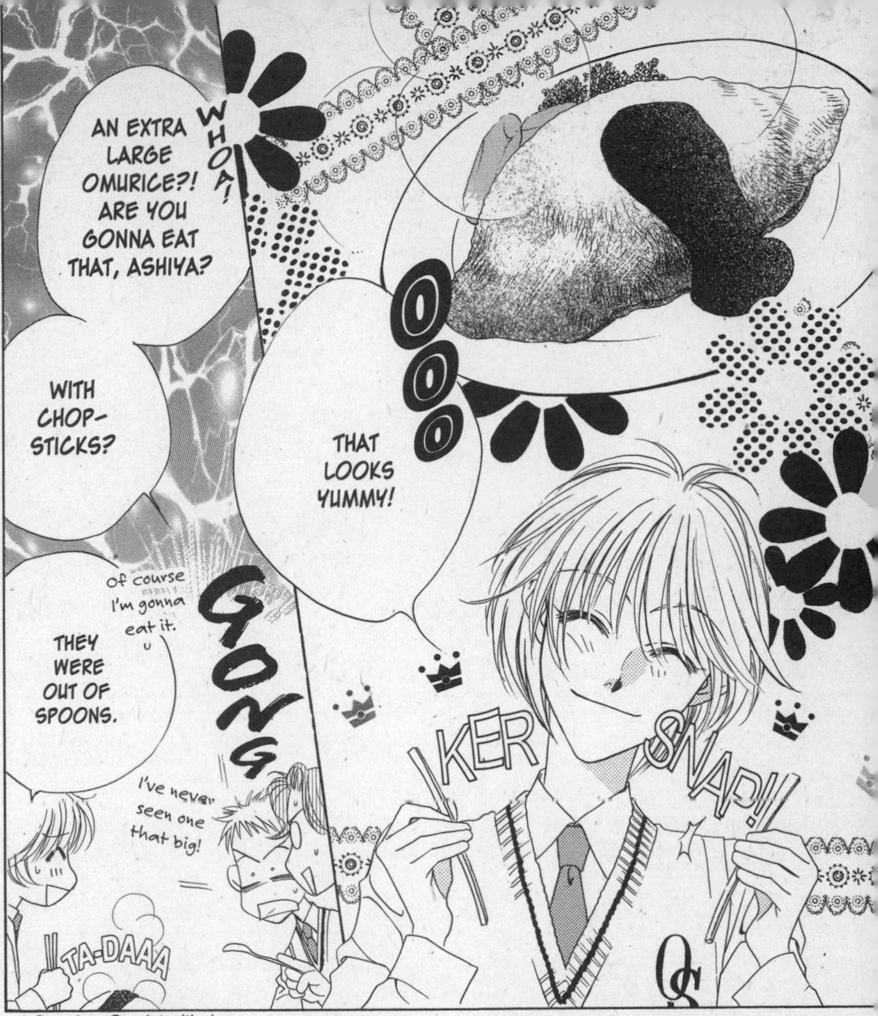
WHOA!
OOOO
THAT LOOKS YUMMY!
AN EXTRA LARGE OMURICE?! ARE YOU GONNA EAT THAT, ASHIYA?
WITH CHOP-STICKS?
KER SNAP!!
GONG
THEY WERE OUT OF SPOONS.
Of course I'm gonna eat it.
I've never seen one that big!
TA-DAAA

* Omurice=Omelet with rice

SUO STORIES

「smell」

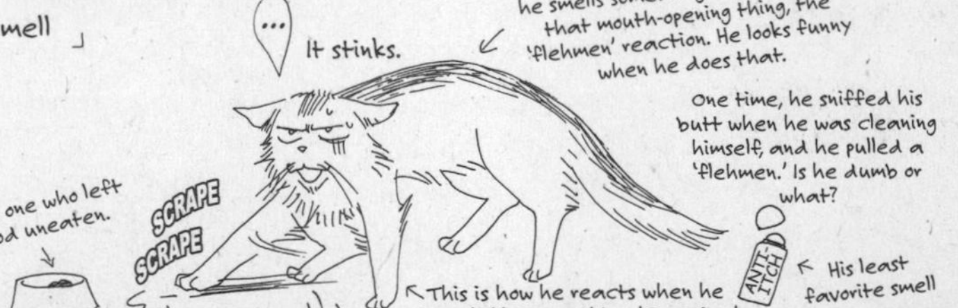
...
It stinks.
He likes to smell stinky stuff, but when he smells something weird, he does that mouth-opening thing, the 'flehmen' reaction. He looks funny when he does that.
One time, he sniffed his butt when he was cleaning himself, and he pulled a 'flehmen.' Is he dumb or what?
He's the one who left his food uneaten.
SCRAPE SCRAPE
This is how he reacts when he doesn't like something. 'Scraping.'
ANTI-ITCH
His least favorite smell

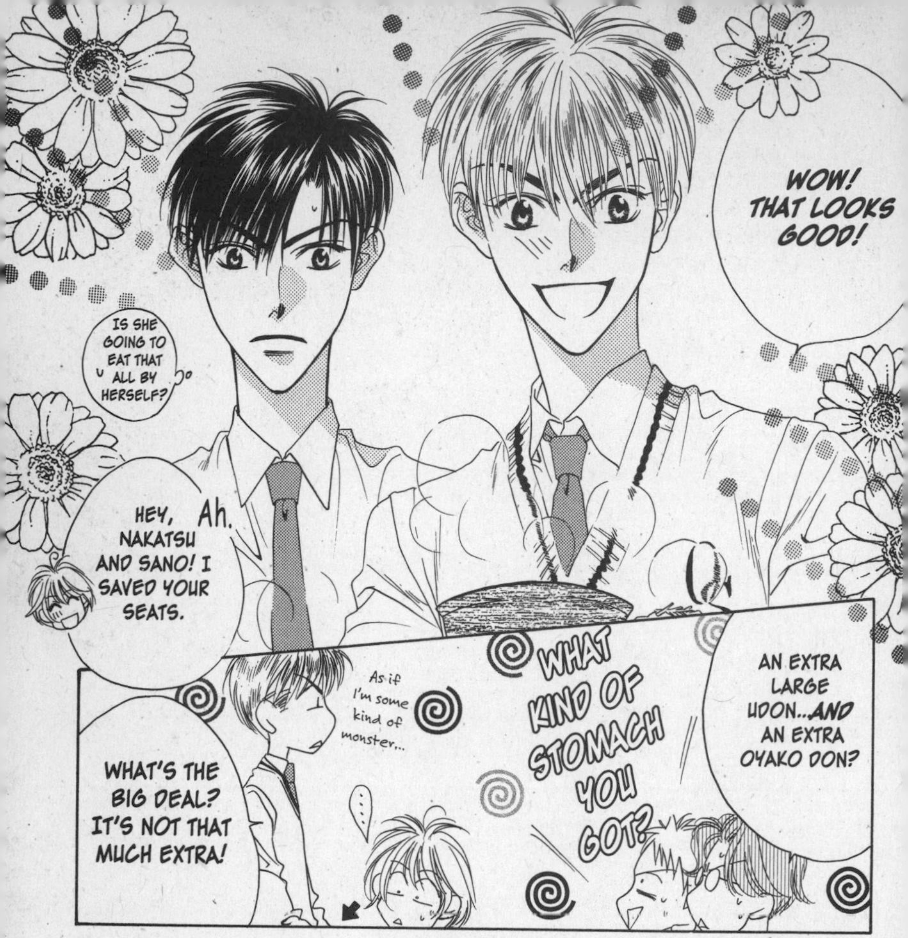
WOW! THAT LOOKS GOOD!
IS SHE GOING TO EAT THAT ALL BY HERSELF?
Ah.
HEY, NAKATSU AND SANO! I SAVED YOUR SEATS.
AN EXTRA LARGE UDON...AND AN EXTRA OYAKO DON?
WHAT KIND OF STOMACH YOU GOT?
As if I'm some kind of monster...
...
WHAT'S THE BIG DEAL? IT'S NOT THAT MUCH EXTRA!

*Udon=thick wheat noodles. Oyako don=Chicken over rice.

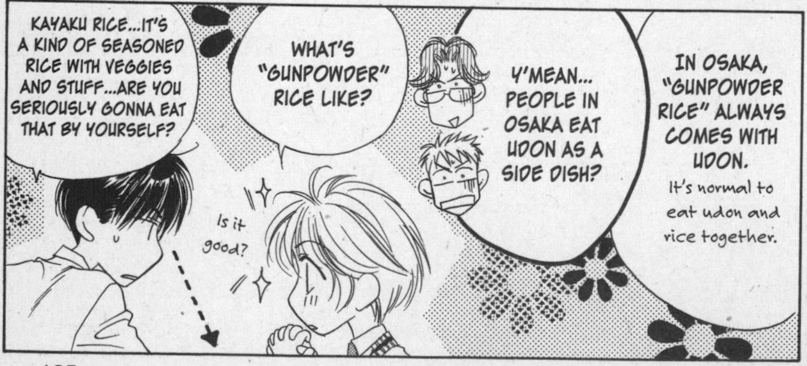
IN OSAKA, "GUNPOWDER RICE" ALWAYS COMES WITH UDON.
It's normal to eat udon and rice together.
Y'MEAN... PEOPLE IN OSAKA EAT UDON AS A SIDE DISH?
WHAT'S "GUNPOWDER" RICE LIKE?
Is it good?
KAYAKU RICE...IT'S A KIND OF SEASONED RICE WITH VEGGIES AND STUFF...ARE YOU SERIOUSLY GONNA EAT THAT BY YOURSELF?

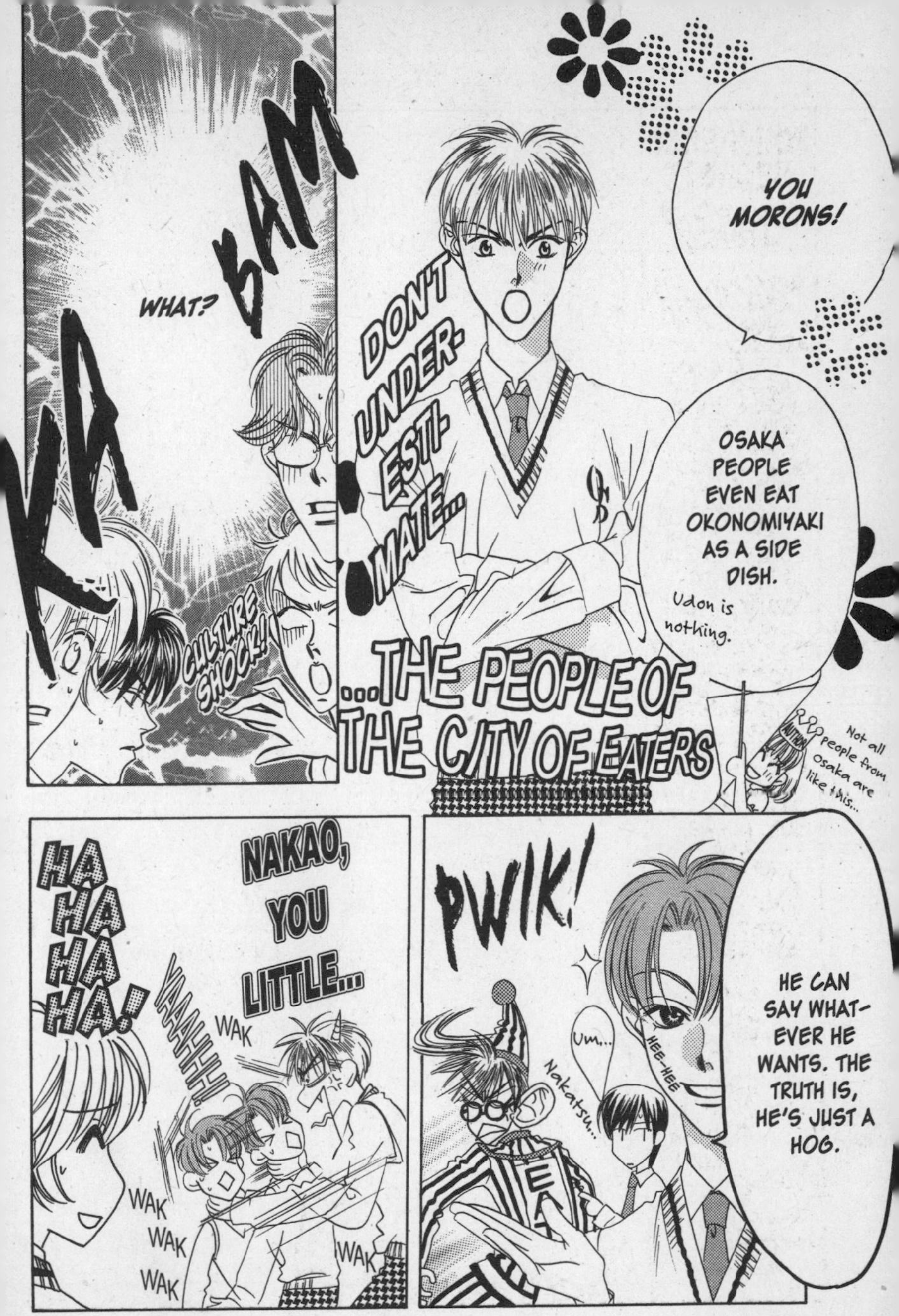
YOU MORONS!
DON'T UNDER-ESTI-MATE...
...THE PEOPLE OF THE CITY OF EATERS
OSAKA PEOPLE EVEN EAT OKONOMIYAKI AS A SIDE DISH.
Udon is nothing.
Not all people from Osaka are like this...
BAM
WHAT?
CULTURE SHOCK!
PWIK!
HE CAN SAY WHAT-EVER HE WANTS. THE TRUTH IS, HE'S JUST A HOG.
HEE-HEE
Um...
Nakatsu...
NAKAO, YOU LITTLE...
HA HA HA HA HA!
YAAAHH!
WAK
WAK WAK WAK
WAK

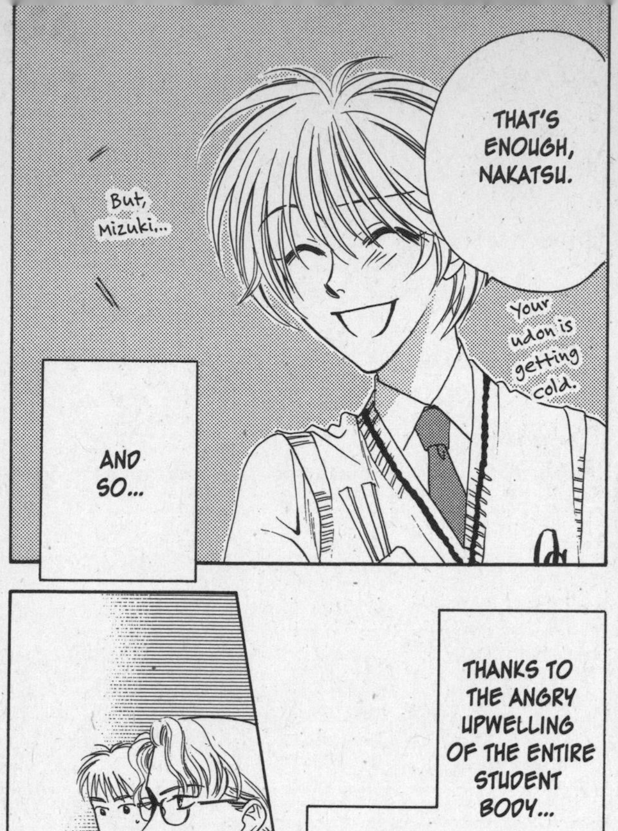
THAT'S ENOUGH, NAKATSU.
Your udon is getting cold.
But, Mizuki...
AND SO...
THANKS TO THE ANGRY UPWELLING OF THE ENTIRE STUDENT BODY...
AND ESPECIALLY SANO'S AGGRESSIVE INVESTIGATION AND THE DARING OF THE R.A.S IN THE *KAÔKAI*...
THE TEACHERS WHO SUPPORTED MR. KITAHAMA REALIZED THAT THEY WERE BECOMING TOO HARSH...

WHISPERED SECRETS

ARANZI AND ARONZO

RIGHT NOW I'M REALLY INTO ARANZI AND ARONZO STUFF! I'D KNOWN ABOUT THEM FOR A WHILE, BUT I WASN'T REALLY CAUGHT UP IN THEM...BUT NOW I CAN'T CONTROL MYSELF. HEH...ONCE I TOOK A LOOK AT THEIR PHOTO BOOK, I WAS HOOKED. THEY'RE REALLY COOL, AND I LIKE THE COMMENTS WRITTEN ALONG SIDE THE PHOTOGRAPHS. MY FAVORITES ARE 'SHIROSA AND KUROSA' AND 'WARUMONO.' BUT I REALLY LIKE ALL THE OTHER CHARACTERS TOO.

I HAVE ONE OF THESE. THIS ONE'S ALREADY BECOME A COLLECTOR'S ITEM. IT'S A 'DANCE WATCH.' ←

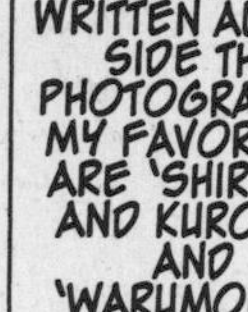

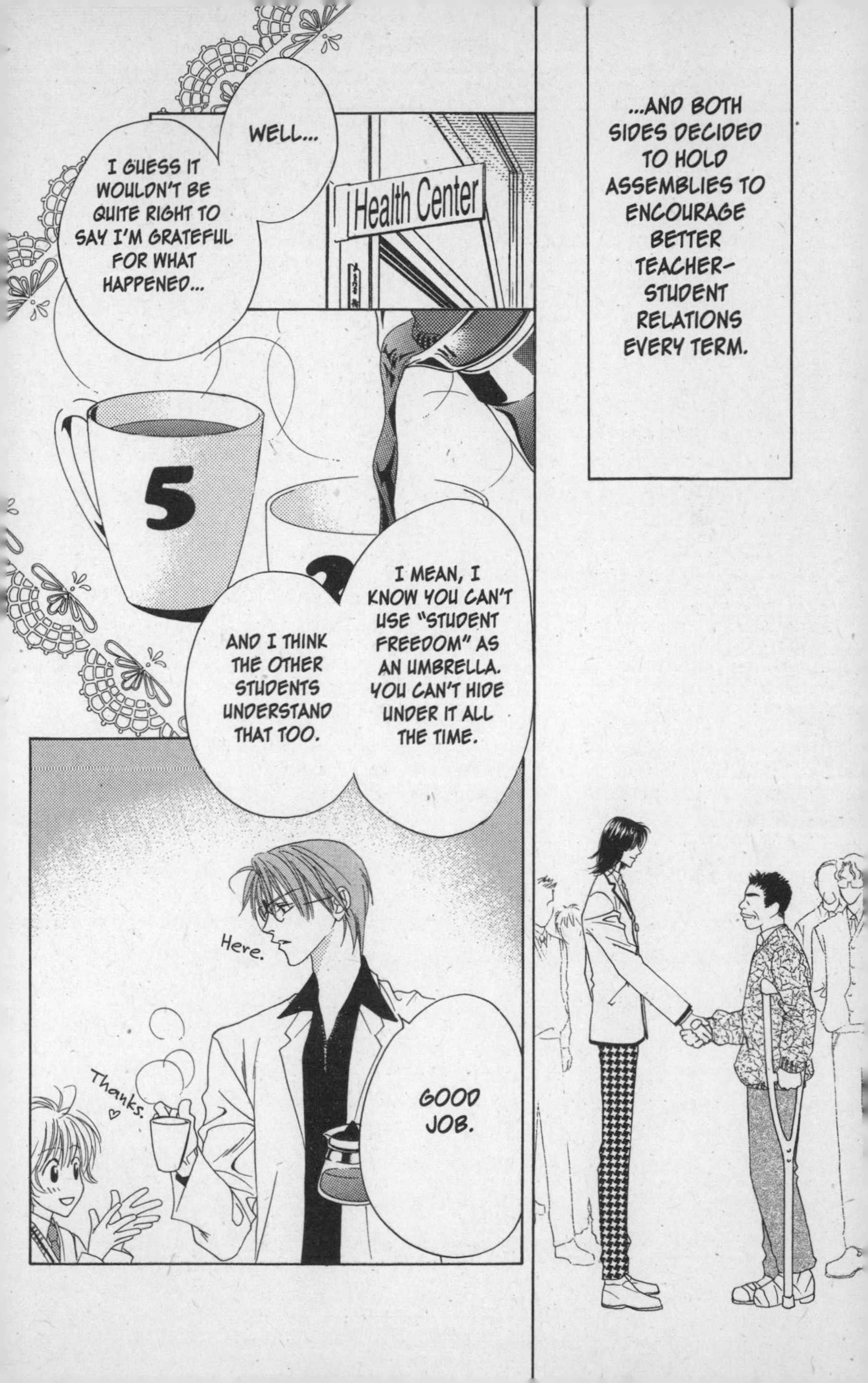
...AND BOTH SIDES DECIDED TO HOLD ASSEMBLIES TO ENCOURAGE BETTER TEACHER-STUDENT RELATIONS EVERY TERM.
Health Center
WELL...
I GUESS IT WOULDN'T BE QUITE RIGHT TO SAY I'M GRATEFUL FOR WHAT HAPPENED...
I MEAN, I KNOW YOU CAN'T USE "STUDENT FREEDOM" AS AN UMBRELLA. YOU CAN'T HIDE UNDER IT ALL THE TIME.
AND I THINK THE OTHER STUDENTS UNDERSTAND THAT TOO.
Here.
GOOD JOB.
Thanks.

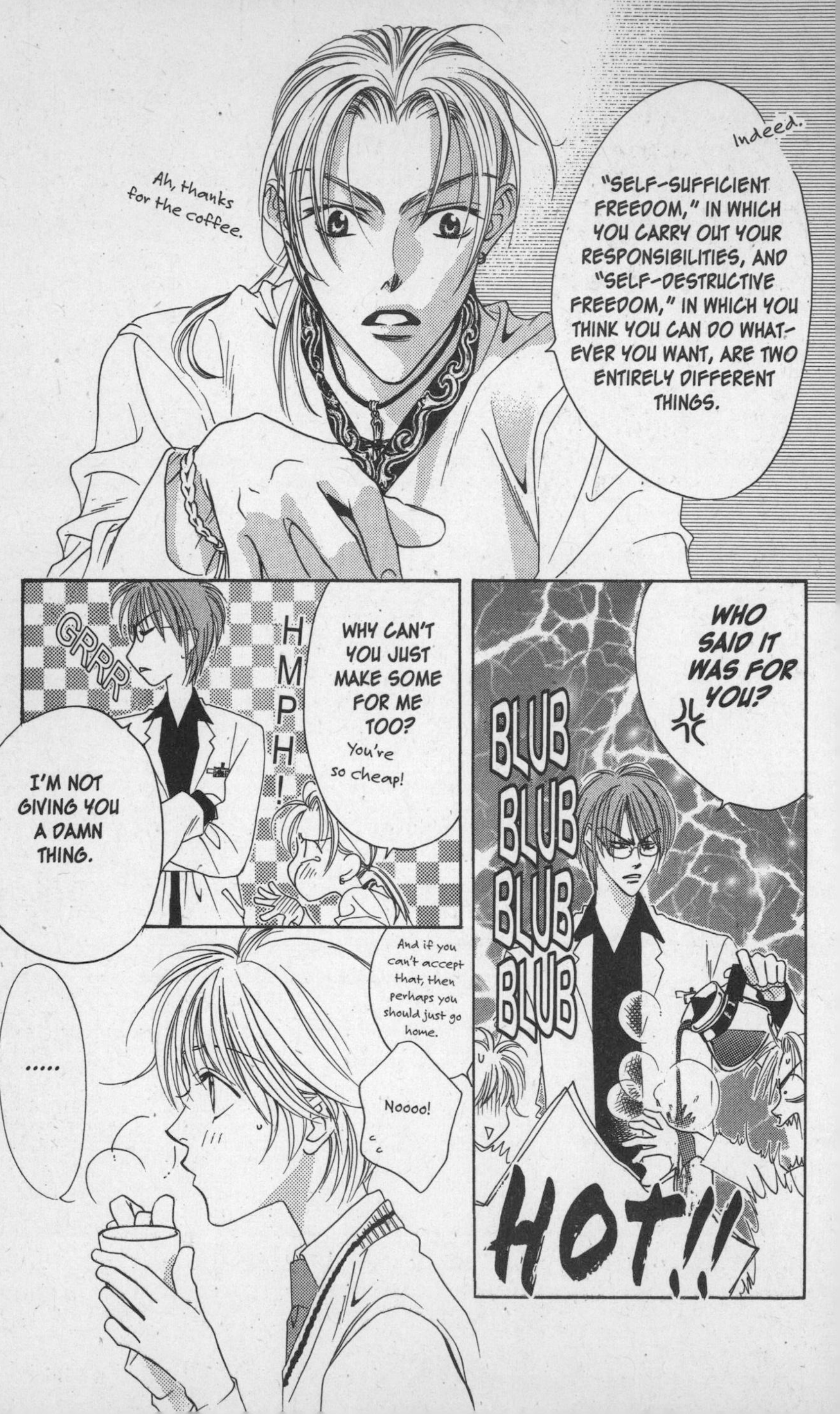
Indeed.
"SELF-SUFFICIENT FREEDOM," IN WHICH YOU CARRY OUT YOUR RESPONSIBILITIES, AND "SELF-DESTRUCTIVE FREEDOM," IN WHICH YOU THINK YOU CAN DO WHAT-EVER YOU WANT, ARE TWO ENTIRELY DIFFERENT THINGS.
Ah, thanks for the coffee.
WHO SAID IT WAS FOR YOU?
BLUB BLUB BLUB BLUB BLUB
HOT!!
WHY CAN'T YOU JUST MAKE SOME FOR ME TOO?
You're so cheap!
HMPH!
GRRR
I'M NOT GIVING YOU A DAMN THING.
And if you can't accept that, then perhaps you should just go home.
Noooo!
.....

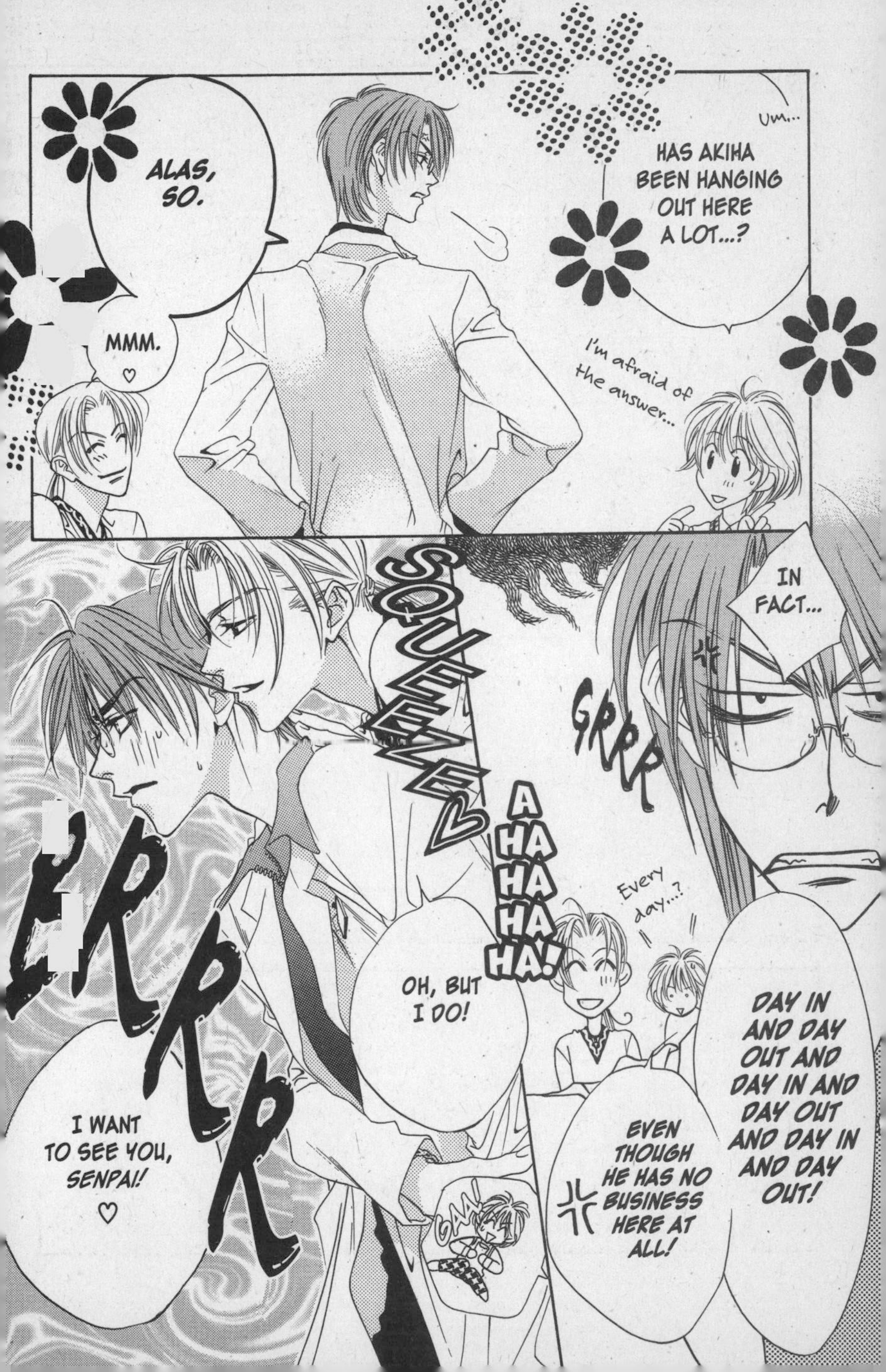
Um...
HAS AKIHA BEEN HANGING OUT HERE A LOT...?
I'm afraid of the answer...
ALAS, SO.
MMM. ♡
IN FACT...
GRRR
DAY IN AND DAY OUT AND DAY IN AND DAY OUT AND DAY IN AND DAY OUT!
EVEN THOUGH HE HAS NO BUSINESS HERE AT ALL!
Every day...?
AHAHAHAHA!
SQUEEEZE♡
OH, BUT I DO!
GAA!
I WANT TO SEE YOU, SENPAI! ♡
ERRR

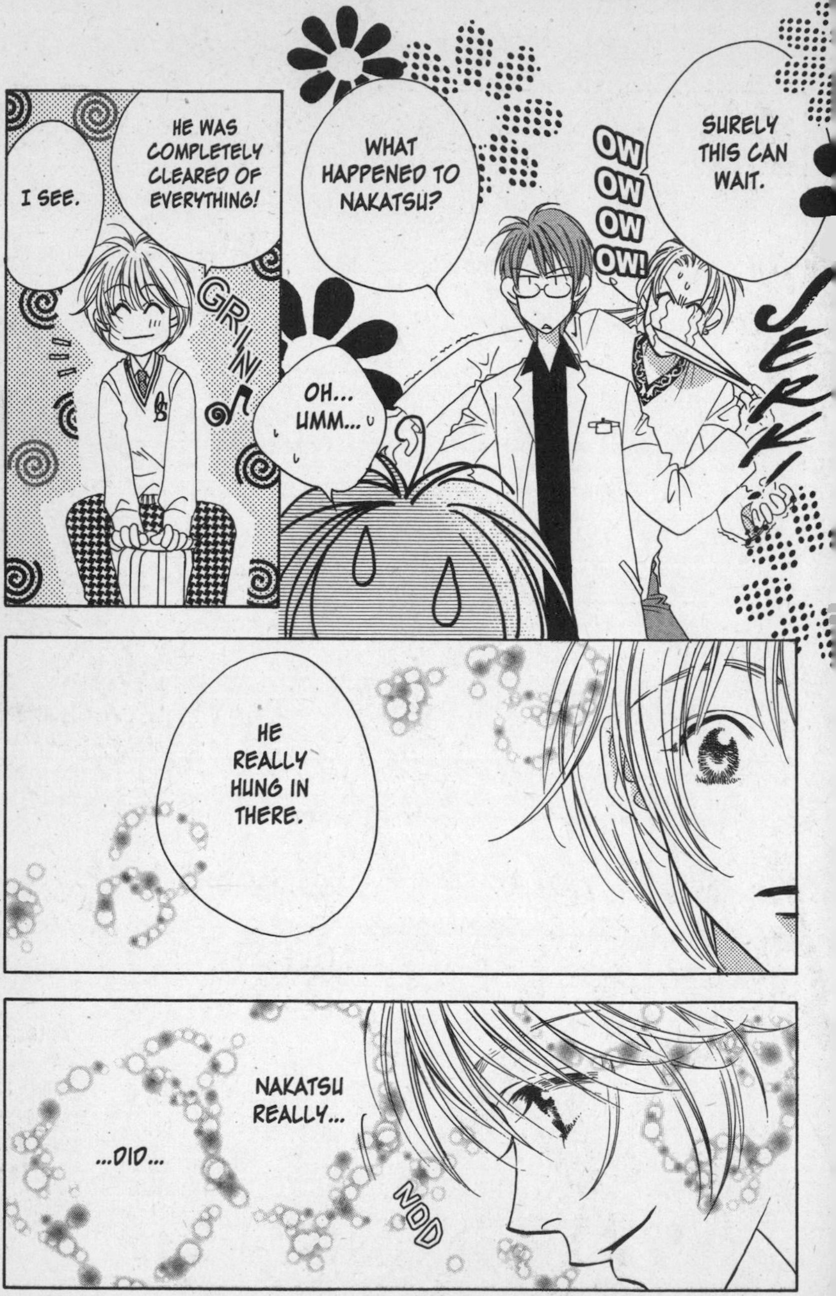

SURELY THIS CAN WAIT.
OW OW OW OW!
JERK!
WHAT HAPPENED TO NAKATSU?
OH... UMM...
HE WAS COMPLETELY CLEARED OF EVERYTHING!
I SEE.
GRIN
HE REALLY HUNG IN THERE.
NAKATSU REALLY...
NOD
...DID...

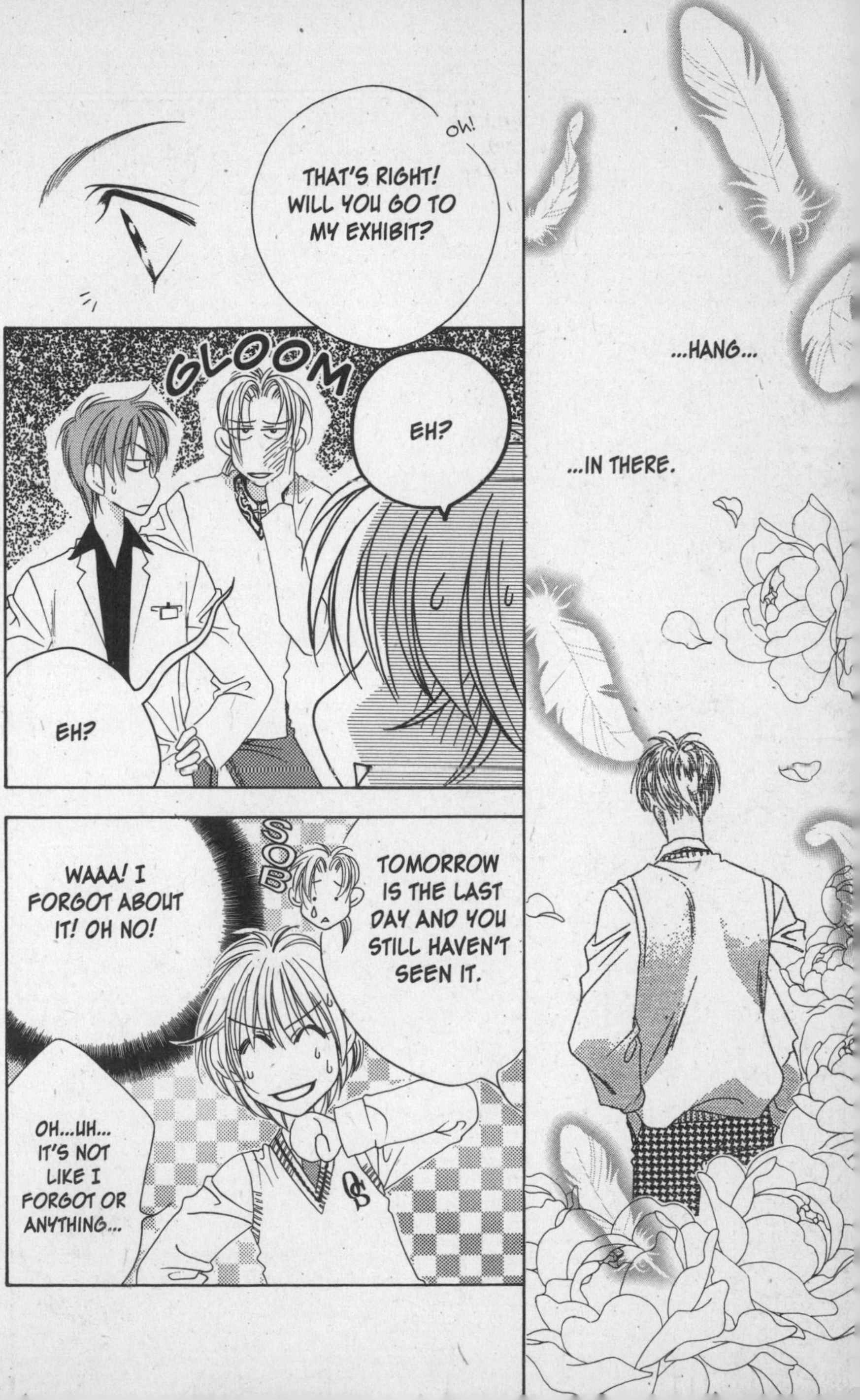
...HANG...
...IN THERE.
OH!
THAT'S RIGHT! WILL YOU GO TO MY EXHIBIT?
GLOOM
EH?
EH?
TOMORROW IS THE LAST DAY AND YOU STILL HAVEN'T SEEN IT.
SOB
WAAA! I FORGOT ABOUT IT! OH NO!
OH...UH... IT'S NOT LIKE I FORGOT OR ANYTHING...

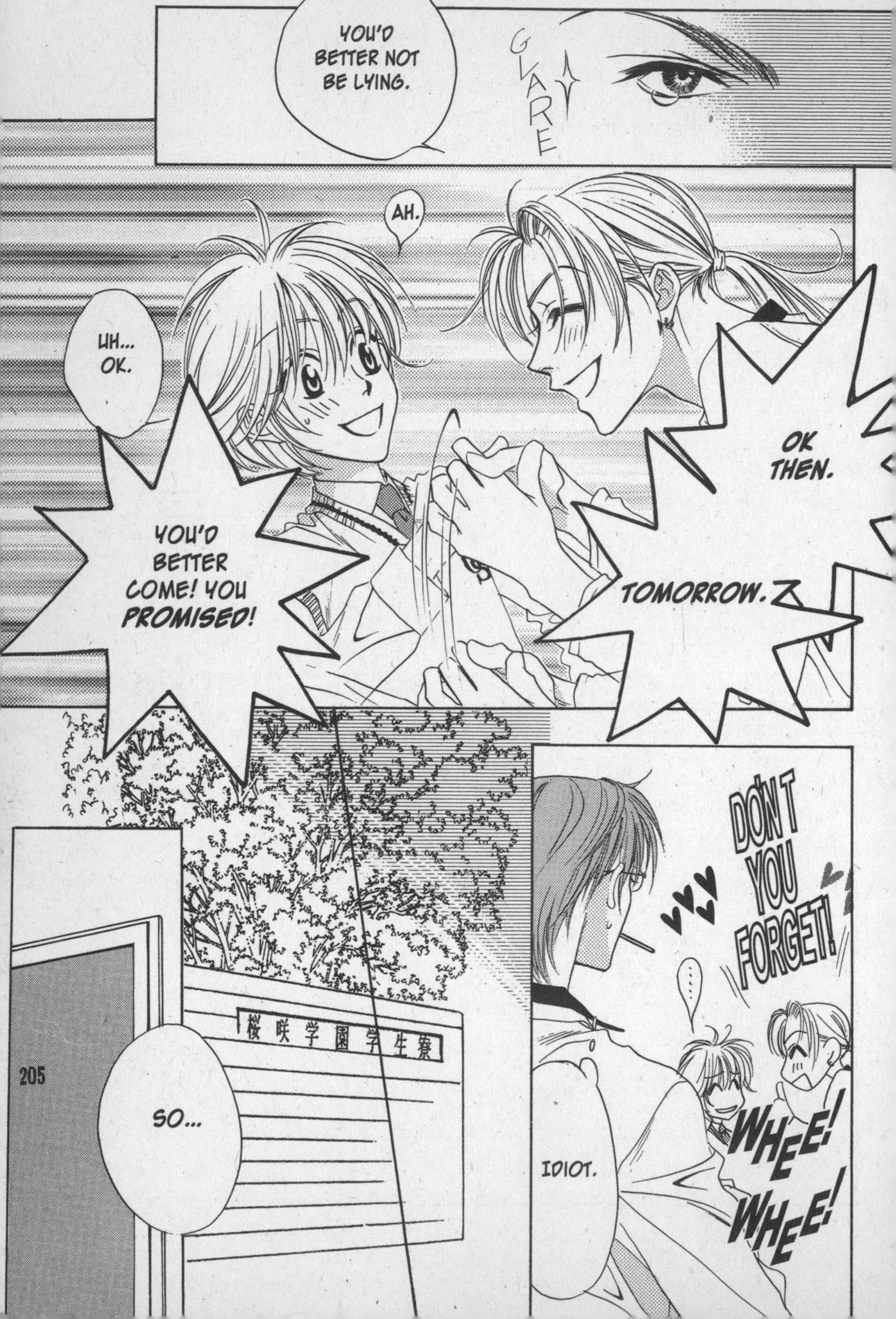
GLARE
YOU'D BETTER NOT BE LYING.
AH.
OK THEN.
TOMORROW.
UH... OK.
YOU'D BETTER COME! YOU PROMISED!
DON'T YOU FORGET!
...
WHEE! WHEE!
IDIOT.
桜咲学園学生寮
SO...

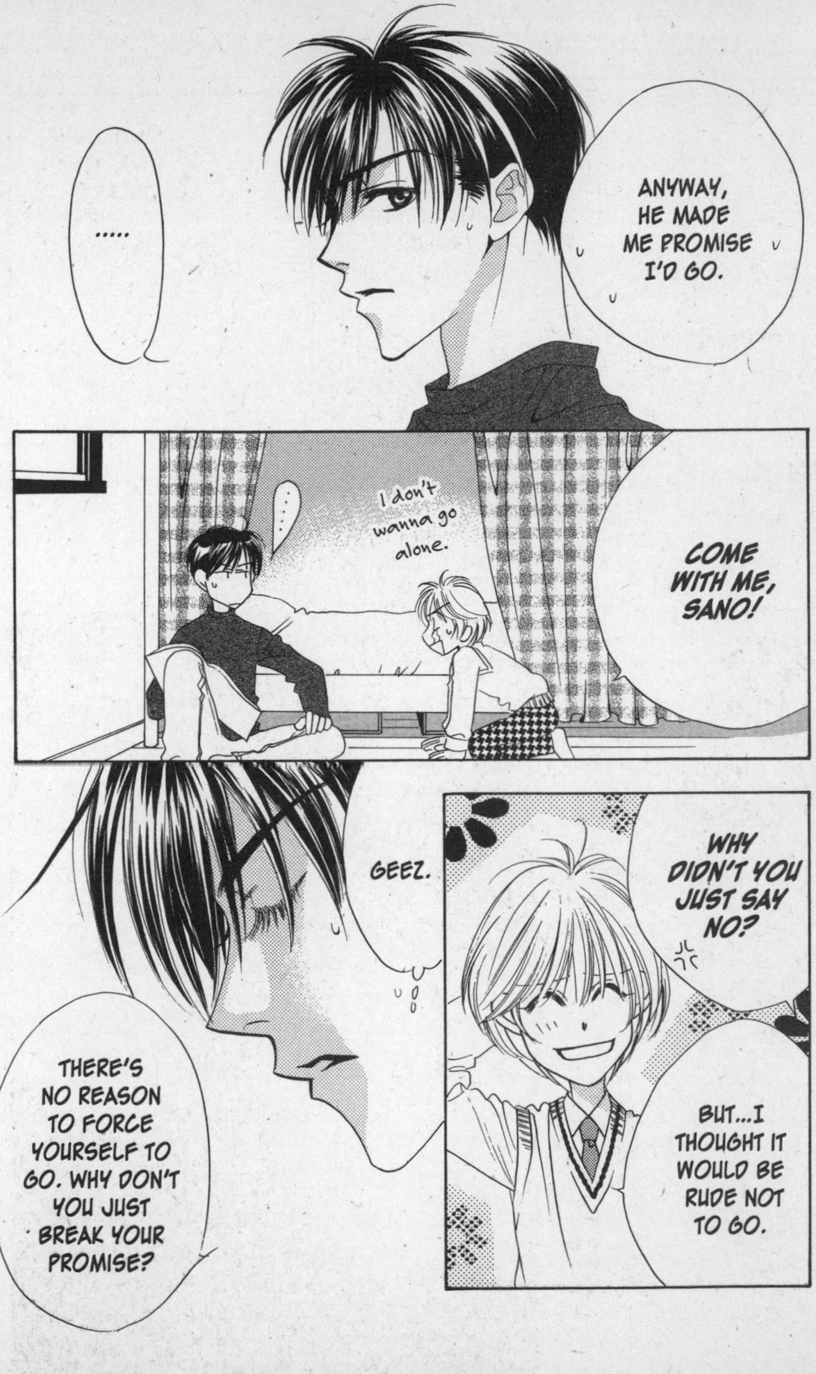
ANYWAY, HE MADE ME PROMISE I'D GO.
.....
COME WITH ME, SANO!
I don't wanna go alone.
...
WHY DIDN'T YOU JUST SAY NO?
BUT...I THOUGHT IT WOULD BE RUDE NOT TO GO.
GEEZ.
THERE'S NO REASON TO FORCE YOURSELF TO GO. WHY DON'T YOU JUST BREAK YOUR PROMISE?

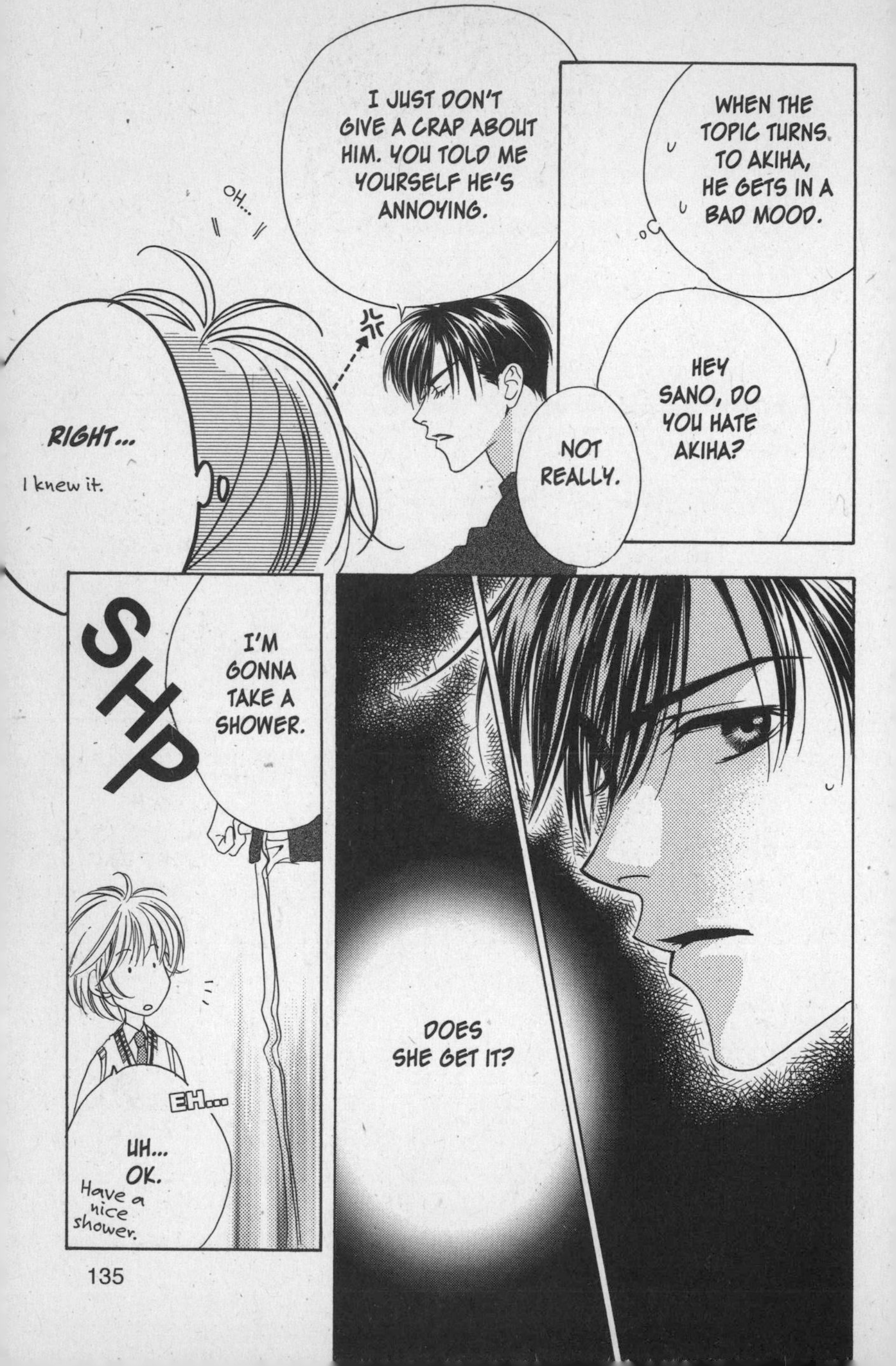
WHEN THE TOPIC TURNS TO AKIHA, HE GETS IN A BAD MOOD.
HEY SANO, DO YOU HATE AKIHA?
NOT REALLY.
I JUST DON'T GIVE A CRAP ABOUT HIM. YOU TOLD ME YOURSELF HE'S ANNOYING.
OH...
RIGHT...
I knew it.
DOES SHE GET IT?
I'M GONNA TAKE A SHOWER.
SHP
EH...
UH... OK.
Have a nice shower.

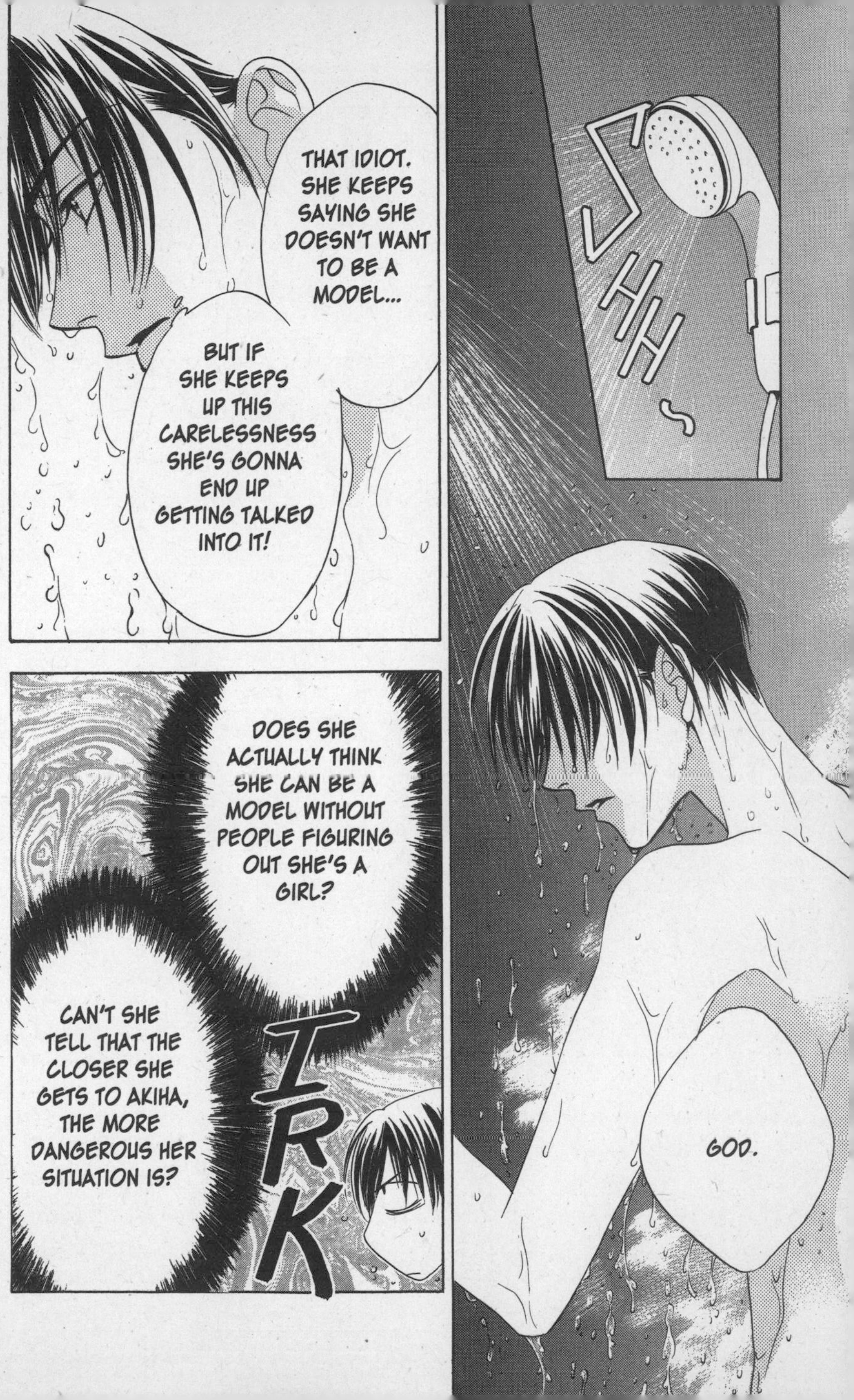
SHHH~
GOD.
THAT IDIOT. SHE KEEPS SAYING SHE DOESN'T WANT TO BE A MODEL...
BUT IF SHE KEEPS UP THIS CARELESSNESS SHE'S GONNA END UP GETTING TALKED INTO IT!
DOES SHE ACTUALLY THINK SHE CAN BE A MODEL WITHOUT PEOPLE FIGURING OUT SHE'S A GIRL?
IRK
CAN'T SHE TELL THAT THE CLOSER SHE GETS TO AKIHA, THE MORE DANGEROUS HER SITUATION IS?

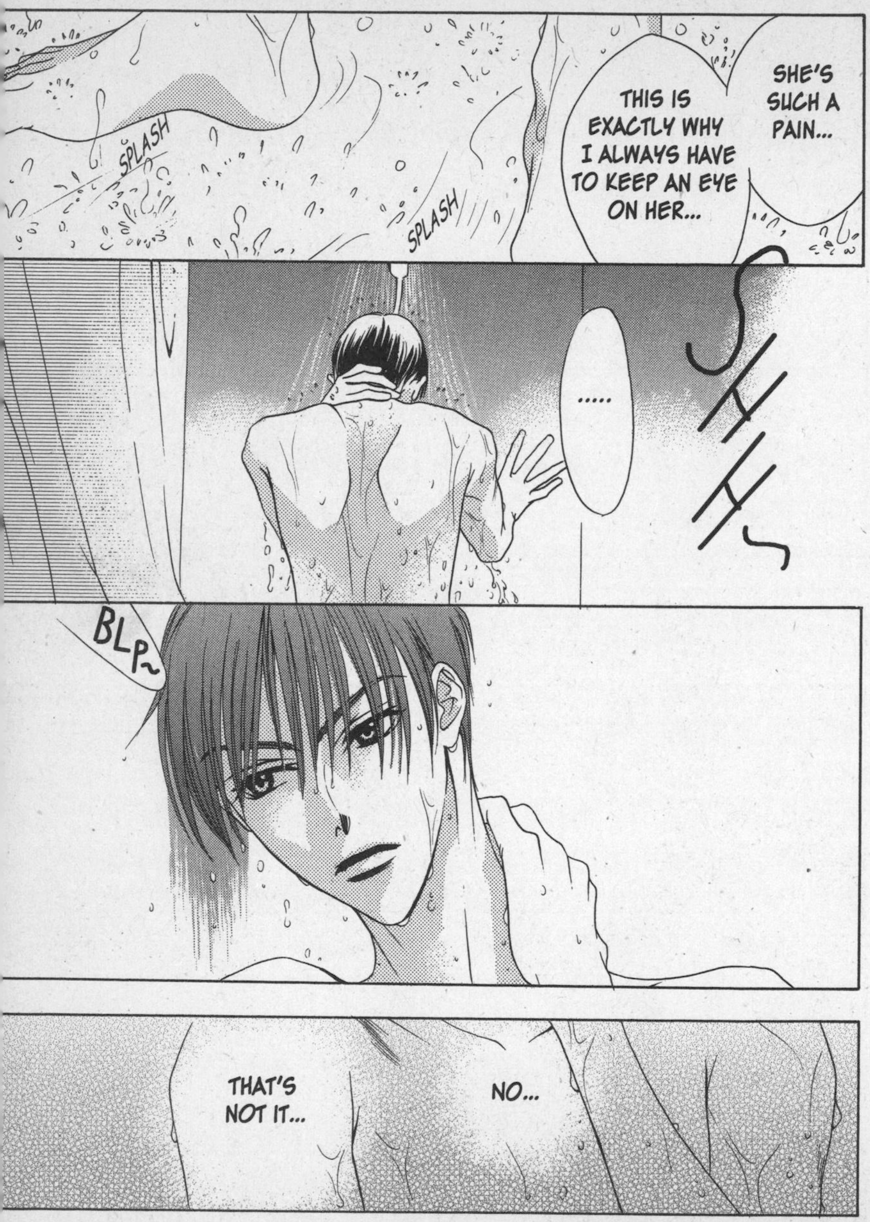
SHE'S SUCH A PAIN...
THIS IS EXACTLY WHY I ALWAYS HAVE TO KEEP AN EYE ON HER...
SPLASH
SPLASH
SHHH~
.....
BLP~
NO...
THAT'S NOT IT...

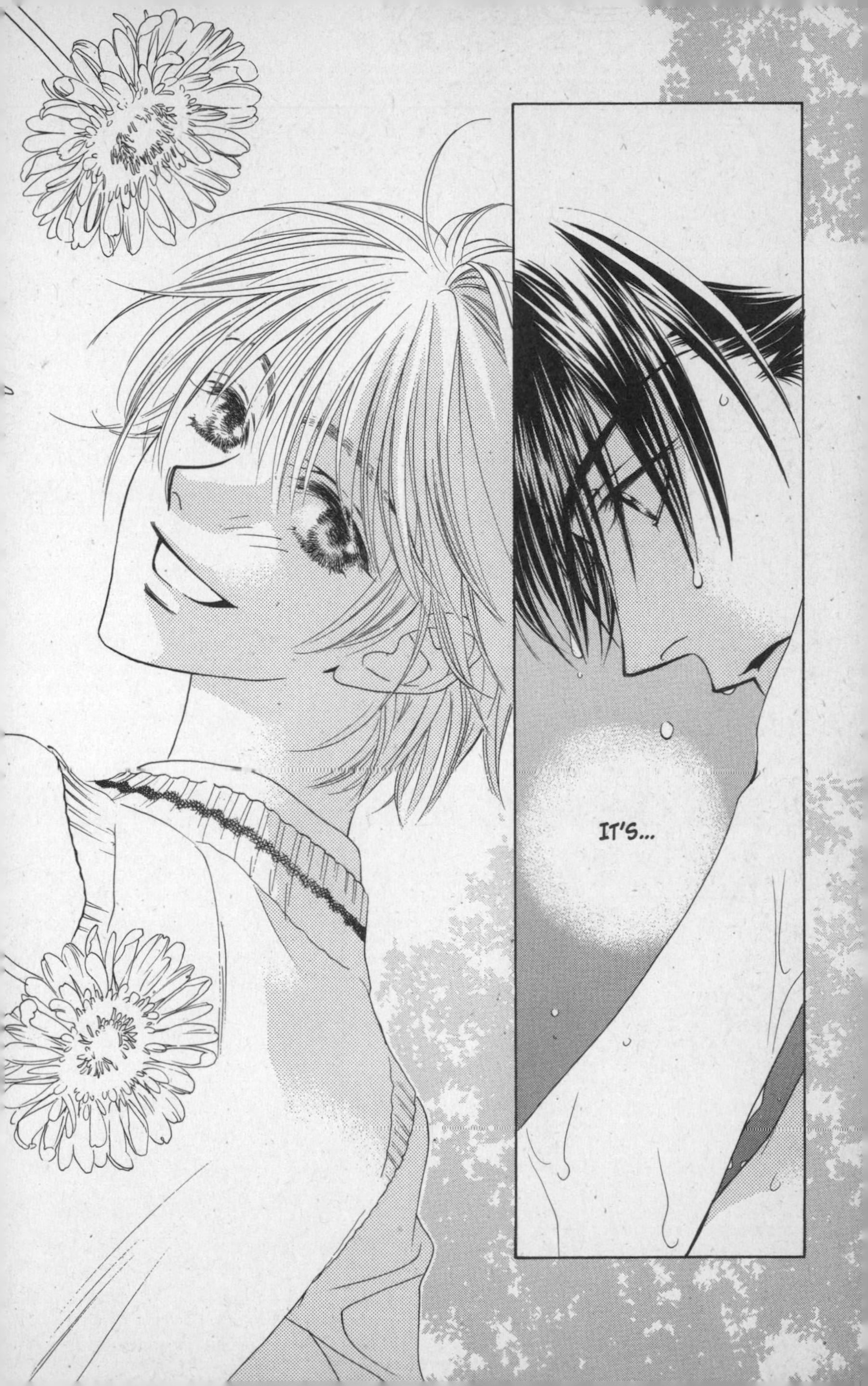
IT'S...

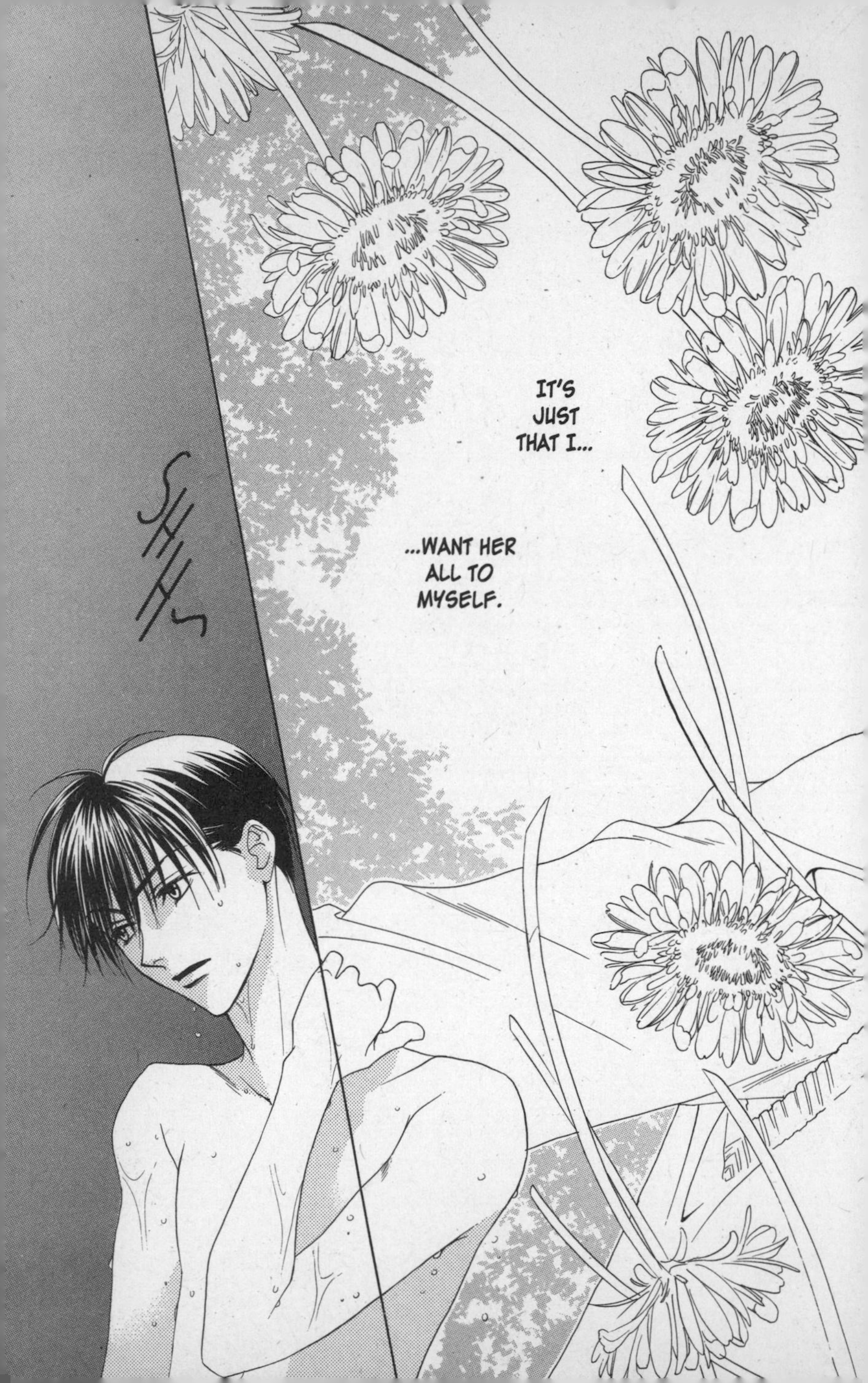
IT'S JUST THAT I...
...WANT HER ALL TO MYSELF.
SHHH

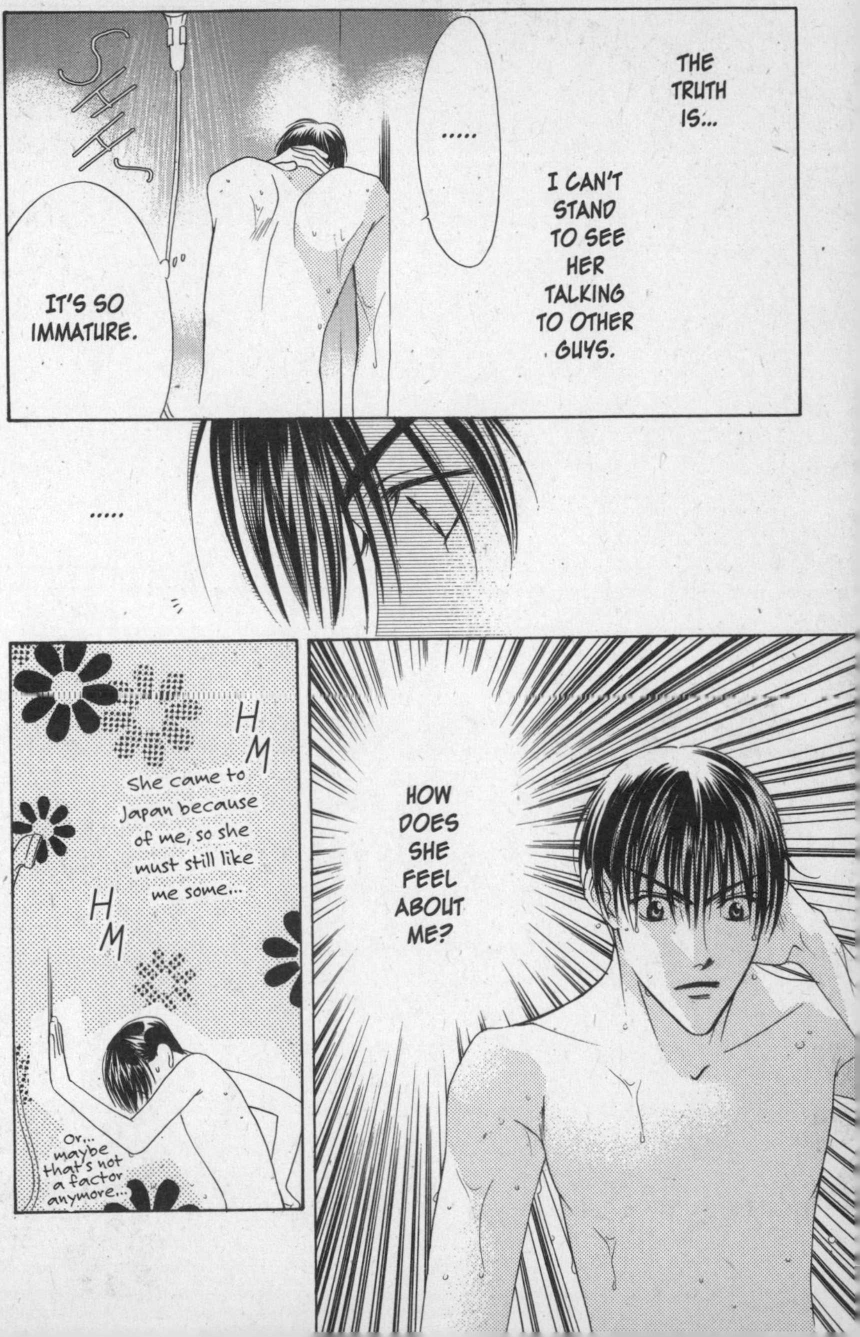
THE TRUTH IS...
I CAN'T STAND TO SEE HER TALKING TO OTHER GUYS.
.....
SHHH
IT'S SO IMMATURE.
.....
HOW DOES SHE FEEL ABOUT ME?
HM
She came to Japan because of me, so she must still like me some...
HM
Or... maybe that's not a factor anymore...

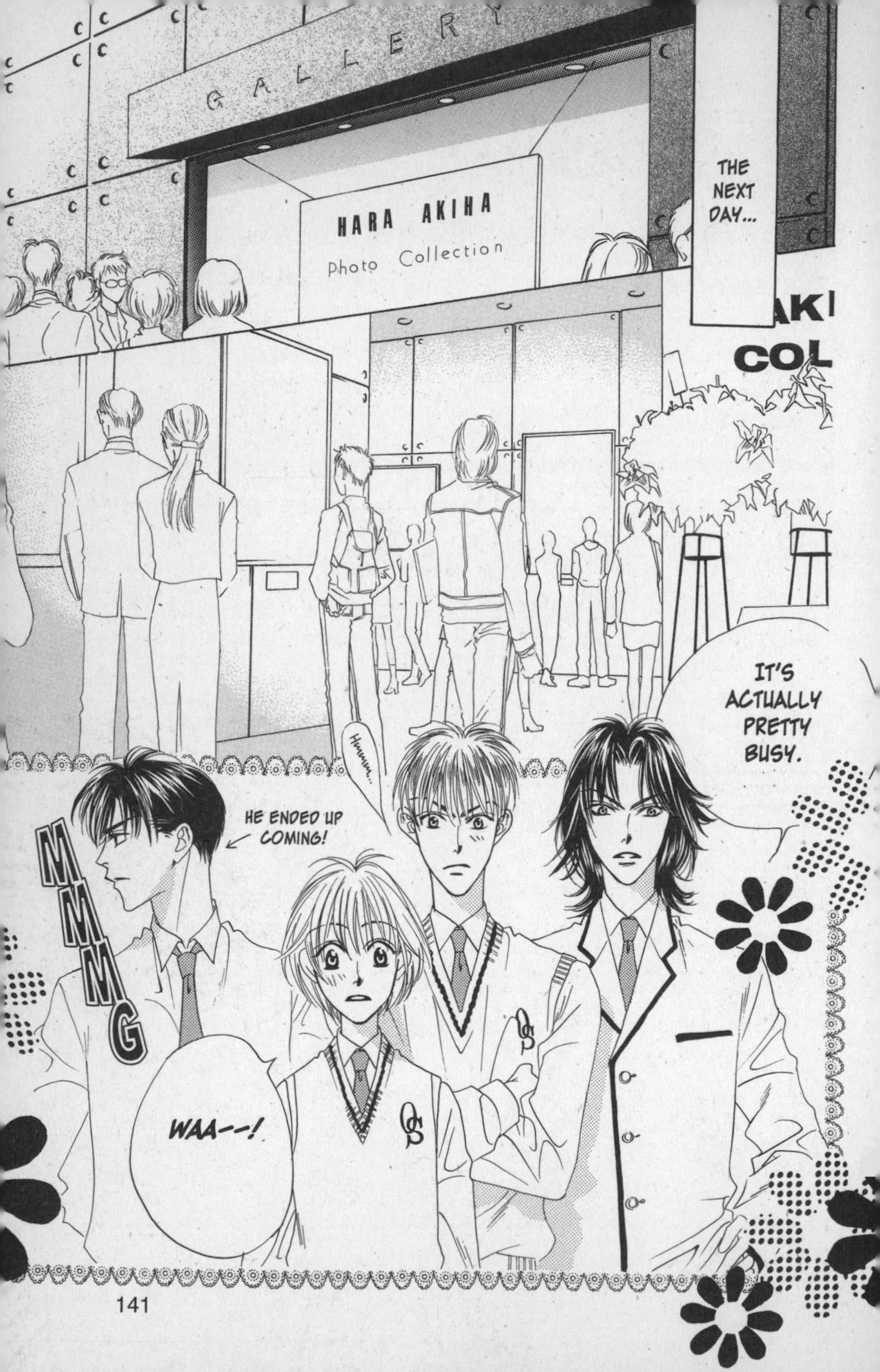

GALLERY
HARA AKIHA
Photo Collection
THE NEXT DAY...
IT'S ACTUALLY PRETTY BUSY.
Hmmm...
HE ENDED UP COMING!
MMMG
WAA--!

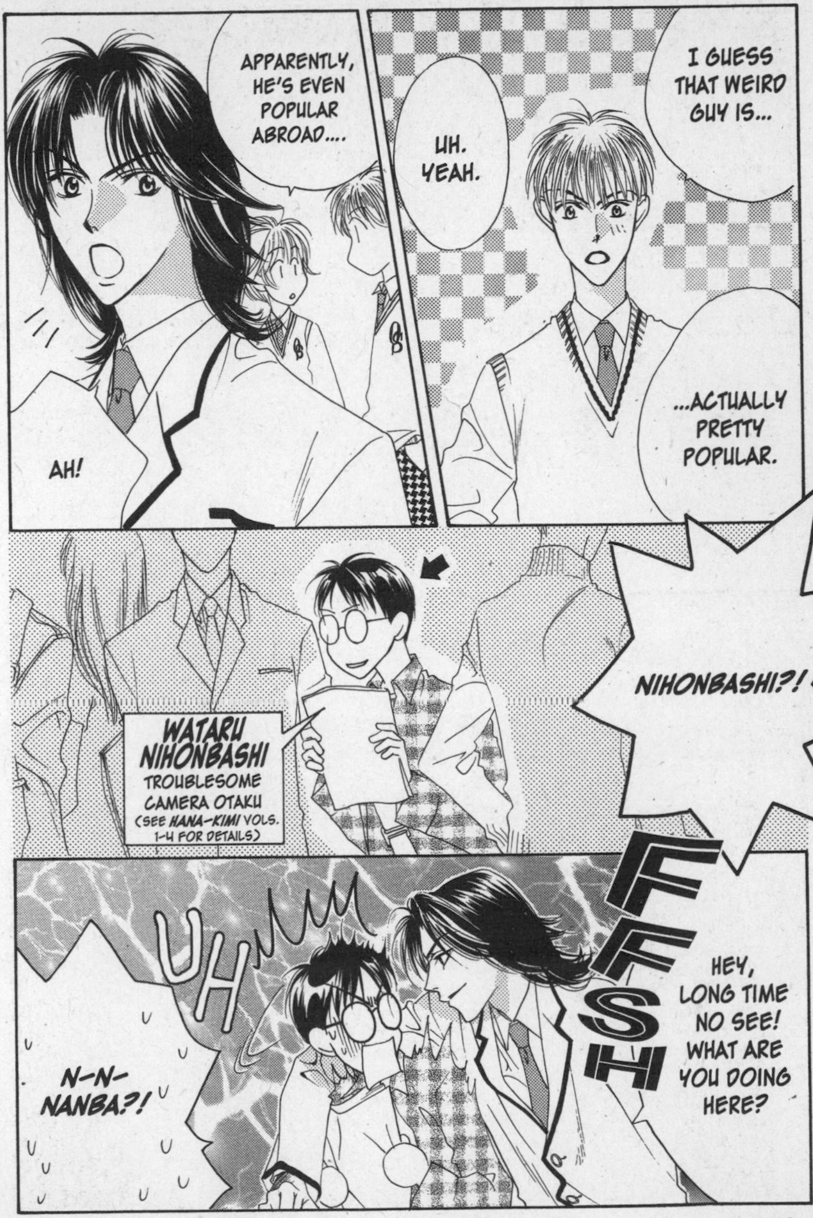
I GUESS THAT WEIRD GUY IS...
...ACTUALLY PRETTY POPULAR.
UH. YEAH.
APPARENTLY, HE'S EVEN POPULAR ABROAD....
AH!
NIHONBASHI?!
WATARU NIHONBASHI
TROUBLESOME CAMERA OTAKU
(SEE HANA-KIMI VOLS. 1-4 FOR DETAILS)
FFFSH
HEY, LONG TIME NO SEE! WHAT ARE YOU DOING HERE?
UHMMM
N-N-NANBA?!

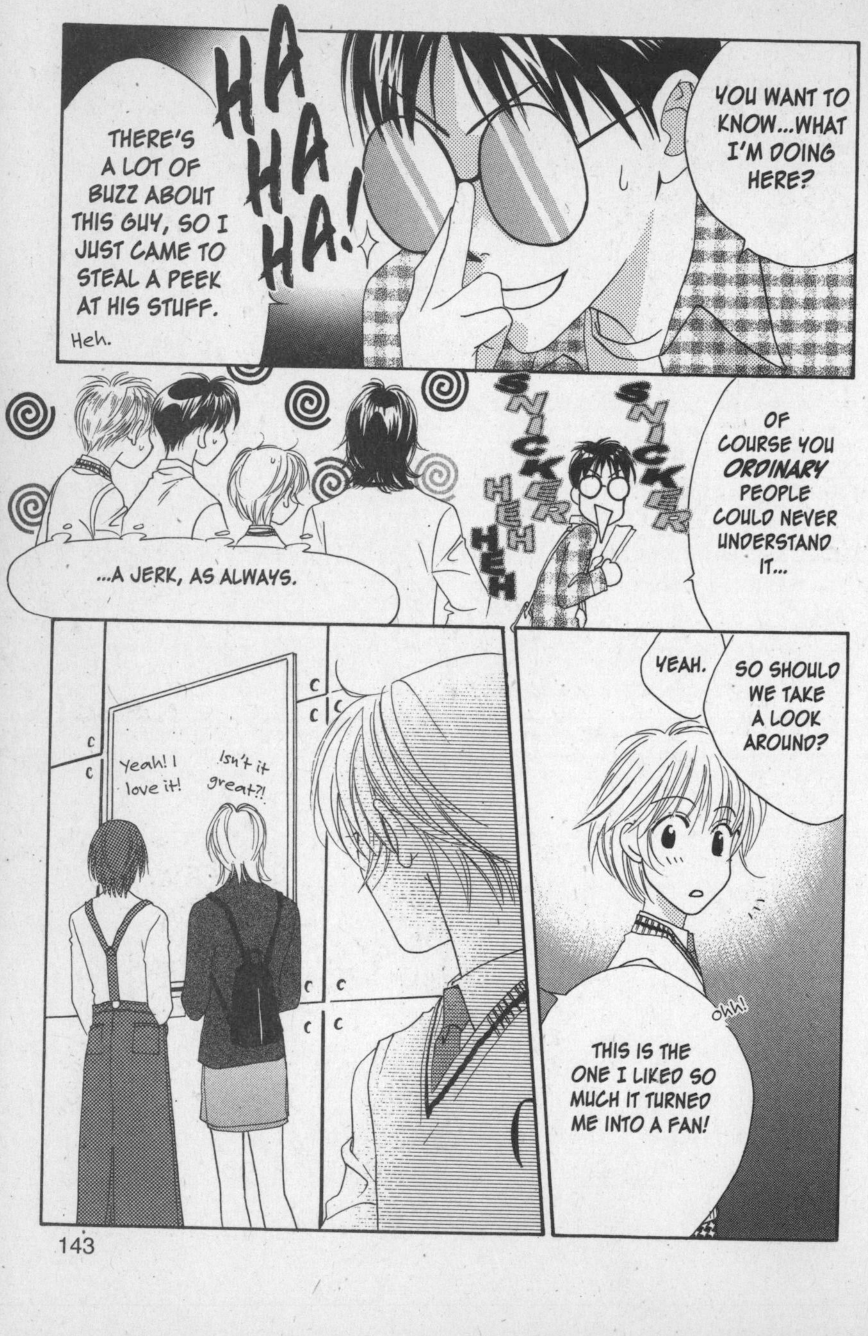
YOU WANT TO KNOW...WHAT I'M DOING HERE?
HA HA HA!
THERE'S A LOT OF BUZZ ABOUT THIS GUY, SO I JUST CAME TO STEAL A PEEK AT HIS STUFF.
Heh.
OF COURSE YOU ORDINARY PEOPLE COULD NEVER UNDERSTAND IT...
SNICKER SNICKER
HEH HEH HEH
...A JERK, AS ALWAYS.
SO SHOULD WE TAKE A LOOK AROUND?
YEAH.
Isn't it great?!
Yeah! I love it!
Ohh!
THIS IS THE ONE I LIKED SO MUCH IT TURNED ME INTO A FAN!

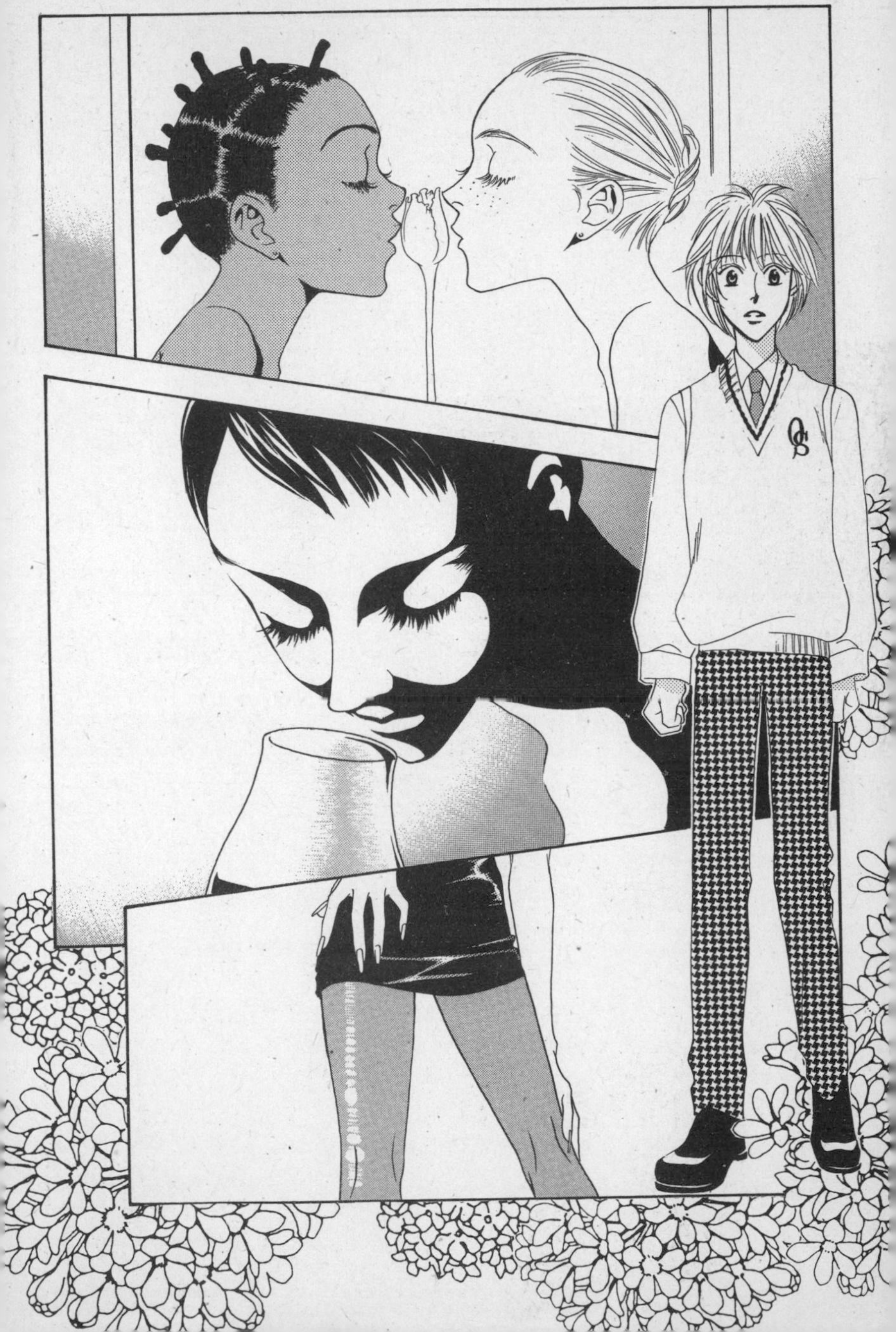

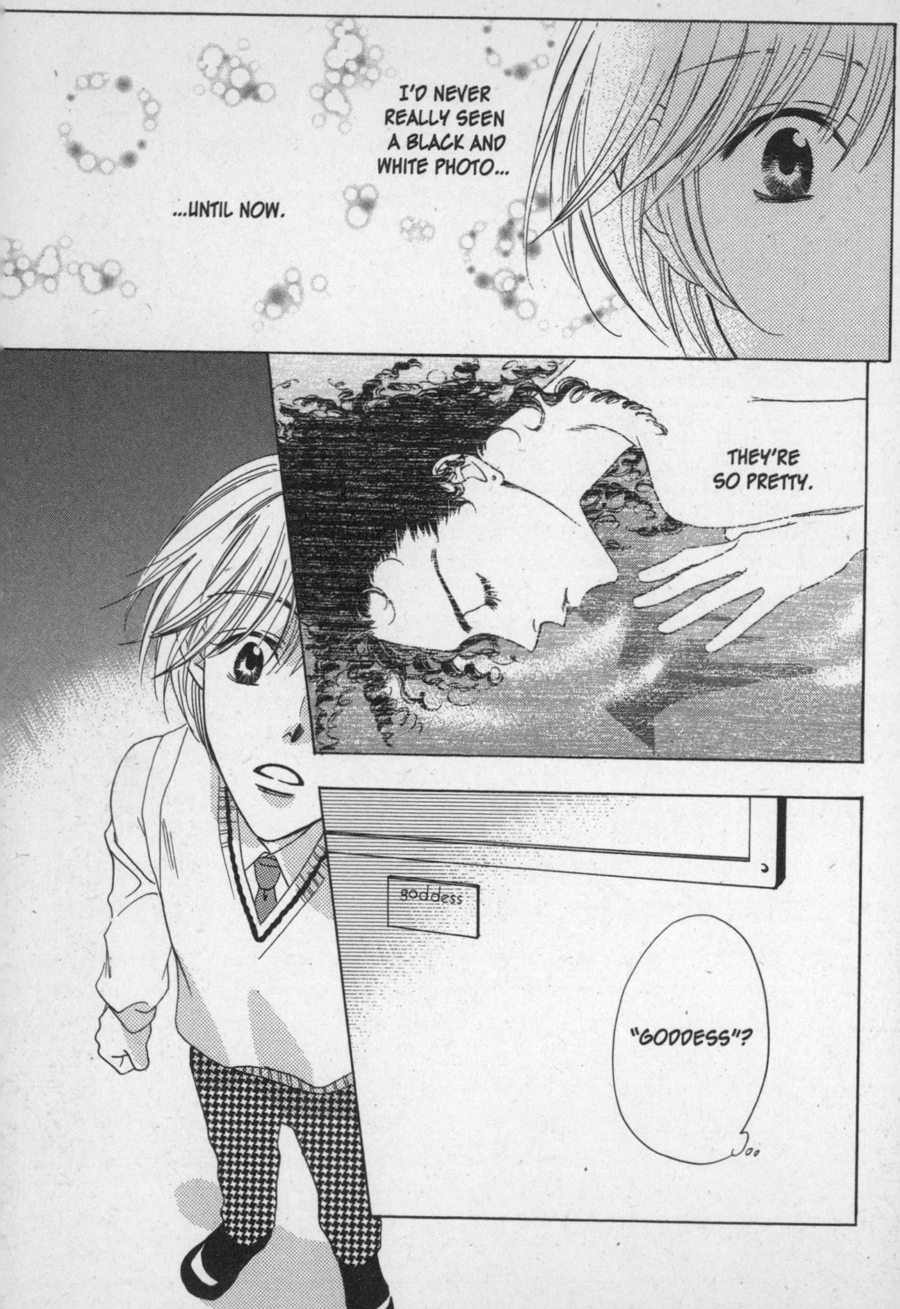
I'D NEVER REALLY SEEN A BLACK AND WHITE PHOTO...
...UNTIL NOW.
THEY'RE SO PRETTY.
goddess
"GODDESS"?

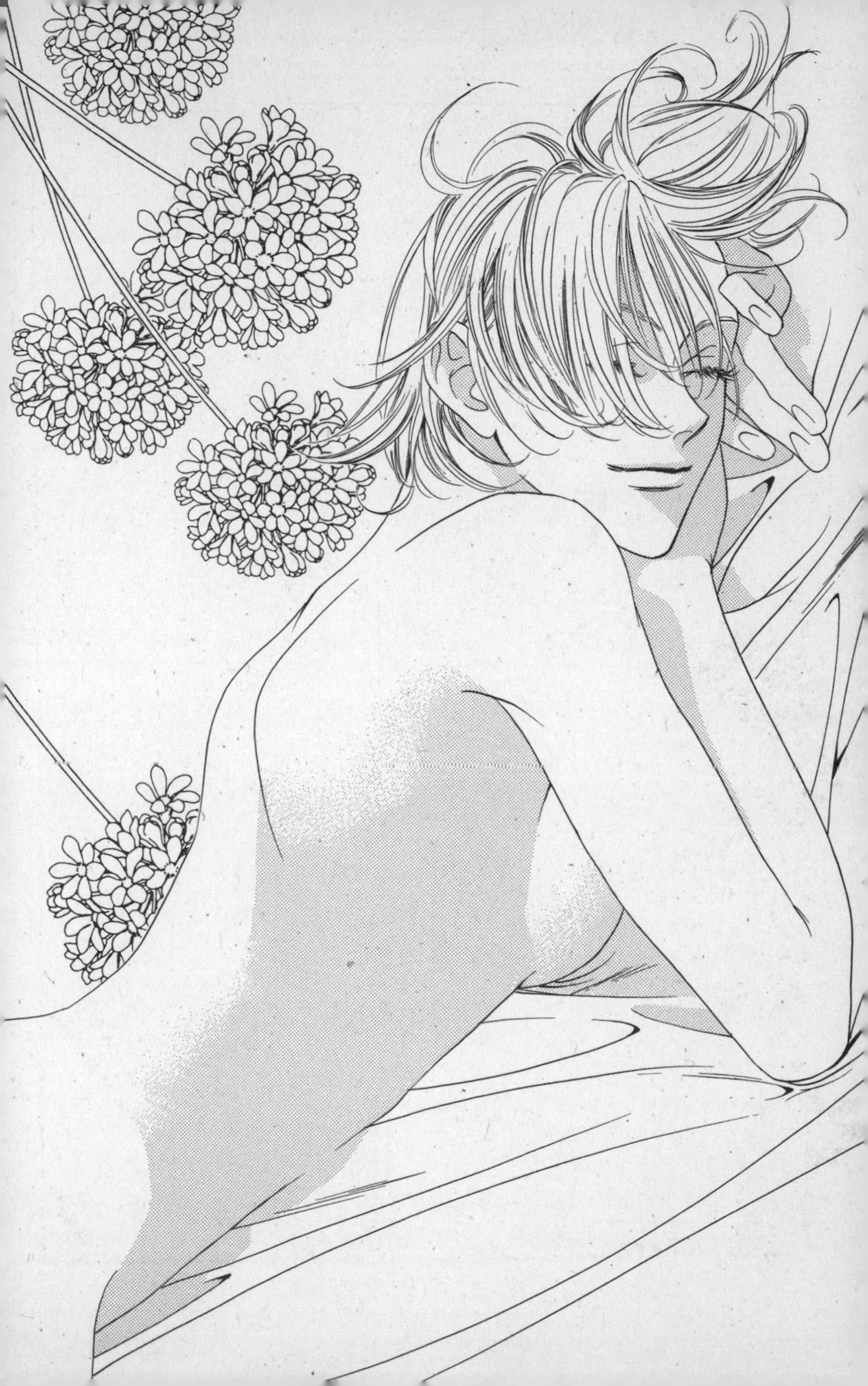

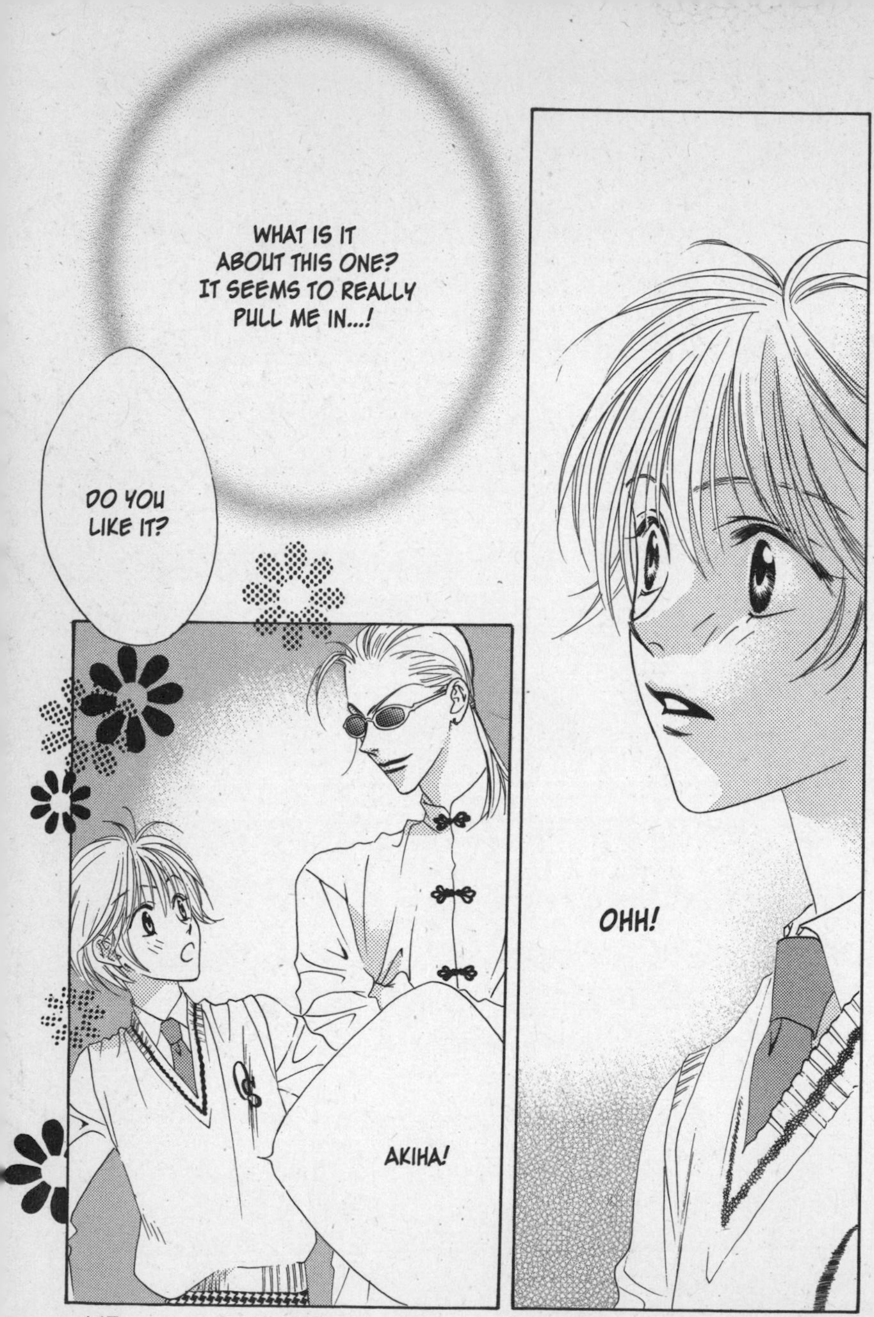
OHH!
WHAT IS IT ABOUT THIS ONE? IT SEEMS TO REALLY PULL ME IN...!
DO YOU LIKE IT?
AKIHA!

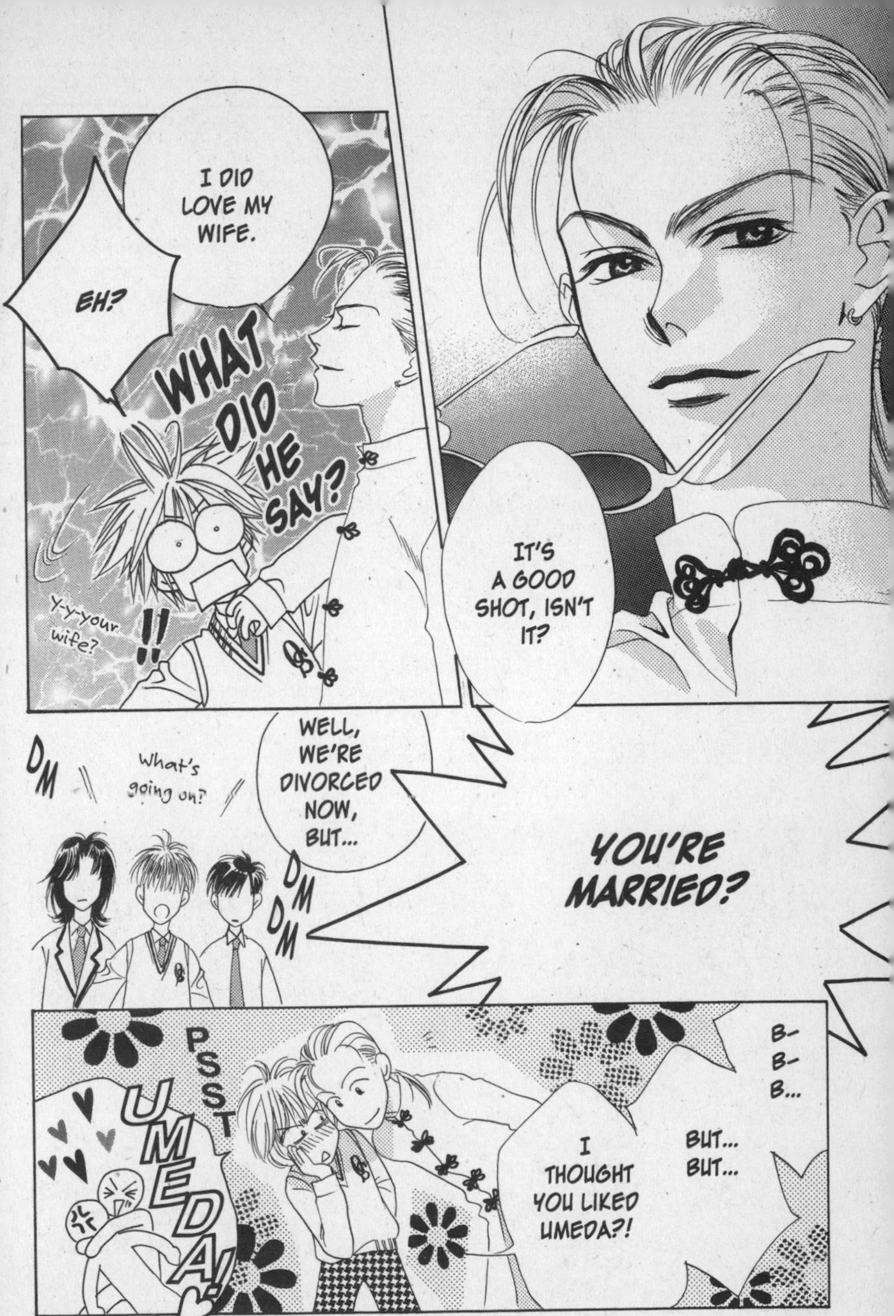

IT'S A GOOD SHOT, ISN'T IT?
I DID LOVE MY WIFE.
EH?
WHAT DID HE SAY?
Y-y-your wife?
!!
YOU'RE MARRIED?
WELL, WE'RE DIVORCED NOW, BUT...
DM DM DM
What's going on?
DM
B-B-B...
BUT... BUT...
I THOUGHT YOU LIKED UMEDA?!
PSST
UMEDA!

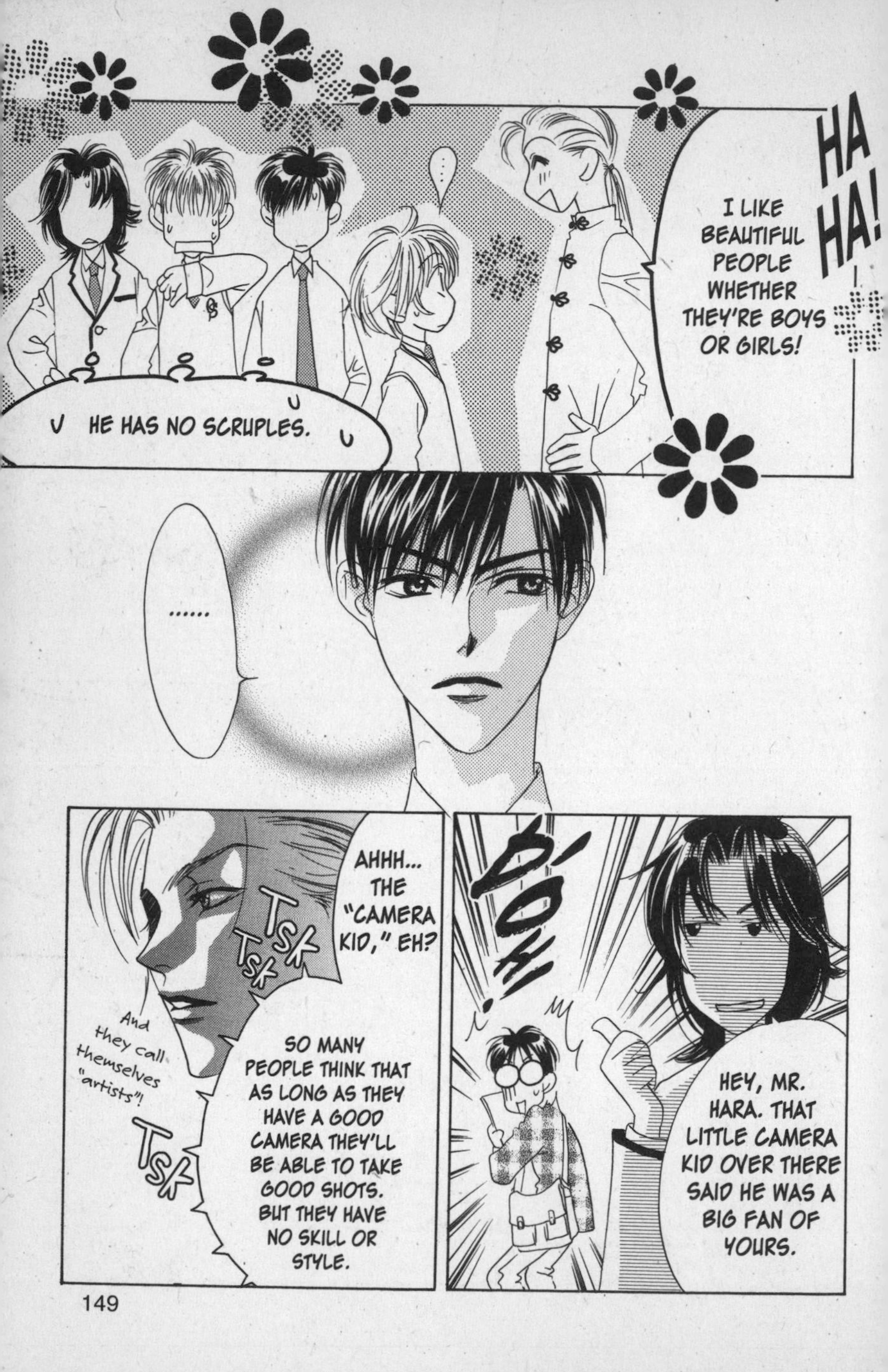
HA HA!
I LIKE BEAUTIFUL PEOPLE WHETHER THEY'RE BOYS OR GIRLS!
HE HAS NO SCRUPLES.
......
DOH!
HEY, MR. HARA. THAT LITTLE CAMERA KID OVER THERE SAID HE WAS A BIG FAN OF YOURS.
AHHH... THE "CAMERA KID," EH?
TSK TSK
SO MANY PEOPLE THINK THAT AS LONG AS THEY HAVE A GOOD CAMERA THEY'LL BE ABLE TO TAKE GOOD SHOTS. BUT THEY HAVE NO SKILL OR STYLE.
TSK
And they call themselves "artists"!

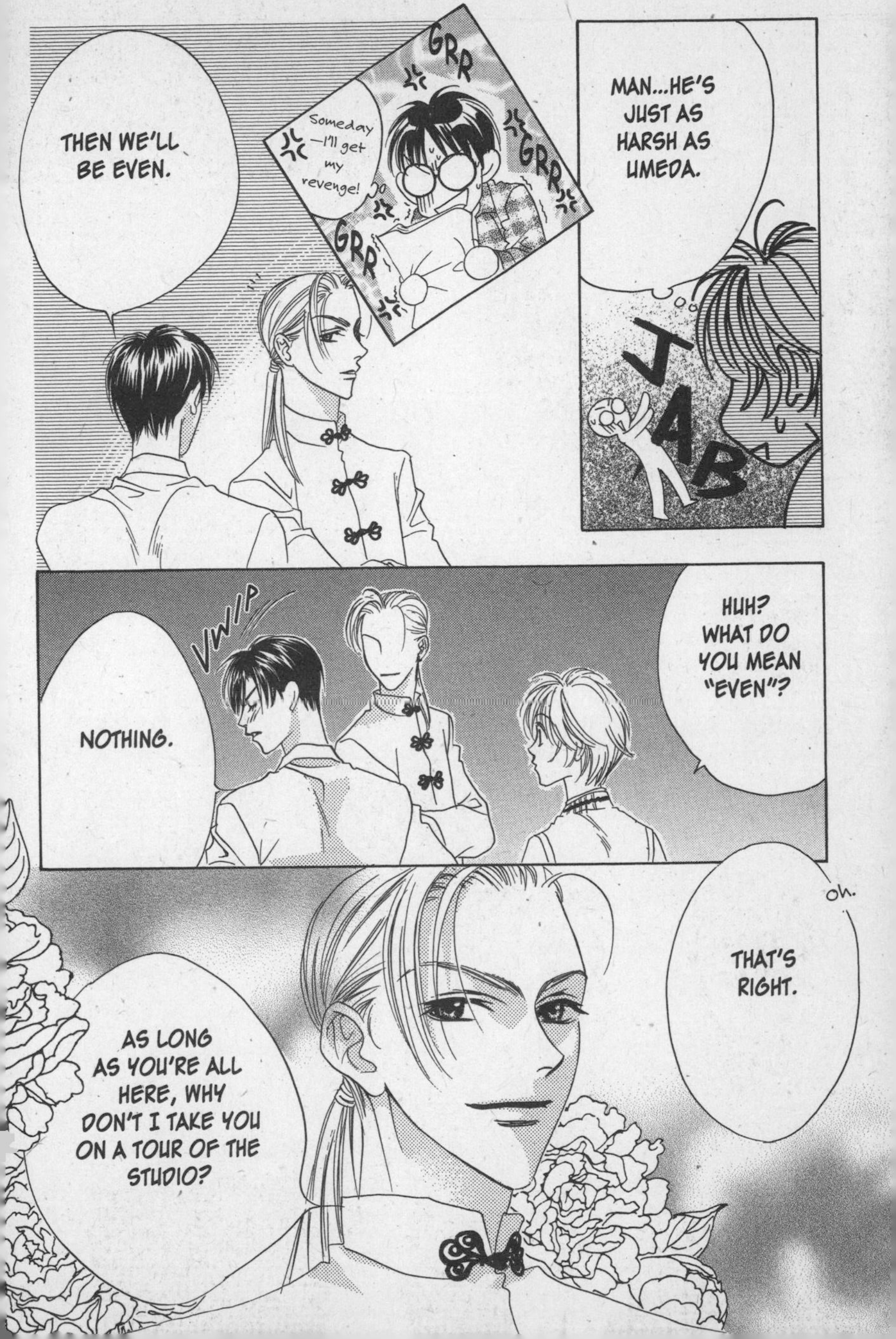
MAN...HE'S JUST AS HARSH AS UMEDA.
JAB
GRR
GRR
Someday—I'll get my revenge!
GRR
THEN WE'LL BE EVEN.
HUH? WHAT DO YOU MEAN "EVEN"?
VWIP
NOTHING.
oh.
THAT'S RIGHT.
AS LONG AS YOU'RE ALL HERE, WHY DON'T I TAKE YOU ON A TOUR OF THE STUDIO?

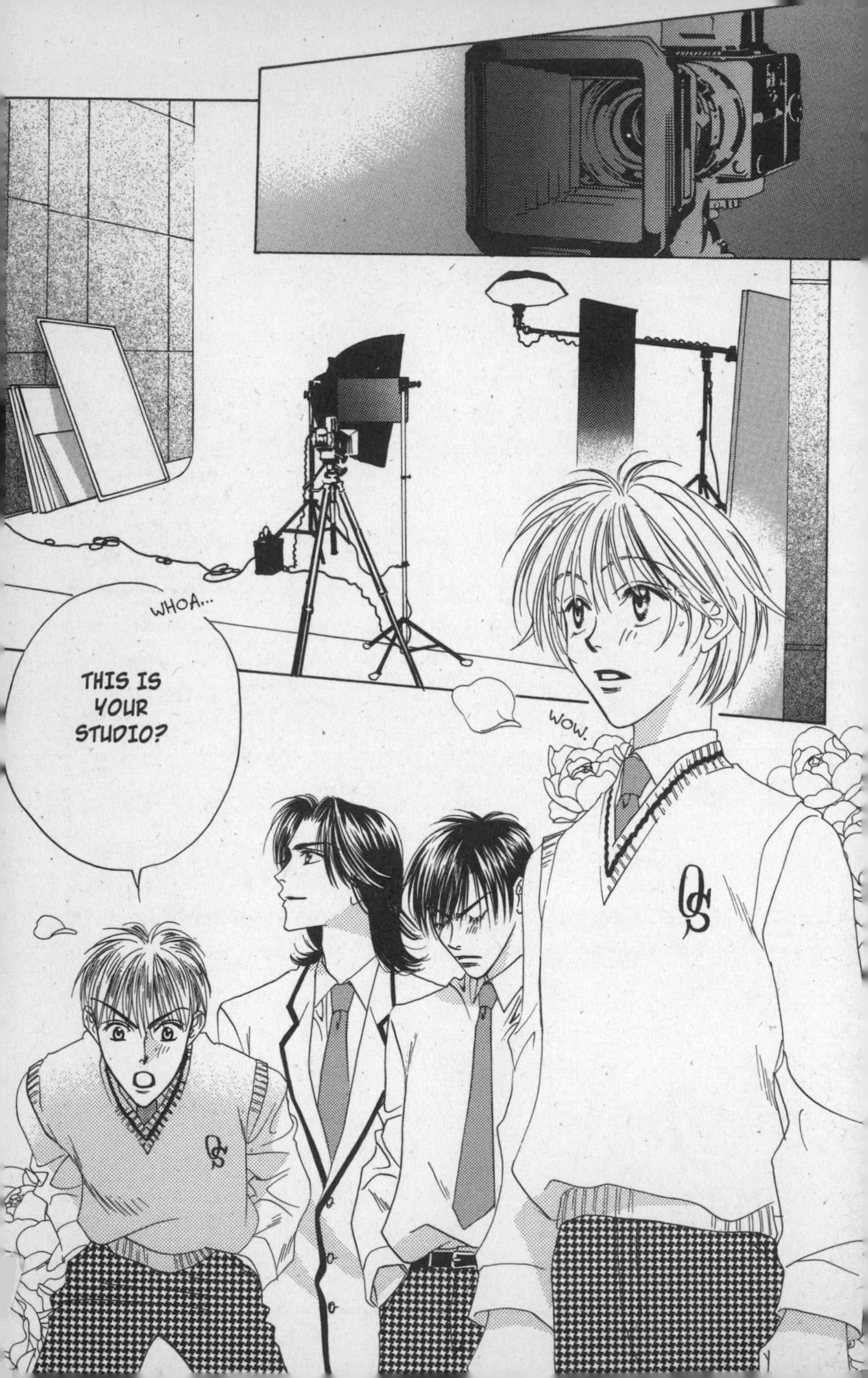
WOW.
WHOA...
THIS IS YOUR STUDIO?

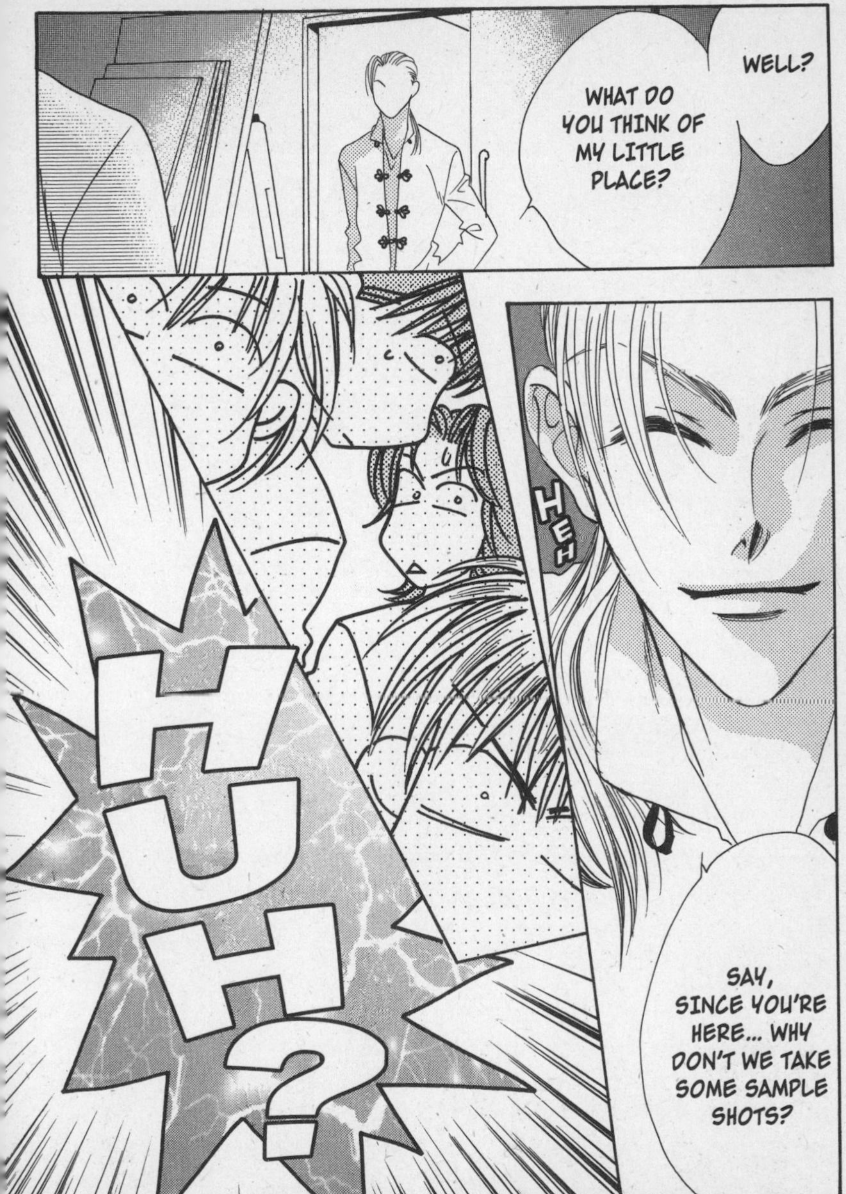
WELL?
WHAT DO YOU THINK OF MY LITTLE PLACE?
HEH
SAY, SINCE YOU'RE HERE... WHY DON'T WE TAKE SOME SAMPLE SHOTS?
HUH?

HANA-KIMI CHAPTER 47/END

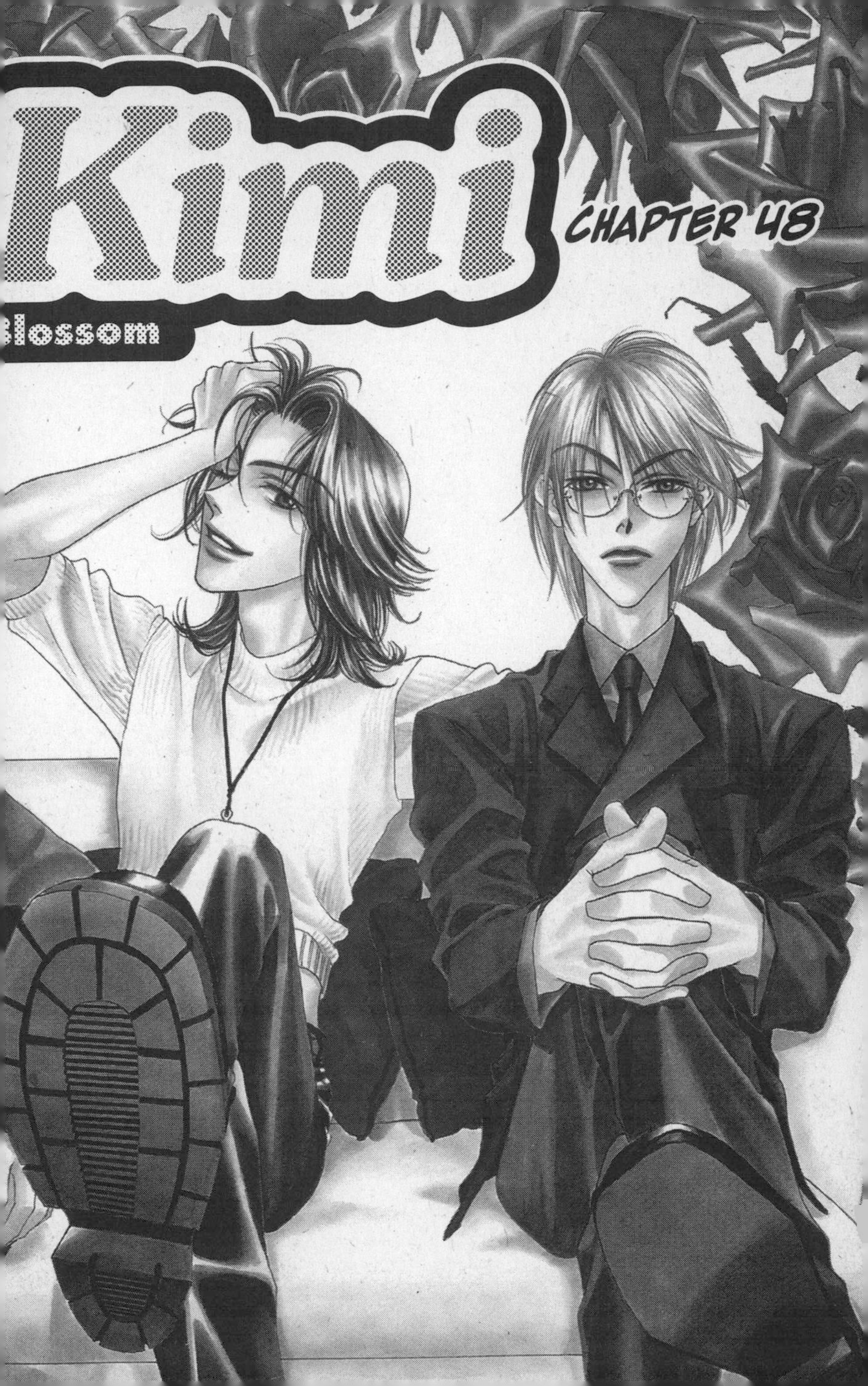
Kimi
Blossom
CHAPTER 48

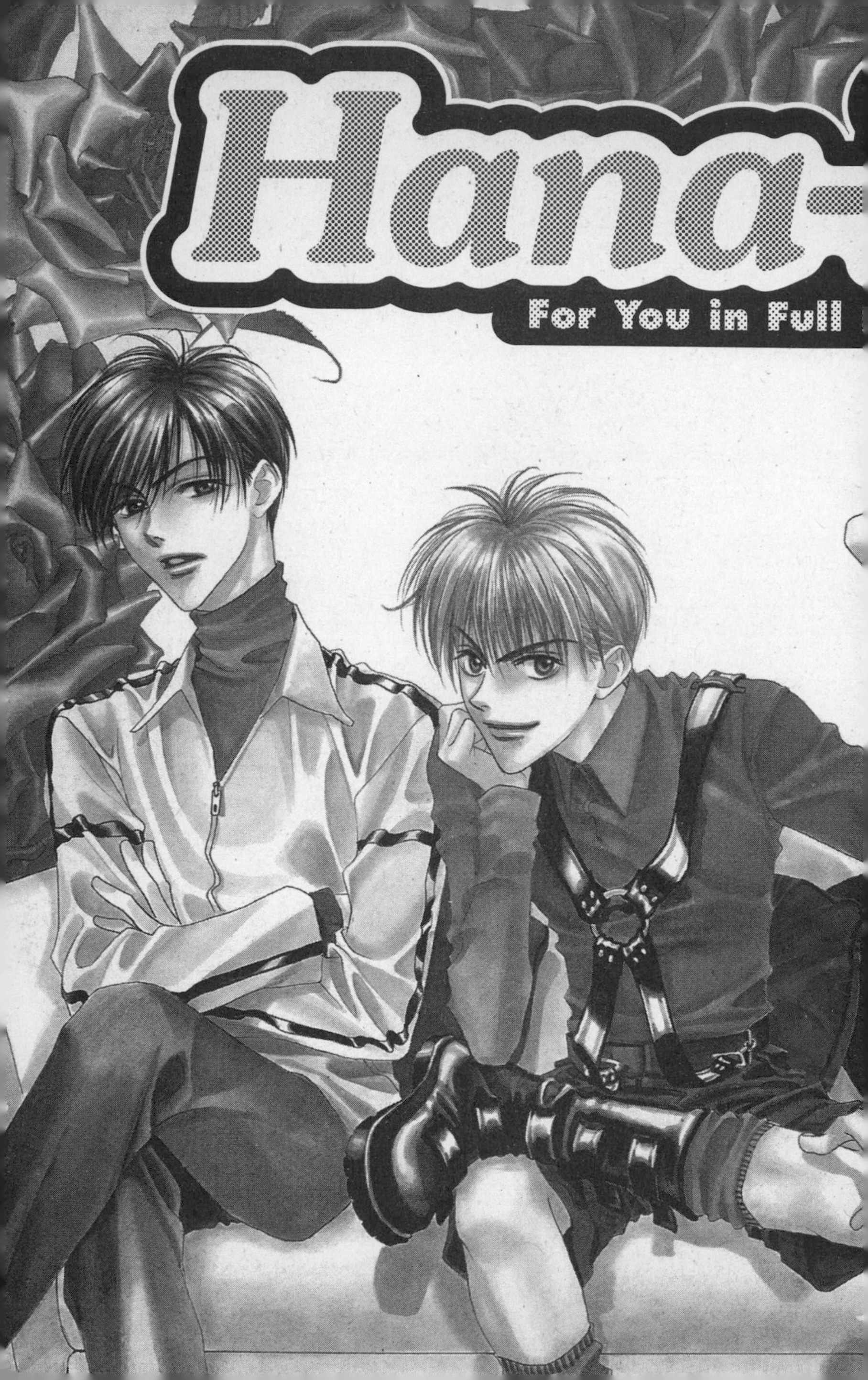
Hana-
For You in Full

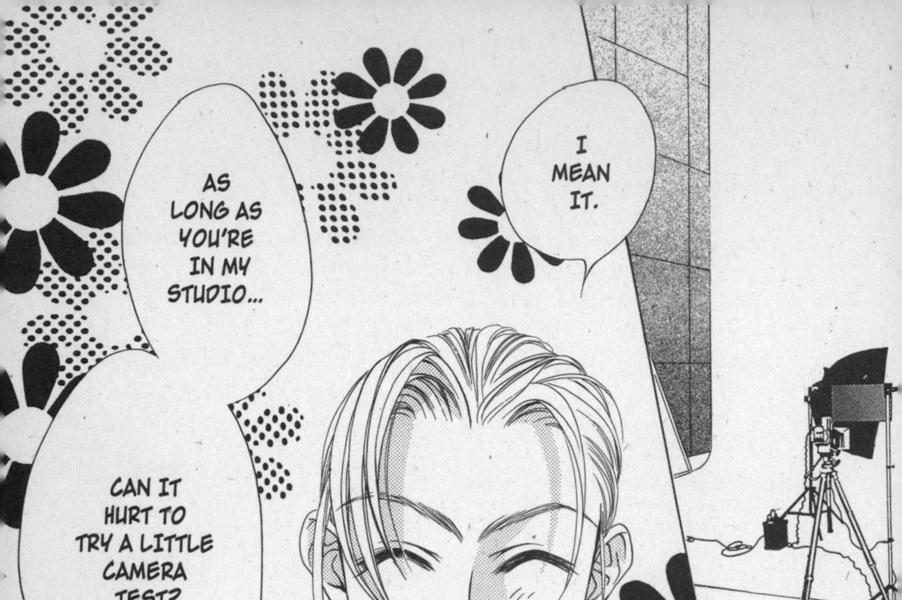
AS LONG AS YOU'RE IN MY STUDIO...
CAN IT HURT TO TRY A LITTLE CAMERA TEST?
I MEAN IT.
GLINT
GLINT

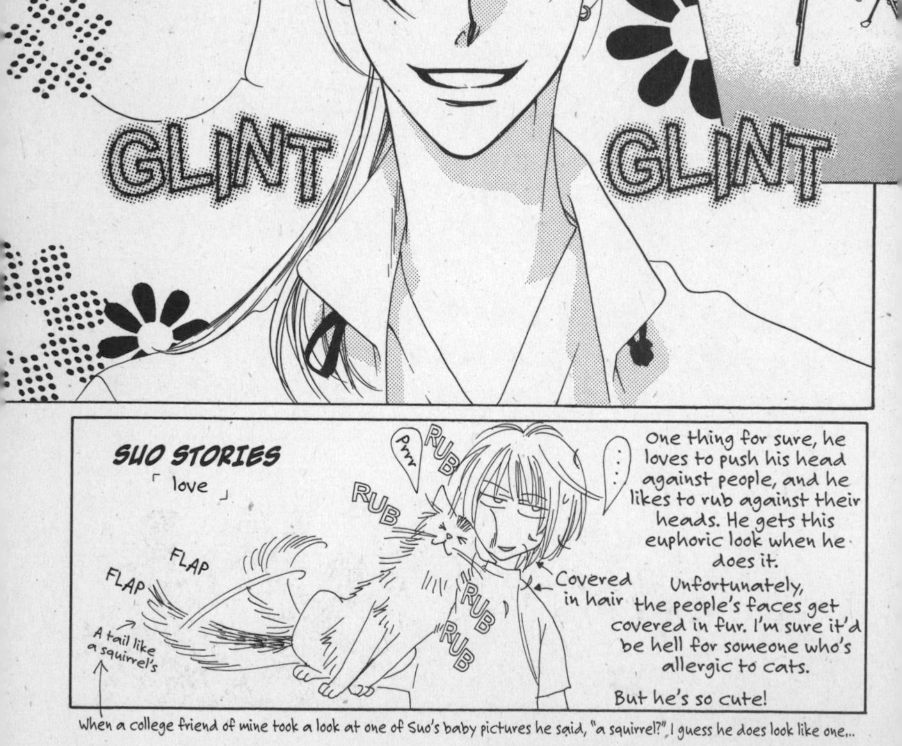
SUO STORIES
「love」
One thing for sure, he loves to push his head against people, and he likes to rub against their heads. He gets this euphoric look when he does it.
Unfortunately, the people's faces get covered in fur. I'm sure it'd be hell for someone who's allergic to cats.
But he's so cute!
...
Purr
RUB
RUB
RUB
RUB
RUB
RUB
Covered in hair
FLAP
FLAP
A tail like a squirrel's

When a college friend of mine took a look at one of Suo's baby pictures he said, "a squirrel?" I guess he does look like one...

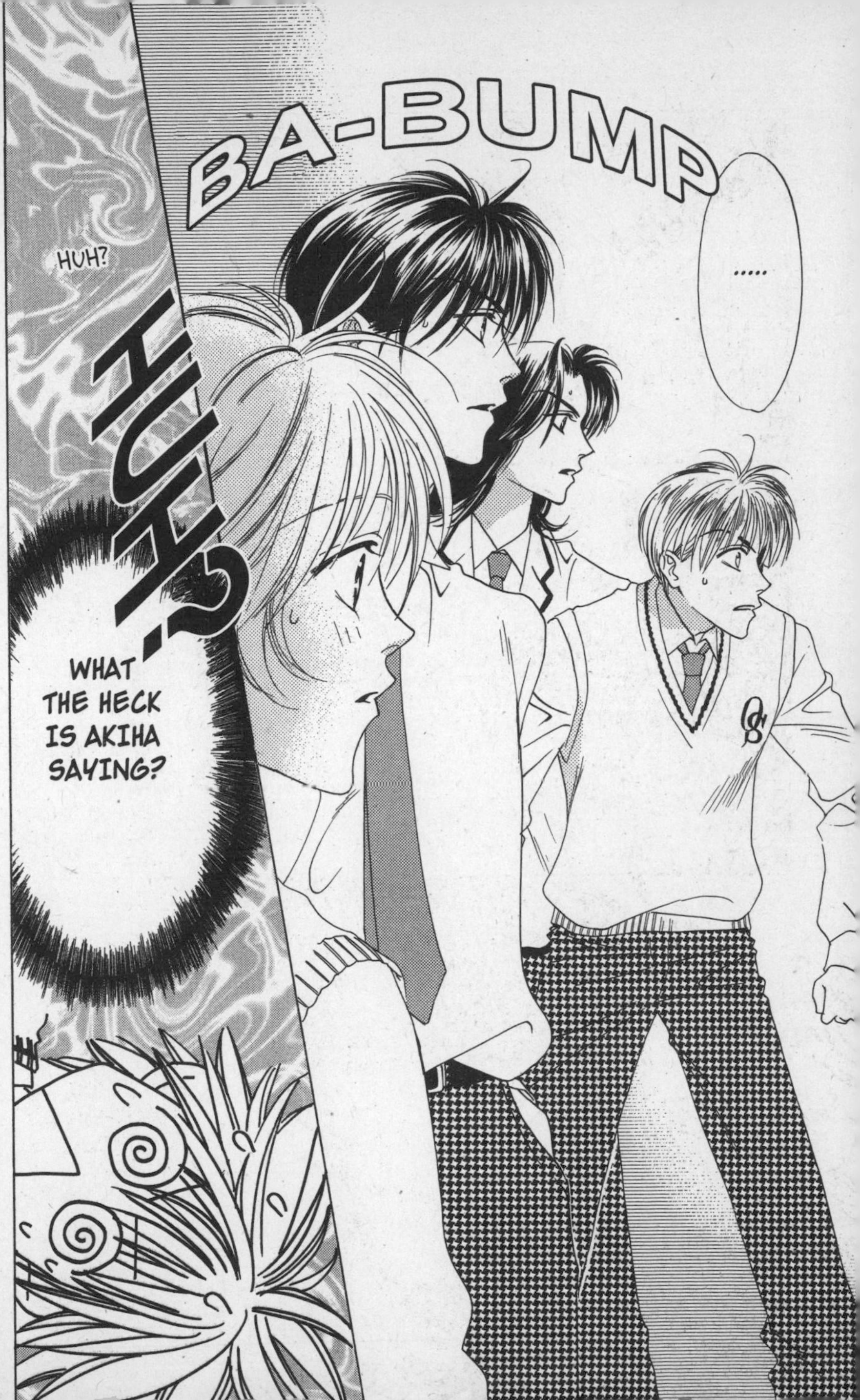
BA-BUMP
.....
HUH?
HUH?!
WHAT THE HECK IS AKIHA SAYING?

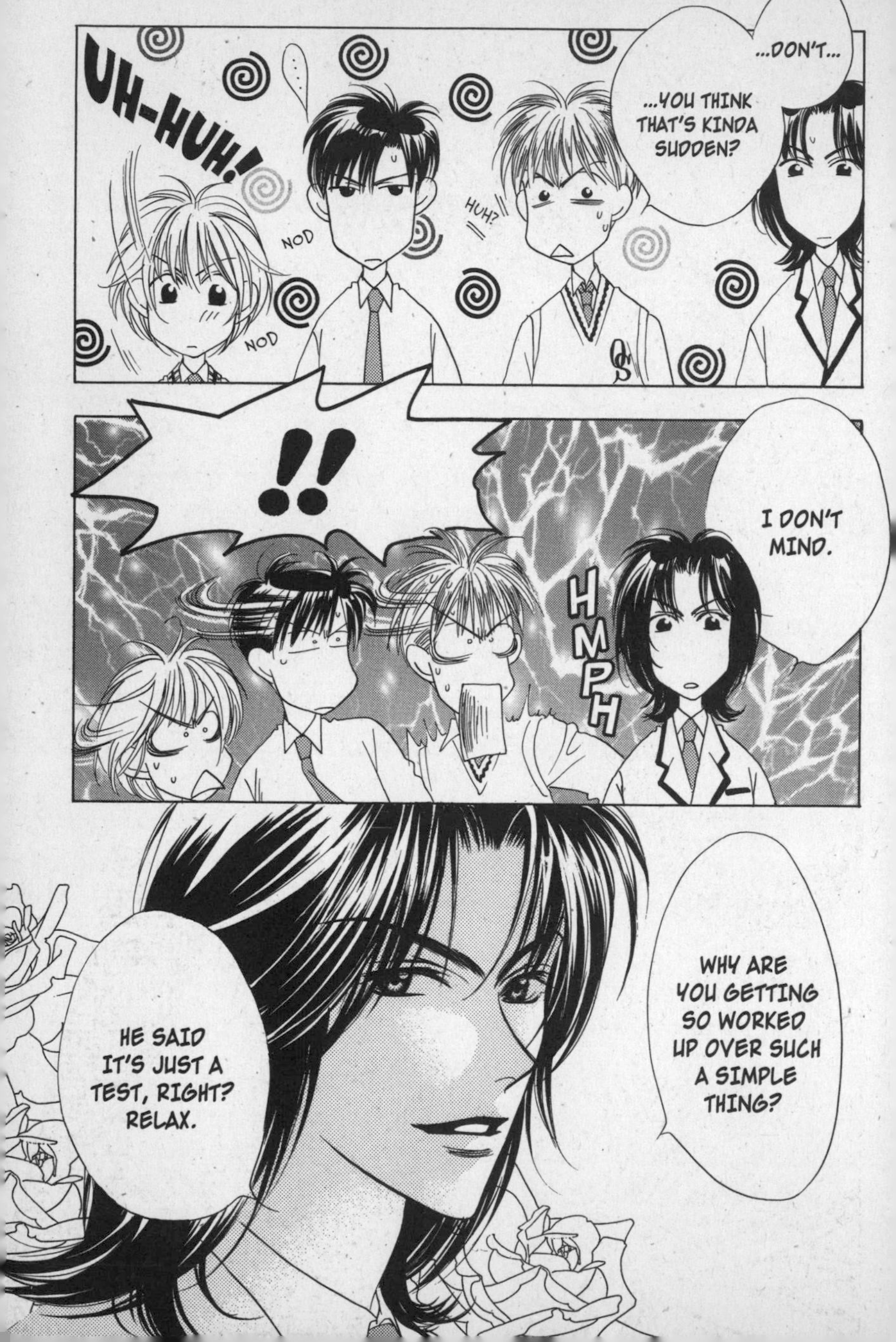
...DON'T...
...YOU THINK THAT'S KINDA SUDDEN?
HUH?
NOD
UH-HUH!
NOD
I DON'T MIND.
HMPH
!!
WHY ARE YOU GETTING SO WORKED UP OVER SUCH A SIMPLE THING?
HE SAID IT'S JUST A TEST, RIGHT? RELAX.

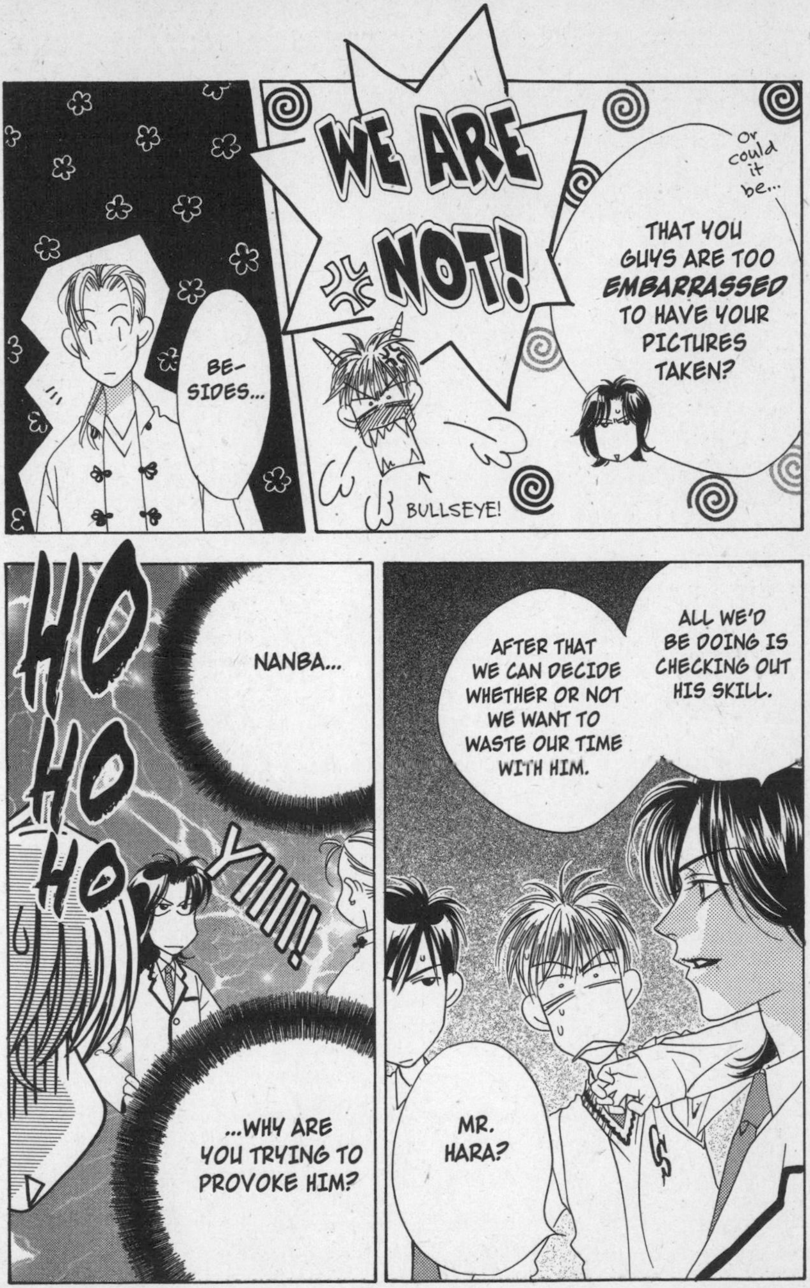
Or could it be...
THAT YOU GUYS ARE TOO EMBARRASSED TO HAVE YOUR PICTURES TAKEN?
WE ARE NOT!
BULLSEYE!
BE-SIDES...
ALL WE'D BE DOING IS CHECKING OUT HIS SKILL.
AFTER THAT WE CAN DECIDE WHETHER OR NOT WE WANT TO WASTE OUR TIME WITH HIM.
MR. HARA?
NANBA...
...WHY ARE YOU TRYING TO PROVOKE HIM?
HO HO HO
YIIII!!

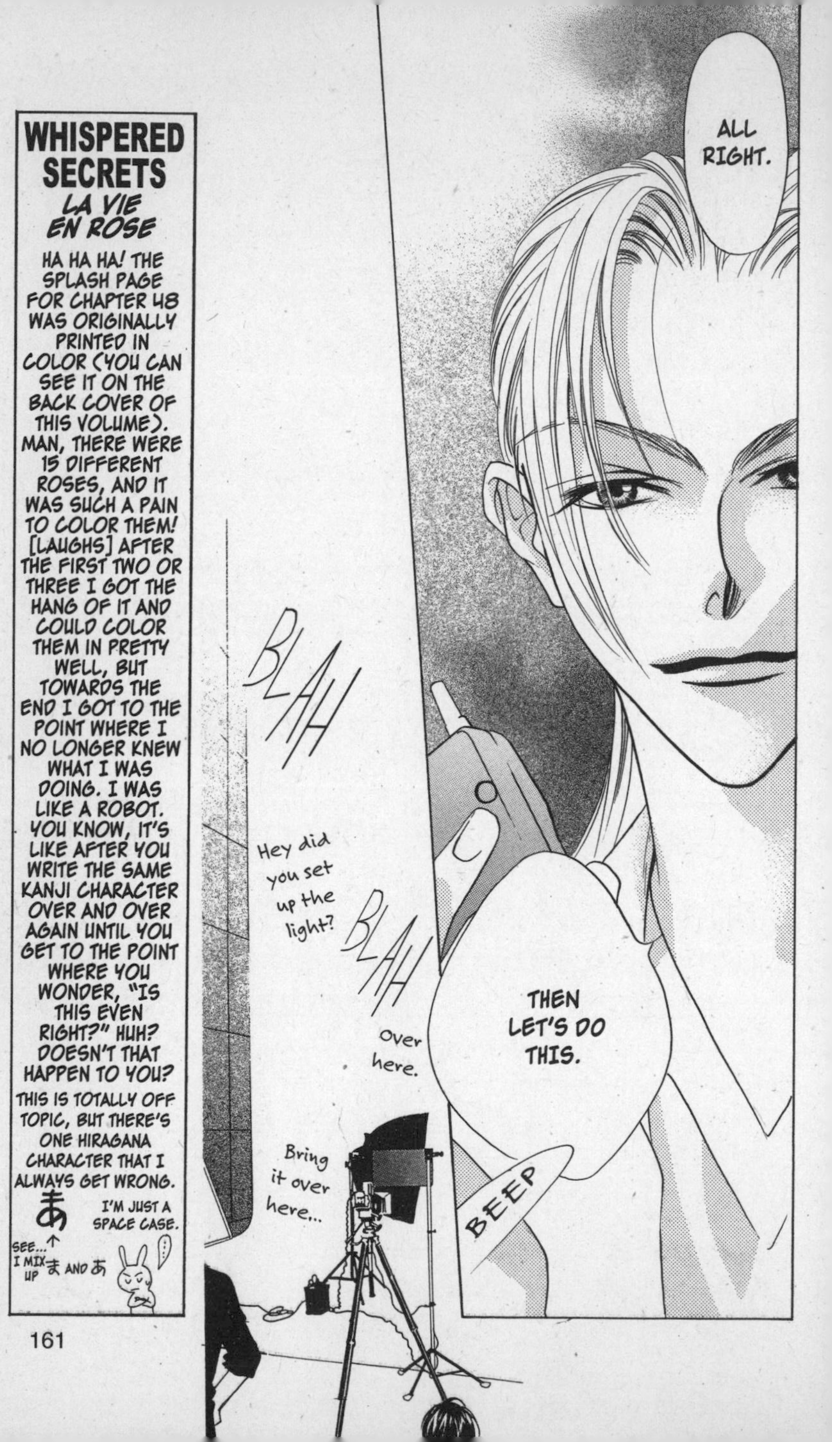
ALL RIGHT.
THEN LET'S DO THIS.
BEEP
BLAH
Hey did you set up the light?
BLAH
Over here.
Bring it over here...

WHISPERED SECRETS

LA VIE EN ROSE

HA HA HA! THE SPLASH PAGE FOR CHAPTER 48 WAS ORIGINALLY PRINTED IN COLOR (YOU CAN SEE IT ON THE BACK COVER OF THIS VOLUME). MAN, THERE WERE 15 DIFFERENT ROSES, AND IT WAS SUCH A PAIN TO COLOR THEM! [LAUGHS] AFTER THE FIRST TWO OR THREE I GOT THE HANG OF IT AND COULD COLOR THEM IN PRETTY WELL, BUT TOWARDS THE END I GOT TO THE POINT WHERE I NO LONGER KNEW WHAT I WAS DOING. I WAS LIKE A ROBOT. YOU KNOW, IT'S LIKE AFTER YOU WRITE THE SAME KANJI CHARACTER OVER AND OVER AGAIN UNTIL YOU GET TO THE POINT WHERE YOU WONDER, "IS THIS EVEN RIGHT?" HUH? DOESN'T THAT HAPPEN TO YOU?

THIS IS TOTALLY OFF TOPIC, BUT THERE'S ONE HIRAGANA CHARACTER THAT I ALWAYS GET WRONG.

あ I'M JUST A SPACE CASE.

SEE... ↑ I MIX UP ま AND あ

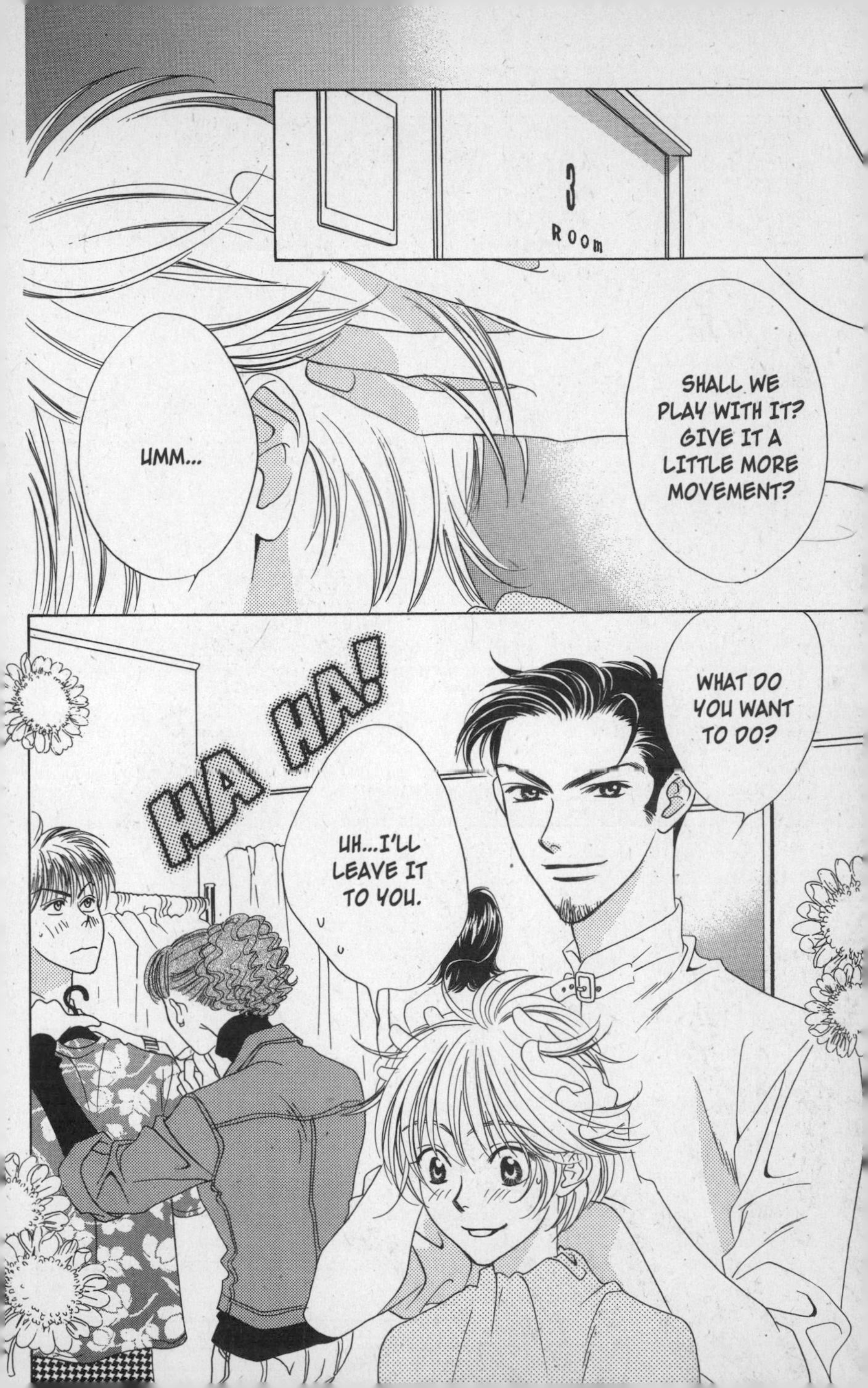
3
ROOM
SHALL WE PLAY WITH IT? GIVE IT A LITTLE MORE MOVEMENT?
UMM...
WHAT DO YOU WANT TO DO?
HA HA!
UH...I'LL LEAVE IT TO YOU.

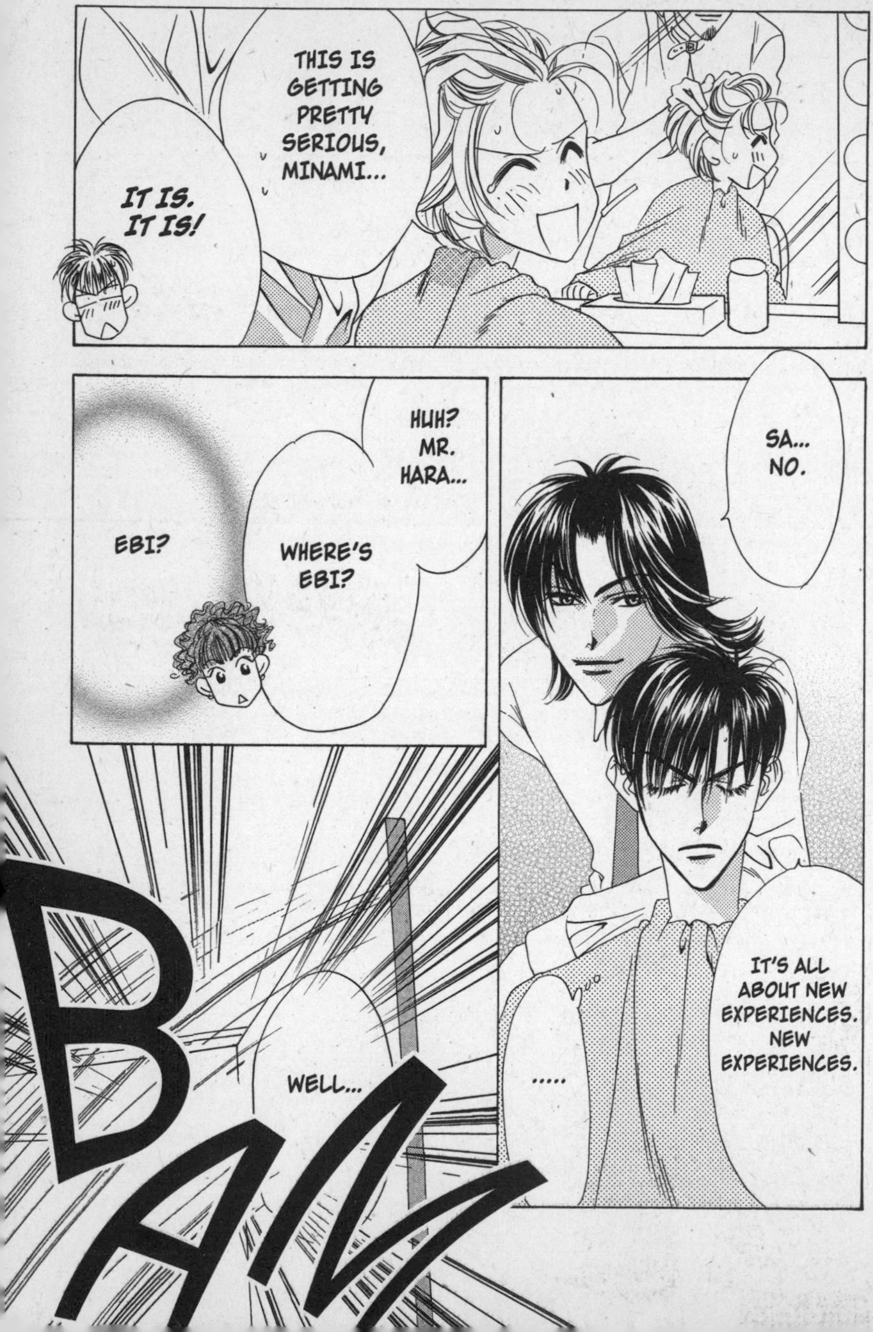
THIS IS GETTING PRETTY SERIOUS, MINAMI...
IT IS. IT IS!
SA... NO.
IT'S ALL ABOUT NEW EXPERIENCES. NEW EXPERIENCES.
.....
HUH? MR. HARA...
WHERE'S EBI?
EBI?
WELL...
BAN

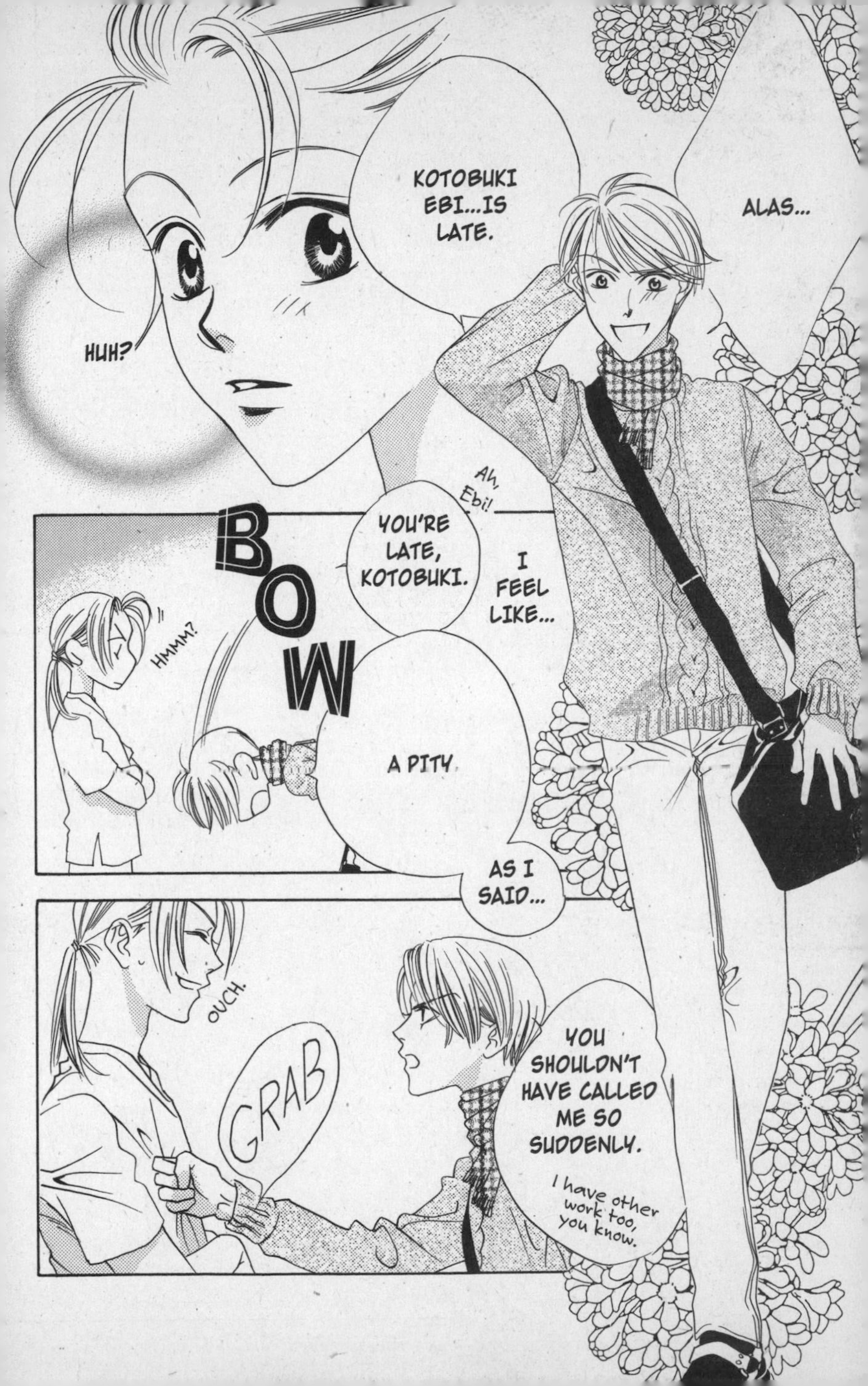
ALAS...
KOTOBUKI EBI...IS LATE.
HUH?
I FEEL LIKE...
A PITY
AS I SAID...
Ah, Ebi!
YOU'RE LATE, KOTOBUKI.
BOW
HMMM?
YOU SHOULDN'T HAVE CALLED ME SO SUDDENLY.
I have other work too, you know.
GRAB
OUCH.

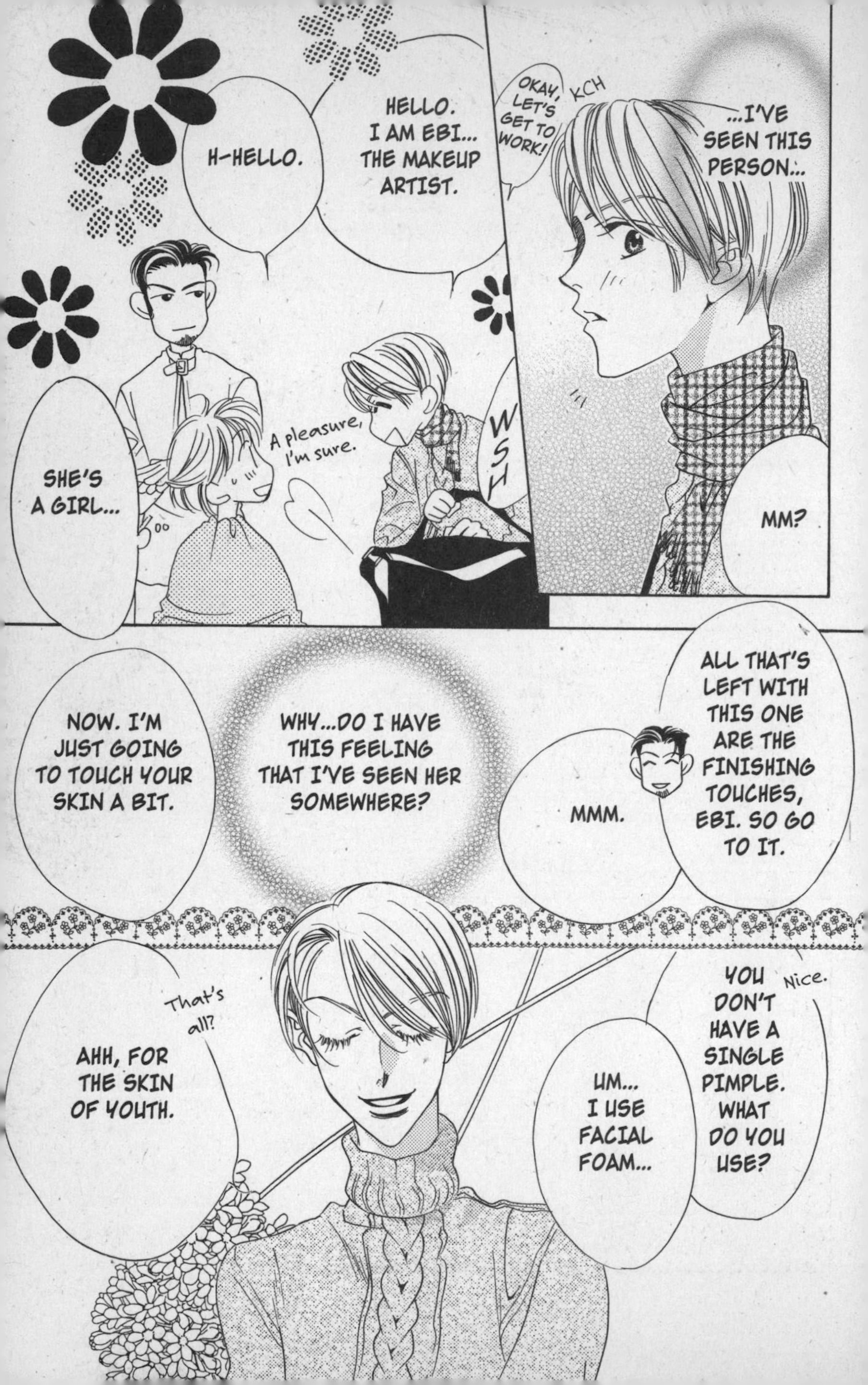
OKAY, LET'S GET TO WORK!
KCH
...I'VE SEEN THIS PERSON...
MM?
HELLO. I AM EBI... THE MAKEUP ARTIST.
H-HELLO.
WSH
A pleasure, I'm sure.
SHE'S A GIRL...
ALL THAT'S LEFT WITH THIS ONE ARE THE FINISHING TOUCHES, EBI. SO GO TO IT.
MMM.
WHY...DO I HAVE THIS FEELING THAT I'VE SEEN HER SOMEWHERE?
NOW. I'M JUST GOING TO TOUCH YOUR SKIN A BIT.
Nice.
YOU DON'T HAVE A SINGLE PIMPLE. WHAT DO YOU USE?
UM... I USE FACIAL FOAM...
That's all?
AHH, FOR THE SKIN OF YOUTH.

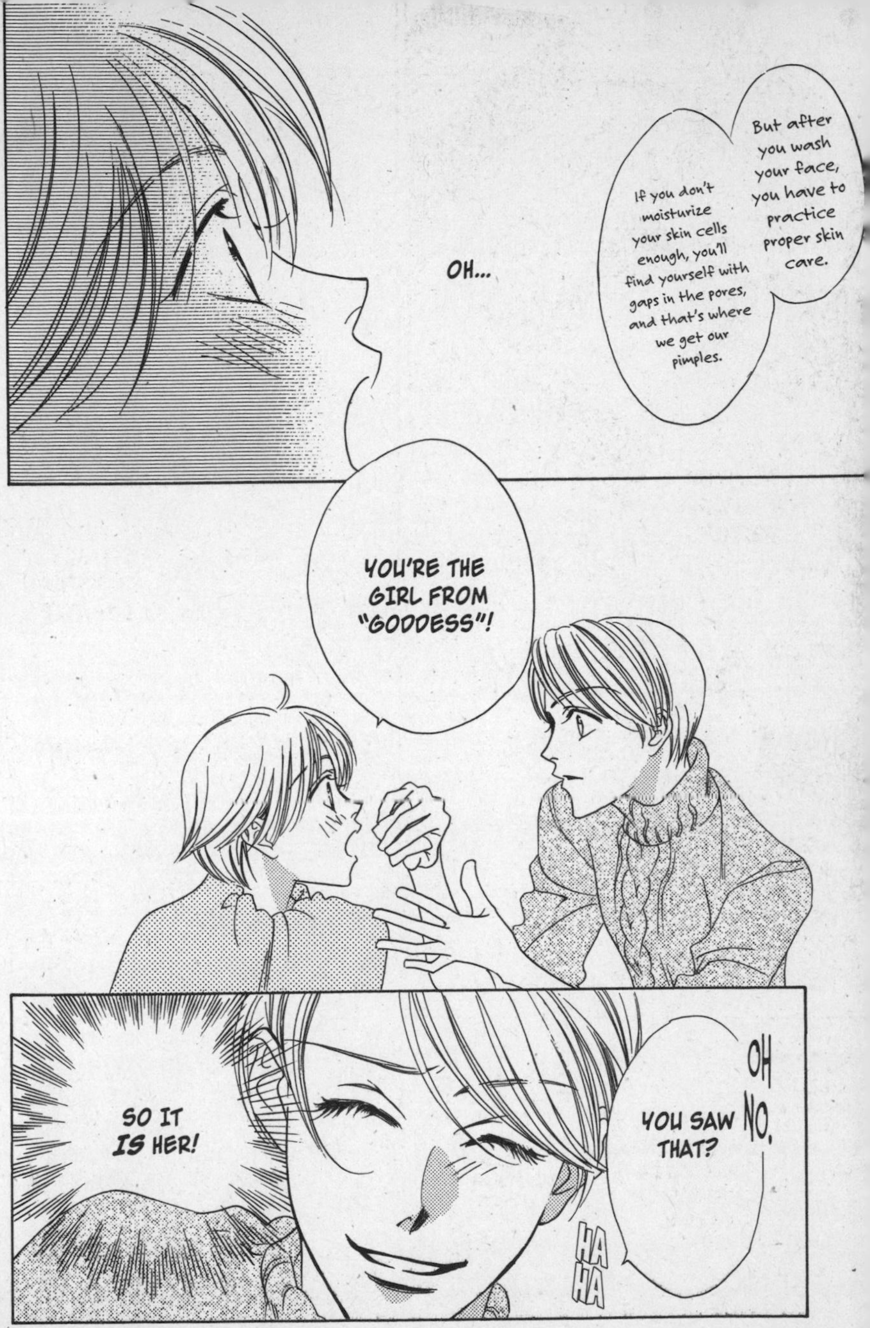
But after you wash your face, you have to practice proper skin care.
If you don't moisturize your skin cells enough, you'll find yourself with gaps in the pores, and that's where we get our pimples.
OH...
YOU'RE THE GIRL FROM "GODDESS"!
OH NO.
YOU SAW THAT?
HA HA
SO IT IS HER!

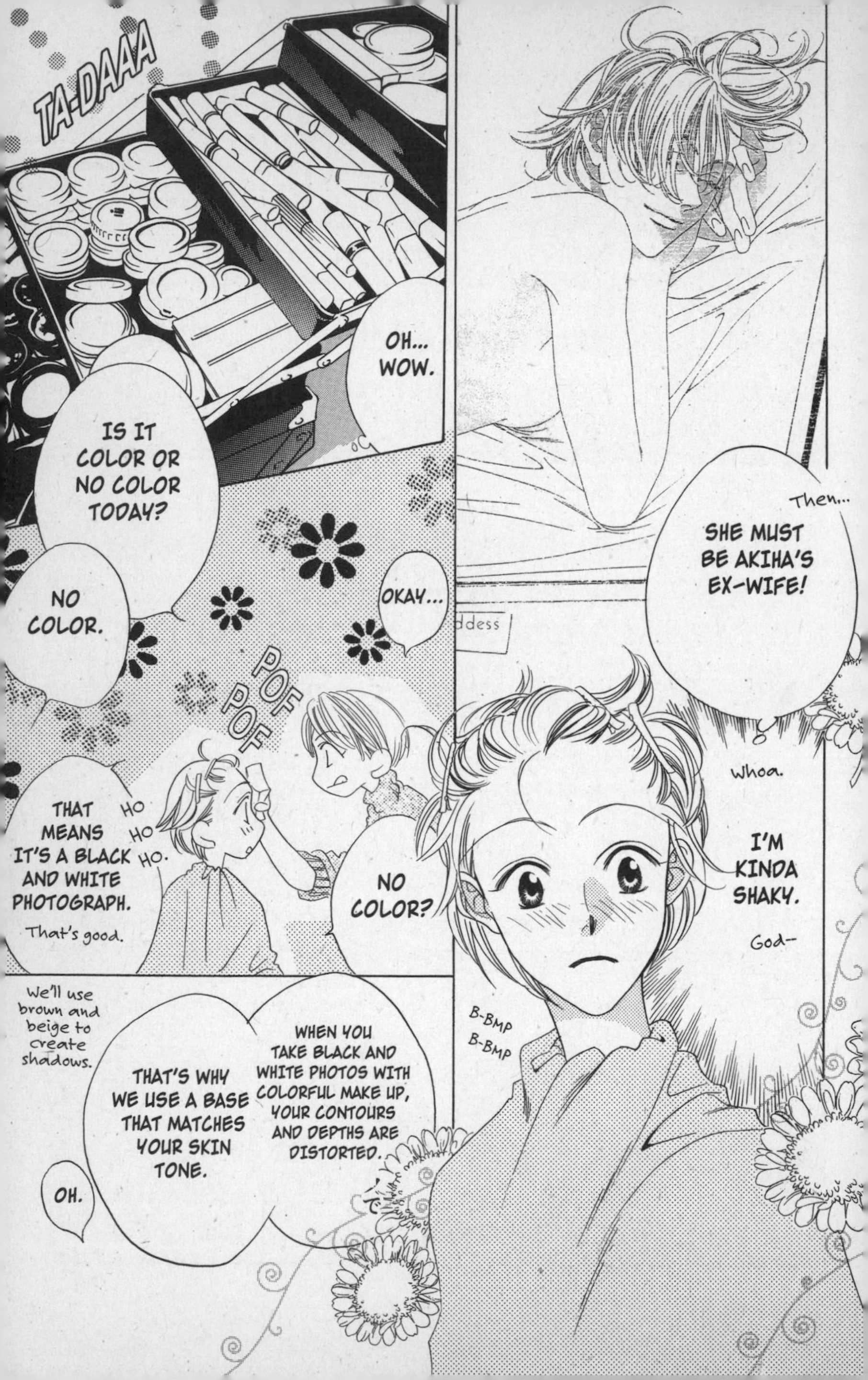
Then...
SHE MUST BE AKIHA'S EX-WIFE!
Whoa.
I'M KINDA SHAKY.
God-
B-Bmp
B-Bmp
TA-DAAA
OH... WOW.
IS IT COLOR OR NO COLOR TODAY?
OKAY...
NO COLOR.
POF POF
NO COLOR?
THAT MEANS IT'S A BLACK AND WHITE PHOTOGRAPH.
HO HO HO.
That's good.
WHEN YOU TAKE BLACK AND WHITE PHOTOS WITH COLORFUL MAKE UP, YOUR CONTOURS AND DEPTHS ARE DISTORTED.
THAT'S WHY WE USE A BASE THAT MATCHES YOUR SKIN TONE.
We'll use brown and beige to create shadows.
OH.

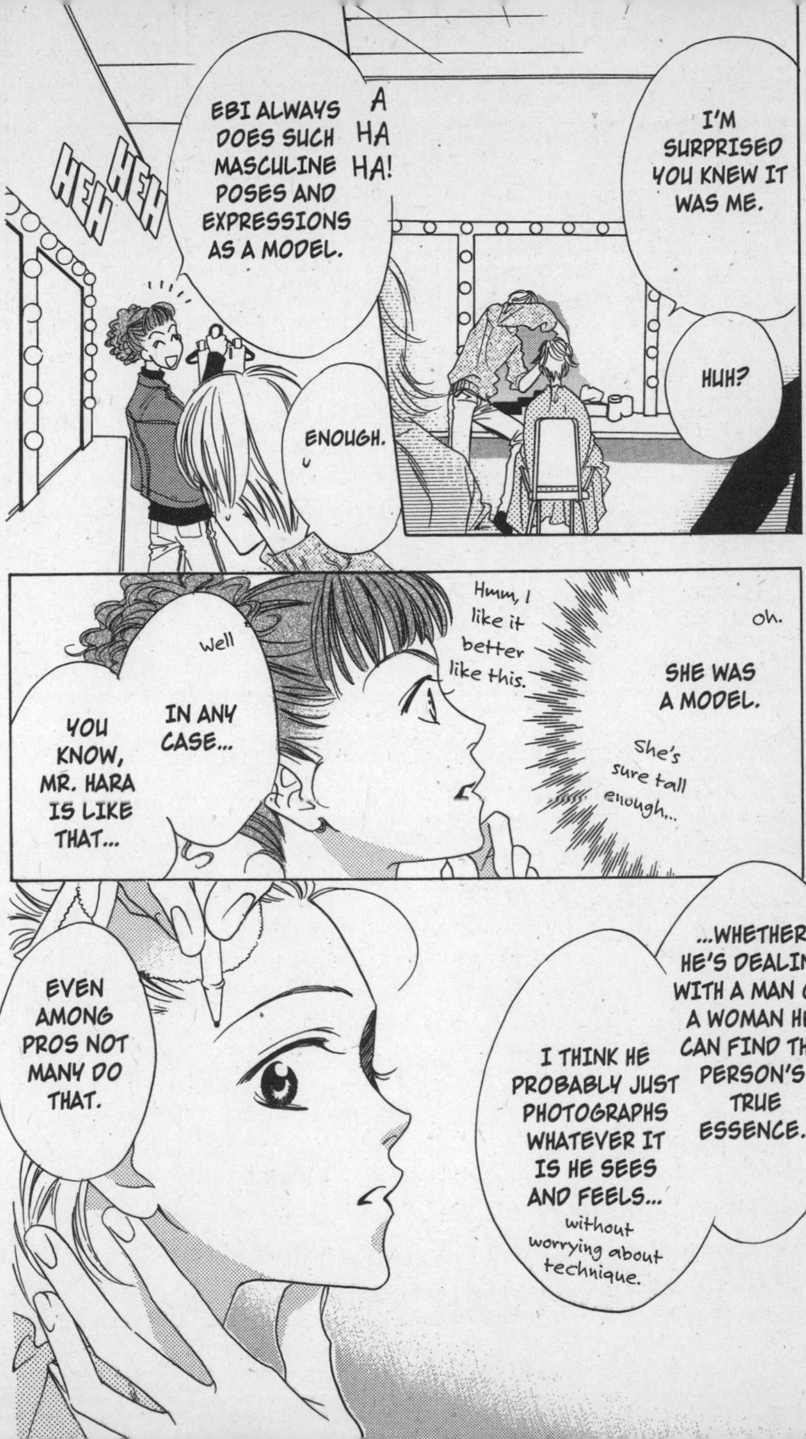
I'M SURPRISED YOU KNEW IT WAS ME.
HUH?
A HA HA!
EBI ALWAYS DOES SUCH MASCULINE POSES AND EXPRESSIONS AS A MODEL.
HEH HEH
ENOUGH.
oh.
SHE WAS A MODEL.
She's sure tall enough...
Hmm, I like it better like this.
well
IN ANY CASE...
YOU KNOW, MR. HARA IS LIKE THAT...
...WHETHER HE'S DEALING WITH A MAN OR A WOMAN HE CAN FIND THE PERSON'S TRUE ESSENCE.
I THINK HE PROBABLY JUST PHOTOGRAPHS WHATEVER IT IS HE SEES AND FEELS...
without worrying about technique.
EVEN AMONG PROS NOT MANY DO THAT.

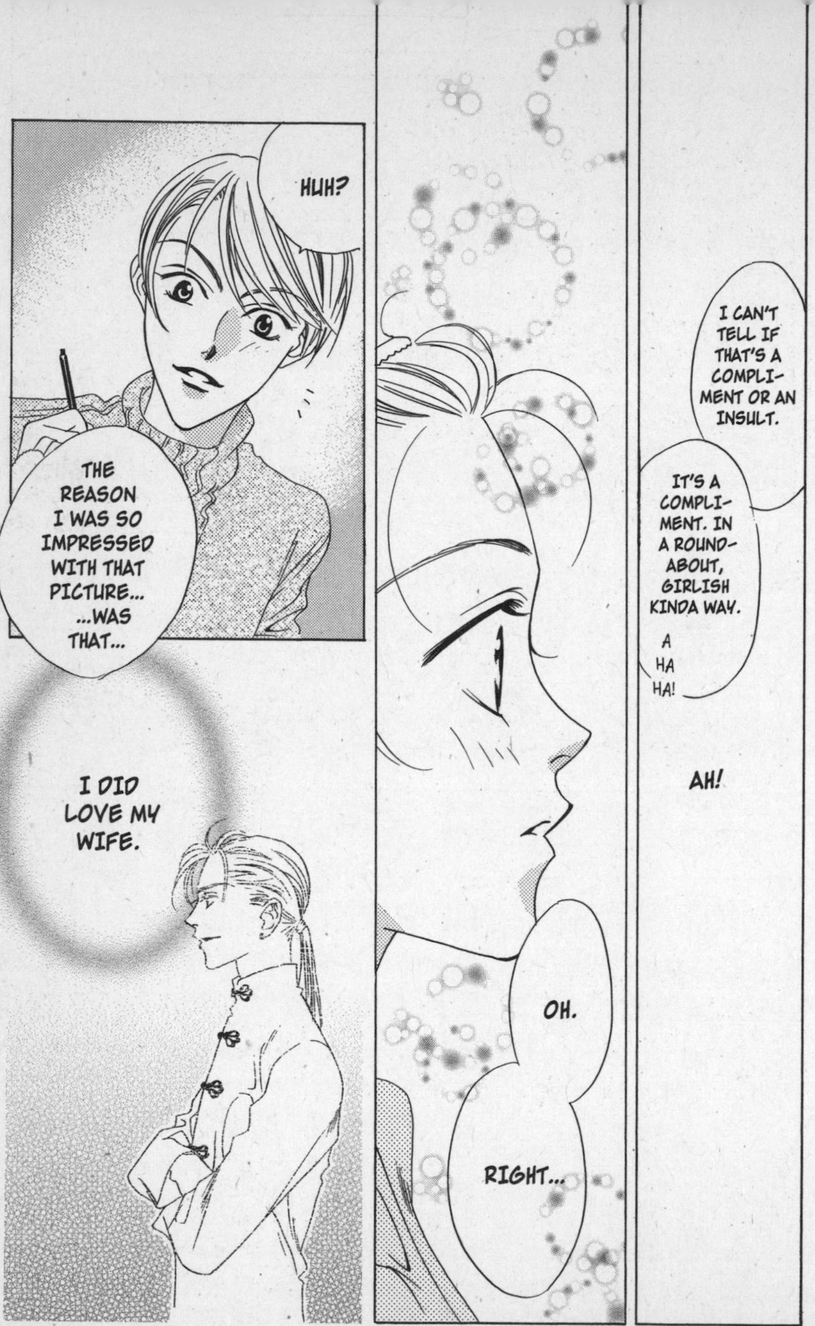
I CAN'T TELL IF THAT'S A COMPLIMENT OR AN INSULT.
IT'S A COMPLIMENT. IN A ROUNDABOUT, GIRLISH KINDA WAY.
A HA HA!
AH!
OH.
RIGHT...
HUH?
THE REASON I WAS SO IMPRESSED WITH THAT PICTURE... ...WAS THAT...
I DID LOVE MY WIFE.

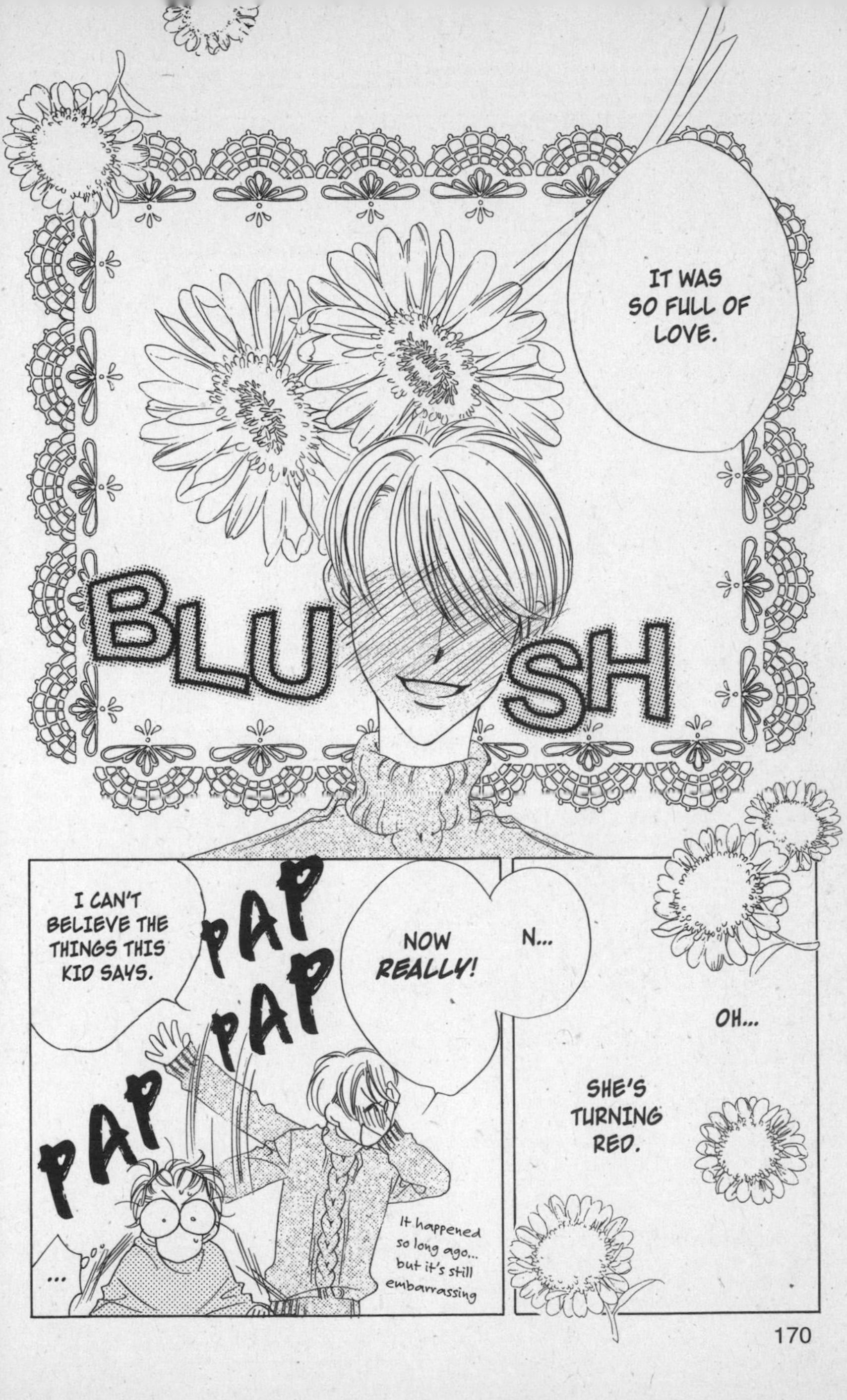
IT WAS SO FULL OF LOVE.
BLUSH
N...
OH...
SHE'S TURNING RED.
NOW REALLY!
PAP PAP
PAP PAP
I CAN'T BELIEVE THE THINGS THIS KID SAYS.
It happened so long ago... but it's still embarrassing
...

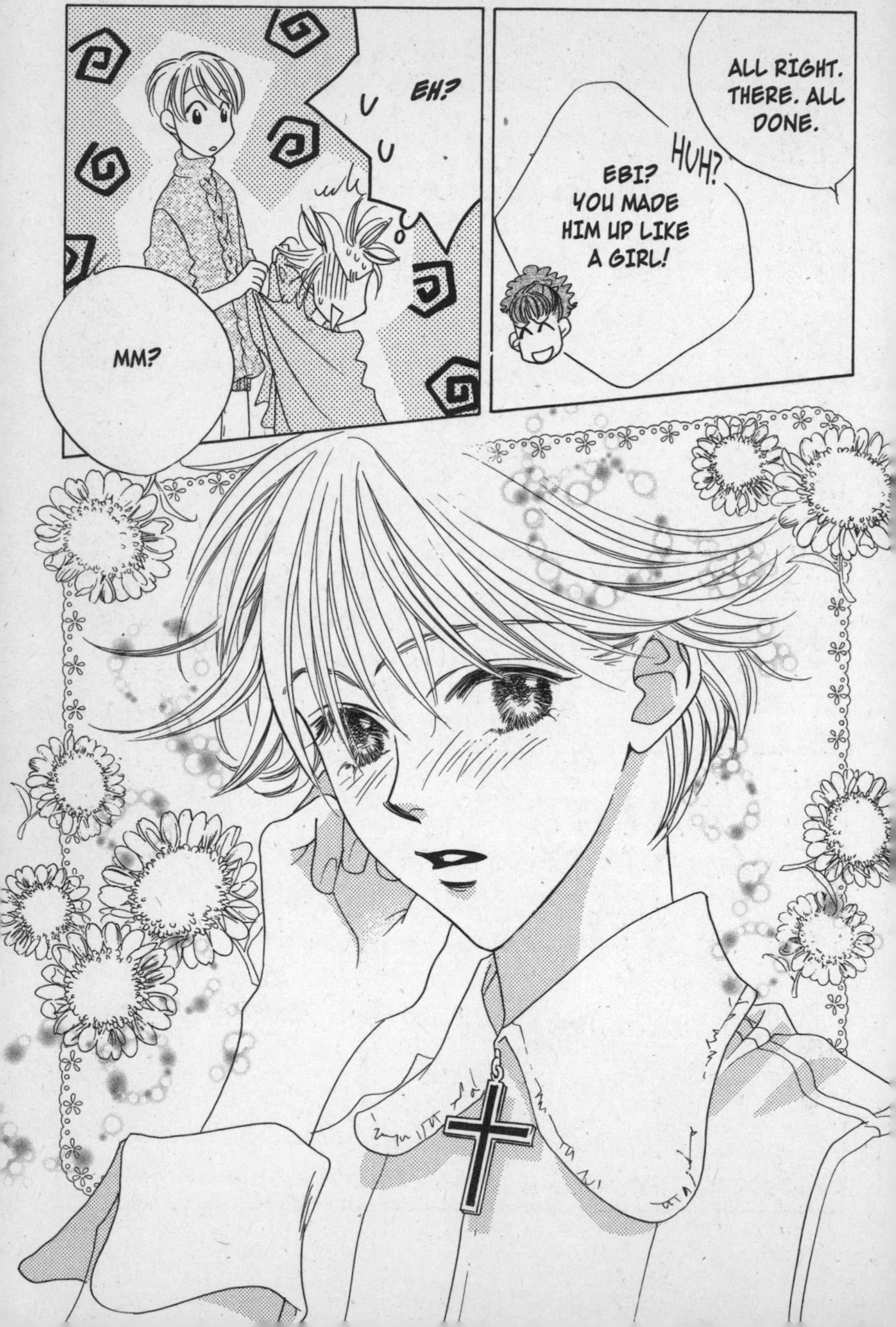
ALL RIGHT. THERE. ALL DONE.
HUH?
EBI? YOU MADE HIM UP LIKE A GIRL!
EH?
MM?

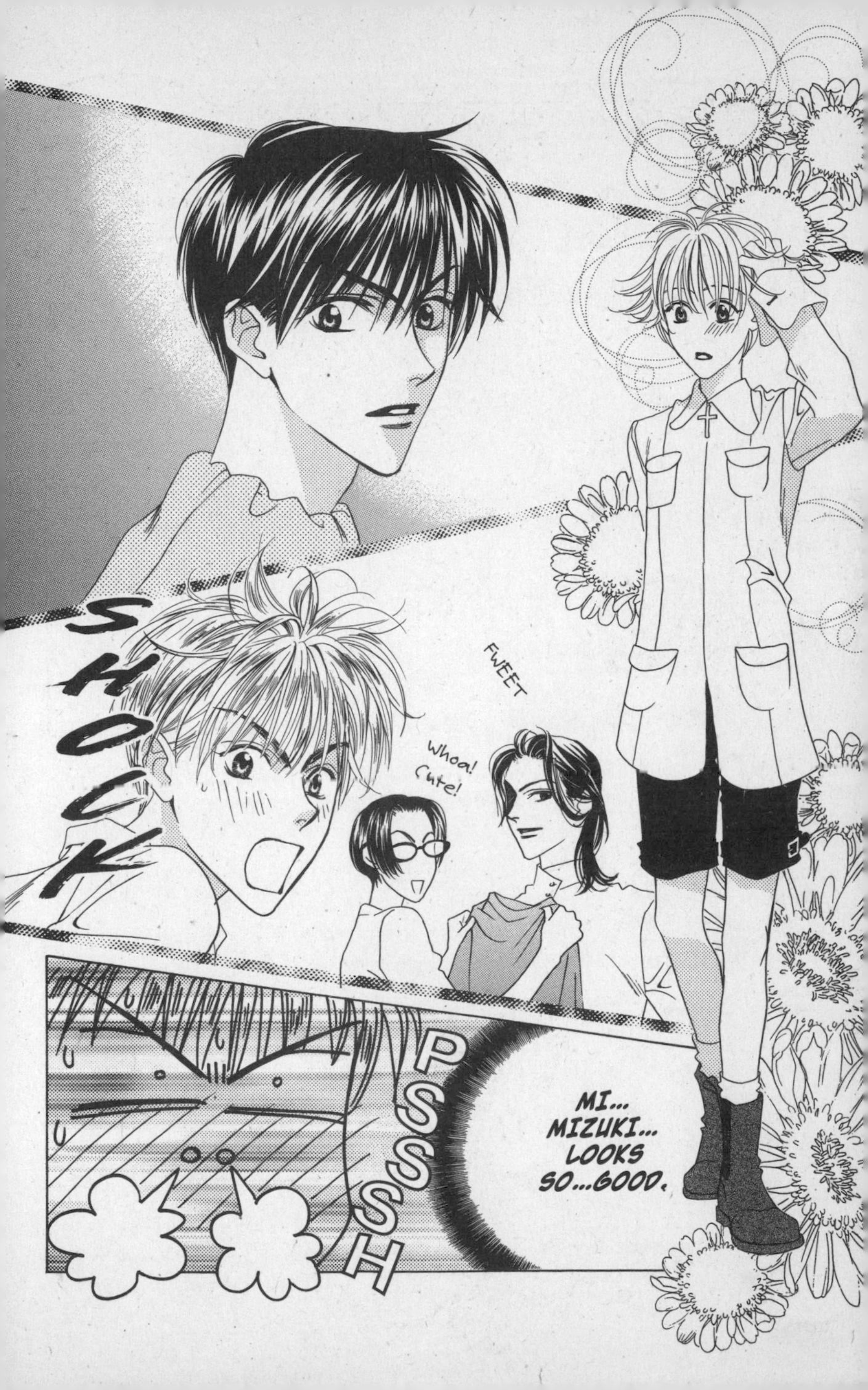
MI... MIZUKI... LOOKS SO...GOOD.
SHOCK
FWEET
Whoa! Cute!
PSSSH

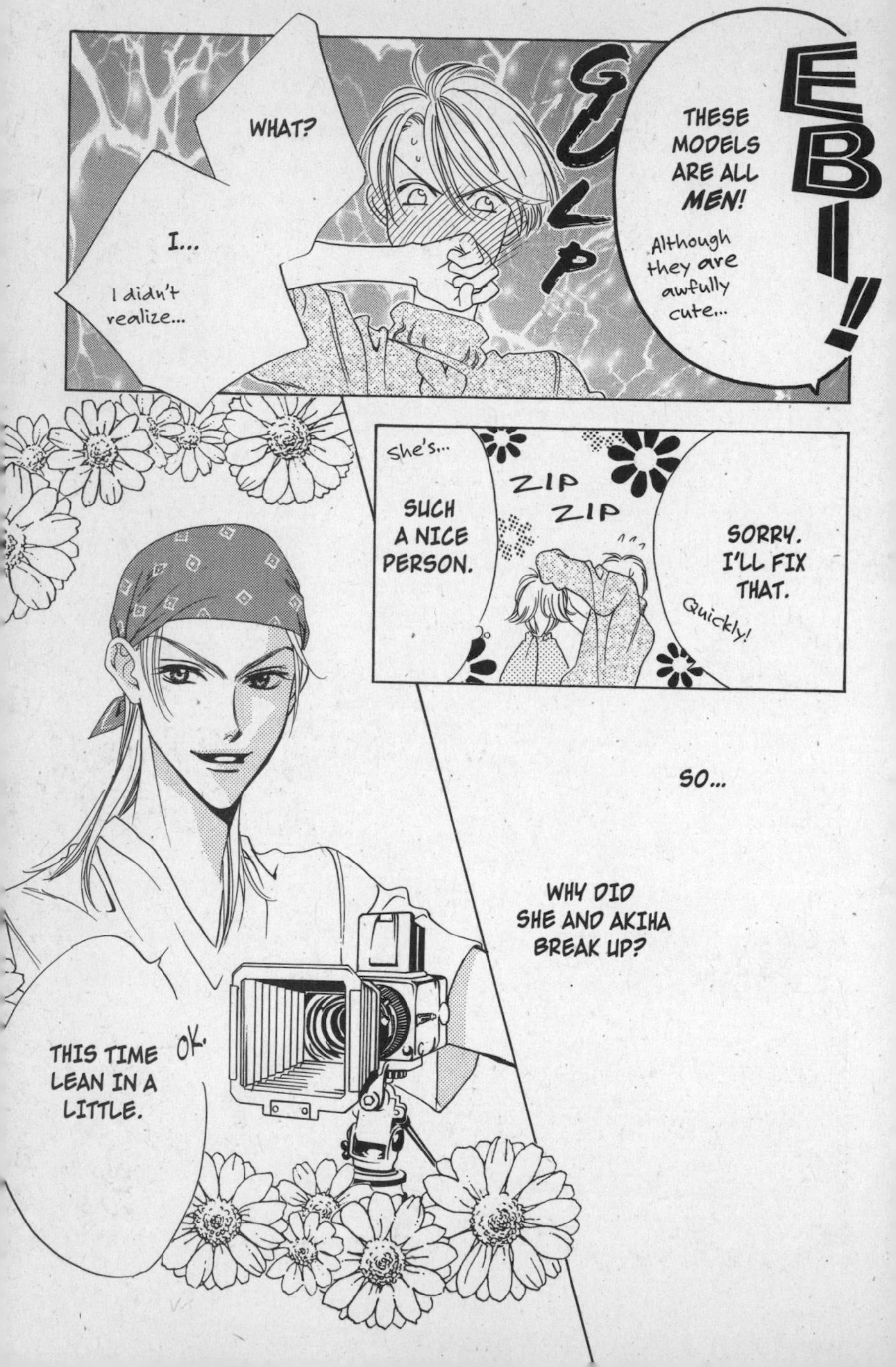
EBI!!
THESE MODELS ARE ALL MEN!
Although they are awfully cute...
GULP
WHAT?
I...
I didn't realize...
SORRY. I'LL FIX THAT.
Quickly!
ZIP ZIP
She's...
SUCH A NICE PERSON.
SO...
WHY DID SHE AND AKIHA BREAK UP?
OK.
THIS TIME LEAN IN A LITTLE.

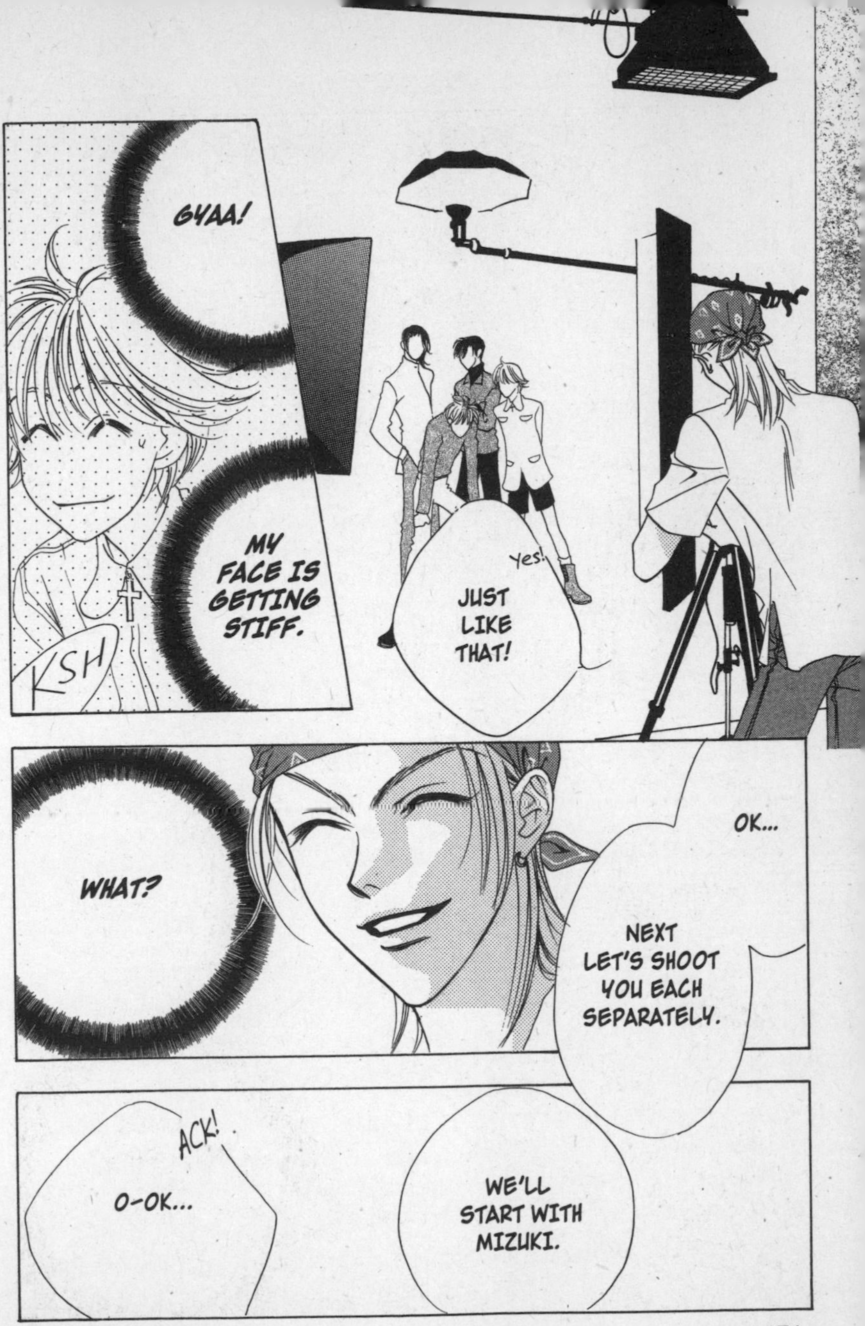
Yes!
JUST LIKE THAT!
GYAA!
MY FACE IS GETTING STIFF.
KSH
OK...
NEXT LET'S SHOOT YOU EACH SEPARATELY.
WHAT?
WE'LL START WITH MIZUKI.
ACK!
O-OK...

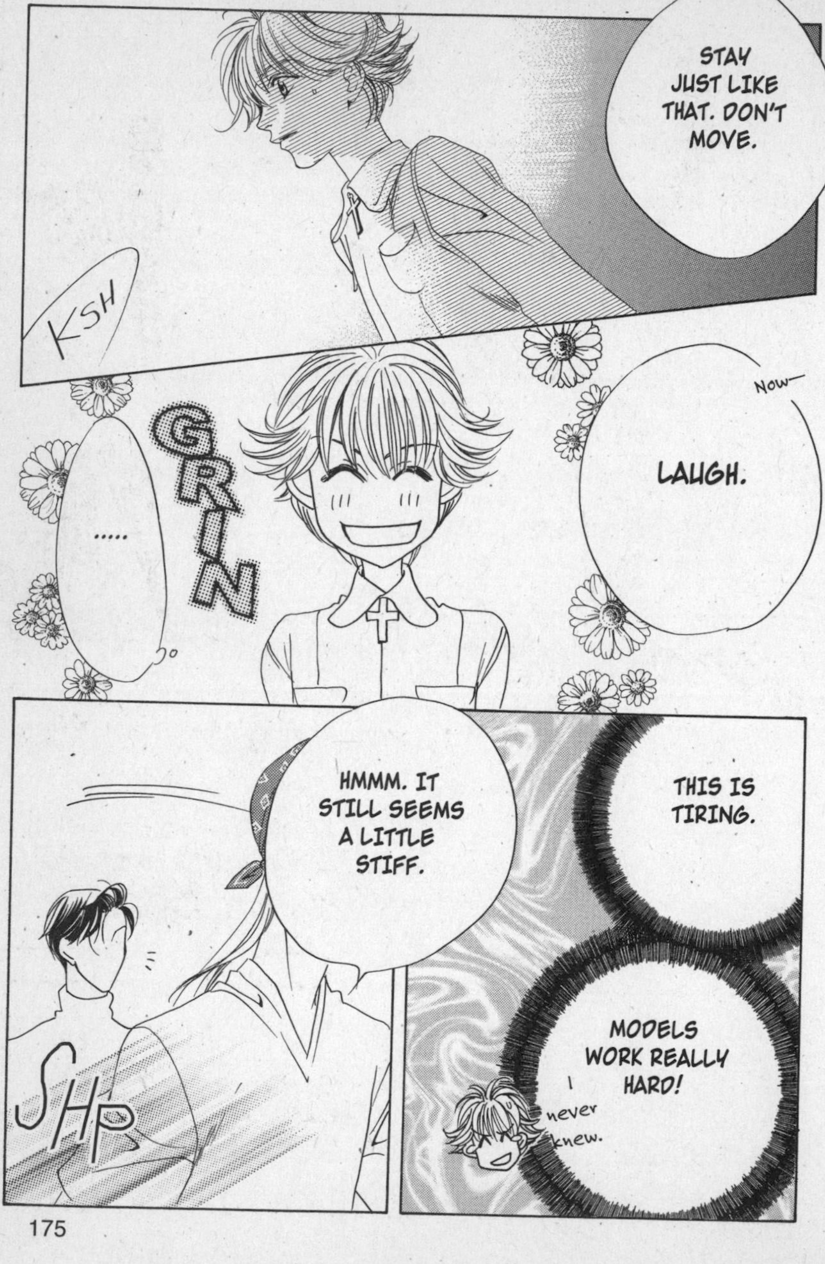
STAY JUST LIKE THAT. DON'T MOVE.
KSH
Now—
LAUGH.
GRIN
.....
THIS IS TIRING.
MODELS WORK REALLY HARD!
I never knew.
HMMM. IT STILL SEEMS A LITTLE STIFF.
SHP

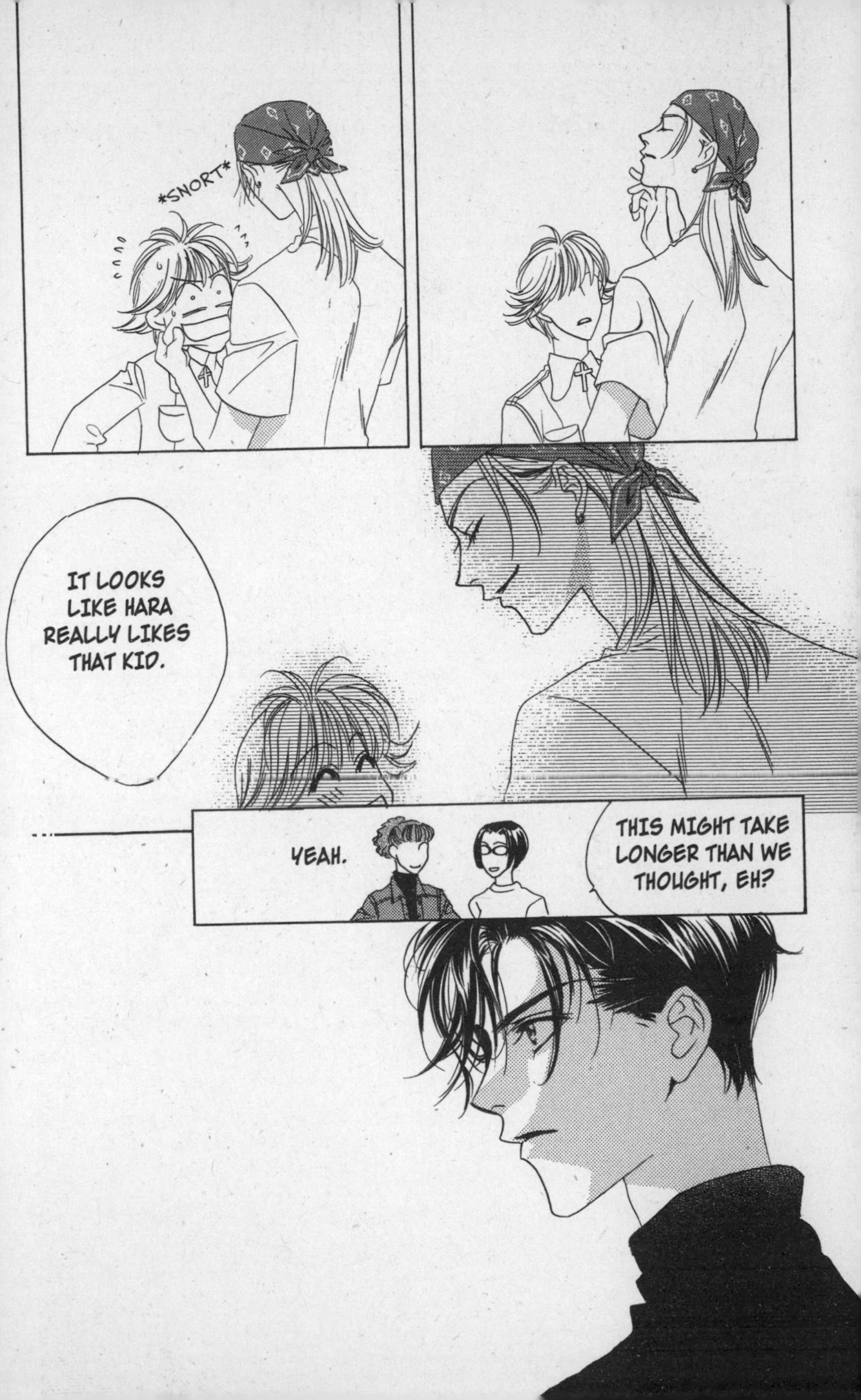
SNORT
IT LOOKS LIKE HARA REALLY LIKES THAT KID.
THIS MIGHT TAKE LONGER THAN WE THOUGHT, EH?
YEAH.

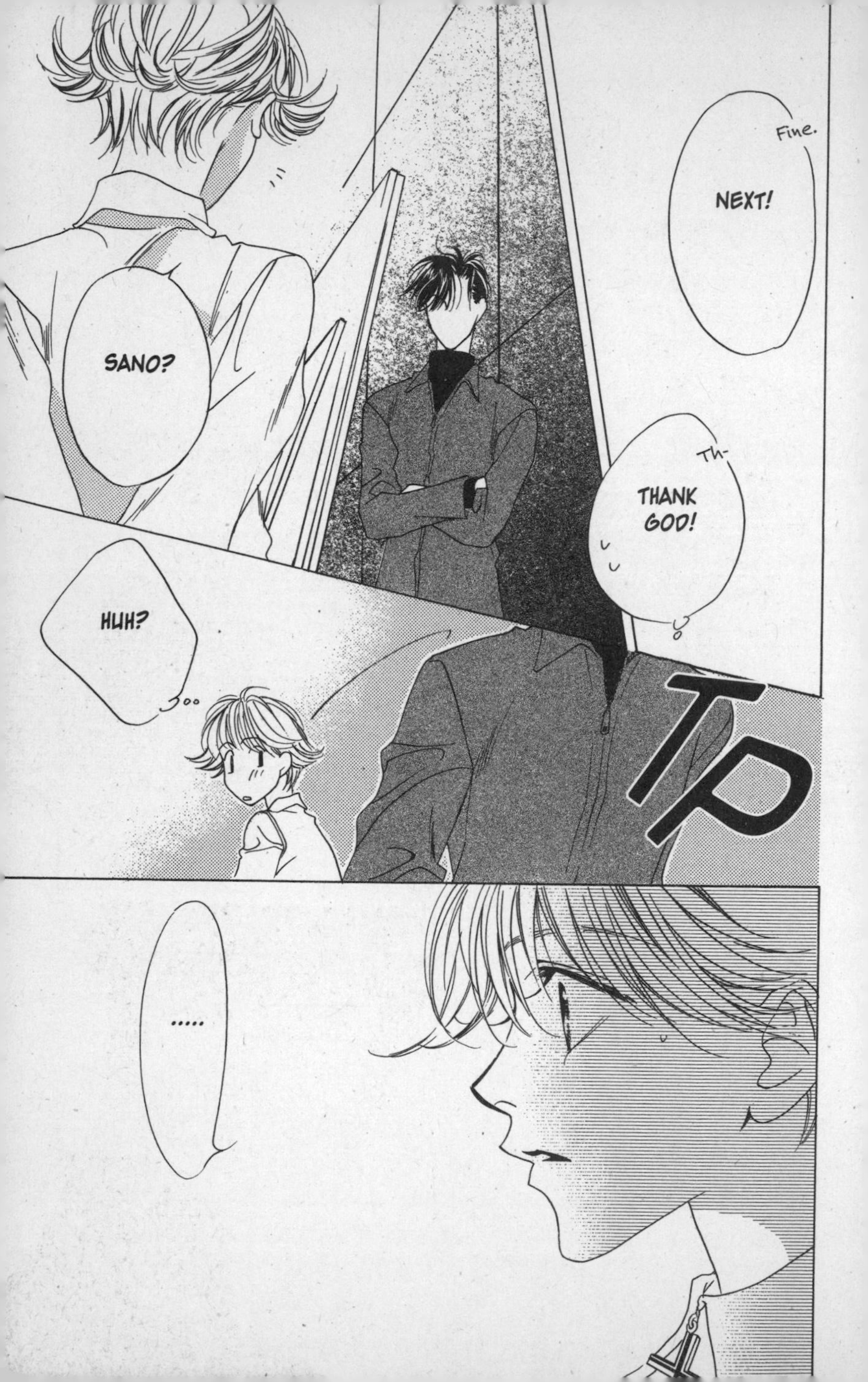

Fine.
NEXT!
SANO?
Th- THANK GOD!
TP
HUH?
.....

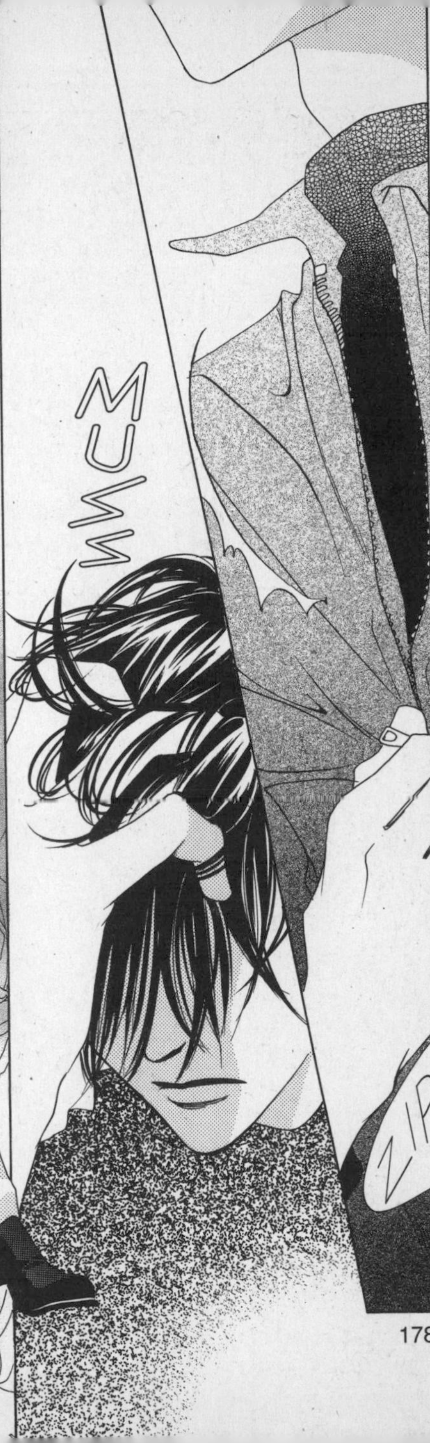
MUWW
ZIP
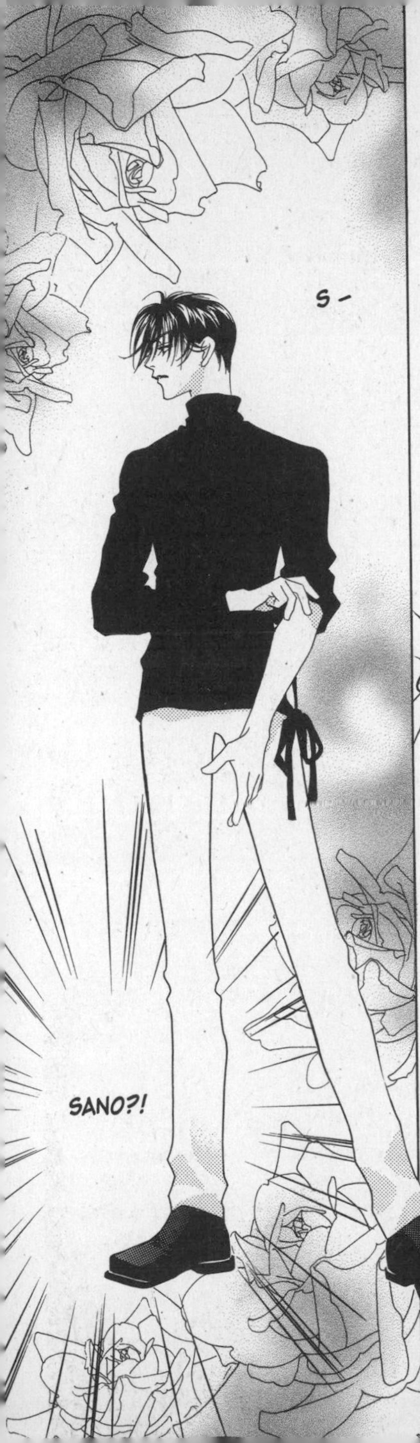
S-
SANO?!

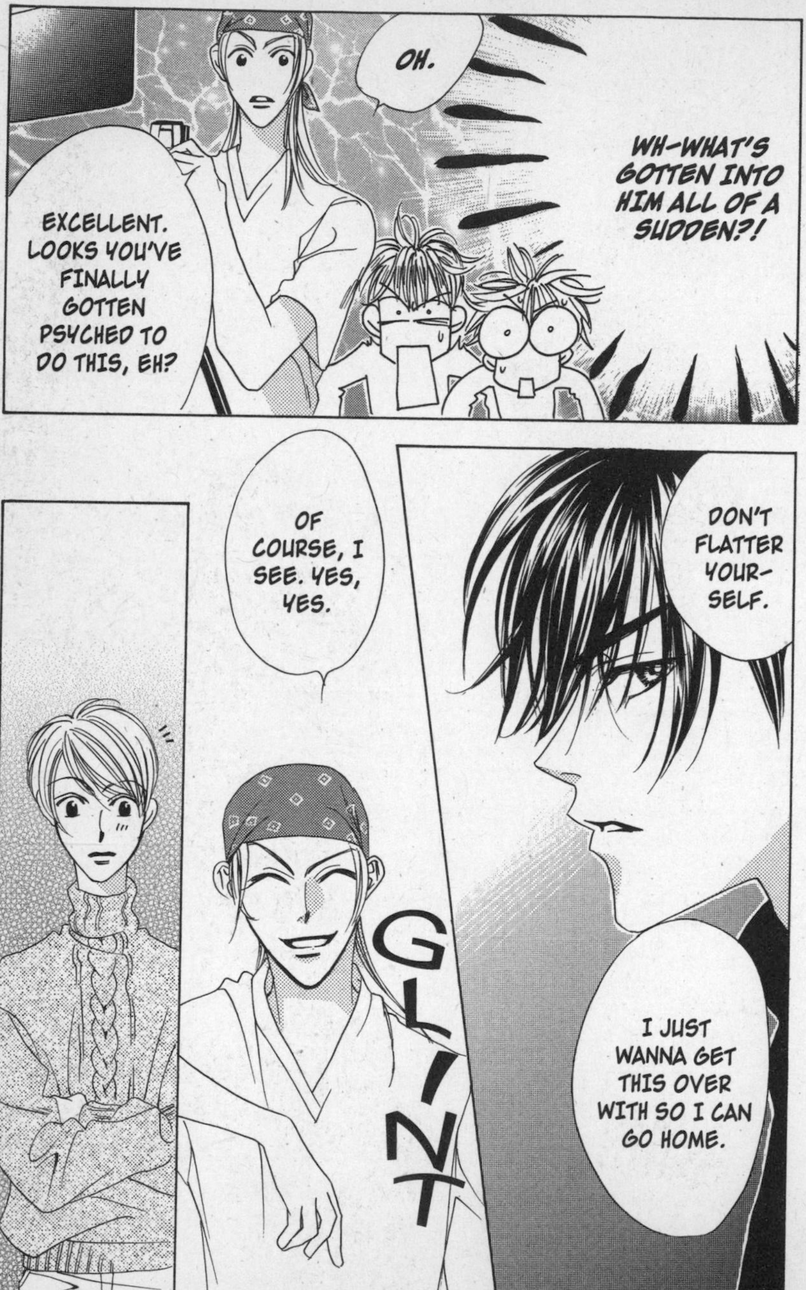
OH.
WH-WHAT'S GOTTEN INTO HIM ALL OF A SUDDEN?!
EXCELLENT. LOOKS YOU'VE FINALLY GOTTEN PSYCHED TO DO THIS, EH?
DON'T FLATTER YOUR-SELF.
I JUST WANNA GET THIS OVER WITH SO I CAN GO HOME.
OF COURSE, I SEE. YES, YES.
GLINT

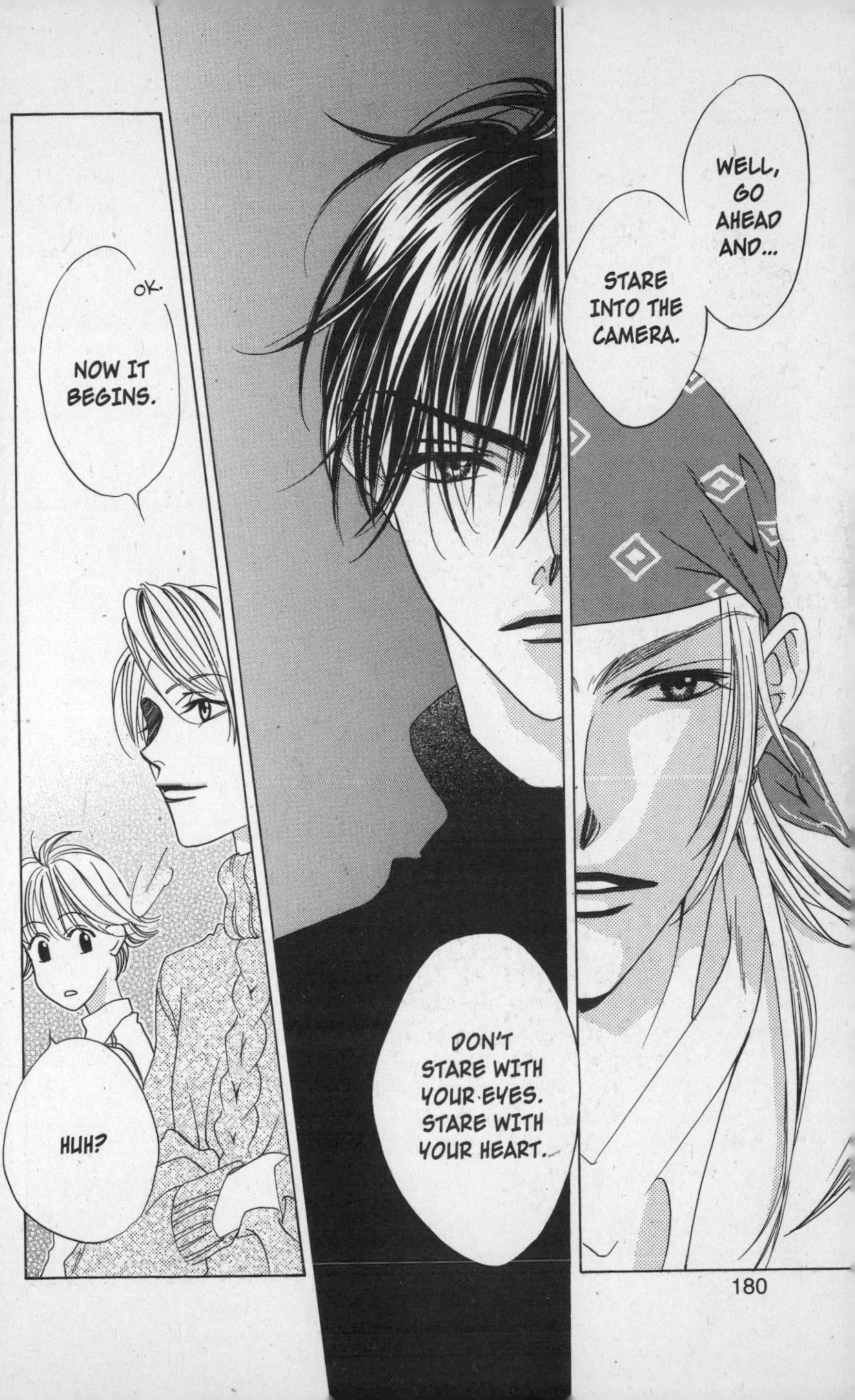
WELL, GO AHEAD AND...
STARE INTO THE CAMERA.
DON'T STARE WITH YOUR EYES. STARE WITH YOUR HEART.
OK. NOW IT BEGINS.
HUH?

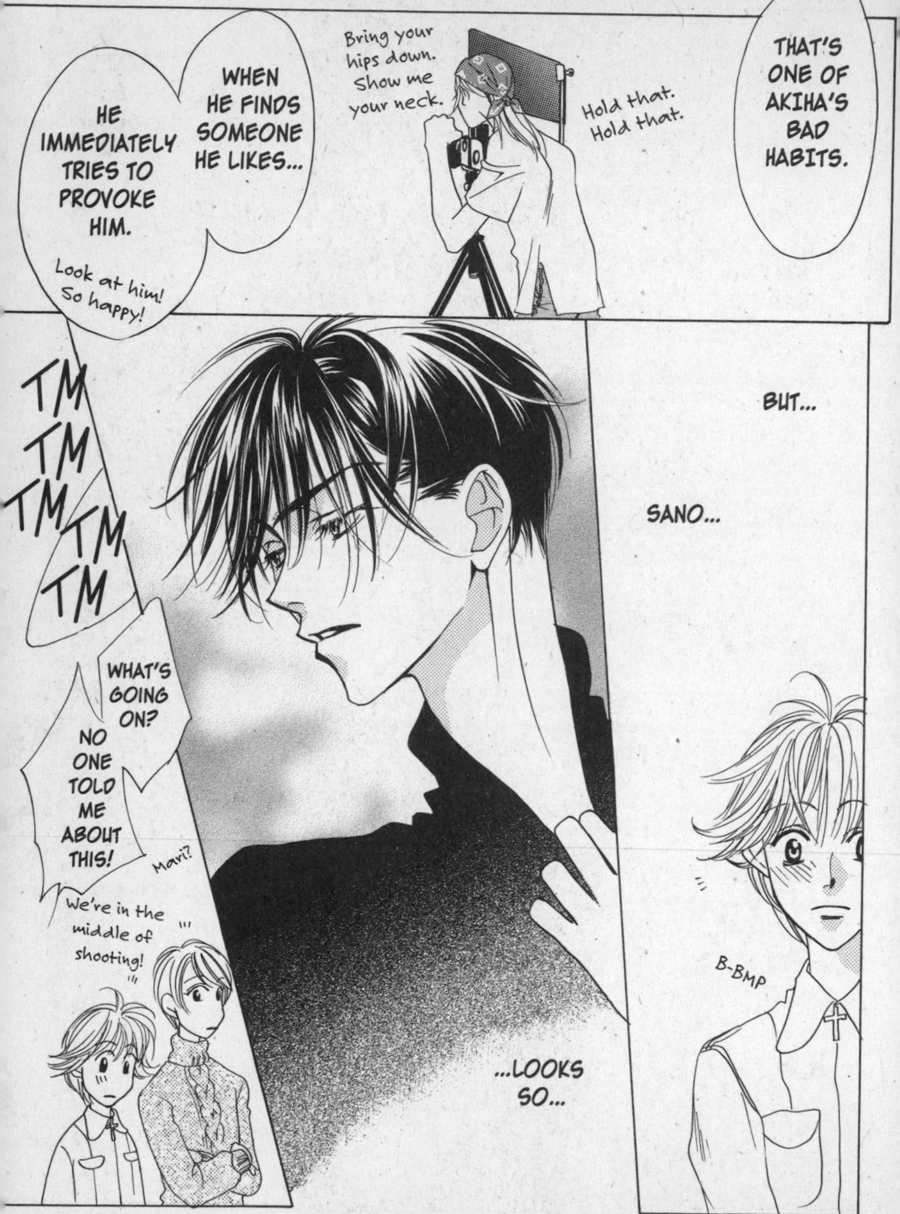
THAT'S ONE OF AKIHA'S BAD HABITS.
Bring your hips down. Show me your neck.
Hold that. Hold that.
WHEN HE FINDS SOMEONE HE LIKES...
HE IMMEDIATELY TRIES TO PROVOKE HIM.
Look at him! So happy!
BUT...
SANO...
B-BMP
...LOOKS SO...
TM TM TM TM TM
WHAT'S GOING ON?
NO ONE TOLD ME ABOUT THIS!
Mari?
We're in the middle of shooting!

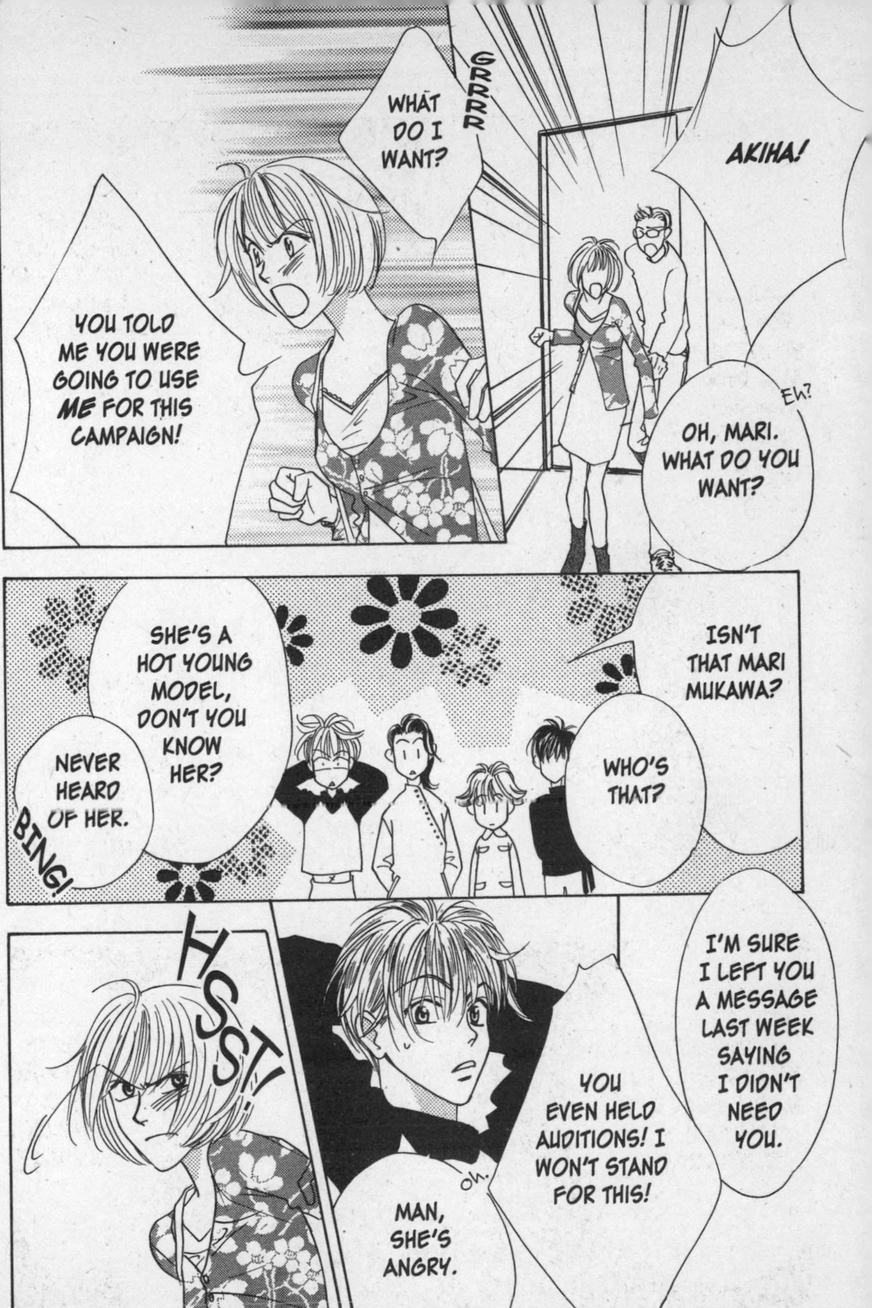
AKIHA!
Eh?
OH, MARI. WHAT DO YOU WANT?
GRRRR
WHAT DO I WANT?
YOU TOLD ME YOU WERE GOING TO USE ME FOR THIS CAMPAIGN!
ISN'T THAT MARI MUKAWA?
WHO'S THAT?
SHE'S A HOT YOUNG MODEL, DON'T YOU KNOW HER?
NEVER HEARD OF HER.
BING!
I'M SURE I LEFT YOU A MESSAGE LAST WEEK SAYING I DIDN'T NEED YOU.
YOU EVEN HELD AUDITIONS! I WON'T STAND FOR THIS!
oh.
MAN, SHE'S ANGRY.
HSST!

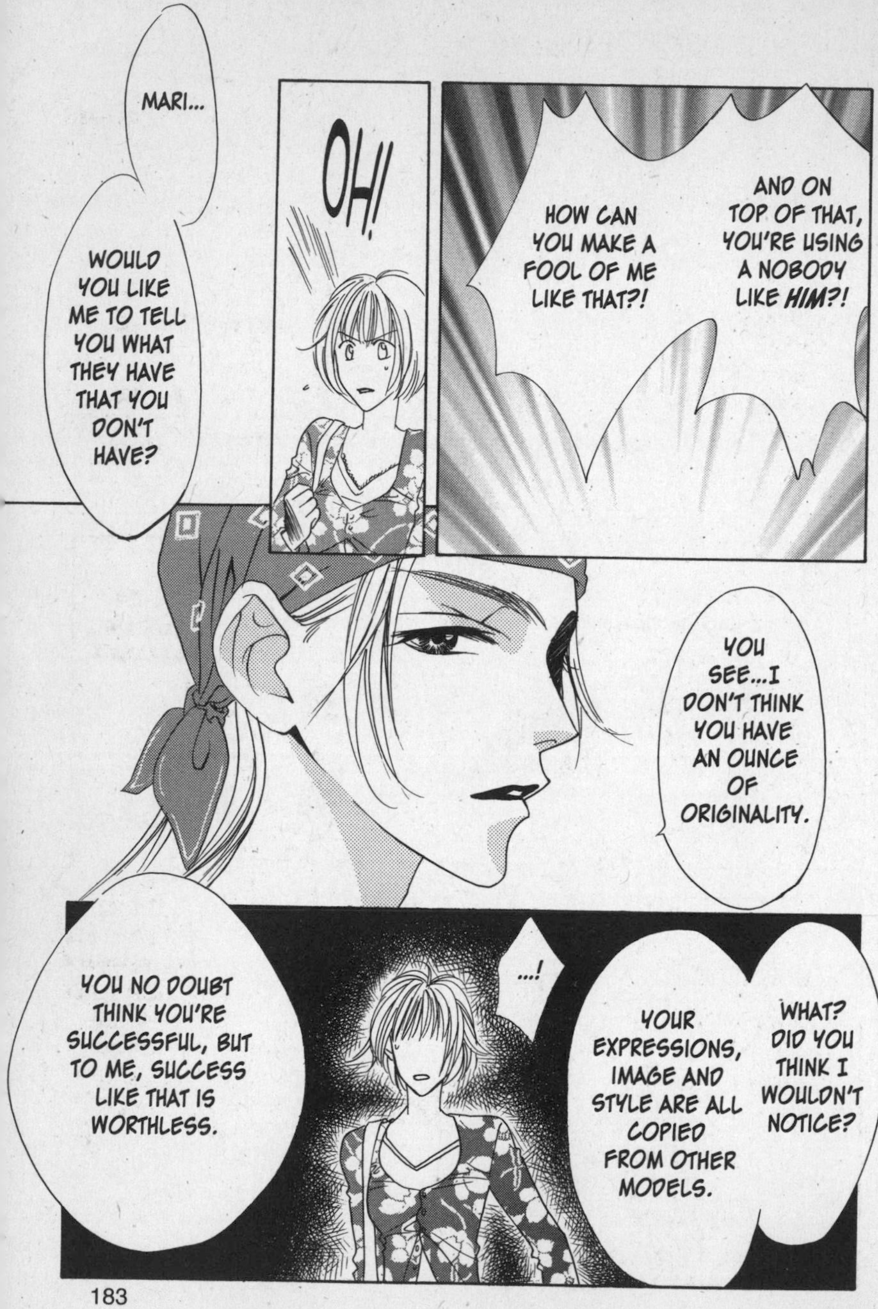
HOW CAN YOU MAKE A FOOL OF ME LIKE THAT?!
AND ON TOP OF THAT, YOU'RE USING A NOBODY LIKE *HIM*?!
OH!
MARI...
WOULD YOU LIKE ME TO TELL YOU WHAT THEY HAVE THAT YOU DON'T HAVE?
YOU SEE...I DON'T THINK YOU HAVE AN OUNCE OF ORIGINALITY.
WHAT? DID YOU THINK I WOULDN'T NOTICE?
YOUR EXPRESSIONS, IMAGE AND STYLE ARE ALL COPIED FROM OTHER MODELS.
...!
YOU NO DOUBT THINK YOU'RE SUCCESSFUL, BUT TO ME, SUCCESS LIKE THAT IS WORTHLESS.

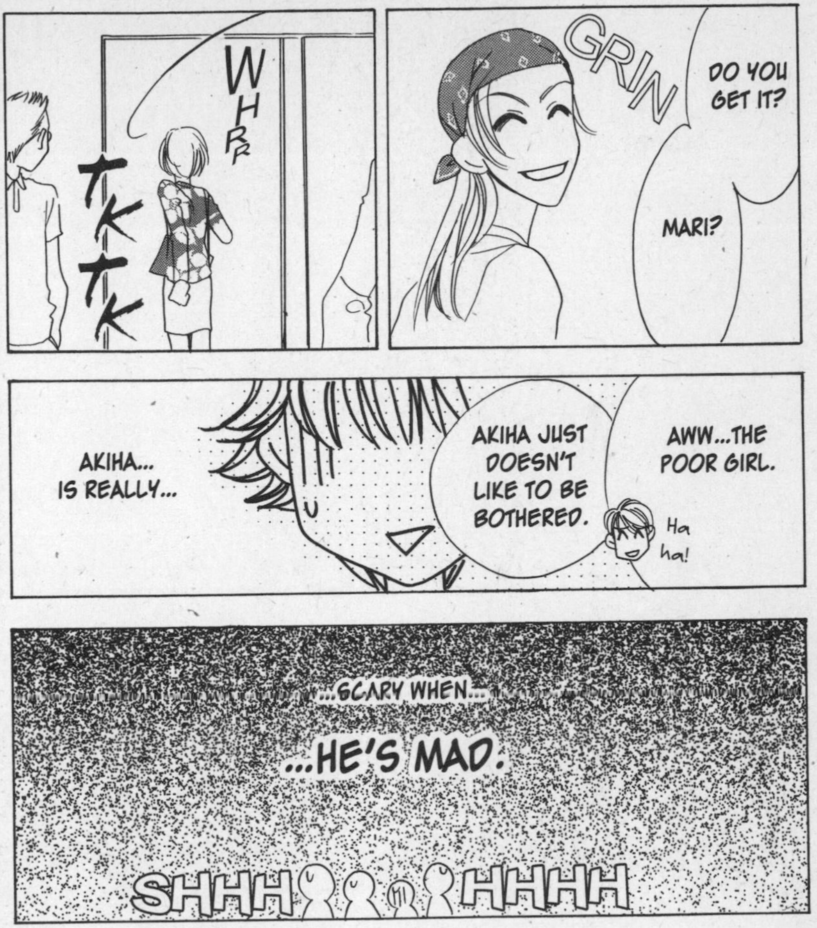
GRIN
DO YOU GET IT?
MARI?
WHRR
TKTK
AWW...THE POOR GIRL.
Ha ha!
AKIHA JUST DOESN'T LIKE TO BE BOTHERED.
AKIHA... IS REALLY...
...SCARY WHEN...
...HE'S MAD.
SHHH HHHH

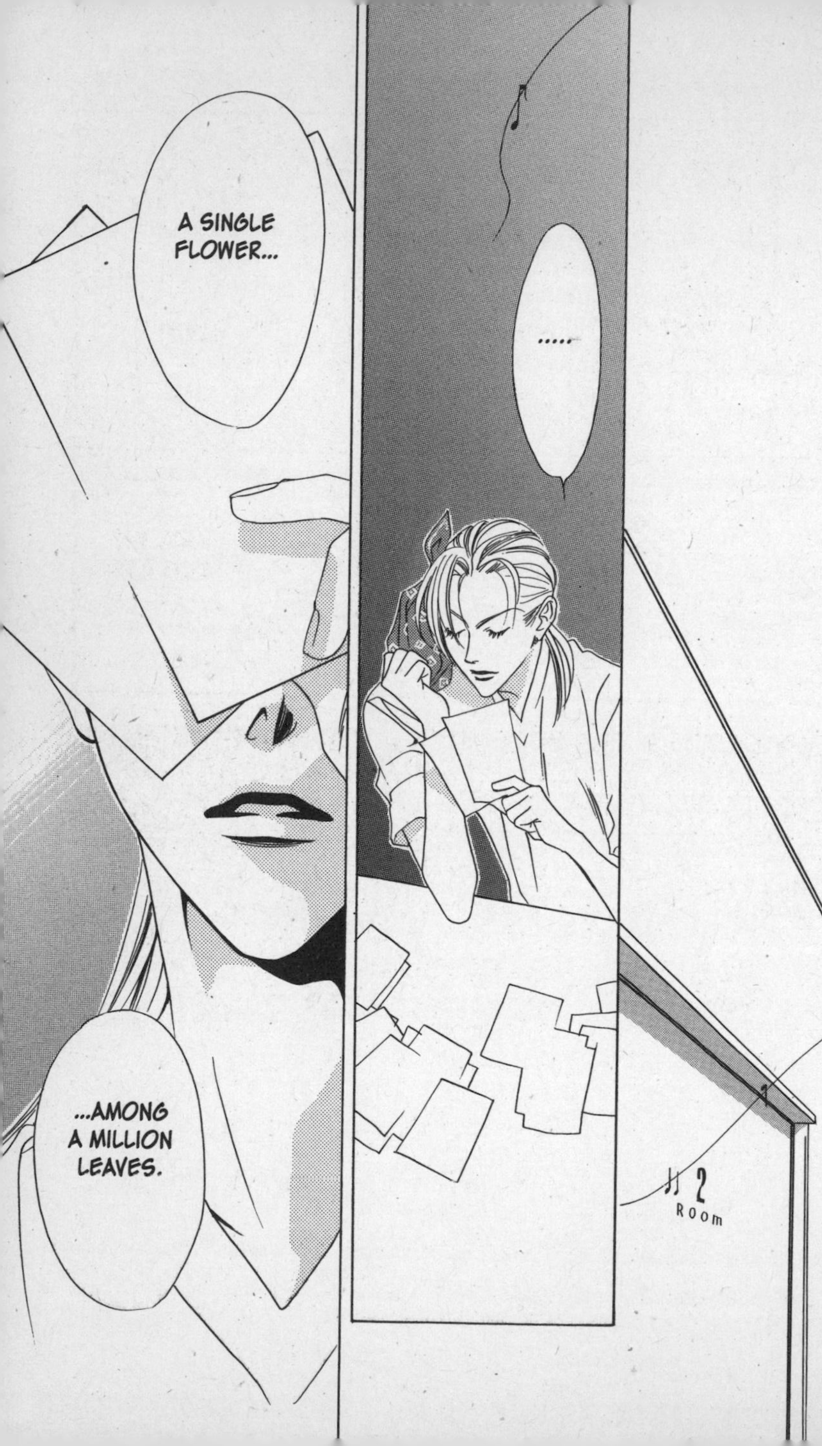
.....
2
ROOM
A SINGLE FLOWER...
...AMONG A MILLION LEAVES.

"A SINGLE FLOWER AMONG A MILLION LEAVES." MEANING THERE'S ONE THING DIFFERENT FROM THE REST... LIKE ONE GIRL SURROUNDED BY BOYS!

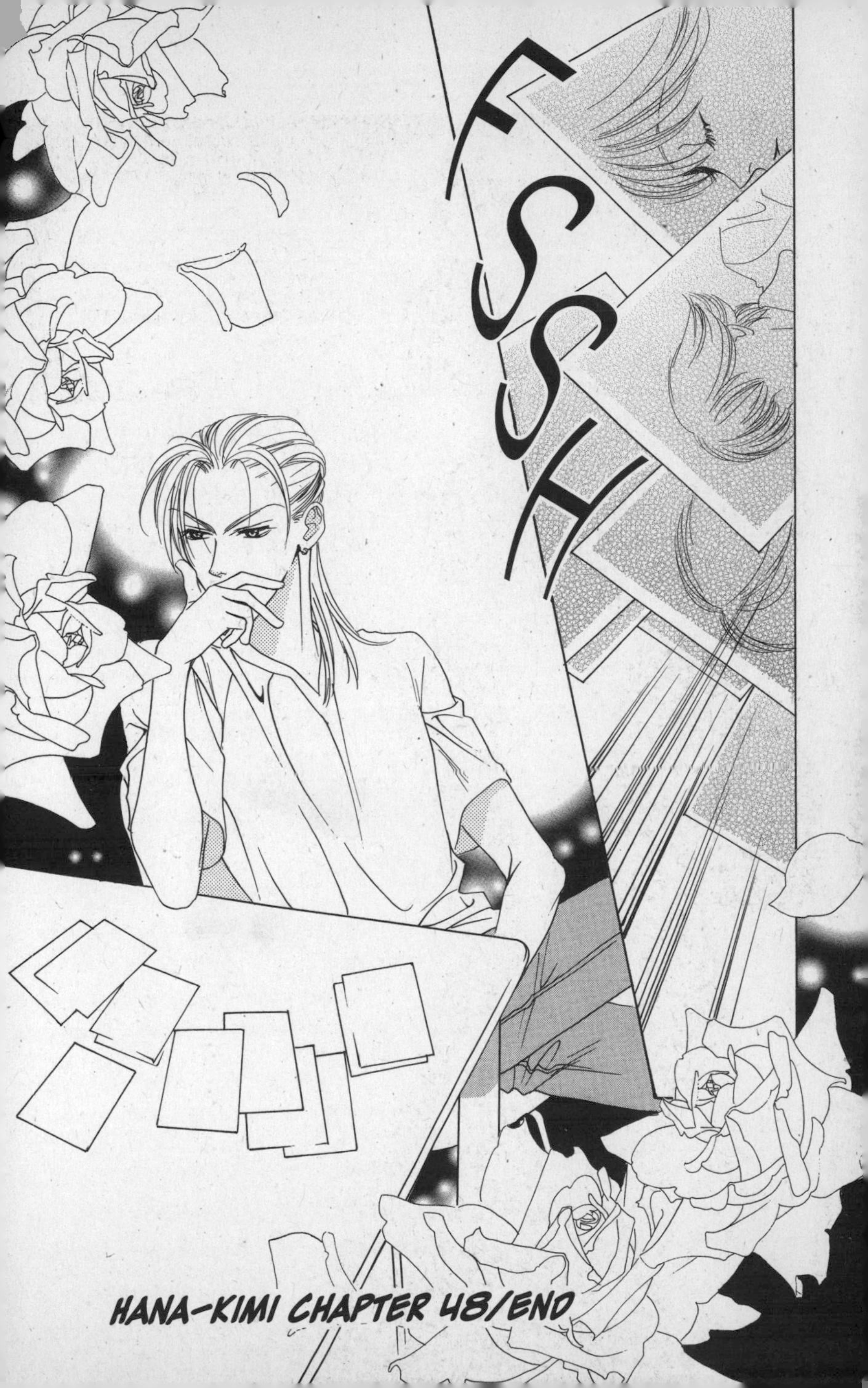
FSSH
HANA-KIMI CHAPTER 48/END

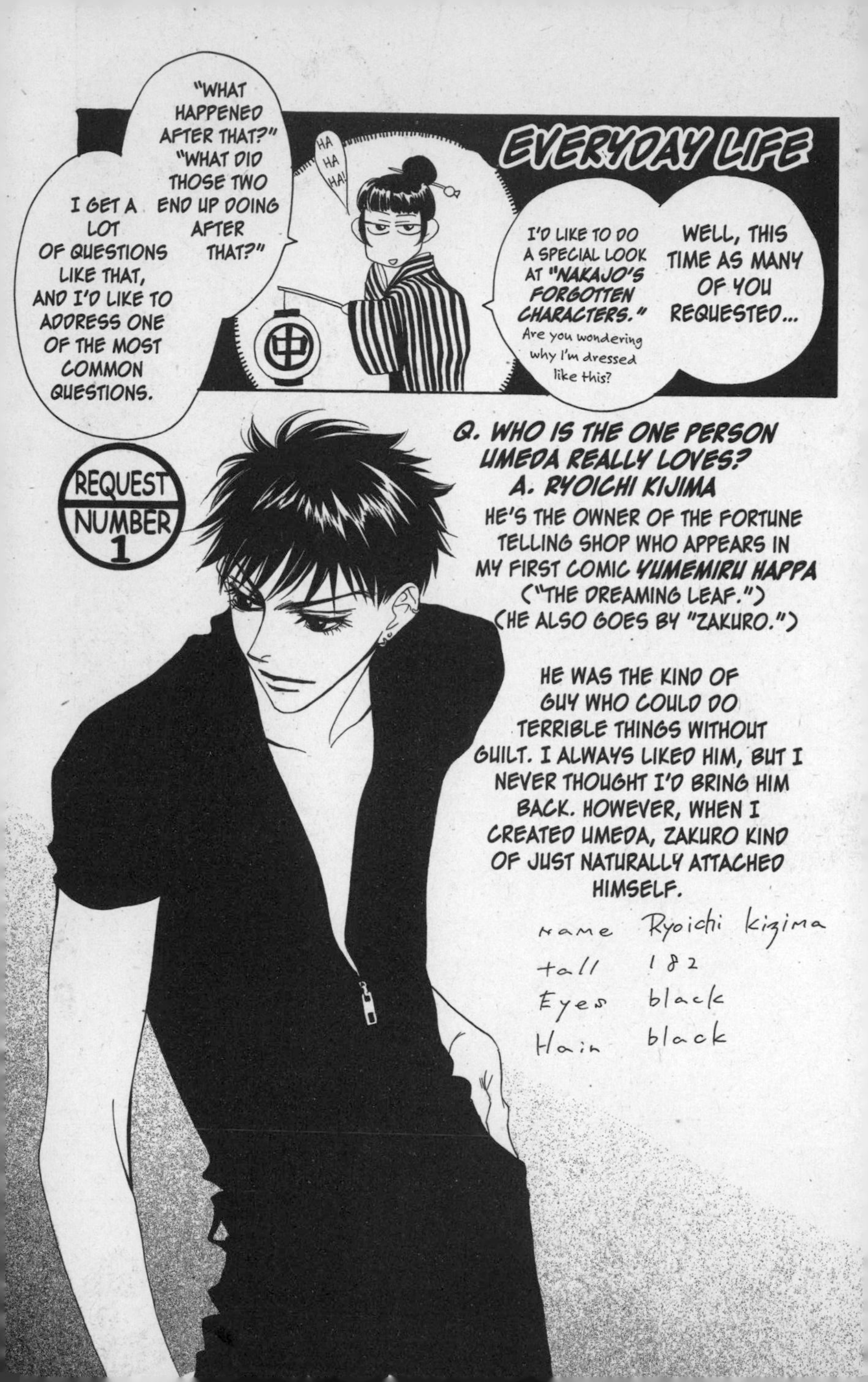
EVERYDAY LIFE
WELL, THIS TIME AS MANY OF YOU REQUESTED...
I'D LIKE TO DO A SPECIAL LOOK AT "NAKAJO'S FORGOTTEN CHARACTERS."
Are you wondering why I'm dressed like this?
HA HA HA!
"WHAT HAPPENED AFTER THAT?" "WHAT DID THOSE TWO END UP DOING AFTER THAT?"
I GET A LOT OF QUESTIONS LIKE THAT, AND I'D LIKE TO ADDRESS ONE OF THE MOST COMMON QUESTIONS.
REQUEST NUMBER 1
Q. WHO IS THE ONE PERSON UMEDA REALLY LOVES?
A. RYOICHI KIJIMA
HE'S THE OWNER OF THE FORTUNE TELLING SHOP WHO APPEARS IN MY FIRST COMIC YUMEMIRU HAPPA ("THE DREAMING LEAF.") (HE ALSO GOES BY "ZAKURO.")
HE WAS THE KIND OF GUY WHO COULD DO TERRIBLE THINGS WITHOUT GUILT. I ALWAYS LIKED HIM, BUT I NEVER THOUGHT I'D BRING HIM BACK. HOWEVER, WHEN I CREATED UMEDA, ZAKURO KIND OF JUST NATURALLY ATTACHED HIMSELF.
name Ryoichi kizima
tall 182
Eyes black
Hair black

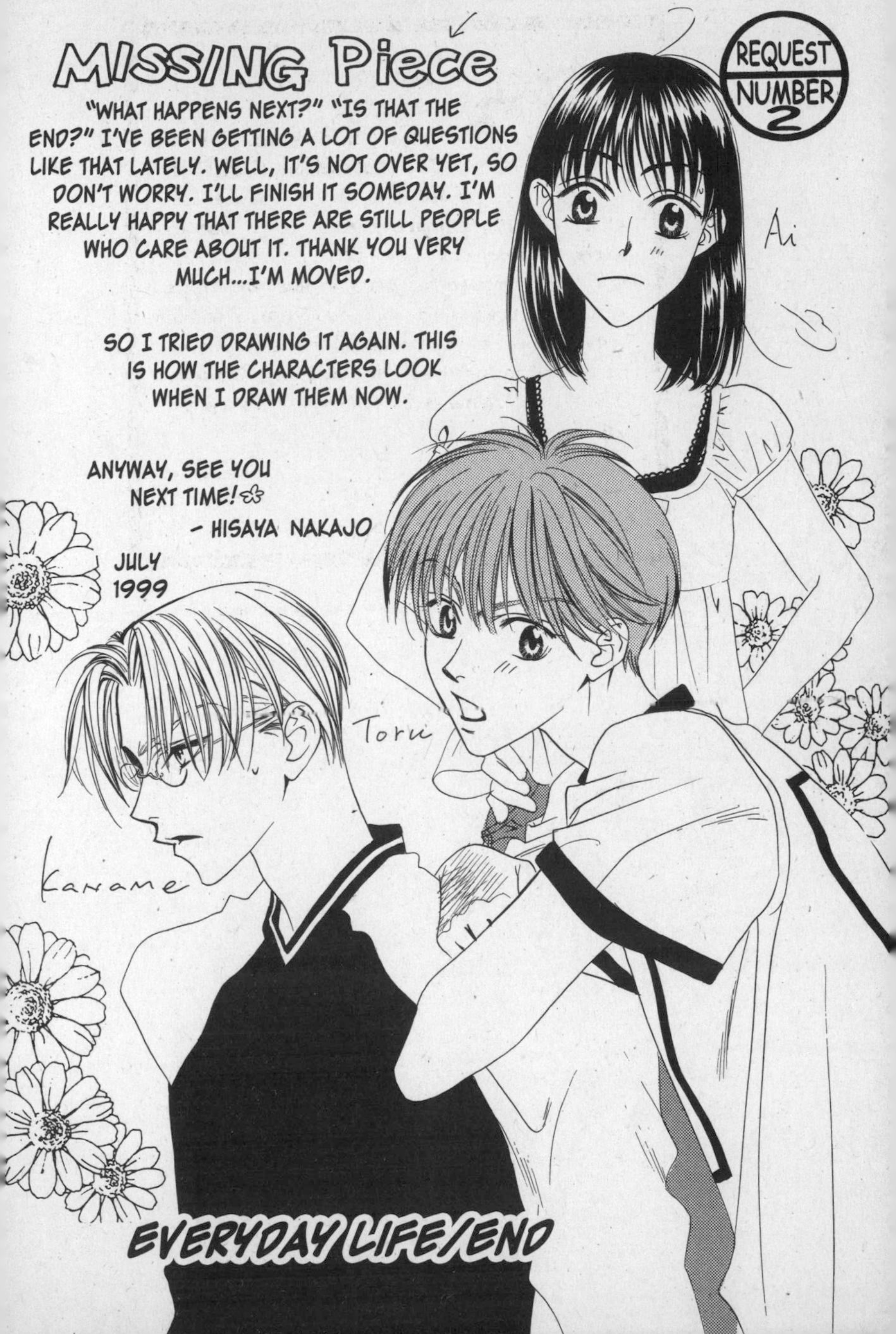
MISSING Piece
REQUEST NUMBER 2
"WHAT HAPPENS NEXT?" "IS THAT THE END?" I'VE BEEN GETTING A LOT OF QUESTIONS LIKE THAT LATELY. WELL, IT'S NOT OVER YET, SO DON'T WORRY. I'LL FINISH IT SOMEDAY. I'M REALLY HAPPY THAT THERE ARE STILL PEOPLE WHO CARE ABOUT IT. THANK YOU VERY MUCH...I'M MOVED.
SO I TRIED DRAWING IT AGAIN. THIS IS HOW THE CHARACTERS LOOK WHEN I DRAW THEM NOW.
ANYWAY, SEE YOU NEXT TIME!
- HISAYA NAKAJO
JULY 1999
Ai
Toru
Kaname
EVERYDAY LIFE/END

ABOUT THE AUTHOR

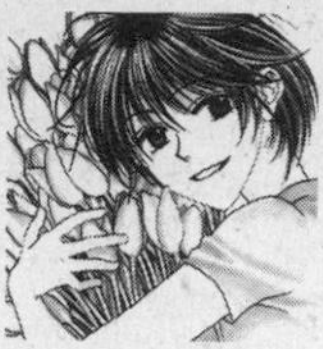

Hisaya Nakajo's manga series **Hanazakari no Kimitachi he** (For You in Full Blossom, casually known as **Hana-Kimi**) has been a hit since it first appeared in 1997 in the shôjo manga magazine **Hana to Yume** (Flowers and Dreams). In Japan, two **Hana-Kimi** art books and several "drama CDs" have been released. Her other manga series include **Missing Piece** (2 volumes) and **Yumemiru Happa** (The Dreaming Leaf, 1 volume).

Hisaya Nakajo's website:
www.wild-vanilla.com

IN THE NEXT VOLUME ...

Akiha Hara isn't out of the picture: he wants even more photos of Sano, Nakatsu, Mizuki and Minami! But the handsome, bisexual Akiha may have a more than professional interest in his models. And has he figured out that Mizuki is a girl? Caught in the treacherous, seductive world of high fashion, will our heroes ever be the same again?

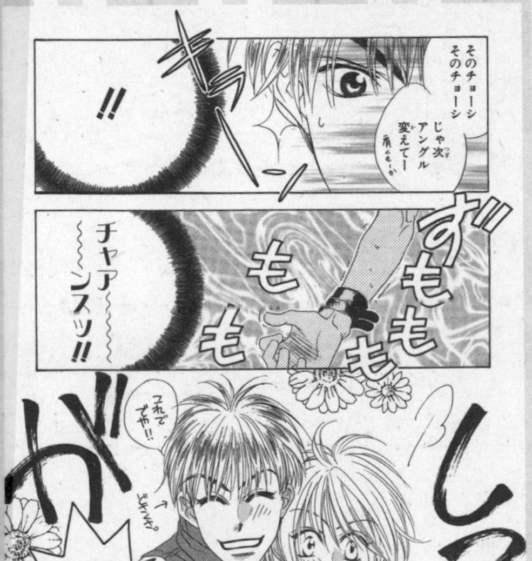
そのチョーシ
そのチョーシ
じゃ次アングル変えてー
キラ
!!
ずももももも
チャア〜〜ンスッ!!
わッ
ガしっ

COMING FEBRUARY 2006!

LOVE SHOJO? LET US KNOW!

☐ Please do NOT send me information about VIZ Media products, news and events, special offers, or other information.

☐ Please do NOT send me information from VIZ' trusted business partners.

Name: _____

Address: _____

City: _____ State: _____ Zip: _____

E-mail: _____

☐ Male ☐ Female   Date of Birth (mm/dd/yyyy): ___ / ___ / ___   (Under 13? Parental consent required)

What race/ethnicity do you consider yourself? (check all that apply)

☐ White/Caucasian   ☐ Black/African American   ☐ Hispanic/Latino

☐ Asian/Pacific Islander   ☐ Native American/Alaskan Native   ☐ Other: _____

What VIZ shojo title(s) did you purchase? (indicate title(s) purchased)

_____

What other shojo titles from other publishers do you own? _____

_____

Reason for purchase: (check all that apply)

☐ Special offer   ☐ Favorite title / author / artist / genre
☐ Gift   ☐ Recommendation   ☐ Collection
☐ Read excerpt in VIZ manga sampler   ☐ Other _____

Where did you make your purchase? (please check one)

☐ Comic store   ☐ Bookstore   ☐ Mass/Grocery Store
☐ Newsstand   ☐ Video/Video Game Store
☐ Online (site:_____)   ☐ Other _____

How many shojo titles have you purchased in the last year? How many were VIZ shojo titles?
(please check one from each column)

SHOJO MANGA	VIZ SHOJO M...
☐ None	☐ None
☐ 1 – 4	☐ 1 – 4
☐ 5 – 10	☐ 5 – 10
☐ 11+	☐ 11+

D0020621

What do you like most about shojo graphic novels? (check all that apply)

☐ Romance ☐ Drama / conflict ☐ Fantasy

☐ Comedy ☐ Real-life storylines ☐ Relatable characters

☐ Other _____

Do you purchase every volume of your favorite shojo series?

☐ Yes! Gotta have 'em as my own

☐ No. Please explain: _____

Who are your favorite shojo authors / artists? _____

_____

What shojo titles would like you translated and sold in English? _____

_____

Garfield County Libraries
Gordon Cooper Branch Library
76 South 4th Street
Carbondale, CO 81623
(970) 963-2889 Fax (970) 963-8573
www.garfieldlibraries.org

THANK YOU! Please send the completed form to

VIZ
media

NJW Research
ATTN: VIZ Media Shojo Survey
42 Catharine Street
Poughkeepsie, NY 12601